AFTER

THE

BALL

○ ○ ○ ○ ○

D O U B L E D A Y

New York   London

Toronto   Sydney

Auckland

AFTER THE BALL

○　　○　　○　　○　　○

How America Will Conquer
Its Fear and Hatred
of Gays in the '90s

MARSHALL KIRK
AND
HUNTER MADSEN
Ph.D.

Published by Doubleday, a division of
Bantam Doubleday Dell Publishing
Group Inc.,
666 Fifth Avenue, New York, New York
10103

Doubleday and the portrayal of an
anchor with a dolphin are trademarks of
Doubleday, a division of Bantam
Doubleday Dell Publishing Group, Inc.

Library of Congress Cataloging-in-
Publication Data
Kirk, Marshall.
    After the ball : how America will
conquer its hatred and fear of
homosexuals in the '90's / Marshall Kirk
and Hunter Madsen. —1st ed.
        p.   cm.
    Bibliography: p.
ISBN 0-385-23906-8
    1. Gay liberation movement—United
States.
2. Gays—United States—Public opinion.
3. Homophobia—United States—
Prevention. 4. Public opinion—United
States. I. Madsen, Hunter. II. Title.
HQ76.8.U5K57 1989
306.7'66—dc19   88-36860
                                    CIP

BOOK DESIGN BY CAROL MALCOLM

PRINTED IN THE UNITED STATES OF AMERICA
JUNE 1989
FIRST EDITION

BG

ACKNOWLEDGMENTS

○　　　○　　　○　　　○　　　○

For their contributions to this book, many deserve our thanks. Marshall DeBruhl, our initial editor, was the one who first sought us out to write a "gay manifesto for the 1990s"; and Mr. DeBruhl steered us through the project's early stages. Casey Fuetsch, our subsequent editor, gamely picked matters up from there and, with enthusiasm and patience, saw us through to the finish. We also received valued editorial advice from Robert Weil, and even filched the book title from a friend of his, Larry Schneer.

Numerous advertising, public relations, and fundraising professionals made suggestions helpful to our analysis: we especially thank Howard Buford, Susan MacMurchy, Rosemary Kuropat, and Alan Dee. Urvashi Vaid of the National Gay and Lesbian Task Force, Sherrie Cohen of the Fund for Human Dignity, Craig Davidson of the Gay and Lesbian Alliance Against Defamation, Katy Taylor of the New York City Commission on Human Rights, and the Waging Peace Committee led by Connie and Corrie in Columbus, Ohio, all took time to share with us some of their thinking on the subject. So did many members of the Positive Images Campaign, which was created by the Fund and GLAAD, and which is spearheading our community's first efforts at national gay advertising.

We also salute those few—including Catherine Coker in Los Angeles, Tom Kalin in New York, and Jay Clark in Virginia—whose organizations have already attempted gay advertising locally to straight publics, and who graciously consented to let us reprint and assess some of their efforts. A debt is likewise owed to Bruce Eves and Tom Steele, who put aside their work at the hectic Christopher Street offices long enough to hunt down various photographs for inclusion in our own ad mock-ups. Kyle Hoepner, Michael Bell, and several others volunteered additional art for our ads.

Intending that this book would have a straight, as well as a gay, audience, we sought 'advance reviews' and suggestions—and got much appreciated encouragement—from many straight friends. Thank you, Robert and Martha, Ron, Linda, Jim, Nora, Rob and Jacqueline, David and Stymean, and our inadvertent benefactress, the Dragon Lady.

There are many other gay and straight individuals who helped us here, but insisted they'd drop dead of embarrassment if acknowledged in our book. We lay a wreath in their memory on the tomb of the unknown soldier. (While we're at it, we should also lay to rest any pat conclusions you might draw about the personal lives of individuals who are mentioned in this book: as the lawyers say, publication of the name, photograph, or likeness of any person or organization here is not necessarily to be construed as any indication of the sexual orientation of such persons or members of such organizations.)

"There is not so poor a book in the world," Dr. Johnson reminds us, "that would not be a prodigious effort were it wrought out entirely by a single mind, without the aid of prior investigators." Even so, while we've benefited enormously from the advice and writings of others, it must be said that the authors alone are responsible for the opinions expressed in this book. Much as we'd prefer, from time to time, to pass it to others, the buck always stops here.

Along with these various acknowledgments to others, the two authors wish, finally, to add a personal word to each other, acknowledging the uncanny survival of their friendship. You readers may disagree over much in this book, but probably not half so much as we did. An auctorial collaboration can be, we've learned, a sort of death struggle between *strong-minded partners, the more so when shaping a manifesto whose complex moral, psychological, and expositional dimensions are bound to raise hackles and snarling demurrers. Gentlefolk simply agree to disagree on such murky matters in casual discourse, but cannot do so when hammering out a coherent argument; someone's opinion must always prevail, and this is no fun for old friends. No, the real fun starts tomorrow, when—as old friends do—we begin shifting the blame as to who said what.*

PART I: PROBLEMS: THE STRAIGHT AND NARROW

1

○　　　○　　　○　　　○　　　○

A FIELD TRIP TO STRAIGHT AMERICA

2

THE ROOTS OF HOMOPHOBIA AND HOMOHATRED

PART II: SOLUTIONS: DRIVING THE WEDGE

3

STRATEGY: PERSUASION, NOT INVASION

4

○   ○   ○   ○   ○

TACTICS FOR EATING THE MEDIA ALIVE: A SOUND-BITE HERE, A SOUND-BITE THERE

5

○   ○   ○   ○   ○

GETTING OUR ACT(IVISTS) TOGETHER: UNITY, OR-GANIZATION, FUNDRAISING

PART III: NOT IN OUR STARS, BUT IN OURSELVES

6

○   ○   ○   ○   ○

THE STATE OF OUR COMMUNITY: GAY PRIDE GOETH BEFORE A FALL

INTRODUCTION

○   ○   ○   ○   ○

THE PERMANENT
CRISIS OF
AMERICAN
HOMOSEXUALITY

*Gay power erected its brazen head and spat out
a fairy tale the likes of which the area has
never seen . . . Watch out. The liberation is
under way.*

—*VILLAGE VOICE,* JULY 3, 1969

The gay revolution has failed.

Not completely, and not finally, but it's a failure just the same. The 1969 Stonewall riot—in which a handful of long-suffering New York drag queens, tired of homophobic police harassment, picked up rocks and bottles and fought back—marked the birth of 'gay liberation.' As we write these lines, twenty years have passed. In those years, the combined efforts of the gay community have won a handful of concessions in a handful of localities. Some of those concessions have been revoked; others may be. We should have done far better.

What has gone wrong? And what can we do about it?

This book is about hope and dread. It explores the dire necessity —and the real possibility—of reconciling America to its large, oppressed, and inescapable minority: gay men and women. It proposes a practical agenda for bringing to a close, at long last, the seemingly permanent crisis of American homosexuality. And it aims to launch upon this task in an era of superlative need and supreme difficulty, the frightening era of 'the gay plague,' AIDS.

We begin by *telling* you that this book is about hope, since you may well think otherwise after reading our opening chapters, which are grim and glum. We catalog and illustrate—as vividly as possible, for too many people are still inclined to complacency— the genuine sufferings of gays in America today, and forecast the future in terms no darker and scarier than what we really believe. Lest gay readers puff themselves up too much as sinless martyrs, we have plenty of uncomplimentary things to say about them, too. Our purpose in these opening pages is to cut through those pleasing but foolish self-delusions that abound in the American gay community, and that prevent it from mobilizing against a present and burgeoning disaster.

The solutions we offer—we could agree on no others that seemed realistic—are presented in later chapters. So, despite our cries of doom, we urge you to read on until the bitter end . . . which, as it turns out, is not so bitter after all.

o

THE GREAT SOCIETY IS RUNNING A TEMPERATURE

It's an unhappily familiar observation that America is a sick society. Not because AIDS has blood-poisoned the billion sexual arteries of its giant body, although this has compounded the national sickness. And not because American culture has been crippled by role breakdown, alienation, narcissism, and moral decay, although these real deformities of the spirit are often lamented bitterly and blamed wrongly by the very carriers of the still more serious sickness we have in mind. On the contrary, America's cruelest illness was not born of the '80s at all. The illness is a grotesque exaggeration of that which is traditional, ancestral, perhaps written into the genes: it is the wholehearted endorsement and practice of unvarnished *bigotry.*

Without apology or even qualm, America hates and eats its own. Generation after generation, it savagely chews apart at least one homosexual child for every nine heterosexual children, and feeds it to them.

The nine lucky enough to be born and raised as heterosexuals usually grow up proud and strong, an eager brood of young American Aryans. The one—representing millions born or raised as homosexuals—is forced to cower and skulk like a German Jew of the '30s. Although at least as numerous as black Americans, and innocent, *as homosexuals,* of every crime save one denounced purely on Biblical grounds by the jurists of the time of Henry II, gays are still hounded from pillar to post by the watchdogs of American society. As children they are humiliated, beaten, even turned out of their homes. As adults, insult and injury are added to insult and injury: exposed gays lose their jobs, their homes, their churches, their friends, their children, and, not infrequently, their very lives.

This pattern of harassment and victimization is strikingly at odds with the way contemporary America likes to see itself. Homophobia—better described as homo-hatred—is its blind spot. These days, America rebukes all bigotry, except that which it imagines is God's. Although sick with the very same sickness it despises in the Ku Klux Klan, straight America fails to see the connection: like a self-satisfied Quasimodo, it inspects its moral hump in the mirror, smiles, and says, 'But on me it looks good!'

○

GAY SUICIDE AND THE BIG LIE

Under these conditions, too many desperate gays do, in fact, take their own lives. Hated and attacked, less thick-skinned gays despair, and—as the Biblical proverb has it—"fold their arms and eat their own flesh." The resulting suicide takes many forms: some escape into drunkenness and drug addiction, others into camouflage marriages or the priesthood. Some martyr themselves to their work or don the robes of the bachelor-scholar and disappear forever into musty library catacombs. Many gays sever old ties, opt out of the wider world, and exile themselves to gay ghettos. Still others, desperately seeking an ersatz approval, from a naïve public contrive assumed identities as 'straight' politicians, pop artists, and entertainers, and hit the campaign trail or the stages of Las Vegas, looking for love.

And some, of course—perhaps even in high school—sadly, quietly, obediently, just lay down and die.*

This, of course, is what straight America really demands: that, one way or another, come hell or high water, gays just *cease to exist.* The easiest means of dealing with a problem is to deny that there is one. And so, the nation squares the burden of upholding the Big Lie—that gays are rare freaks—on the backs of gays themselves.

Perhaps precisely because they want so desperately to fit in, members of oppressed minorities have a distressing tendency to buy into the lies and false values of their oppressors. Gays are no exception. With varying degrees of willingness, they have sustained the Big Lie through an all-too-necessary self-erasure. Just as blacks allowed whites to render them 'invisible' until the 1960s, so have gays made of themselves 'invisible' men (and women). Until a very few years ago, 'gay rights' was a non-issue in American history, simply because, in effect, whenever the roll was called, there *were* no gays to speak up!

Consequently, gays are assumed to be quite rare. Although, when polled, the average American now estimates the proportion of gays in the general population at roughly 10 percent—which is quite correct—he is only parroting back a much-bandied-about and, to him, meaningless statistic. He doesn't understand its implications, and certainly doesn't believe that that '10 percent' lives anywhere near him, still less that it might include some of his friends and acquaintances. Rather, his belief is, 'Maybe 10 percent

---

* It may anger bereaved parents who get wind of this, but we cannot help wondering, in this connection, just how much of the 'epidemic' of 'unexplained' suicides of teenagers who were 'attractive, popular . . . with everything to live for' could be explained, if truth were known, as the result of hidden homosexuality, guilt, and, finally, despair. As the AIDS Coalition To Unleash Power has declared, Silence can, indeed, equal Death.

nationally, but not in my backyard!' As a telling sign, a 1985 *Los Angeles Times* survey showed that over 50 percent of Americans believe that they are not personally acquainted with even one gay person . . . which is, of course, statistically preposterous. In John Reid's autobiographical *The Best Little Boy in the World,* the closeted protagonist's father constitutes an example of this sort of invincible ignorance; when asked about homosexuals, he notes that, "Thank God, those sick, twisted people are very few."

Matters aren't helped by gays' own perfectly natural recognition of the expedience of obliging this national ignorance. As a lesbian from a small town in Tennessee recently explained in *The Advocate,* "It makes life a whole lot easier. We don't get our church burned down, we don't get our bar burned down, and less people are murdered on the streets as a result of being quiet about our lifestyles." For gays and straights alike, mum's the word.

It is not, however, as though straights were not repeatedly given broad, heavy-handed hints, by television glimpses of throngs at gay pride marches and so forth, that the Big Lie is just that. But they don't take the hint; they *need* to believe in the rarity, and—by illogical extension—illegitimacy, of any way of life, any thoughts or feelings, other than their own. In psychiatric terms, this is 'denial of reality,' a mark of serious mental illness when it occurs in individuals. Any society that flatly denies the fact that one or two citizens in every ten have strong homosexual interests, and structures its laws and values around this denial, is, to this extent, seriously ill. Such an illness leaves the citizenry vulnerable to nasty, opportunistic infections of the mind, such as prejudice, distrust, and dissembling, cruelty, violence, perversion, and despair. And all these maladies reinforce the Big Lie in their turn.

We'd like you to think carefully for a moment about just how peculiar and appalling this social situation really is. We are all so used to the present state of affairs that it's quite hard to see it afresh, as hard as for a goldfish to inspect the water in its bowl. Try to picture it: the public denial of widespread homosexuality in America is like having some 25 *million* human skeletons stuffed into a single closet. The circumstance is grotesque, foul, and absurd.

We've noted that the majority of Americans are sick on this issue. Although they believe in a Big Lie, they are not liars in the full, deliberate, and morally culpable sense. The same cannot be said of certain Americans in positions of power who are fully aware of their lying and fully responsible for its consequences. Knowing the truth—that, in denying gays' existence, they impose untold misery upon millions of citizens—they manufacture, nevertheless, a clumsy, creaking, heavily orchestrated social falsehood. They are judges and politicos, government bureaucrats and their hired thugs, unctuous televangelists—may they fry in their own unction!—and even certain beer manufacturers, each ladling out hypocrisy by the metric ton. Theirs is, frankly, the sort of exaggerated and hollow joke one might expect more readily from Orwell's Ministry of Truth than from the institutions of American democracy. And we think the joke stinks.

o

THE LEFT-HANDED COMPLEMENT: AN ALLEGORICAL TALE

To sharpen your sense of the absurdity of gay life in homo-hating America, consider an appropriate analogy. *Imagine what might have happened if society had come down with and pursued a grudge against* the left-handed *the way it has against gays.*

As with gays, there is roughly one left-handed person in America for every nine right-handed. In our imaginary society, 'Lefties' find themselves born into a world in which left-handed behavior, and even being left-handed, are reviled in all fifty states, and illegal in half of them! The sight of a person writing with his left hand arouses a storm of disgust . . . as though the lefty had done so with his bare, unwashed foot. Such 'perverse' behavior is punished stiffly by state law, with malefactors facing ejection from their jobs and homes, disbarment from the company of children (sometimes including their own), and prison.

Harsh laws have not eradicated loathsome Lefties from plain view, so America reinforces its laws with left-hating social sanctions. From an early age, children learn abusive names for left-handed people: names like 'lefto,' 'southpaw,' and 'queer.' Before they are old enough to know what they mean, children learn to call one another by these names. They invent silly little 'telltale signs' of hidden left-handedness, and try to catch one another showing these signs.

Boys, especially, seem obsessed with left-handedness, left-baiting, and left-bashing. Liberal psychologists allege that this is because nearly 40 percent of all males are drawn to commit left-handed behavior at least once in their life—usually while still young, perhaps while drunk ('God, was I drunk last night! I didn't even know which hand I was using!')—and spend the rest of their lives hiding that fact by viciously persecuting open Lefties. Some psychologists go so far as to claim that all humans are 'polydextrously perverse,' potentially ambidextrous. (In fact, in the daring '70s it was almost fashionable to claim that one was 'ambi.')

Raving and waving their scriptures, Judeo-Christian leaders encourage discrimination against Lefties, because some old Testament or other views left-handedness as the mark of Cain: 'For it is an abomination before God that a man shall do with his left hand what he would do with his right.' Right-handedness is the only normal and natural way for humans to be, reason the preachers, and this is self-evident: why else would the right hand be *called* the right hand? Conservative homiletics is especially fond of identifying 'Lefties' with 'leftists.' (But, strangely enough, despite all this excoriation, every so often another fundamentalist minister is caught in a motel room with an underaged youth—teaching him to scribble with his left hand.)

Some of the more forgiving churches have taken a lenient stand: they will permit the left-handed to remain in their congregations so long as these unfortunates renounce vile, left-handed *practices*. Love the sinner, hate the sin! After all, it is plainly the pursuit of the godforsaken Lefty *lifestyle* that makes these creatures so suicidally miserable.

Pity, then, the child who feels drawn to the use of the left hand. (The American Psychodramatics Association reports that most of these pariahs secretly recognize their peculiarity from an early age.) Pubescent male Lefties fear the coming high school and college years, when their peers will expect them to be aggressive, strong, and graceful at right-handed sports. Instead, they are painfully awkward—just 'shy,' some say—and rumors begin to circulate. Left-handed girls privately wince when their girlfriends chat excitedly about the cutest boy in the class: '. . . and did you notice the *size* of his *right hand?*'

Bit by bit, therefore, young Lefties come to realize that they are outcasts in American society. They spend countless lonely hours wondering: are they the only ones? What went wrong with them? Were they, so to speak, *born* on the left-hand side of the bed, or did something in their home life produce this disaster?

Unable to face a future of deception or shame, some Lefties kill themselves. Others seek out physical 'therapy,' hoping to be 'converted' to right-handedness through aversive conditioning with electrical shocks. Still others deliberately marry right-handed people, raise children (hoping anxiously their kids will 'turn out right!'), and plunge themselves into careers requiring a lot of dexterity.

Among a small but growing segment of these left-handed victims, however, a sliver-thin but unquenchable light begins to dawn. They ask themselves: why does it *matter* which hand I prefer to use? Why does it matter whether I draw, grasp, or write with my left hand? Are not the love letters I write with my left hand still love letters? *(No!* shout the preachers: they are *lust* letters!) Are not the religious signs I make with my left hand still sincere gestures of my faith? Why am I persecuted for a handedness I came by naturally?

Eventually, in our allegorical America, such questions lead to so-called Lefty Liberation. Quietly, Lefties form social clubs and publish magazines extolling the 'gauche' way of life. Stories of 'gloved' Lefties in positions of national prominence and power are rife. Lefties note proudly their overrepresentation among the world's greatest artists and writers. With breathless enthusiasm, they point out that in other, more progressive parts of the world, such as Western Europe, citizens are not only allowed but encouraged to drive on the left-hand side of the road.

As time passes, the sheer number of left-handed Americans creates a thriving hidden economy catering to their tastes and needs. In Greenwich Village—America's 'Left Bank'—little boutiques pop up, selling clothing and implements designed especially for the convenience and 'kinky' enjoyment of Lefties. Gradually, police, politicians, and public get wind of these developments, in a vague way, but generally cause little trouble for Lefties unless they become too 'overt' or 'militant.'

Then—just when it seems that discrimination against Lefties is waning—Acquired Dextral Degeneration Syndrome strikes America. First paralyzing the muscles of the hand, then spreading fatally throughout the body, ADDS is caused by a small, burrowing worm transmitted via handshakes. To their disastrous discredit, ADDS spreads first among Lefties, who are fond of 'gladhanding' frequently and warmly—naturally, with their *left* hands. Now the 'Lefty Plague' begins to spread rapidly through right-handed shaking, as well, and the public reacts with a vengeance. Once again, oppression and left-hating violence are on the rise.

o   o   o

Three questions: Is our tale of 'Lefties' ridiculous? Yes. Is their invented plight pathetic and cruel? Certainly. Is this allegory of gay life in America overdrawn? Not in the least. But the reality isn't amusing, either. It's a story of bitter suffering, fear, and feeling sick at heart every day. It means mutilated spirits, mutilated lives. Only by forcing another hapless minority to 'don our gay apparel' can we recognize the naked silliness of our predicament: only then can we see plainly that homo-hatred has no clothes.

Still, it marches its shriveled privates down Main Street with ugly self-righteousness, daring anyone to smirk. Few dare.

○

WHAT'S IN A WORD? OR, A ROSE ISN'T ALWAYS A ROSE

Homophobia or homo-*hatred?* Does it make a difference?

To make a point, an exasperated President Lincoln once interrupted his quibbling Cabinet and demanded, "How many legs does a sheep have, if you call a tail a leg?" "Why, five," replied the Cabinet. "Wrong!" exclaimed Lincoln. "It's still four. Calling a tail a leg doesn't make it one!"

Our point is similar. 'Homophobia' is a comforting word, isn't it? It suggests that our enemies, all who oppose, threaten, and persecute us . . . are actually scared of us! If we must be hated, it's comforting to imagine that we have, at the very least, the power to inspire fear. The very term 'phobia' ridicules our enemies (and intentionally so), evoking images many would find comical, such as the old lady standing on the dining-room table, hiking up her skirts, and shrieking—at a mere mouse.

The trouble with this, as with so many 'empowering' euphemisms—like 'alternatively' enabled for 'disabled'—is that it's false and misleading, lulling us into complacency rather than rousing us to necessary action. The implications of this comforting distortion go something like this: if we inspire fear, we must be strong, and our enemies weak. Therefore, we needn't take our enemies seriously. In the words of *Mad* magazine's Alfred E. Neuman, "What, me worry?"

But is it phobia, or is it hatred? Common sense tells us that many of our enemies come by their queerbashing actions the old-fashioned way: by hating. Fear need have nothing to do with it. A well-designed 1985 study by researchers S. Shields and R. Harriman proved this quite nicely, demonstrating that although some "homonegative" males respond to homosexual stimuli with the 'tell-tale (racing) heart' of phobia, plenty of others don't.

Clearly, when we call our enemies 'homophobes,' we run the risk of underestimating them, which is a big mistake. Worse, the specious 'diagnosis' suggests an equally specious 'cure': that if straights just got to know us, they'd necessarily get over their fear —which, as with fear of tarantulas, is simply not true.

No, Lincoln was right, after all: a tail may equal a leg in the realm of metaphor, but not when you're carving the beast for a stew. Gays are *in* quite a stew, and we insist on calling the ingredients by their right names, not by medically exculpatory euphemisms. Let's reserve the term 'homophobia' for the psychiatric cases to which it really applies, and find a more honest label for the attitudes, words, and acts of hatred that are, in any event, our real problem. (After all, if it never actually *said* or *did* anything about it, straight America could hate us until the cows came home, for all that we'd care!)

We've cast about in vain for a term that would, at once, (a) clearly signify 'homo-hatred' for the layman, (b) satisfy the pedant's demand for etymological consistency, and (c) for everyone, look as impressively scientific and clinical as the term 'homophobia.' Well, Greek roots failed us; 'homomisia' would be etymologically satisfactory, but it don't mean a thing if it ain't got that swing —and it ain't. The plain English has the advantage of being blunt. *Homohatred* it is, and a dirty sock by any other name would smell as sour.

From now on, therefore, when we really do mean 'fear of homosexuals,' 'homophobia' it will be; when we're talking about *hatred* of homosexuals, we'll speak (without the hyphen) of 'homohatred,' 'homohating,' and 'homohaters.' We urge the reader to follow suit.

○
AIDS: THE INSURMOUNTABLE OPPORTUNITY

We have spoken of the 'permanent' crisis of American homosexuality. But in truth, that crisis will necessarily come to a head during the 1990s, thanks-but-no-thanks to the deadly spread of AIDS in the gay community and well beyond. Though the crisis may not end, it must necessarily *change*. Seldom in history has there been a disease simultaneously so horrid, so mortal, so relentless—and transmitted in a manner whose regulation is so nearly impossible without massive disruption of the fabric of society. America has only just begun to scratch the infected surface of AIDS and its implications. However, one implication is already clear: like Godzilla meeting King Kong, AIDS will confront the Big Lie—and bash it to bits.

The confrontation is, of course, under way. Americans, surrounded by the carnage of AIDS—at this point still mainly a 'gay disease'—cannot escape the conclusion that this is because they are, and have always been, surrounded also by *gays*. As friends, relatives, and admired celebrities fall down dead on all sides, straights are being forced to admit, for the first time, that homosexuality is more widespread than they'd ever dreamed. Legions of blue-haired American matrons who had previously managed the really staggering balancing act of *hating* faggy men while *adoring* their hairdressers are being forced, kicking and screaming, to add two and two to arrive, not at four but at a big, queer three. Ironically, gay activists used to wish that every gay person in America would turn lavender for a day, so that straights would be made to recognize their vast numbers. Now this ill-considered wish is, in effect, coming true—at least for gay men—through the gruesome agency of Kaposi's purple lesions.

Thus, AIDS presents us with what Pogo once termed "an insurmountable opportunity." The disease has brought us unprecedented public recognition and—along, of course, with a blast of increased hatred—a gratifying sympathy. It remains unclear whether we can and will turn this attention and sympathy into progress for gay rights.

By its very nature, the unwelcome 'opportunity' of AIDS puts us at a crossroads where we cannot dawdle for long. Even if we do not mobilize for action, the impact of the disease will shove us willy-nilly down one path or the other. As the death toll rises to the quarter-million mark in the early 1990s, gays fighting for their rights will see either significant victory or utter collapse before a wave of renewed oppression, violence, shame, and mass panic such as few would think possible in America.

The AIDS avalanche could slide in either direction. Public recognition of the formerly invisible gay community has finally come, but in an atmosphere of dread. Public sympathy is partly genuine, partly *pro forma*, and always intertwined with moralistic revulsion. Furthermore, whatever derived attention and sympathy we now enjoy cannot last much longer: the so-called gay men's health crisis will lose its special claim to the limelight as the disease spreads among the general population.

For these reasons, AIDS, though a loose cannon, is a cannon indeed. As cynical as it may seem, AIDS gives us a chance, however brief, to establish ourselves as a victimized minority legitimately deserving of America's special protection and care. At the same time, it generates mass hysteria of precisely the sort that has brought about public stonings and leper colonies since the Dark Ages and before; it has already produced a striking increase in reported antigay violence.

This, therefore, is the question and the challenge: how can we surmount our 'insurmountable' opportunity? How can we maximize the sympathy and minimize the fear? How, given the horrid hand that AIDS has dealt us, can we best play it? If, on the one hand, AIDS is actually conquered via therapy and vaccine, how can we position ourselves to take full advantage of the brief moment of reconciliation and good feeling toward gays that might follow? Could we keep straights from eventually rendering us once more invisible and illegitimate? On the other hand, if we are to assume that no vaccine will be found, and that AIDS will spread until society is profoundly altered, what should we be doing *now* to protect ourselves against the inevitable scapegoating?

Daunting questions, about a menacing future. If you think we overstate the menace, read on: we will summon up ample evidence of the threat of homohating backlash. If, instead, you feel overcome with gloom, and are unsure whether there's even any point to reading on, we promise to show you that conditions are not hopeless, and that there *are* opportunities to turn our predicament to our advantage, even now. To do so will require a clear understanding of the problem, and a practical—we emphasize, *practical*—plan. That's just what gays haven't had. That's why we wrote this book. And, though we expect to take some flak from the very people we're trying to help, the only alternative to a sensible plan is more gay suicide.

The campaign we outline in this book, though complex, depends centrally upon a program of unabashed propaganda, firmly grounded in long-established principles of psychology and advertising. Some readers will be disappointed with the seemingly tame idea of a propaganda campaign; they'd rather 'storm the barricades,' or at least parade defiantly in pink cha-cha heels on the next Gay Pride Day. Alas—in a way, we, too, would like to storm some barricades, but such tactics have proven themselves impractical—ineffective or even harmful—and *their day is past.* After all, it is hostile public opinion that has thwarted the gay movement at every turn, so it is hostile public opinion that we must address. Does this seem boring? If so, make no mistake: in its own way, this will be a 'hot' campaign, with all the excitement and theatrics of any other approach—and with a better chance of at least partial success.

In all candor, we're not convinced that the whole of our scheme will work as intended. Some elements, though potentially highly effective, will probably be rejected by gays out of hand, because they require too much effort or too much discipline or too much self-restraint or too much money or because, as Oscar Wilde once dismissed socialism, their accomplishment would take up too many nice evenings. To be blunt, we can only recommend. It is up to you, fearless reader, to act.

PART I

PROBLEMS:
T H E
STRAIGHT
A N D
NARROW

1

A FIELD TRIP TO
STRAIGHT
AMERICA

○ ○ ○
UP AGAINST IT

Consider what gays are up against: the wall. It stretches high and broad, like the Great Wall of China, across the full expanse of American society. Today there is almost no social interaction between straights and gays wherein the latter can safely ignore the barricade of dislike and fear which separates them from the rest. In the first part of this book we seek to understand exactly what that wall is made of, so that, with the plan proposed in Part II, we can proceed to tear it down.

For our purposes, homohatred and homophobia are best viewed from a detached, even unfamiliar distance (if one can manage it), because that's the best way to see the situation clearly—perhaps the way the Great Wall of China can be seen in its entirety only from outer space, or the way a visiting anthropologist would disinterestedly record the folkways of a primitive culture.

The goal here is to develop a list of negative things that straights believe and feel about gays—summarized as seven deadly myths —and harmful things that straights do to gays in consequence of those myths. *This list of prejudices and harmful actions shall stand as our specific agenda for change.*

But such a list can report only the symptoms and effects of homohatred, *not* its underlying causes. It catalogs the what, not the why. To understand the deep psychological roots of the problem, the reader will have to wait until Chapter 2, which explains how most heterosexuals come to hate and fear gays in the first place.

The distinction between the symptoms and the causes of homohatred is essential, yet the two are invariably confused by gay activists, who, consequently, approach the problem like the proverbial blind men groping their way around an elephant, focusing on all the wrong things instead of the whole. This confusion has caused the gay avant-garde to mount clumsy, inconsistent attacks on the superficial symptoms of homohatred—and has caused them to address the items on our list in a piecemeal fashion—with only haphazard success.

We have a different, and more systematic, approach. First we concern ourselves with getting the symptoms of homohatred/homophobia down in a list. Our observations are grouped under two simple questions:

• *What, exactly, do most straights* think *of gays?*
• *How do they* treat *gays?*

To answer these questions, we set off on a field trip to heterosexual America, a reconnaissance mission into the living rooms, boardrooms, and locker rooms of the nation, to get a closer look at the supposed opposition.

Some gays will scoff at such an excursion. They may feel patronized: doesn't every gay man and woman raised in this society already know its blind spots and bigotries only too well? Doesn't each gay person have straight friends and family which remind him daily, in a hundred ways, of his estrangement from their society?

The answer to such protests is both yes and no. Yes, every gay person knows plenty about his own experiences with straights;

they are etched indelibly, like red scrimshaw, on his heart. No, though valid, those personal experiences are not necessarily representative of the big picture of gay life in America today.

Personal experiences may not even be typical. For instance, based on their own lives within the social ceasefire zones of America's larger cities, many ghettoized homosexuals have come to imagine that heterosexuals across the nation are more tolerant today than they really are. (A Greenwich Village troglodyte, not long ago, earnestly assured the *New York Times*, "Now the vast majority understands that to shun gay people is wrong.") Such gays have evidently forgotten about blue-collar and rural America, about the Midwest and the South. Most ghetto gays have either never been to Texas, Maine, Alabama, or Kansas, or else, like Dorothy in Oz, they've been swept up dizzily in the cyclone of urban gay life and, in the process, have come down with amnesia about whence they came.

If forewarned is forearmed, such refugees from the heartland had best hop aboard the bus for our field trip back to Kansas, with their ruby slippers and Toto too.

○
WHAT STRAIGHTS THINK OF GAYS

1. THEY DON'T.

"[Homosexuals are] the filthiest, dirtiest human beings on the face of the earth," asserted a town commissioner from Traverse City, Michigan, to the *New York Times* in 1987. He then explained, in defense, that his opinions were based on something he once read about gays. "They are not my opinions because I don't know anything about homosexuals, and I don't want to know anything."

This is the first point for gays to understand: *straights know very little about homosexuality and would prefer to know even less.* Because they find the subject distasteful and disturbing—in any but titillatingly small doses—most heterosexuals simply put it out of their minds with a shudder or a shrug of indifference. They go about their lives as though the issue had no bearing on themselves or anyone they know. Their meager fund of knowledge about homosexuality is constructed from hoary myths, rumors, jokes from their school days, and lurid news stories; and, for most straights, that is enough. More direct exposure to homosexuality or homosexuals—say, during a trip to Rudy's Salon for Fabulous Hair, or to see a film with a kinky gay subplot—is merely brushed aside, since straights will go to great lengths *not* to think about such things.

Straight indifference to, or avoidance of, the subject is hard for gays to bear in mind, since they perforce must think about their sexual and social predicament daily. Still, gays who come out to their family or straight friends often experience such shunning of the subject firsthand. After the initial brutal or tearful confrontations with loved ones, the topic of homosexuality somehow has a way of slipping silently, awkwardly off the menu of discussable subjects. "You're homosexual?," said a straight friend, "O.K., that's your business. But I'd rather not hear the details, if you don't mind. And *please* don't invite me to visit a gay bar with you; I'm not ready for that." (And as the years went by, this friend was never to prove ready.)

Observing American society as a whole, its refusal to think too much about homosexuality takes on the appearance of deliberate collusion in what we earlier called the Big Lie—the nationwide public pretense that in America there are really no gays to speak of.

Avoidance of Gay News Events and Issues. One sees, for example, blackouts of, or deliberate inattention to, gay news events, in ways both small and big—everything from the tearing down of gay speakers' posters on college campuses to the refusal by the *Washington Post* to cover a large Gay Pride Day celebration in the nation's capital some years back.

One sees efforts to minimize the significance of gay public events. The *New York Times* and other newspapers, for example, evidently underestimated by half the number of gays participating in the momentous Gay & Lesbian March on Washington during October 9–12, 1987. If, as the most reliable gay-news sources maintained, the number of demonstrators totaled roughly half a million, then the event rivaled the largest civil rights marches of the sixties. At least the *Times* put the news of "200,000 protesters" on page one: not a single word about the event appeared in the nation's two largest newsweeklies, *Time* and *Newsweek*. Theirs was so blatant a breach of reporting standards that, had any other minority's mass demonstration been likewise neglected, the omission itself would have become the big news story.

While the press's coverage of gay news is inadequate, even this scant attention is more than enough for most Americans. In an ABC News survey conducted in 1984, for instance, fully half of the public felt that the broadcast press gives altogether *too much* attention to gays. As a conservative columnist has complained acidly, homosexuals have always been around, of course, but, like children, should be seen and not heard.

One also observes the profound *reluctance of society to engage in public discussion of issues that concern gays,* such as homohating violence and AIDS. Indeed, there can be only one reason why it took President Ronald Reagan four years of epidemic to utter the word 'AIDS' for the first time in public—years during which twelve thousand citizens fell ill and some six thousand died: Reagan knew that broaching the subject would require that he acknowledge publicly the existence of a large and growing number of gay Americans suffering from a sexually related disease. Homosexuality remains such a ticklish subject that, as late as 1987, Vice-President Bush felt compelled to confess that there was still a "giggling factor" about AIDS within the administration. As one aide to right-wing congressman Jack Kemp observed with irony, "Everyone's trying to avoid this issue because it combines homosexuality, sexual disease and death, matters in which most of us wish to be unenlightened."

Willful Perpetuation of Ignorance About Homosexuality. America is not only reluctant to recognize news events or address public issues concerning gays; it also *refuses to educate citizens on the nature of homosexuality itself.* Prodded by the AIDS crisis, a few school boards have gritted their teeth and begun to teach schoolchildren the meaning of words such as 'homosexual' and 'bisexual.' But, apparently mindful of George Orwell's warning that words have the power to stimulate dangerous thoughts and deeds, most educators have not been eager to expand their pupils' vocabulary. "I've talked to school superintendents around the country," one educator from Montgomery, Alabama, told the *New York Times* "and they don't want AIDS education to broach homosexuality or safe sex practices. As far as they are concerned, that's unconscionable." Arch-conservative pundit Phyllis Schlafly expressed the same sentiment in more inflammatory terms: "The American people will not put up with teaching safe sodomy in the classroom." So, because a blanket of silence continues to smother the subject, whispering little boys and girls are left, on the playground during recess, to teach one another their stereotypic myths and unschooled prejudices about 'faggots' and 'queers.'

Just as the American public will not educate its children, neither will it educate itself about homosexuality. *Straight Americans do not care to read serious treatments of gay life.* This also holds true for straight literary critics, who have little good to say about the burgeoning genre of 'gay literature.' Reviewing a gay novel, one book critic for the *Wall Street Journal* recently carped that the love that dare not speak its name has become "the love that can't shut up."

Not that it really matters whether gay writers scream or shut up about their lives, since few straights are listening in any case. You may convince yourself of this by visiting the deserted Gay Studies aisle of your local bookstore or library. The Gay Studies aisle (or, more likely, shelf) is seldom hard to find: it's usually near the Psychology/Therapy section, even though Gay Studies may include works of fiction, history, sociology, or political science, as well as psychology.

Even straights who are curious do not wish to be seen showing interest in that aisle, for fear of what others may conclude about their sexual proclivities. In contrast, no emotionally normal white male would harbor fears of venturing into the Black Studies or

Women's Studies aisle; no one is likely to conclude that he's secretly black or female. One might, on the other hand, wonder about the fellow in the Psychology aisle who is perusing a book about sexual impotence. And, in exactly the same way, the Gay Studies shelf has come to be regarded as a kinky apothecary of psychotherapeutic self-help remedies and aphrodisiac romances written exclusively for gays themselves. So straights stay the hell away. And learn nothing.

Neglect of Gays in Mass Culture. Indeed, if straights were to learn anything about gays, it would not be in schoolrooms or from serious books: it would be from mass entertainments like television shows, films, and plays. *But heterosexuals do not want to watch homosexuality portrayed in their mass entertainments with any frequency.* Most straights haven't the patience to watch sustained portrayals of gay characters in television series, for example, even though such portrayals could provide genuine education, and help counteract the two-dimensional cardboard stereotypes one usually sees whenever gays are introduced briefly on TV shows and in films.

Of course, there have always been public entertainments which featured clownish homosexual men (but, significantly, seldom lesbians) for comic effect. Homosexuals are least frightening to straights when portrayed, like Step'N Fetchit, as harmless, childish eunuchs. The film and Broadway hit *La Cage aux Folles* followed this hoary formula and prospered in the 1980s. (Though, as Robert Sandla noted in the *Advocate,* the musical's publicity poster curiously chose to feature one of the show's only truly heterosexual women doing a high kick, which "has about as much to do with *La Cage aux Folles* as a giraffe has to do with *Cats.*")

But the public has shown mixed interest in the recent spate of TV shows and movies with more serious gay themes. These have featured two subjects: (1) young men dying of AIDS, and/or (2) confused gay women or men who must agonize over their 'choice' to become straight or gay. (Story lines of the second variety represent, of course, a concession to the public's insistence upon the myth of moral choice in such matters, and typically include—

alongside the infatuated gay innocent—at least one male or female Temptress of Debauchery who displays in his or her coarsened person the just deserts of 'excessive' commitment to the homosexual lifestyle.)

These shows have been produced partly because gay Hollywood itches to indulge itself; partly because straight Hollywood understands that sexual exotica clad in the diaphanous fig leaf of social relevance is always a sure bet to attract jaded viewers. (Surely this was one motive behind low-rated ABC's abrupt—and encouraging —addition of gay characters to three of its prime-time dramas in the late 1980s.) Yet the public's interest in such productions is ambivalent and basically prurient. Most straights watch stories about 'gays in crisis' with the lurid, reluctant, peekaboo fascination that attends a bloody roadside car wreck.

But nobody wants to see a car wreck *every* time she hits the highway. The public's patience and voyeurism tend to wear thin when gay characters are made likable leading characters on TV shows. Early 1980s sitcoms, such as *Love, Sidney*—which was to have featured a kindly, avuncular gay man residing with a woman and her daughter—were muzzled from the start by protesting conservatives. On the other hand, the long-running evening soap opera *Dynasty* made sensational headlines by introducing the leading character of a handsome, masculine boy who struggled valiantly, episode after tiresome episode, to resolve his bisexuality.

What, then, was the key difference between these two series? In the first, homosexuality was portrayed as a permanent condition, while in the second it was portrayed as a big but temporary problem to be resolved. The public is bothered by the portrayal of homosexuality as a settled fact of life but rather enjoys watching it portrayed as a disease or mental illness from which the victim will either perish or recover.

This distinction between homosexuality as *problem* and *condition* is crucial to the way in which straights think—when they do— about the subject. By definition, a problem both admits of, and requires, a solution. A condition, on the other hand, is *not* subject to solution: it is simply an aspect of life that must be accommodated. You needn't think too much about a problem until it directly confronts you, whereupon you solve it, then turn your attention elsewhere. But a permanent condition may require your permanent tolerance; you must come to terms with it practically, psychologically, and somehow morally. Homosexuality in America should be recognized as a condition but instead is still perceived as a problem.

No wonder TV writers continue to let Steven teeter-totter on the fence, without settling into gayness. If he ever falls for homosexuality permanently, they'll face some mighty irate viewers. "The public is happy the writers have dropped Steven's 'gay' character, especially with the AIDS scare," gushed one delighted fan in the *Star* after one of randy Steven's straighter episodes, "Now that he is straight, keep him that way and have him remarry Sammy Jo." (Sorry, Sammy Jo is *not* another boy.)

Viewing homosexuality as a problem rather than a condition, straights offer advice to gay America: why not be done with this homosexual stuff once and for all? Let life imitate TV art: just get over it and remarry Sammy Jo. And if you stubbornly resist, then we'll have no choice but to switch channels to a more wholesome and believable show, like *MacMillan and Wife*.

There Are No Gay Heroes. Which brings us to the matter of Rock Hudson and other all-American heroes who happen to be gay. Just as straights don't like to see homosexuality portrayed in their mass entertainments, neither do they wish to contemplate it among their celebrities and heroes. *Straights who have come to admire closeted heroes refuse to accept their homosexuality, even when it seems a fact beyond dispute.*

The Rock Hudson scandal provides a classic case of public self-delusion, and even collusion in the Big Lie. Hudson had been actively homosexual throughout his career as Hollywood's ultramacho leading man, but, like so many other famous gay actors, had hidden the fact from the public, and even entered an arranged marriage for a few years to protect his reputation. When Boze Hadleigh asked him confidentially, in 1982, how many top actors in Hollywood were homosexual, Hudson replied, "Whew! Too many for me to name. If you mean gay, or 'bisexual' . . . then maybe most . . . Trust me, . . . America does not want to know."

As it turned out, Rock was right: America did *not* want to know. Shortly before his death from AIDS in 1985, Hudson contracted with a publisher and coauthor to tell the story of his life, homosexuality and all. When the book (like its subject) came out, the coauthor, Sara Davidson, went on promotional tour and was appalled by her book's incredulous and resentful reception. Writing in the *New York Times Magazine* about her experiences on tour, Davidson said she had "underestimated how devastating it would be for many to learn that a star they had cherished as a symbol of manliness was gay." She was astounded when asked repeatedly by reproachful reporters across the country, "Do we need to know the truth about Rock Hudson?" Davidson said that the low point in her tour came during a talk show stint in Detroit, when an entertainment columnist implied that "the book was 'fiction' and that Rock wasn't gay . . . The audience cheered."

In reaction to Davidson's article recounting these experiences, a disgruntled reader wrote back, "It may be the writer's job '. . . to seek out the truth,' but who wants to know? Leave some heroes untarnished for us to foolishly admire."

The myth that there is no significant homosexuality in the American character (hence none in its heroes) is being abetted in this instance by the public's desperate denial of an awkward datum—that Rock Hudson was gay. How could his millions of fans have deluded themselves for decades about the cause of that heart-throb's protracted bachelorhood? After Hudson's death, they were comforted by his onetime wife, Phyllis Gates, who proclaimed reassuringly in her autobiography and news interviews that, with her, Rock had been "a passionate, if quick, lover," and "I never suspected he was gay." Well, then, if his own *wife* didn't suspect, why should the rest of us?

It's harder to imagine, however, how straight America could have deceived itself about another beloved and seemingly gay entertainer, the flamboyant pianist Liberace, who died from AIDS in 1987. Liberace turned ultra-campy effeminacy into a schtick, and the public, for the most part, loved it. They bought his records, swarmed to his performances, and made him very, very rich. In the conservative 1950s, Liberace became television's first matinee idol, with a syndicated show carried by more stations than *I Love Lucy*. Even after an embarrassing and much-publicized palimony suit for $113 million was filed against him in 1982 by his self-alleged lover Scott Thorson, Liberace denied all accusations and remained popular.

How did he pull it off? With the help of his fans, no doubt, who chose not to recognize in him what any ordinary person might have considered obvious and otherwise discreditable. Liberace was not exactly, crudely homosexual, they seem to have told themselves with a wink. Rather, Liberace was Liberace, an eccentrically lovable character, a harmless, sexless one-of-a-kind. In viewing him this way, the pianist's elderly fans could avert the repugnant issue of homosexuality while enjoying Liberace's showmanship and his music. Ironically, they would probably have had a much harder time stomaching Liberace if they'd met him as a stranger on the street. But then, straights would hardly expect to meet anyone like Liberace on the street because . . .

2. 'THERE AREN'T MANY HOMOSEXUALS IN AMERICA'

MR. THURMOND: *And how many members do you say you have?*

MR. LEVI: *We have about 10,000 members [of the National Gay and Lesbian Task Force], and we represent various organizations around the country.*

MR. THURMOND: *Ten thousand members? . . . I was interested in one statistic you gave, that one-tenth of the population are gay or lesbian. I'm shocked to hear that, if that's true. Are you sure that figure is correct?*

—Excerpted in the *New York Times* from an exchange between Senator Strom Thurmond, Chairman of the Judiciary Committee, and Jeffrey W. Levi, Executive Director of the NGLTF, at August 1986

hearings on William Rehnquist's nomination to be chief justice of
the Supreme Court.

Gays must understand that, just as straights decline to think
deeply about homosexuality, *straights also refuse to believe there are
many homosexuals around for them to think about.*

This is not, of course, the case. During 1938–63, Alfred Kinsey
and his colleagues at the Institute for Sex Research gathered nationally representative data, drawn from many thousands of in-
depth interviews, on the incidence of homosexual experience
among American men and women. Their survey method had minor flaws and the results are now, in any case, dated, since their
research ended years before the 'sexual revolution' of the '60s and
'70s got under way. Still, the Kinsey surveys provide the most
reliable data yet available on this sensitive topic. The Institute
found that quite a large proportion of the public—roughly one in
three men and one in five women—have had at least *some* overtly
homosexual experience between their teen years and middle age;
and, for many of these, such experience has been rather more
than incidental. Some 21% of white college-educated men and 7%
of white college-educated women report having had sex with two
or more persons of their own gender, and/or having had gay sex
six or more times. Percentages for noncollege white men and
women are 28% and 5%, respectively. Fewer blacks report such
extensive gay experience; e.g., only 16% of black college men and
3% of black college women. Across the board, for some reason,
homosexually inclined males seem to outnumber their female
counterparts by two or three to one (which is, incidentally, why
this book so often is actually speaking of gay *men* when generaliz-
ing about the 'gay community').[1]

Are all of these homosexually experienced individuals 'gay'? In
our society, where getting caught in the act *just once* can brand a
person for life as a 'homo,' it is tempting to say yes. Certainly,
anyone who repeatedly engages in gay sex, or seeks out multiple
partners, displays strong homosexual proclivities. On the other
hand, as Kinsey explained, sexual orientation isn't an either/or

situation: people array themselves along a spectrum ranging from exclusive heterosexuality to exclusive homosexuality. If we must draw the line somewhere and pick a specific percentage for propaganda purposes, we may as well stick with the solidly conservative figure suggested by Kinsey decades ago: taking men and women together, *at least 10% of the populace has demonstrated its homosexual proclivities so extensively that that proportion may reasonably be called 'gay.'* But we stress that this figure is, if anything, an *under*estimate. When the *Los Angeles Times* conducted a national poll by telephone in December 1985, fully 10% of those who answered the question described themselves as "gay"; one can only imagine how many more actually saw themselves as gay but declined to admit this to a complete stranger, under suspicious circumstances, on the telephone.

So much for the hard facts. Now, does the general public understand them? Straight awareness of the size of the gay population exists in a weird psychological twilight, half there and half absent, known and yet not known. The public's estimates of the number of gays in its midst range widely. Based on their personal experience, most straights probably would put the gay population at 1% or 2% of the general population. Yet, Senator Thurmond's quaint ignorance notwithstanding, when straights are asked by pollsters for a formal estimate, the figure played back most often is the '10% gay' statistic which our propagandists have been drilling into their heads for years.

Do not be overly encouraged by such polls, however, since straights show no real understanding of what '10%' actually means. Although it implies that one out of every ten people they know well is predominantly homosexual, *more than half* of all straight Americans continue to believe (according to the *L.A. Times* poll we just mentioned) that they are not personally acquainted with *any* gays. It's a case of "Ten percent, maybe—but not of *my* friends." Many if not most straights would undoubtedly find it hard to believe—ten percent or no—that there are very nearly as many gays as blacks in America today, half again as many as Hispanics, and more than three times as many as Jews.

Straights do not appreciate that, with at least one tenth of the public extensively involved in it, the practice of homosexuality may be a more commonplace activity in America than, say, bowling (6%), jogging (7%), golfing (5%), hunting (6%), reading drugstore romance novels (9%), or ballroom dancing (2%) on a regular basis.[2] (Ballroom dancing—now, *that's* abnormal.)

Nor, we suppose, do straights understand what '10%' means in absolute numbers: that there are some 24 million to 25 million homosexual Americans of both sexes, all ages, races, and creeds. That's a whopping big number—as big, in fact, as the total population of California. It means there are as many gays in the United States as there are Swedes in Sweden, Danes in Denmark, Austrians in Austria, and Irish in Ireland—combined. When we make simple comparisons like this, our straight friends gape with astonishment, as though we'd added one plus one and come up with sixty-nine. When we further point out that the social trauma of gay orientation directly touches the lives of more than one third of the American populace (25 million gays, their 50 million parents, plus countless siblings), our friends look downright queasy.

And no wonder this is news to straights: the fact that there are teeming millions of American gays has been suppressed to corroborate the Big Lie. We've noticed that this fact is spookily absent from all kinds of discussions of gay politics and lifestyle in the mainstream press; nor is it to be found even in textbooks on American history, culture, or demography. Sometimes this omission is conscious and deliberate, as when, for example, a major Boston publishing house recently excised from a new high school history text the neutral observation that there are "millions" of homosexual citizens in the United States. The publisher feared that inclusion of this mild statement would cause the entire text to be rejected by incredulous school boards across the South. Thus the Big Lie perpetuates itself.

Society similarly refuses to recognize the heavy concentration of gays within its esteemed core institutions, its government and churches. For instance, the public both knows and yet refuses to know that gays make up a disproportionately large part—probably one third to one half—of the Catholic and Episcopalian clergy. So when this is asserted candidly by the press or by clergy themselves, ruffled members of the flock put up a flap: typically, one angry parishioner, writing in the *Boston Globe*, recently dismissed the claim as a "bizarre assertion," an "utterly incredible suggestion," and a "deliberate and systematic attack" on the church. Anxious church leaders likewise repudiate the allegation with heated rhetoric (but how would they know?)—and so, quite willfully, the blind lead the blind. One can almost *see* the three monkeys settling into formation: see no evil, hear no evil, confess no evil.

You should grasp clearly why America's persistent underestimation of the number of homosexuals in its citizenry and core institutions is so dangerous to the cause of civil rights. The public conflates two distinct senses of the word 'abnormal'—'infrequent' and 'pathological'—into just one. In doing so, it unwittingly commits what philosophers call a naturalistic fallacy, judging the rightness of sexual conduct only by how often it occurs in nature. Literally, the more the better. As Kinsey, Pomeroy, and Martin explain dryly in their classic study *Sexual Behavior in the Human Male:*

> To those who believe, as children do, that conformance should be universal, any departure from the rule becomes immorality. The immorality seems particularly gross to an individual who is unaware of the frequency with which exceptions to the supposed rule actually occur.

Thus, when it comes to fighting the charge that homosexuality is statistically abnormal hence immoral, there *is* strength in numbers.

But how can the gay community show its numerical strength when most of its members remain closeted and incognito? Many think this will be accomplished involuntarily through the highly visible spread of AIDS among homosexuals. "Five years ago," gay activist Eric Rofes told the *Boston Globe* in 1987, "individuals and institutions were still arguing over whether we existed, how many there were, and whether we had special needs. AIDS has brought all our issues fully into the public domain."

Rofes is right about this, but he jumps to a conclusion that is blithe and dangerous: "We no longer have to fight for society to recognize that we are an identifiable and substantial community with a culture all our own." On the contrary, we think gays must *never* underestimate straight society's desire and capacity not to see them, to make them invisible, even during the AIDS epidemic. Gays must struggle unceasingly to become *real* to straights, to advance from vaporous myth to living flesh and blood, even as a virus threatens to transform our decimated community from flesh to myth once again.

3. 'ALL GAYS ARE EASY TO SPOT: THERE ARE TELLTALE SIGNS!'

The Big Lie that there are not many gays in America is further supported by the myth that all gays are easy to identify by their outward appearance and manner. 'Fags' and 'dykes,' it is believed, can be identified by a short checklist of telltale signs so simple, blatant, and unambiguous that most kids know them before they leave grade school. That relatively few gay people actually exhibit those 'telltale' signs—Kinsey's institute has estimated that only one in seven male and one in twenty female homosexuals are recognizable as such to the general public—reinforces straight America's misconception that its gay neighbors are very few in number.

Once, while showering in the communal bathroom of his graduate school dormitory, one of the authors was cornered by a Mormon friend in what appeared, for an instant, to be a sexual advance: stepping unnervingly close to the (closeted) author, the young man smiled knowingly and whispered, "Hunter, I've got something to tell you. I think Jerry's a queer." Jerry was an ordinary-looking resident of the dorm who nonetheless exhibited, on occasion, vaguely effeminate mannerisms. When the author demanded evidence of Jerry's homosexuality, our Latter-Day Saint shrugged and replied, "Well, of course, he hasn't *admitted* anything, but I can always tell a queer when I see one; there's just something about them that gives them away."

In a similar tale, a gay Manhattan police officer told the *New York Times* about the time when he and another officer had broken up a fight between two men. On the way back, his partner observed, "That younger man—he's a homo." "How can you tell?" asked the covertly gay officer. "I can always spot them," came the confident reply.

This blackly comic scenario, *mutatis mutandis,* has been experienced innumerable times by those many homosexuals who are not recognizably gay: sooner or later some straight friend will pull them aside and disgustedly point out a third person as a homosexual.

How can straights be so sure—and so wrong—so much of the time? Because their confident assessments are never checked against reality: there is no external authority to step in from the wings and affirm or repudiate their suspicions, nor is there anyone to point out when they have *failed* to recognize a gay person.

The only evidence straights have to go on is the accumulated American folk wisdom about homosexuals. This amounts to a lengthy checklist of surefire, telltale signs which are, for the most part, misleading, silly, and irrelevant. Consider the following mythology of gay attributes, culled from what we've overheard in the straight world. One is struck by the richness and complexity of the gay caricature that emerges. If a 'social myth' is defined as 'what the public is dreaming'—as the mythologist Joseph Campbell has suggested—then it is apparent from the highly developed myths about gays that the shadow of homosexuality has haunted the public's dreams for a very long time.

Telltale Signs: Gay Names. Let's ease into more serious matters of stereotype by dispensing, first, with the most patently preposterous one: name-calling. Many straights grow up believing that you can identify gay males by their pansy-ish first names. (Significantly, the same is not true for lesbians, to whom no particular

names have become linked; and whose detection and chastise-
ment have historically been of far less interest to our male-ori-
ented society.) The names that parents give their male infants fix
their sexual destinies—or at least predestine the amount of harassment they'll suffer from classmates for being fags. Hardly a lad in
America, straight or gay, doesn't wince inwardly and thank his
parents that at least he is not, as the old Johnny Cash song put it,
"A Boy Named Sue."

Fatedly homosexual names include those which sound a bit too
fancy (for example, Byron, Miles, or Guy), or those which lend
themselves to derisive pronunciation with a 'gay' lisp, such as
Percy or Bruce (pronounced 'brooth' or 'broothee'). Pretty much
any blueblood name, unless shortened sportily by its owner, is
asking for trouble. Cyril, Neville, Maxwell, and Christopher, for
instance, will conjure up in some minds the prissy young men
who staff the fragrance counter at Bloomingdale's.

Dual-gender names—Leslie, Gene, Dana, Marion, Hilary, Fran-
cis—are also suspect, and will cause their male bearers much
locker-room woe from grade school on. No wonder Marion Morri-
son and Marion Robertson had to do what a man's gotta do:
switched to the names John Wayne and Pat Robertson. (Obviously
Rev. Robertson didn't quite get the hang of things: even 'Pat' is a
dual-gender name.)

Wimpy names—e.g., Cecil, Clarence, and Wendell—also seem
to carry homosexual overtones, because we all know that fairies
are meek and wimpy, just as we know that all wimps are 'fags' in
one sense or the other. Finally, we should add that diminutive
nicknames (e.g., Ricky, Bobby, Stewy, Stevie), when retained
much past elementary school, can be telltale too. Gay males supposedly like to address one another by precious, infantile names
rather than by the names of Real Men.

Telltale Signs: Gay Voices, Bodies, and Demeanors. We will leave
aside, for the most part, the diverse array of signals of (male) homosexuality that children devise among themselves in grade
school—even though they have only the dimmest notion of what
homosexuality itself might be. There is no limit to the list of silly

criteria, and kids rewrite that list weekly. Generally speaking, however, children will say that others are 'fags' and 'homos' if they:

- Show signs of unusual intelligence (i.e., are eggheads or teacher's pets);
- Speak a certain way;
- Dress a particular way (e.g., wear white socks or boxer shorts, or button their shirts up to the top button, or fail to remove the 'fairy hook' or 'fruit loop' found on the back of some dress shirts);
- Move in specific ways (e.g., 'all fags cross their legs like girls');
- Fail designated tests of manly courage (e.g., if they flinch when socked in the shoulder);
- Participate voluntarily in certain school activities (e.g., sing in the chorus or show an interest in school plays).

These childhood indicia certainly show us where the telltale checklists compiled by straight grownups get their start.

Virtually every adult knows how gay males are supposed to sound: campy, like William Hurt's impersonation of one in *The Kiss of the Spider Woman*. Their voices are excessively musical, either all high warbles and whines or else deep and ridiculously theatrical. Their tone of voice is arch and pissy, except when wracked by self-pitying sobs (they cry a lot). When agitated, they shriek and coo like schoolgirls. When sexually aroused, they hiss or purr languorously, like catty old barmaids. And, naturally, all gay males lisp like Truman Capote.

In physique, gay males are still widely perceived to be either ectomorphs or endomorphs, seldom solidly muscled mesomorphs (except in California, where a new 'narcissistic body-builder' stereotype is developing). That is, gay men are either frail, willowy, nervous creatures ('neurasthenic,' psychologists used to say), or else they are larger, but with the pudgy contours of a woman. Put these two types side by side and you have a duo resembling Laurel and Hardy.

When gay male bodies move, according to myth, their joints

swivel smoothly—too smoothly—particularly at the languid wrist, and sometimes in the wayward pinky. Where other men put their feet down firmly and clomp along heavily, homosexual men are said to be 'light of foot' and to flounce or mince gaily forward. At the same time, their unconscious body language is recognizably prim, tight and constrained, not free and open in the manner of Real Men. In films and plays, one discerns something tentative, even fearfully cautious, about the movements of gay characters. Except for their handshake, which is always bonelessly limp, gay men grasp objects the way weak people do: with a delicacy, deliberate precision, and unmanly grace that suits them for their inevitable careers as antique dealers and floral designers.

(Perhaps one other reason why gay men have such difficulty grasping objects pertains to their nails, since, as many straights know, gays are prone to grow their fingernails to creepy and incriminating lengths: one man recently complained to the *Boston Globe* that he had been verbally attacked as a homosexual "simply because, as a classical guitarist, I have long fingernails on my right hand. Now, unless I'm out with my wife, I take extra care to drink a beer or collect my change—with my left hand." With his *left* hand? It's certainly a good thing that the poor fellow wasn't born into a leftophobic society or he'd be in for *real* trouble.)

In countenance, the gay youth is often supposed to be tellingly pretty, endowed with small features and full lips. He grooms with particular care, wears bracelets and earrings, has unnaturally smooth skin that hints of makeup (!), and he takes fashion risks with his clothing. In manner and attire, he is an extravagant fop.

As the boy grows older—past thirty—and uglier, his clothes and demeanor become more fastidious, and his vanity curdles in noticeable ways. An overly formal manner and outmoded courtliness are stereotypic for the middle-aged gay. The myth paints his expression as that of the embittered schoolmarm or the officious librarian. He is defensively censorious; he clucks disapproval at the 'insensitive brutes' around him. He's the annoying sort of prig who wears an exquisitely trimmed pencil-thin mustache and an ascot, purses his lips a lot, and taps his foot too often—hand to hip, one eyebrow raised—in impatient indignation. In sum, middle-aged gays are supposed to come off like sour old biddies. Or like Tony Randall's character in *The Odd Couple*.

Now a few words about the less well-developed stereotype of lesbians. They are pictured—when American straights bother to picture them at all—as just the opposite of gay males. They are supposed to have 'butch' voices: low and gravelly. Their speech is abrupt, monosyllabic, profane, and tough. Who knows whether they ever actually cry, or just take everything like a man.

Where gay male bodies are either birdlike or as diffuse and soft as jellyfish, lesbian bodies are reputed to be stout, broad-shouldered, thunder-thighed, and athletic. Their body movements are graceless and abrupt. Their handshake—as well as their vaginal grip, according to William Burroughs—could crush a lead pipe. They have no breasts (having cut them off, Amazon style), but they may have noticeable mustaches. For that matter, according to the old joke, their armpit hair is long enough to braid, and they need to shave their legs daily but don't. No wonder they never wear anything but pants. As a matter of fact, they seem to dress like men in all regards and keep their coiffures cropped short. (A straight friend insists that butch-cut hair *with long dangling earrings* is a sure sign.)

In countenance, the lesbian is thought to be homely and humorless—rather like Picasso's appalling portrait of Gertrude Stein. The lesbian never wears makeup, both because she is acne-prone and because she hates all men, who might find such artifice attractive. (Many straights will suspect from these supposed traits that the lesbian is merely an unhappy heterosexual *femme manquée* who has ultimately sought the affection of other women because she couldn't get a man: see our discussion later on.)

No myth specifies how a lesbian's countenance and demeanor change as she gets older, primarily because she is not thought to change much at all, unless she goes bald. Ironically, it is the aging straight woman—with her thickening skin, coarsened features, and resort to pants and short-cropped gray hair—who eventually evolves to resemble the stereotypic lesbian.

Telltale Signs: Work, Play, and Property. As for myths about gay occupations, let's make this simple: all gay men (except for the fungus-covered ones who live in alleyways and abduct boys) are florists, hairdressers, interior decorators, waiters, clothing-store sales clerks, librarians, ballet dancers, or nurses. All lesbians are gym teachers, physical therapists, East European swimmers, masseuses, teamsters, or the headmistresses of girls' boarding schools.

Gay men supposedly live their solitary lives in the city (may we suggest San Francisco or New York?), in homes decorated in the French Provincial style. Their apartments are cluttered with precious, breakable knickknacks and oval photographs of their mothers—who may, in fact, be living on the premises. There are flowers, fresh cut or dried. And slipcovers on the furniture, which is good because there is lots of beloved cat hair everywhere. Otherwise, there's not a mote or smudge to be found on the home's surfaces: if pressed to do it, a traveling cosmetic surgeon could safely perform an emergency nose job right there on the living room carpet. Or in the impeccable garage.

The hobbies of gay men are reputed to be strictly domestic: they garden if they can, naturally, and collect toys, butterflies, glass things, and (hidden) male erotica. Big art books, too. Gay men absolutely love to cook, but on the nights when they want to cut loose and get out of the kitchen, they go to the opera or ballet. On their vacations, they travel, alone or in small groups, to Fire Island, southern Europe, or in search of Haitian youths.

Lesbians, on the other hand, are supposedly communal animals, always living together in large prairie-dog towns (a.k.a. 'women's collectives') in either urban or rural communities. Housing, as they do, the full defensive line-up of the NFL, lesbian homes purportedly lack the 'feminine touch' and are not particularly clean. A traveling cosmetic surgeon could *not* safely perform a silicone breast implantation anywhere on the premises.

According to their caricature, lesbians are too glum to have much fun. Still, they do enjoy donating their free time to run local V.D. clinics or shelters for battered women. They also attend militantly anti-American demonstrations, and go to feminist poetry readings. Dykes drink too much and get into barroom brawls. Where gay men have strictly domestic, indoor kinds of hobbies, lesbians mostly entertain themselves outside. They may be seen every Saturday afternoon in their driveways, contentedly overhauling the engines of their Harley Davidson 1200cc motorcycles, or of the gargantuan 18-wheel rigs that so many of them drive for a living.

Telltale Signs: AIDS! These days, gays are even easier to spot than usual, many straights believe, because *they're the ones with AIDS.* Over the past few years, a bit of vicious graffiti has been scrawled repeatedly across the public bathroom walls of America: "GAY = Got Aids Yet?" This equation does not even distinguish, as it ought, between gay men (the group at highest risk for AIDS) and lesbians (least at risk). So whether you are male or female, if *you* get AIDS—or begin to lose weight for any other reason—don't be surprised if others jump to conclude that you must be gay. One sex education instructor who worked for the St. Paul, Minnesota, school system told a *Newsweek* reporter in 1987 that many young people are "terrified of getting AIDS and being labeled homosexual. That's the issue—they are more afraid of having people call them gay than they are of dying."

As it happens, the social concern is reversed for most homosexuals: their fear is that people who find out they're gay will assume that they must have AIDS and will shun them. Perhaps the only thing worse than being a 'Mary' in this society is being a Typhoid Mary. Here, alas, homosexuality itself becomes a 'telltale sign' of the century's most dreaded disease. With everyone's attention focused on the plague itself instead of gay rights, the pretzel logic of homohaters such as Rev. Pat Robertson begins to make sense: "Since when does a virus have civil rights?"

Indeed, images of AIDS and of homosexuality have begun to fuse in an eerie way: one critic, Andrew Sullivan, recently complained in the *New Republic* that American advertising is being "infected" with displays of "homosexual erotica and the milder forms of sadomasochism . . . The ADS virus, once restricted to high-risk publications such as *GQ, Vanity Fair,* and *Vogue,* is now breaking out in the general circulation." The real infection spreading here is not gay 'ADS,' of course, but homochondria.

○   ○   ○

So far we have argued that straights: (1) don't like to think much about gays, (2) prefer to believe that there are very few homosexuals in America, and (3) think their tiny band of gay neighbors can be identified easily by a glittering array of telltale signs. Now it is time to consider a few additional straight beliefs about gays—beliefs about the origins and social behavior of this outgroup that serve specifically to make gays look loathsome.

4. WHY GAYS ARE GAY: 'SIN, INSANITY, AND SEDUCTION'

One major reason why many straights dislike and distrust gays is that they disapprove of the things which, they believe, *cause* homosexuality. Like the rest of us, straights ask the question, why are some people drawn to homosexuality when everybody else prefers heterosexuality? And the answers they come up with can be divided, for our purposes, into two kinds: those which attach no blame or moral culpability to gays or their families, and those which do—and how!

Theories of the first kind might include, for example, the notion that homosexuality is innate and immutable in certain people; that some are simply born gay as a genetic or biochemical fact of life, so leveling blame against them (or against those who brought them up) is unreasonable and unjust. There is some concrete evidence to support theories of this sort, but straight Americans generally don't believe them. In a Roper survey conducted in 1979, only 14% of the American public agreed that heredity determines whether a person is heterosexual or homosexual; 53% said orientation is determined entirely by the person's "environment" (presumably including everything that he does to himself or that is done to him after birth); 11% felt heredity and environment play equal parts; and a sizable number, 22%, said they couldn't answer the question. (Incidentally, it's tempting to speculate that a large proportion of those who declined to answer the question as phrased felt they could not do so because the simple choice of "heredity" or "environment" implies that, in any case, homosexuals are created by forces beyond their own control, whereas many religious conservatives insist on believing that homosexuality is a sin that is utterly voluntary and the product of a corrupted soul.)

No wonder theories of the second, blaming kind dominate straight folk beliefs about the cause of homosexuality. That such theories tend to be either unprovable or demonstrably false is quite beside the point: their chief purpose is to lay blame for homosexuality at someone's door. These theories presume that homosexual inclination is a matter of *choice,* to a greater or lesser extent, and that gays themselves therefore deserve blame, anathema, and ill-treatment. Gays are not the only ones blamed, however, since their basic 'moral weakness' supposedly can be exacerbated by their families, who 'don't raise them right,' and by contact with other homosexuals, who help 'corrupt' them. Theories of blame, then, amount to three general hypotheses:

A. HOMOSEXUALITY IS CAUSED BY SINFULNESS. Gays are willfully perverse and wicked, so they fall into sin and choose to be homosexual.

B. HOMOSEXUALITY IS CAUSED BY MENTAL ILLNESS. Everybody's born basically straight, but some kids give in to homosexual vice (and related insanities) because they've been screwed up by a misguided childhood or bad family 'taint.'

C. HOMOSEXUALITY IS CAUSED BY RECRUITMENT. Tender youths and maidens who have a weakness for the vice become homosexual because they are seduced by older gays—and the sinister oldsters actively recruit youngsters because it is the only way for them to reproduce their own kind and perpetuate their sordid pleasures.

An unpromising list, isn't it? What one senses running through the black heart of these 'theories' of homosexuality is hatred and fear—to say nothing of a willful ignorance that would be laughable if it weren't so meanspirited. But why sit there trying to sense such things, when you can hear them directly from the mouths of homohatred's most vocal theoreticians? Let's take a closer look at homosexuality as sin, insanity, and seduction.

Theory A: Homosexuality Is Caused by Sinfulness

"Is homosexuality a disease? No! It is a sin," thunders a white fundamentalist preacher in Paw Creek, North Carolina; verily, it is "an abominable sin in the sight of God," intones a scowling black minister from Boston. And faithful heads nod in vigorous agreement all the way to the Vatican, which has defined "the inclination itself" as an "objective disorder" and, at the same time, "an intrinsic moral evil." (In other words, according to Rome, homosexuality has all the repellent characteristics of a leprous disease or psychotic affliction *plus* the blameworthiness of a personal sin; makes you wonder how gays can bear to get out of bed in the morning.)

Not one to be bested in vitriol, televangelist Jerry Falwell likewise denounces gays, gay ministers, and gay churches as "part of a vile and satanic system" of corrupters and corrupted. Falwell's dysangelic political organization, the Moral Majority, harps regularly on the sinfulness of gay rights in its direct-mail fund-raising campaigns, as do many other groups. Dr. Murray Norris's Christian Family Renewal operation, for example, has sought donations by sounding ominous warnings about a "Gay Rights Bill" now marching through Congress (by which, presumably, he means one of the mild antidiscrimination ordinances currently stalled there): "Just when you thought your children were safe from homosexual advances," this bill comes along that would enable "children to legally participate in perverted sex acts."

Religious straights believe homosexuality is a sin—this they know—because the Bible tells them so (in Leviticus 18:22 and

Romans 1:27); but also because it seems to display the chief characteristics of sin per se. The first trait of sin is that it is *voluntary and deliberate.* As a Christian tract put it, "The gay mentality or lifestyle aren't things you just 'stumble' into—you walk into them step by step."

The second distinguishing trait of sin, from the perspective of traditional Christianity since the days of Thomas Aquinas, is that *it defies the apparent Law of Nature;* it isn't natural so it must be immoral. And what things are 'unnatural'? Those behaviors which are seemingly uncommon, such as homosexuality.

Both alleged traits of homosexuality—deliberate sinning and defiance of what is natural—come together in a view held widely by straight Americans, and expressed in 1983 with characteristic nastiness by President Reagan's speechwriter Patrick Buchanan: "The poor homosexuals—they have declared war upon nature, and now nature is exacting an awful retribution [i.e., AIDS]." In other words, you know homosexuality must be a sin, *because it is punished.* Jerry Falwell has pounded home the same point: "The Scripture is clear: we do reap it in our flesh when we violate the laws of God." The Vatican has called AIDS a "natural sanction" against immoral behavior; and the Roman Catholic cardinal of Philadelphia, John Kroll, once made the sin/punishment equation explicit: "The spread of AIDS is an act of vengeance against the sin of homosexuality." This is a casebook example of the public's treatment of illness as metaphor, a metaphor equating sex with sin, sin with death. In the 1985 *L.A. Times* survey, more than one in four citizens agreed that AIDS is God's chosen punishment for gays, and nearly as many thought that AIDS victims get just what they deserve. They are actually "dying of sodomy"—as James J. Kilpatrick put it in his syndicated column in 1988—and such deaths are not really "tragic deaths" at all. (If the reasoning about AIDS as divine punishment were true and consistent, one might conclude, of course, that lesbians are God's Chosen People, since they are 'punished' by AIDS less often per capita than gay males or straights. But then, truth and consistency are not the objectives of the GAY = SIN theory.)

Religious zealots are not the only ones who view homosexuality as the fruit of sinfulness. Even some 'secular humanists' have managed to hammer together philosophical arguments justifying their revulsion toward homosexuality. One of the wackiest efforts has come from the so-called Aesthetic Realist movement. The Aesthetic Realists maintain that homosexuality commits the sin of being unaesthetic, or something of the sort. According to their literature, "All homosexuality arises from contempt of the world, not liking it sufficiently. This changes into a contempt for women." So it's all a matter of gay contempt, a secular sin. To us *un*-aesthetic realists, of course, such contempt—like beauty—is actually in the eye of the beholder.

One last, and important, point about the notion of Homosexuality-as-Sin, before we move on: that notion is straights' answer to a lot of loose talk among gays about sexual 'preference' and 'lifestyle'—as if one's sexual identity were all merely a matter of choice verging on whim or caprice. Cast in that light, the decision to 'remain' homosexual looks like nothing more or less than the deliberate perverseness of a nose-thumbing libertine—and that's always annoying, if not sinful.

Conservatives have taken the supposition that gays can make a sexual choice and have linked it with a secular sin: *the sin of social contrariness,* the gleeful tweaking of traditional values, contempt (dare we say?) for the established way of things, a malignant urge to crimp the social fabric. Sexual 'choice' makes homosexuality look like nothing more than a stubborn mind-set, like the arrogant decision to become a scofflaw. No wonder some straights react coolly to that 'decision' in the way AIDS-basher Paul Weyrich has: "I'm not gay-bashing. I have compassion for those people who've *gotten themselves* into a reprobate mindset . . ." (Stress added.)

Even the *language* in which homosexuality is discussed by Americans prejudges the notion of choice in a way that opens gays to the charge of sinfulness. The United Methodist Church, for example, maintains a formal prohibition against "self-avowed, practicing homosexuals." The phrasing implies that some people "practice" homosexuality, and so become gay by dint of effort; just as one might choose to practice the violin and become a virtuoso, or practice demon worship . . . and become a sinner. The notion that somebody is an "avowed homosexual" suggests that he has confessed a vow to be gay, as though that condition were a chosen creed. By contrast, it seems vaguely humorous to call somebody an 'avowed, practicing heterosexual,' because obviously it is much more than just a creed, and does not develop as a result of practice: rather, sexuality of the conventional sort is taken to be, in Michel Foucault's words, the very "truth of our being." Homosexuality, on the other hand, is not believed to be a deep need: it's just a sinful practice.

Homosexuality-as-Contrariness was at the root of Midge Decter's classic indictment of gay culture on New York's Fire Island during Gay B.C. (Before Crisis) days, a microstudy titled "The Boys on the Beach," published in *Commentary* during the fall of 1980. The essay's concluding paragraph is worth quoting at length here because it shows how the notion of sexual 'choice' has been misconstrued by hostile heterosexuals to imply that gays could simply go straight if they weren't so darned contrary.

> One thing is certain. To become homosexual is a weighty act. Taking oneself out of the tides of ordinary mortal existence is not something one does from any longing to think oneself ordinary (but only following a different "lifestyle"). Gay Lib has been an effort to set the weight of that act at naught, to define homosexuality as nothing more than a casual option among options. In accepting the movement's terms, heterosexuals have only raised to a nearly intolerable height the costs of the homosexual's flight from normality. Faced with the accelerating round of drugs, S-M, and suicide, can either the movement or its heterosexual sympathizers imagine that they have done anyone a kindness?

Flight from normality? Taking oneself out of the tides of ordinary existence? Is *that* what those willful gays are up to? The nerve of them! In the naïve mind of Decter and many other straights, "to become homosexual" *is* an arrogant and sinful act of volition. In reality, however, because sexual orientation usually is set at an early age and cannot be changed, Decter's indictment makes no more sense than if she had somberly observed instead, "To become a Negro is a weighty act." This much is true: both blacks and gays do appear to have committed the unforgivably irksome sin of social contrariness, just by being different from the straight, white majority.

Theory B: Homosexuality Is Mental Illness

"Health consists in having the same diseases as one's neighbors."
—QUENTIN CRISP, *THE NAKED CIVIL SERVANT*

This second popular hypothesis about the origins and nature of homosexuality has many variants, but here we'll review only the most enduring:

- Homosexuality is one aspect of general mental illness.
- Homosexuality is the crazed result of masturbation.
- Homosexuality comes from being confused about one's gender, and desiring to be a member of the opposite sex.
- Homosexuality is caused by ingrained fear or dislike of the opposite sex.

The idea behind all these variants is that some children with a moral weakness for this 'vice' end up giving in to its madness, because of the way they are raised, the bad habits they develop, or a genetic 'taint.' In other words, under these theories, gay persons still deserve blame, somehow, for the depravity of their character, but here their depravity is rendered more awful and tragic because it also involves genes or twisted parenting—the bad seed or Frankenstein's monster. Consider these notions in turn.

Homosexuality Is One Aspect of General Mental Illness.

Never mind that the American Psychiatric Association removed homosexuality from its official list of psychiatric disorders in 1973, or that in 1975 the American Psychological Association likewise recommended "removing the stigma of mental illness that has long been associated with homosexual orientation." Such professional pronouncements have gone unheard by the straight mainstream, whose resilient folk beliefs on the subject can instead be traced back, rumor-like, to the theories of the early sexologists. And *they* regarded homosexuality (a.k.a. inversion, urningism, uranism, etc.) as a mental illness.

There are three reasons why most sexologists from the very start portrayed homosexuality as a sickness. First, they tended to portray *all* variation in sexual behavior as pathological because severe cultural norms would permit no other interpretation. Second, the goal of providing medical treatment for homosexuality and comparable 'illnesses' may have helped to explain to suspicious others (and to themselves) why they, as physicians, were engaged in the clinical examination of sexuality at a time when the very word was unmentionable in polite society.

Third, and most important, in the Stone Age of psychiatry there was a search for simple, unifying explanations of all mental illnesses. Many supposed that a person's susceptibility to one apparent disorder signaled an underlying constitutional or hereditary susceptibility to other illnesses, both physical and mental, as well. In other words, a sicko is a sicko is a sicko—a supposition surviving as folk wisdom to this day.

The linkage of homosexuality to general mental illness can be traced to the work of pioneering sexologists such as Dr. Richard von Krafft-Ebing. In the numerous editions of his classic 1886 treatise *Psychopathia Sexualis,* Krafft-Ebing reports the case histories of homosexuals who came to him for therapy, and seeks to explain the origin of their condition.

Consider Case 126, the lesbian "Ilma S., aged twenty-nine; single, merchant's daughter." Krafft-Ebing notes: "The patient never had any severe illnesses" and was "bright, enthusiastic and dreamy." So whence her lesbianism? Alas, poor Ilma was "of a family having bad nervous taint":

Father was a drinker and died by suicide, as also did the patient's brother and sister. A sister suffered with convulsive hysteria. Mother's father shot himself while insane. Mother was sickly, and paralysed after apoplexy.

After all this trouble—enough material to supply a TV soap opera for a decade—Ilma's lesbianism appears as just another deviant twist in the crooked family tree, another horrific fire-breathing head on the lineage's hydra-headed *taint.*

Such reasoning sounds archaic, but some clinicians still associate homosexuality with general physical and mental frailty. As recently as 1974, Dr. Walter C. Alvarez—professor emeritus at the Mayo Clinic and a syndicated columnist sympathetic to gays — was assembling, from his own practice, case studies that have a familiar ring. Here is just one of countless examples from Alvarez's text, *Homosexuality and Other Forms of Sexual Deviance.*

I once had a brilliant homosexual male patient whose daughter was homosexual, while a sister and a cousin were deaf mutes, and an uncle had a congenital deformity of his spinal cord . . . His mother was a diabetic; one of her cousins went insane; a brother of the patient, a paranoid schizophrenic, was in a mental hospital; and another brother had an idiot child. This sort of family history convinces me that much of homosexuality is inherited as an equivalent of neurosis or psychosis.

Thus, psychiatry has added 'clinical' weight to the popular notion that some people, by dint of their homosexuality, will also be 'screwy,' degenerate, and odd in other ways as well. We'll describe those other ways presently. (In the meantime, gays are advised to check themselves daily for congenital deformities of the spinal cord.)

Homosexuality Is the Crazed Result of Masturbation.
Then there is that other notorious route to deviance, the path

bumbled down by those whom Krafft-Ebing described as "untainted, mentally healthy" individuals: masturbation.

You've probably always wondered how *that* wive's tale was cooked up; you've probably joked about it among your friends and relegated it to the wastebin of superstitions, along with 'toads give you warts.' And yet, whether you're now certifiably gay or straight, doubt lingers: isn't it *possible* that, during adolescence, receiving too much sexual pleasure by your own hand, while staring into the mirror, *could* leave you liking your sexual apparatus (hence others having apparatus like yours) too much?

You need doubt no more: Krafft-Ebing gives us the rigorous technical explanation of this process, and you may decide for yourself whether it lays bare your own sordid personal history:

> Very frequently the cause of such temporary aberration [i.e., homosexuality] is masturbation and its results in youthful individuals . . . It despoils the unfolding bud of perfume and beauty, and leaves behind only the coarse, animal desire for sexual satisfaction. If an individual, thus depraved, reaches the age of maturity, there is wanting in him that aesthetic, ideal, pure and free impulse which draws the opposite sexes together . . . If the youthful sinner at last comes to make an attempt at coitus, he is either disappointed because enjoyment is wanting, . . . or he is lacking in the physical strength necessary to accomplish the act [and this] . . . leads to absolute psychical impotence . . . Passive and mutual onanism [masturbation] now become the equivalent of the avoided act.

This elaborate 'scientific' explanation of the several steps from masturbation to homosexuality, when laid out in linear fashion this way, probably seems as farfetched to you as it does to us (even though the authors do, in fact, suspect that masturbatory conditioning and imprinting may play some part in the development of some homosexuals). Yet Krafft-Ebing's hoary theory has shown astonishing hardiness as folk wisdom. In the early 1970s, at age fifteen, one of the authors heard the same jerking-off-makes-you-gay theory recited in all its essential details by another anxious boy. He had heard it from still another boy, who had learned it from his father. Doubtless this theory will be circulating still in the next century, because it serves as a pejorative weapon against both masturbation and homosexuality. Why is masturbation naughty? Because it makes you homosexual. Why is homosexuality naughty? Because it is the punishment that comes from masturbating too much.

Homosexuality Comes from Being Confused About One's Gender, and Desiring to Be a Member of the Opposite Sex.

Karl Ulrichs, Edward Carpenter, and other sympathetic (indeed, gay) sexologists germinated this notion in the late 1800s, and we have been reaping the rich harvest of public misunderstanding ever since. Ulrichs, a lawyer without training in psychology or medicine, alleged that gay males have a "feminine soul confined by a masculine body," making them a "third sex." He titled his monograph—eventually expanded to twelve volumes—"The Race of Uranian Hermaphrodites, i.e., the Man-Loving Half-Men." Sounds a bit like a horror film, doesn't it? The authors have never thought of themselves as Man-Loving Uranian Hermaphroditic Third-Sexed Half-Men from Outer Space, but we've had the misfortune to be treated as such by many straights.

It's easy to see why this idea has become entrenched as folk wisdom about gays. After all, many straights believe that gay people visibly resemble, and behave like, the opposite sex. Gay males presumably wish to be mounted by other men just as women are mounted. And dildo-strapped lesbians apparently seek to ravish other females the way males do. Moreover, effeminacy is the stereotypic trait of gay males, and bullish masculinity in women is believed to signal lesbianism. This certainly *looks* like gender confusion, no?

And then there is the matter of transsexuals and transvestites, whom many straights take to be gay, and for whom the term 'gender confusion' seems tailor-made. Truth is, transsexuals make up an exceedingly small group with psychosexual peculiarities all their own, while the vast majority of transvestites—surprise!—are exclusively heterosexual. (Indeed, however mindboggling it may seem, clinical research by Wardell Pomeroy, C. A. Tripp, and others suggests that homosexuality may actually be *less* prevalent among cross-dressers than it is in the general population.) For their part, most gays wouldn't change their sex for all the mascara in the late Divine's makeup chest. On the contrary, they are inclined to glorify their own sex and, in the case of gay males, idolize and model themselves physically after its icons. A visitor to Greenwich Village is far more likely to see a parade of body builders, leather bikers, and Marlboro men than cross-dressers.

Still, straights often view transsexualism and transvestism as closely kindred to homosexuality, even as extreme manifestations of the homosexual impulse. Sexologists have contributed to the gender-confusion confusion. Dr. Magnus Hirschfeld, the eminent German founder of the Institute for Sexual Science (and himself both gay and transvestite), was neither the first nor the last to group 'urnings' (i.e., homosexuals) and cross-dressers together. In his *Sexual History of the World War* (1946), Hirschfeld noted sagely that "the informed person" can identify gays "in every department of the [military] service":

> I once saw a vigorous artillery man who didn't look to me at all like an urning, but after a short time I got two pictures of him, one dressed as a chauffeur in a military costume and beneath that a little inset showing him dressed in female garb. Whosoever lacks the capacity or knowledge for detecting what is typical to urnings will not see a homosexual even when he is sitting right next to him.

If the confusion between transvestism and homosexuality persists today, it is partly because some drag queens *are* gay, partly because transvestites and transsexuals are occasionally seen in the more accepting company and more tolerant neighborhoods of gays, and partly because gays themselves lean into the transvestite stereotype by donning outrageous gender-bending costumes for comic effect and self-mockery at public gay-pride festivities. Drag queens make an indelible (mis)impression on straight observers because those observers operate under psychology's 'principle of availability': flamboyant types determine the gay stereotype because they provide the most visible and vivid—hence the most immediately available—mental image.

But how does gender confusion come about in the first place, and how is it supposed to lead to homosexuality? Many straights believe that kids get 'confused' about their gender, and become homosexuals, *because of misguidance by their parents.* As we said earlier, such theories are really about who is to blame for homosexuality, and here the rap is laid on Mom and Pop. Maybe they never encouraged their son to get over his Oedipal love for his mother. Perhaps the lesbian's parents wanted a lad instead of a lass, and therefore turned her into a tomboy. Perhaps the 'sensitive' son became a porcelain princess instead of a ruff-'n'-tuff Real Man because he was mollycoddled by his smotheringly attentive mother and neglected by his weak, bespectacled father. Perhaps the young homosexual lacked an appropriately masculine or feminine role model. One way or another, goes the argument, there must have been something deviant in the deviant's early home-life.

Thus, K. S. Lynn's recent biography of Ernest Hemingway implies that the obsessively macho writer suffered from suppressed homosexual concerns and "trans-sexual fantasies" which could be traced directly, as Alfred Kazin aptly summarized it in a review, to "a pretentious, overbearing mama who kept the babe in dresses, paired him with his sister, and so dominated her husband that he committed suicide." This is the theory of Smothering Motherism, as cut and dried as beef jerky.

While there is nothing inherently farfetched about the idea that gender confusion brought on by abnormal parental/familial relationships might contribute to homosexual orientation, it is nonetheless clear to most homosexuals and many modern sexologists that gender confusion induced in children by their parents is only occasionally associated with homosexuality. Conversely, the vast majority of gays have grown up under parenting of the garden variety, according to Alan Bell, Martin Weinberg, and Susan Hammersmith, whose *Sexual Preference: Its Development in Men and Women* was published in 1981. That pathbreaking study sought to identify consistent factors in the family backgrounds of homosexuals that might distinguish their upbringing from that of heterosexuals. Despite an exhaustive search based on in-depth interviews with some fifteen hundred individuals, no master factor was found: most gays came from normal households and had conventional relationships with parents, siblings, and—except where effeminate males were concerned—peers. The researchers concluded that, having failed to find it in childhood environment, the secret of sexual preference probably lies in biology.

And yet the myth persists: mothers and fathers are to blame for their 'sexually messed up' children.

Homosexuality Is Caused by Ingrained Fear or Dislike of the Opposite Sex.

People turn to homosexuality, according to this theory, as a miserable last resort. Certain individuals settle for gay sex because they are too frightened, angry, or otherwise inadequate to compete successfully for what they'd *really* like to have: a normal heterosexual relationship.

This 'sour grapes' theory supposes that people stop wanting certain things simply because they have trouble getting them—a supposition which has seldom held true in sex or any other realm of life. Even if true, it would hardly apply to gays, who usually have plenty of opportunity to sample straight sex, and do so. As Bell, Weinberg, and Hammersmith found in their study, homosexual men and women are "not particularly lacking in heterosexual experiences during their childhood and adolescent years. They are distinguished from their heterosexual counterparts, however, in finding such experiences ungratifying." Nevertheless, gays are viewed derisively as the low-status wolves of the pack: frightened runts who can only go through the motions of mounting one another because the lead wolf has his way with all the bitches, or because the bitches themselves bite back. Midge Decter made this smug argument in her 1980 study of Fire Island gays:

> The meaning of those undeniable marks of dread that collected around the boundaries of the homosexuals' actual erotic life, then, is that for many if not all of them homosexuality represented a flight from women far more than a wholehearted embrace of men. This was understood in her bones by every heterosexual woman on the beach.

And was understood in *his* bones as poppycock by every homosexual on the beach. No doubt Decter's straight matrons sincerely believe that, at some deeply suppressed level, their gay companions must actually share their own heterosexual drives. It's human to think this way, it being fundamentally inconceivable to most persons that others might genuinely and legitimately hold values and feel desires that differ profoundly from their own. It is, all the same, a brute fact that intimate contact with partners of the same sex is the ardent *first* choice of most homosexuals, not a booby prize for the ill-favored or skittish.

Indeed, history has left little room for cowardice or meekness among our kind. Many if not most gay men and women throughout history have halfheartedly yet stoically conformed to the norm by entering heterosexual marriages and parenting children —but have saved their secret passion for partners of their own sex. In any case, it can hardly be argued that the pursuit of one's homosexual desires is for the passive and lily-livered: it takes strength to swim against the riptide of society, and no little courage to face the savage, lawless, and unrelenting sexual competition which distinguishes the gay (male) from the straight dating scene.

None of this is to say that physical advances by the opposite sex do not make gays quail. For the covert gay there is always the fear that one's unresponsiveness to such advances will raise suspicions. Or, if one goes along with the advance and ends up in the bedroom, there is the dread that a humiliating failure to perform capably will likewise reveal one's true preference. But this is merely a fear of exposure and condemnation, not a fear of the opposite sex per se. The distinction, however, is lost on those straights who insist that gays must feel the same attractions and fears that they do.

Another popular variant of the flight-from-heterosexuality theory suggests that homosexuality is an act of spiteful rebellion by those who so dislike and distrust the opposite sex that they'd rather stoop to self-abuse or perversion than become entangled with it.

This folk theory is often invoked by straights to explain lesbianism, because it is temptingly easy to apply. After all, some lesbians are radical feminists who make no secret of their resentments toward men in general: understandably, they hate American society's male chauvinism and pervasive discrimination against women. Some feminist literature even seems to verify the lesbianism-as-rebellion theory by its nearly paranoid insistence that the brass bed is no more than a battleground for *Machtpolitik*, wherein the field objective of the man is—as Andrea Dworkin explains it in *Intercourse*—to "occupy," "violate," "invade," and "colonize" the woman; the implication of such an outlook being that all aware, self-respecting women should resist this assault, even avoid it altogether. And it may also be true that some lesbians have come to realize their attraction to other females only as they have discovered their physical revulsion toward the panting male beasts who urgently, and sometimes forcibly, straddle them in bed.

But, once again, none of this means that lesbians acquired their sexual orientation out of spite. Sexual attraction is a positive passion: it stirs of its own accord, and for no other reason. Given a moment's thought, it should strike straights as most improbable that gays can conjure up a lifelong passion for peaches, as it were, merely because they don't care for plums.

Theory C: Homosexuality Is Caused by Recruitment

Along with the popular beliefs that homosexuality is the product of sinfulness and of various kinds of mental weirdness, the notion of homosexuality-through-seduction also deserves mention here.

This theory hardly requires detailed explanation: indeed, it tolerates no close scrutiny. It merely asserts that—whether homosexuality is a sin or a mental illness—ordinary folks can be craftily lured into its sordid pleasures by 'hardened' homosexuals, whereupon the novitiates become addicted to the vice themselves. In a 1970 survey conducted nationwide by the Institute for Sex Research (the only poll we've seen that asked the question), 43% of the public believed that all or most "young homosexuals became that way because of older homosexuals."

Older gays recruit innocent young straights, it is believed, because—not unlike vampires or werewolves—the long-nailed old poufs love to sink their teeth (and other things) into young flesh, and know that only in this way can they make their creepy race multiply.

Raising up his cross to fend off this unspeakable predation, preacher Jerry Falwell has warned parents, "Please remember, homosexuals do not reproduce! They recruit! And many of them are out after my children, and your children!" Such warnings are almost never taken lightly by heterosexuals. Why is it so easy to believe that, as one alarmed citizen said recently about a gay rights advocate she scarcely knew, "That man wants to sodomize my son"? There are several reasons.

First, American straights generally lump homosexuals into a broad class of 'sexually depraved' and 'mentally unstable' types, none of whom can be trusted around children. Moreover, they believe that gays are disproportionately involved in child molesting—and straights have frequently treated the terms 'homosexual' and 'pederast' as interchangeable.

In 1986, for example, a conservative group in Seattle easily got the forty-one thousand signatures it needed to put an antigay referendum on the ballot by inciting voters to "repeal special rights for transvestites, child molesters, rapists, and other persons with a deviant sexual orientation." Similarly, columnist Jasper Dorsey, writing in 1985, thought back over the notorious Atlanta child-murder cases, then gravely concluded: "Homosexual sodomists are too much favored by politicians and the news . . . How many of the murdered and missing Black children in Atlanta were sexually molested, then murdered by sexual perverts? Maybe all of them."

Of course, the gay community does, sad to say, have some shady connections with suspected child molesters. The ample press attention given to small fringe groups such as NAMBLA, the North American Man-Boy Love Association, has only further blackened our reputation. (And later in this book we will offer some methods for cauterizing this disfiguring wart on our communal face.)

But the fact remains that the statistics suggest no disproportionate homosexual involvement in pederasty: about 10% of all detected child molesters are gay, just as 10% of the general population is thought to be gay; the other nine tenths of this vile business is monopolized by heterosexual men (and, to a lesser extent, women). But straights don't seem to know this.

If it is plausible that homosexuals seek to seduce young and innocent straights, it seems just as easy to suppose that certain boys and girls fall prey—out of an innocent curiosity, or a longing for affection, or general adolescent horniness, or lack of a 'normal' heterosexual outlet, or a sinful nature, or an unstable mind—and are seduced.

The exact psychological process by which a promising heterosexual teenager is caused suddenly to convert to homosexuality remains obscure in the minds of straights who subscribe to the recruitment theory (though the process must imply, if nothing else, that the homosexual act itself is enticingly delightful!). Whatever the supposed process, however, the actual statistics of childhood sexual experience indicate that the 'conversion' is anything but sudden and does not usually involve old poufs. Most gays interviewed for the Bell, Weinberg, and Hammersmith study remembered having homosexual feelings some two to three years before their first consummated physical encounters. Moreover, in its tomes on sexual behavior in the human male and female, the Kinsey team presented evidence that about two thirds of all boys, and one third of all girls, have rudimentary homosexual experiences (not necessarily involving orgasm) with other children roughly their own age, before they even enter adolescence. This preadolescent activity appears all the more common among kids who become predominantly homosexual in adulthood.

But such statistics are not widely known among straights, so the recruitment theory is alive and well. Perhaps the persistent notion that homosexuality is just an acquired taste, and one acquired under duress, can be traced back to the public's familiarity with the 'institutional homosexuality' that has sprung up among otherwise straight men during their time in prison and on ships at sea, ever since prison bars and nubile cabin boys were first invented.

Examining the recruitment myth from a psychological perspective, we are tempted to speculate that it persists among many straight adults—despite all evidence to the contrary—because it resonates with what went on in their heads during their own youth, when they first felt the allure of gay sex unexpectedly grip them like an unbidden stranger, and then struggled to free themselves of its thrall.

The myth serves additional psychological functions for straights. For parents, the recruitment theory makes it possible to deal with the dimly recognized but profound dread that their child might turn out gay. If homosexuality is caused by recruitment, then all parents need do to protect their child and themselves from its shameful contagion is to avoid the company of gays. And if their child does turn out to be gay, then belief in recruitment is still more imperative. It means that homosexuality is not intrinsic to their child, but can be viewed as something separate and foreign, like a cancer. Parents can place blame outside themselves and their gay child if he has been seduced, since plainly someone else, some crafty and wicked outside force—pictured perhaps as Satan or an incubus—has lain with the child, had its way with him, and injected something awful into his system which is now an addiction.

In short, heterosexuals in general, and parents in particular, may *need* to believe in the recruitment theory of homosexuality for a whole host of reasons. Those intrepid champions of common sense, Dear Abby and Ann Landers, must tire of reassuring wary parents, letter after letter and year after year—to no apparent effect—that (as Landers put it) "straight people cannot become gay by association. If, by chance, your son should turn out to be gay in a few years, it means the seeds of homosexuality were already present. Seduction alone doesn't do it." Alas, on this issue, few distressed straights have ears to hear.

Summary: Folk Theories of Homosexuality

We have now reviewed a full range of theories concocted by hostile straights to explain the causes of homosexuality. These theories always trace the condition back, one way or another, to sinfulness, recruitment, and/or some kind of mental illness (via family taint, masturbation, gender confusion, or fear and dislike of the opposite sex).

Our purpose has not been merely to debunk such theories. (Indeed, some of them—such as those tracing homosexuality to conditioning or heredity—may have a basis in fact.) Rather, our intention has been to show how all these folk beliefs are designed to point toward a common conclusion: *that straights are logically justified in condemning and blaming gays (and, to a lesser extent, their families) for their 'deviant' sexual preference.*

What we see operating here is the ordinary fellow's (or gal's) need to *rationalize* an underlying and basically arational dislike or fear of homosexuality. In Chapter 2 we shall offer our thoughts on the naked roots of homohatred and homophobia, those pure emotions of prejudice for which the folk theories serve as intellectual fig leaves.

5. 'GAYS ARE KINKY, LOATHSOME SEX ADDICTS'

A moment ago we noted that straights tend to group homosexuals into a broad class of 'sexually depraved' types. You should appreciate how important this perception is to the mainstream's revulsion toward gays. Almost by definition, homosexuals are thought to be sex maniacs.

The well-adjusted homosexual comes to view her or his romantic feelings and sexual practices as perfectly *natural*—just a mirror image of straight love and sex. After all, when it comes to the mechanics of sex, most gays make love the way straights do: with petting, kissing, intercourse, and oral-genital stimulation. Compared to more exotic and specialized forms of sexual desire, the flavor of conventional homosexuality is strictly vanilla.

It is easy to forget, then, that most straights lump homosexuality into the 'creepy weirdo' class—alongside necrophilia, bestiality, pedophilia, feces fetishism, and snuff sex. To straights unused to thinking about such things, even the most conventional homosexual practices are shocking, sickening, ludicrous—in a word, completely *perverse*.

Hostile straights seem particularly fond of the analogy to bestiality, probably because the latter calls to mind a picture which is inhuman and vulgar, and which surely must stake out the farthest hinterland of sexual abnormality. Thus, a small national stir was caused in 1986 when a Yale sophomore mocked his university's annual GLAD (Gay and Lesbian Awareness Days) celebration with his own satirical flier advertising BAD—"Bestiality Awareness Days." His poster offered a list of fictitious activities, such as a lecture on "Pan: the Goat, the God, the Lover." On a different occasion, but with comparable wit and sophistication, conservative syndicated columnist Cal Thomas directly questioned how homosexuals could "claim special privileges" for their practices any more than "those who prefer sex with animals can."

It is just one small step from the equation of homosexuality with bestiality to the inference that the former is an unbridled, piggishly indiscriminate appetite that knows no decent bounds. Gays begin to resemble sexual monsters, the more so after the press has printed indelible news stories about sociopaths whose demented tastes happen to have been homosexual rather than heterosexual. Who could forget the gruesome torture-murders of twenty-seven boys in Houston in the early '70s, by Elmer Wayne Henley and two other deranged men?; or replays of the same horror show, 'starring' John Wayne Gacey in Chicago, Juan Corona in California, and Wayne Williams in Atlanta?

As these stories mount up, the distinction between normal, victimless homosexuality and psychopathy begins to blur: in December 1987, United Press International disseminated a lurid story about a California professor charged with shooting to death a young male prostitute, then dismembering his body with a chain saw in what prosecutors described as a "homosexual rage"—as though this were a specific kind of rage, a particularly *sordid* rage. Such crimes-*qua*-media events seal and re-seal the reputation of gays as sex fiends of the first order.

In the days before AIDS, libertines deliberately compounded the gay community's wild, felonious reputation with public paeans to sexual liberation, experimentation, and the virtues of promiscuity. Then, as the AIDS disaster unfolded, nightly newscasts shocked ordinary citizens with their reports that the disease was surfacing first among those gays who had had *five hundred or more* sexual partners, those who had been infected repeatedly with venereal diseases, and those for whom drugs and alcohol were an integral part of their hard-driving sex lives. To the happily married Lutheran couple in Ohio, watching TV with the kids at dinnertime, this didn't look like your typical sexual appetite; it looked more like a manic and deadly eating disorder, a kind of sexual bulimia. No wonder one third of all respondents in a 1985 Gallup poll acknowledged that AIDS had worsened their opinion of homosexuality.

Alas, it turns out that, on this point, public myth is supported by fact. There *is* more promiscuity among gays (or at least among gay men) than among straights; and in Chapter 6 we'll explain why this is so. Correspondingly, the snail trail of promiscuity—sexually transmitted disease—also occurs among gay men at a rate five to ten times higher than average. Even so, outsiders have often exaggerated the extent of gay promiscuity far beyond what is known from sex research. To get a more accurate perspective, Alan Bell and Martin Weinberg conducted a large survey, published as *Homosexualities: A Study of Diversity Among Men and Women*, in the mid-1970s, at the height of the 'free love' era. They found that, among their sample, roughly one in four gay men and one in six lesbian women had little or no sex with anyone. One in seven men and two-fifths of the women were involved in stable, completely monogamous gay relationships. Altogether, that means that roughly four in ten gay males, and over half of all lesbians, were found to be leading decidedly *un*promiscuous sex lives. The rest ranged from the most typical pattern—singles who occasionally dated and had sex, just as straight singles do—to the most exotic: hungry male adventurers who sought out multiple, anonymous sexual encounters on a daily basis.

In the years since that survey was done, AIDS has thinned out the number of eager sexual wantons: there is reason to think that the proportion of sexually restrained gay men has risen dramatically. But this news has not spread among straights. As the old saying goes, a lady's reputation is unlikely to improve. What is remembered, instead, is the dramatic evening news report about an airline steward named Gaetan Dugas—the infamous 'Patient Zero' blamed for triggering the AIDS epidemic—who was reported to have made some twenty-five hundred homosexual contacts over a ten-year period.

Not only has the reported *quantity* of gay sex alienated straight America, so has its *quality*. The health crisis has confirmed publicly what had only been rumored before: that homosexual men (and, for all the masses know, lesbians as well) have been groping one another's naughty bits anonymously and furtively, two by two and in larger orgies, in the filth of gas station toilet stalls, in public parks, in steamy red-lighted bathhouses, at highway rest stops, in tawdry porn theaters, in 'vaseline alleys' behind bus stations, on the dunes of county beaches in broad daylight, and beneath the coastal piers at midnight. The AIDS epidemic first brought these cruising spaces into public discussion, and has required that many of them be shut down or abandoned. Never mind the gay community's angry retort, that these anonymous rendezvous points are the only places left for gays to express their affections and passions since American society has banished them from more decorous settings and discouraged more permanent romantic liaisons. The fact remains: what straights have now heard about gay sex is not so far removed from the barnyard.

And then there is the delicate matter of exactly *what* gays have been doing to one another during these encounters. Any straight who had ever read the raunchy personal ads of certain urban weeklies—ads which encrypted and telegraphed a wide variety of specific erotic desiderata from one gay to another—already knew vaguely about the many kinks in gay proclivities. They may have caught on about the meaning of ads offering 'B/D, S/M, FF, golden showers, Grk active, Frnch passive, headcheese, toe jam, and scat.' Fortunately for gays, however, the vast majority of straights had never come across those ads.

Then AIDS yanked aside the curtain. Brochures alerting the public to 'safe sex' practices for the epidemic began to make only too clear what had been going on in darkened corners: gays should stop licking one another's anuses; gays should stop shoving their fists up one another's rectums; gays should stop urinating into one another's mouths; gay sadists should stop drawing blood during their tortures of gay masochists, etc., etc.

Just as most straights do, the vast majority of gays wince to hear such a list, and have had little or no personal experience with the activities it proscribes. But because ignorant heterosexuals have no way of knowing which gay behaviors are common and which rare, they seem inclined to assume that the grossest, kinkiest practices they've heard about are enjoyed nightly by *all* gay people. Conservative pundit Norman Podhoretz recently concluded that, "in the name of compassion," those who have worked toward an AIDS vaccine and fairer treatment of the disease's gay victims "are giving social sanction to what can only be described as brutish degradation."

Our enemies have not been slow to encourage these misimpressions. Some have argued that the entire gay community is sliding sleazily into sadomasochism; others decry gays' purported fascination for filth. A Seattle councilor tells reporters he is working to repeal his county's fair employment ordinance, which protects gays against job discrimination, because "government should not give special privileges to a group of people that practices water works [sic]." A venomous Nebraskan 'psychologist' named Paul Cameron has gratified the religious and political right with wild accusations linking gays to all manner of depravity. (Cameron was booted from the American Psychological Association for violating its code of ethics.) The net result of all these revelations and this hostile mudslinging is that, more than ever, homosexuals are perceived to be both sexually compulsive and bizarre.

A remarkable new canard has developed in the wake of the AIDS scare: that most gays are so addicted to wanton sex that they cannot give it up and curb their unsafe sex practices, even if this means courting AIDS and death. The public finds gay profligacy especially disturbing in this era, of course, because for the first time such behavior seems to present a direct and grave health threat to straights themselves.

This threat is increasingly portrayed as a *deliberate* one. News coverage of the Patient Zero story placed great emphasis on Dugas's continued, and apparently vengeful, pursuit of promiscuous sex after physicians advised him that he had contracted an infectious 'gay cancer.' "Some AIDS sufferers," warns William F. Buckley, Jr., "would rather contaminate other people, causing them to die a miserable death, than to control their own perverse appetites." This new paranoia has been splashed eagerly across the front page, especially of tabloids:

• "Gay Terror Group Vows: 'We're Going to Infect Everyone with AIDS' " [Weekly World News]

- "Soldier Who Knew He Carried AIDS Virus Faces Assault Charges" *[New York Times]*
- "Vengeful AIDS Victim Infects 50 Gays in 2 Weeks" *[The Sun]*
- "The Monster Who Gave Us AIDS: He Was a Globe-Trotter with 250 Sex Partners a Year—Even After Doctors Told Him He Had 'Gay Cancer' ". *[The Star]*

All this paints a grisly image of gay sex and smears homosexuals as dissolute outlaws. But it does something still more damaging: it compels straights to think in terms of homo*sexuality* instead of homo*philia:* "Homosexuality Is Lust, Not Love," screamed one placard at an antigay demonstration in 1984. Events since that time have only reinforced the impression that homosexuality is all about sex and nothing but. There is little appreciation that homosexuality is also about love, intimacy, and romance—the possibility of which seems to unnerve some straights more than any other term in the equation. Our public image suggests that the gay experience consists of wanton promiscuity, not fidelity and bonding. The image of gay promiscuity reminds straights that such behavior cannot lead to marriage and offspring, so it must be dirty and profane. Homosexuality is just sex, of the kind that usually takes place on all fours.

In the United States, such a perception is disastrous. Although they've loosened up considerably in recent years, Americans retain a prissy Victorianism about the naughtiness of sex. Sex is only decent and legitimate when wrapped in a gauze of romantic sentiments and happily-ever-afters. Before the AIDS crisis, the public image of gay sex was evolving very, very slowly toward that kind of legitimacy through an increasing number of sympathetic and romantic portrayals on TV and in films and literature. From the viewpoint of straights, the overwhelming ugliness of its AIDS connection now threatens to taint every aspect of the gay sexual experience.

6. 'GAYS ARE UNPRODUCTIVE AND UNTRUSTWORTHY MEMBERS OF SOCIETY'

If gays are good at having sex, reportedly they're not good for much else: *many straights believe that homosexuals lead dissolute and unaccomplished lives.* This is supposedly true for two reasons.

First, because gays are sex maniacs, they cannot discipline their unruly impulses and devote their energies to more worthy endeavors. This notion crops up in the strangest places. For example, Joan Peyser, author of a 1987 book on the American conductor/composer Leonard Bernstein, was interviewed in *People* magazine, in a piece titled "A Frank Biography Finds That Leonard Bernstein's Passions, Like His Talents, Are Boundless." During that interview, the author was pointedly asked about the impact of Bernstein's "promiscuous homosexuality" upon his life's work. After observing nicely, "Whether he is heterosexual or homosexual is not of primary importance," the book's author went on nonetheless to opine that whenever the composer was "rampantly homosexual" his artistic accomplishments declined. Peyser insists that "More recently he has again been promiscuously homosexual, and he has done work that is less likely to last." Peyser's argument is dubious at best, since Bernstein's homosexual phases have happened to coincide with high points in his conducting career. But what we find noteworthy here is the author's, and the interviewer's, exact phrasings of the problem: Leonard Bernstein's creative doldrums have not persisted because he is 'homosexually *promiscuous,*' but because he is "promiscuously *homosexual.*"

Second, gay males do not accomplish much in life (and this myth generally concerns gay males more than females) because they have a basically feminine disposition, and we all know how debilitating *that* can be. This feminine disposition is thought to make them oversensitive and constitutionally unstable—"emotional derelicts," as someone once put it—causing them to be as giddy and overwrought as lovestruck teenage girls. No wonder gays flock to the arts: because they view Art from the vantage of callow young women, as a drainage duct for the gush of emotion. No wonder they flit back and forth among short-lived, ill-planned careers as minor actors, histrionic dancers, and unaccomplished painters—lifelong dilettantes. Such is the vainglorious ambition of perpetual adolescents. These people lack the macho grit, the gravity, to tackle life's more serious challenges. Somehow, it is charged, gayness robs grown-ups of their adulthood and makes them silly.

Furthermore, the feminine disposition of gay males inclines them to small, domestic kinds of endeavors rather than manly, heroic careers. So they spend their quiet, tidy little lives as hotel clerks, nurses, waiters, clothiers, and jewelrymakers. As for "basic industry or government service or . . . such classic professions as doctoring and lawyering," says Decter, "for anyone acquainted with [gays] as a group the thought suggests itself that few of them have ever made much effort in these directions."

This is hogwash, of course. In the New York area alone, one can attend regular meetings of FLAG (Federal [Government] Lesbians and Gays), Gay People in Medicine, GovernMen, Lesbians in Government, the Bar Association for Human Rights, the Gay Officers Action League, the Greater Gotham Business Council, Gaytek (for lesbian and gay engineers and scientists), and the Wall Street Lunch Club, to name but a few. Alas, the local gay hotline has no listing for a jewelrymakers league.

Not only are gays believed to be relatively unproductive members of American society, *some straights even think they're untrustworthy citizens.* Part of this indictment is personal and part is political. On the personal side, homosexuality itself is often taken as a sign that its bearers have *other* degenerate defects of character—cowardice, perfidy, selfishness, malevolence, cruelty—which make them unreliable company, if not an actual menace to oneself and society. Some filmmakers have even incorporated homosexuality into their melodramatic, black-and-white symbolism for good and evil: you can readily pick the bad guys out of the story's lineup from the very start, because they're the ones whose sleazy, faggy mannerisms or gay leer make the audience want to hiss. The

'heavies' and their henchmen are so marked in films as diverse as
Frenzy, Dune, Road Warrior, The Damned, Mona Lisa, and *No Way Out.*
The message is clear: gays are personally treacherous, not to be
trusted.

Nor are they trustworthy citizens on political grounds. The insult 'commie-pinko-faggot' rolls the two most reviled adversaries
of right-wing yahoos into a single hate object—the imaginary object, in fact, of Senator Joseph McCarthy's assault on the Department of State during the early 1950s. Although sociological studies
have shown gays to be only moderately less conservative than
straights on most political and religious issues, much of the public
continues to regard them as godless radicals.[3] Indeed, a Texan
political scientist may as well have spoken for the entire nation
when, in 1985, he observed, "Down here, homosexuals rank in
overall public opinion with atheists and communists."

The most vociferous attacks on godless gay liberalism, of course,
come from the political right. When a movement took shape in
1987, for example, to recall conservative Arizona governor Evan
Mecham because of his alleged racist remarks and financial im-
proprieties, the embattled governor dismissed his critics as "a
band of homosexuals and a few dissident Democrats." (This very
remark produced further outrage, and contributed to Mecham's
eventual ouster; but—lest gays take too much encouragement
from this—the public probably was less resentful that gays were
being denigrated than that straight critics were being slurred as
homosexuals.)

Back east, Jeffrey Hart, a commentator for the *National Review,*
applauded the previously mentioned Yale sophomore (who had
lampooned the university's gay awareness events in 1986) for "attacking the homosexual liberal icon." Merely because the "radicals are calling the shots" in America today, and because "the
animals are running the farm"—he declaimed—a decent young
American was being unjustly castigated for his "parody of perversion." This injustice supposedly illustrates the "heterophobia, hatred of the normal," which abounds among the "soft socialists"
who now dominate academic life and support "behavior previ-

ously considered deviant." It's the same at all liberal Eastern colleges, Hart implied: the "totalitarians" take over and then the only ones guaranteed freedom of speech are either "Blacks, homosexuals, or leftists," who are all in cahoots anyway.

Too many Americans share this mistrust of gay citizens. As will be shown presently in our discussion of gay civil rights, one in three straights considers gay people to be so subversive in sexual/political/religious terms that they should be denied freedom to speak in public and teach in universities. Not surprisingly, this is about the same proportion who would oppose free speech for other untrustworthy Americans, such as fascists and communists.

Another reason why homosexuals are distrusted as a class is that they are believed to act like a self-interested ethnic group, one that sticks together and favors its own whenever possible. Such special membership groups have traditionally been regarded with resentment and suspicion by Americans. A gentile straight man in the film industry recently complained to one of the authors, "You need two things to succeed in Hollywood—be Jewish and queer; otherwise they'll shut you out." (Indeed, in October 1988, *TV Guide* took millions of readers through an exposé of the "Gay Mafia" that "has always existed in Hollywood.") A book editor in New York says that he hears the same thing in the publishing trade: supposedly there is a "lavender clique" of literary types—gay writers, poets, reviewers, and publishers who nurture their own and discriminate against straights. "It's absurd," says the editor. "I've never hired anyone just because they were gay. Unlike other minorities, perhaps, gays aren't as clubby that way. But recently I've been thinking maybe I *should* start to hire gays, since they're shunned by others and since I'm accused of favoring them anyway."

What makes gays particularly suspect as a special interest group is their conspiratorial invisibility. They seem to constitute a secret society whose members can be as collusive as spies, or guerrillas. Straights can never be entirely sure whether gays are up to something behind their backs, because they're never entirely sure who —telltale signs notwithstanding—might be gay.

Even identifiable gays can be suspiciously reticent. When a straight ventures into gay environs, she may be treated as a distrusted outsider. She may feel like a tourist invading a small Sicilian village: the clamor subsides and the intimate conversation dies away just ahead of her, as she proceeds under watchful eyes. Heterosexuals resent being shut out this way, just as the drama critic Frank Rich plainly did whenever he visited the gay-chic nightclub Studio 54 during the late 1970s. In an *Esquire* article titled "The Gay Decades," Rich recalls:

> To be there as a peon, as I was on a few occasions, was to feel that the Continental Baths crowd had finally turned nasty toward the intruding straights and was determined to make them pay (with overpriced drinks and condescending treatment). Even as everyone was telling you that this was where the action was, you felt that the real action, not all of it appetizing, was somewhere in the dark periphery, out of view—and kept there, to make you feel left out.

Some straights—those inclined to such paranoia—come away from their exposure to the gay world with the impression that a devious plot or well-organized rebellion is taking shape among the downtrodden. (With the support of Jerry Falwell, for instance, Reverend Enrique Rueda published a 680-page tome in 1982 titled *The Homosexual Network,* elaborately documenting the ideology and muscle of the movement.) Some allege that the gay mafia is expanding its base of operation beyond the ghetto, that it is deliberately inserting its pink tentacles into the nation's chambers of power, intent upon a hidden agenda of social upheaval that poses a serious threat to the fabric of the nation. AIDS, in turn, makes this imagined threat seem more insidious than ever: conservatives have charged the gay lobby with cowing or manipulating both the media and the medical profession to block the exposure and quarantining of gay AIDS-carriers. As Richard Goldstein has observed, homohatred is now being validated by "the myth of the powerful homosexual, first cousin to the myth of the powerful Jew."

Thus, in January 1987, when Roper asked the public to rate which of twenty-two "special interest groups" wield *too much influence* in America today, 48% said "gay rights groups." The only group whose purported influence aroused more hostile concern than did gays—on a list which included big business, pro- and anti-abortion movements, fundamentalist church groups, left-wingers, and the military—was labor unions (52%).[4]

The public's fearful perception of gay power is, then, outlandishly inflated: if the gay movement actually loomed as large as the shadow it casts in straight minds, the era of gay rights would be at hand. And there would be no need to write this book.

7. 'GAYS ARE SUICIDALLY UNHAPPY BECAUSE THEY ARE GAY'

Straights are inclined to believe that all gays are—by dint of their emotionally unstable nature and the intrinsic horribleness of their vice—dreadfully unhappy. This belief is longstanding and has received indirect support from prominent psychologists, some of them gay. When in 1946, for example, Magnus Hirschfeld published his *Sexual History of the World War,* he observed the "remarkably" courageous behavior and "war enthusiasm among urnings" on the battlefield and concluded:

> Among the causes which drive homosexuals to war perhaps the most tragic one is that wish or hope, expressed by more than one of their number, that a bullet might put an end to their life which they regard as being a complete failure from the point of view of present conditions and notions. Driven by this feeling, many an urning officer exposed himself to the thickest rain of bombs and the most deadly attacks.

That these urnings might be genuine patriots driven primarily by motives other than self-destructive despair was scarcely imaginable, then as now. When misery and self-hatred explain so much so easily about gays, why look farther afield? A recent book on the treatment of gays and lesbians in the American theater tallies up the gay subplots for plays in the earlier part of this century: among the handful of lesbian characters who graced the stage, "one was forced into prostitution; three were driven to suicide, two were abandoned by the heterosexual object of their affection; one succumbed to a heart attack." As for gay males, except for those implicitly portrayed in the plays of Noel Coward and Eugene O'Neill, "one was an alcoholic, two were on drugs, another insane, and the other two murdered."⁵ Do these gays sound like happy, well-adjusted people to you?

The portrayal has little changed today. The modern blueprint for gay misery was drawn up in 1968, in Mart Crowley's controversial and 'sympathetic' play, *The Boys in the Band;* and again in the 1970 film version directed by William Friedkin. At the end, after the other sorry fairies attending a melancholy birthday party have gone their solitary ways to ponder the dead-end hopelessness of their lives, the central character dissolves into tears and utters a pathetic prayer that he and all other homosexuals might, one day, learn to hate themselves just a little bit less. "It's not always like it happens in plays," he insists, with little heart. "Not all faggots bump themselves off at the end of the story." Maybe not, but faggots certainly do so in movieland: go watch *Advise and Consent.* The same lachrymose stream runs through more recent films having gay characters and subplots, such as *Ode to Billy Joe, That Certain Summer,* and *Another Country.*

Straights look for signs of gay unhappiness, and in fact count on finding them. After all, Americans have followed the rest of Western civilization down the garden path toward hedonism and moral relativism, and so they increasingly judge 'lifestyles' in terms of their capacity for producing something called 'happiness.' Since there persists in the most modern of heterosexuals an underlying emotional revulsion against homosexuality, many moderns feel an urgent need to rationalize against the 'gay life' by concluding that it must not be so gay after all. This need is still greater in an age of narcissism and self-absorption, wherein the bohemian, carefree lives of gays—freed of the shackles of nestbuilding and parenthood—might seem vaguely appealing at first glance. As *Esquire* writer Frank Rich acknowledged, "You didn't want to believe that [gay] men might actually be living out the much-promised (but rarely delivered) Hugh Hefner fantasy of unlimited sex without monogamous attachments."

So straights cast a searching, critical eye upon the few homosexuals they know, especially those who seem to be successes. As Michael Musto has noted in the *Village Voice,* when a supposedly homosexual celebrity becomes unhinged or falls apart—as the popular and buoyant rock star Boy George appeared to do when his heroin addiction was made public—skeptics are "suddenly able to argue that he wasn't so in control after all, that 'those people' [are] innately decadent and self-destructive, it just goes to show." In sum, all such signs of maladjustment are taken as *prima facie* evidence that—in the words of 82% of Harvard and Stanford students recently surveyed—homosexuality must be an "inferior lifestyle."[6]

Now, the most distressing thing about this American myth of the unhappy homosexual is that it does have some basis in fact. Studies suggest that, while most gays are remarkably well adjusted in light of their stigma, on the whole, gay men (and to a lesser extent lesbians) are more prone to feelings of loneliness, anxiety, paranoia, depression, and unhappiness than are straights. (Moreover, the often unpleasant quality of social life among gays themselves is, to a considerable degree, the result of these individual maladjustments: see Chapter 6.) This comes as no surprise. More straights would react likewise, no doubt, if *they* were compelled to live their lives estranged, in constant fear of exposure and attack, and with a clear-eyed comprehension of their bleak predicament. As someone once observed, even a paranoid man can have real enemies. And when his enemies proceed to persecute him on the novel ground that he *is* a bit paranoid—or is socially maladjusted in some other way—then the cycle becomes as vicious as can be. And in the end, the poor maligned fellow is seen hurling himself off a skyscraper ledge in a desperate effort to escape his tormentors once and for all. Did he jump or was he pushed?

We say he was pushed. Gay suicide is, as we've noted, America's prescription for preserving the Big Lie. The prospect of homosexuality makes most heterosexuals unhappy; their answer is to make homosexuals, in turn, so *very* unhappy that they just go away, self-destruct, vanish.

As noted in our Introduction, gay suicide takes many symbolic and figurative forms. But there is reason to think that it's also common in the literal sense. In the 1970s, Alan Bell and Martin Weinberg conducted a large survey of gays and lesbians, and inquired directly about suicide. While their sample group was not perfectly representative of gay demographics, their findings generally agree with those gathered by Eric Rofes and other experts on gay suicide. In the Bell and Weinberg survey:

- Nearly one in every four lesbians and one in every five gay men surveyed had attempted to kill themselves at least once during their life. (Among straights, the numbers were about one in ten and one in thirty, respectively.)
- Roughly one quarter of gay whites who attempted suicide were driven to their first attempt by the time they were seventeen years old; the proportion was even higher for gay blacks.
- Well over half of those attempting suicide for the first time did so, they indicated, for reasons of unhappiness concerning their homosexuality; and the problems of trying to fit into a hostile world.

So it turns out that, while a majority of gays are as well adjusted and content as straights, a sizable minority of homosexuals *are* deeply unhappy. Straights generally suppose that homosexuality itself is to blame for this. Gays, on the other hand, insist quite rightly that what makes them unhappy is the way straights treat them.

The entire situation reminds one of "The Ugly Duckling," the fairytale in which a despairing young swan learns to hate itself because its odd appearance has elicited ridicule and scorn from the ducks into whose company it has fallen. That touching tale was penned by Hans Christian Andersen. Andersen, as it happens, was himself a particularly effeminate gay man who probably knew a thing or two about the unhappiness produced by social rejection. Fortunately for the cygnet in the story, it grows up to become a majestic white trumpeter, leaves the astonished (and, ultimately, admiring) ducklings behind, and joins the grand company of others like itself. The swan lives happily ever after. But that's a fairytale. In the real world, many gays grow up feeling ugly and scorned, continue to feel that way as adults, join an unhappy ghetto of same, and sometimes end up killing themselves. The unsparing game is still Duck-Duck-Goose, and gays are still 'it.'

Summary: What Straights Think of Gays

Our discussion has ranged widely but has touched upon the seven hallowed public myths of homosexuality. Gays are:

(1) Hardly worth thinking about
(2) Few in number
(3) Easy to spot
(4) Homosexual because of sin, insanity, or seduction
(5) Kinky, loathsome sex addicts
(6) Unproductive and untrustworthy members of society
(7) Suicidally unhappy

While all are exaggerations, a few of these myths do, as we've hinted, have some basis in fact; and in Chapter 6 we'll take an unblinking look at misbehaviors within our community that contribute to gays' seamy reputation. But whether these beliefs are true or false, what all seven have in common is their purpose, and combined effect, among heterosexuals: to rationalize an intense feeling of disapproval toward homosexuals and homosexuality. This gut feeling of disapproval is widespread in America and has been stable over the years. When asked whether homosexuality is acceptable behavior, 70–75% of Americans can reliably be expected to answer no. The persistence and extent of this disap-

proval are peculiar: there are other modern Western countries—
France, for example—where an equivalent proportion of the public would answer yes.[7]

No! is an emotional bottom line, the inexhaustible fuel that
keeps intellectual rationalizations about homosexuality burning
brightly (just as raw anti-Semitism has sustained various exaggerations about Jews and Zionism over the years). We add the excla-
mation point to no! in order to signify the intensity and self-righteousness of this disapproval. Indeed, the rejection of gays is so
emotionally grounded and charged that it feels, to straights, like a
moral act, even among those without religious scruples on the
subject. (Indeed, as G. K. Chesterton once remarked, "The people
who are most bigoted are the people who have no convictions at
all.")

Largely for this reason, homohatred—though a bigotry as
wicked as any other—is still sanctioned in America today, and the
gay community remains the last large outgroup in our society that
it is still acceptable to despise and ridicule. True, one hears jokes
about niggers, kikes, chinks, and spics from time to time. But they
are not often heard without the circumspect tone that admits to
the listener, 'I really shouldn't be saying this, but . . .' By contrast, cruel humor against queers is still vented with an unguarded
voice, without the slightest self-conscious giggle.

Just as no! is expressed through the eager perpetuation of certain *beliefs* about gays, it is also expressed through a broad array of
direct, hostile *actions*—if you wish, the 'body language' of bigotry.
We've saved that filthy language for the second leg of our field trip
to Straight America.

O

HOW STRAIGHTS TREAT GAYS:
THREE CLASSES OF BEHAVIOR

*"In learning how a community chooses its
freaks and invents its deviants we construct a
photographic negative of its social life."*

—MICHAEL LEVENSON,
WRITING IN THE *NEW REPUBLIC*

On his best days, the recognizable gay person is treated as a
harmless freak, enjoying all the respect accorded to the Bearded
Fat Lady at the circus. On not-so-good days—which, since AIDS,
have been most every day—he is treated more as a leper, menace,
moral cretin, and third-class citizen.

Beliefs and actions go hand-in-glove. A small, sinful, and dangerously diseased band of sex addicts is easily subdued: just impose laws that criminalize their practices; keep them out of your
neighborhood, workplace, school system, church, government,
and—if they're foreigners—your nation; and do not forbear to
taunt and beat them from time to time. This is the way to control
an undesirable minority.

We must concern ourselves with these actions for two reasons.
First, they bring profoundly unjust suffering upon gays. Second,
these actions, perfectly visible to the friends and enemies of gays,
are thus powerful symbols for manipulation by both sides. So long
as antigay discrimination is encouraged to persist in its most overt
forms, the public is reassured that homohatred itself must be appropriate and virtuous; whereas the opposite message is conveyed
when antigay aggression is deplored and outlawed.

For this reason, our battle for the hearts and minds of Americans must take place both above and below the surface. Antigay
actions are the brutal tip of an enormous iceberg otherwise sub-
merged. An effective plan to smash homohatred must steer directly at the great mass underneath: hostile feelings and beliefs

among the general public. But our success will be judged by how well we topple the exposed peaks of blatant discrimination and violence. Antigay actions, therefore, deserve equal priority with antigay beliefs in our agenda for change.

There are three broad classes of antigay behavior:

1. Actions which prevent homosexual behavior per se.
2. Actions which deny gays their fundamental civil rights.
3. Actions which otherwise vent public disapproval of gays.

The first class of actions is orchestrated by our government at the local, state, and national level, in the form of laws which criminalize the sex acts commonly associated with homosexuality (and usually summarized as 'sodomy'—oral-genital sex and/or anal intercourse), as well as court decisions which support those laws.

The second class of actions invites more direct participation by the straight citizenry and includes all efforts to keep gays from speaking, fraternizing, organizing, working in the jobs and residing in the neighborhoods they would choose, marrying and acquiring property together, and parenting children.

The third class takes homohatred into the spotlight; that is, into the pulpit and onto the streets. Known commonly as 'queerbashing,' it entails the public shunning, harassment, and brutalization of gay people. Its sneering legion of 'activists'—Baptist ministers, Hollywood comedians, ghetto thugs, and the like—are drawn together in an alliance of hate as thick as blood.

You can see readily that these three classes of antigay actions are distinct yet related: to eliminate just one of them would not make the other two tuck tail and slink away. But if society were, in fact, persuaded to eliminate completely any one of the three, its change of heart would eventually make the remaining classes untenable. Thus, gays are best advised to recognize which categories of antigay actions they have the easiest chance of eliminating first, concentrate on eliminating those, and leave the least tractable one for last. Later in this book, we'll suggest that gays begin by concentrating on the second and third classes.

CLASS 1: PREVENTING HOMOSEXUAL BEHAVIOR

Sodomy Laws on the Books. Homohaters expect that three arms of the state will work together to prevent gays from doing what comes unnaturally: (a) the laws must criminalize homosexual sodomy; (b) the police must apprehend sexual criminals under these laws; and (c) the courts must convict these criminals and mete out punishment. For the system to prevent gays from making love, the lawmakers, police, and courts must all be zealous in their duty.

Fortunately for gays, this strategy doesn't work. The system itself is an erratic patchwork. There is no uniform federal law, pro or con. (There is only an immigration regulation classifying homosexuals as "psychopathic personalities" who can therefore be refused entry—a policy that, until softened somewhat a few years ago, made American gays feel right at home.) In the absence of federal legislation, control of sodomy falls to state governments. Until 1961, all fifty states outlawed homosexual acts. By 1988, however, the picture had changed dramatically. New laws and court decisions had decriminalized private homosexual acts between consenting adults in twenty-six states—primarily in New England, in the upper Midwest, and on the West Coast—in which a majority of the nation's population resides.

The remaining twenty-four states, most of them Southern, still have (anti)sodomy laws: four of these proscribe only *homosexual* sodomy, while the broadminded remainder criminalize both homosexual and heterosexual sodomy.

What price love? At present, the penalties that may accompany a sodomy conviction also vary widely from state to state. According to the Privacy Project of the National Gay and Lesbian Task Force (NGLTF), an adult who makes love just once to another of the same sex must be imprisoned for a *minimum* of five years in Idaho; and can be locked away for up to ten years in states such as Maryland, North Carolina, Mississippi, and Montana; up to fifteen years in Tennessee and Michigan; and up to twenty years in Georgia and Rhode Island. A pair of lovers caught in the act repeatedly could get imprisonment *for life* in Michigan—till death do them part. Evidently we are to be thankful that, unlike the Iranian mullahs, American straights temper their injustice with mercy: for some mysterious reason, gay lovemaking between consenting adults is not currently punishable by hanging anywhere in the United States.

Enforcement of the Laws. As we said, however, it takes more than having laws and penalties on the books to effect oppression. It also takes vigorous enforcement; yet the patchy inconsistency of the sodomy laws (as is true for other laws against victimless 'vices') seems to have robbed them of moral authority and dampened the zeal of their official guardians. Fortunately for gays, the close monitoring of homosexual behavior has proved so distasteful—and the laziness of cops and the reluctance of courts so persistent—that gay sex can be had privately, with only slight fear of discovery and punishment, in every state of the Union. Many millions engage in 'sodomy' each year, yet sodomy convictions over recent years have numbered only in the hundreds.

Even when gay couples are caught red-handed having sex in private, authorities frequently decline to prosecute. This is just what happened to Michael Hardwick, arrested for sodomy in Atlanta in 1982. He immediately challenged the arrest as a violation of his rights of privacy and due process; the district attorney refused to submit the sodomy charge to a grand jury and left it to Hardwick to press the case further. (He did so, and the case resulted in a notorious landmark decision by the U.S. Supreme Court, discussed below.)

Many gays think, because of this lax enforcement, that they are getting off lightly; that the system is tolerably lenient. But they are misled. They haven't understood how sodomy laws are intended to function.

Such laws *can't* be enforced vigorously. As written, most sodomy laws apply to both homosexuals and heterosexuals; if impartially enforced, they'd snare more straights than gays (since studies by Kinsey and others suggest that well over half of the heterosexual public is fond of oral-genital play), and that would be unacceptable: it would mean mass rebellion, culminating in the repeal of such laws altogether. The sheer scale of the task of enforcement would make it impossible: after all, no law officer wants to sneak out every midnight to peek through bedroom windows, when instead he could be at home, in bed, performing natural and unnatural acts with his own Significant—or Insignificant—Other.

Even if gay sodomy alone were prosecuted, the court docket would be overwhelmed. As noted earlier, more than a third of American males and a fifth of all females have experimented with homosexuality at least once in their lives. Virtually all of those citizens could be branded as criminal in states having gay sodomy laws. So the laws are deliberately unenforced.

The Real Purpose of Sodomy Laws. Why, then, are these laws even on the books in nearly half of the United States? And why should gays care? There are several reasons. First, so long as gay-targeted sodomy statutes remain, they can be reactivated with a vengeance whenever the public—swept up, for example, in AIDS hysteria—so chooses.

Second, laws and penalties are applied haphazardly, in the meantime, to a few unfortunates—an injustice in itself—while in twenty-four states the possibility of arrest hangs over every gay person like a broadsword.

Third, sodomy laws make all active homosexuals presumptive felons; this warrants limiting their civil rights, like those of other criminals—with direct implications of gays' unsuitability as teachers, parents, military officers, etc.

Fourth, in the AIDS era, the very illegality of sodomy also means that authorities (e.g., in schools and prisons) may refuse to educate citizens about safer oral and anal sex practices, protesting that such education verges on incitement to commit crime.

Fifth, gay-targeted sodomy laws are kept on the books to support and police the Big Lie. The very fact that such laws exist, yet don't seem to produce many convictions, reassures straights that there can't be more than a handful of Americans who would fall into the homosexual 'criminal' class. At the same time, that sodomy laws can still be, and sometimes are, selectively enforced serves as a threat to gays in conservative regions: Don't *you* dare stand up and be counted.

The existence of such laws in nearly half the country may even reinforce the Big Lie elsewhere by exerting a chilling effect on gays in 'free' states. Like most citizens, gays are often a bit foggy about the sex laws of the states in which they live, and tend to suppose the worst. Moreover, knowing that homosexuality is treated harshly elsewhere, even gays who realize they live in a free state are inclined to see their local freedom as a privilege—lucky, merciful, and conditional—rather than a right. Because 'things could be worse,' gays in free states still keep their heads down to remain invisible, conduct their sex lives furtively, and avoid rocking the boat. The Big Lie goes unchallenged.

The sixth reason is paramount: the survival of gay sodomy laws, even unenforced, sends a message to both straights and gays that homosexuality is intrinsically wrong, sinful because it's 'unnatural.' And that, really, is the underlying purpose of such laws: to stand bolt-upright on the social plain as ugly monuments, visible symbols of society's moral condemnation of gays. Thus, sodomy laws function less as statutes than as parliamentary *resolutions:* through them, straights have passed a resolution against homosexuality.

Lest this purpose be missed, consider the titles which some states have given to their sodomy statutes:

- "Crimes Against Nature" (Arizona)

- "Unnatural or Perverted Sexual Practices" (Maryland)

- "Sodomy and Buggery" (Massachusetts)

- "Unnatural and Lascivious Acts" (Florida)

- "Unnatural Intercourse" (Mississippi)

- "Sexual Psychopaths" (District of Columbia)

Nor does the name-calling stop with acts of sodomy. Even the most casual public displays of gay affection—e.g., holding hands or kissing, just as straights do—have been castigated under state and municipal statutes banning "lewd and lascivious behavior." Gay affection is defined, in effect, as a kind of obscenity.

How can we free ourselves of this legal curse? When homosexual behavior is characterized this way by law, repeal becomes exceedingly tricky. How does one knock down a symbol of moral condemnation without seeming to raise up an opposite symbol—that is, without formally *approving* of homosexuality?

Our enemies understand this dilemma well and deliberately put lawmakers on the spot whenever the question of repealing outdated sodomy laws arises. While straight legislators might admit that gay sodomy statutes are unfair and ineffective, few have the public courage to reverse the moral valence of the laws. So proscriptions linger on the books, gathering dust.

Now you can see how all this works together. What looks, at first glance, disorganized and irrelevant, turns out to be a rather neat and enduring system for sexual oppression, even if suboptimal from the viewpoint of conservatives. Straights preserve sodomy laws, unenforced, on the books here and there, so that homosexuality will continue to bear society's tattoo of disapproval. This legal tattoo legitimizes all other forms of social discrimination against gays—the forms that really hurt. At the same time, sodomy laws intimidate homosexuals, lest their behavior become too overt and foil the Big Lie. In return, grateful gays oblige straight norms by lying low and not fighting the laws so long as they remain largely unenforced.

Instead of accepting this sinister system, America's 25 million gays might do better to turn themselves in—*en masse*—at local police precincts as admitted sodomites. That, at least, would be an unprecedented act of civil *obedience* with the impact of massive *dis*obedience, because it would rattle America's false construction of reality to its foundations and might force a formal, public repudiation of the sodomy laws. But, for now, that is just a daydream, because gays are not sufficiently brave or adequately mobilized for such a display.

Perhaps the best we can hope for, instead, is that straights themselves will move to repeal remaining sodomy laws out of self-interest, since most such laws proscribe both homosexual and heterosexual variants of the practice. A 1986 *Time* poll reported that only 26% of the public approved of actions by federal or state authorities to limit or outlaw "certain sex acts between adult men and women." On a more ominous note, however, 45% said they definitely would allow authorities to limit or outlaw "certain sex acts between two adult men." The public became particularly squeamish when asked about *specific* sex acts: 30% would allow the authorities to limit or outlaw "acts of oral sex," and nearly half (47%) would allow restraints on "acts of anal sex." Interestingly, the prospect of anal penetration is more appalling to men (51% would limit/outlaw it) than to women (44%). Clearly, what matters is whose ox is being gored.[8]

At the very least, one might hope that America is now too sociosexually mature to restore sodomy laws where they've been dropped. After all, extant laws were written in a much earlier era, and were built upon Old Testament attitudes that seem less relevant today. 'Sodomy,' the very term itself, sounds like a religious archaism to many Americans.

Nevertheless, we can't be too sure that new laws won't be written. Since AIDS, the public has shown increasing willingness to crack down. According to Gallup, the proportion of Americans decidedly against "legalization of homosexuality" has actually been rising (e.g., from 39% in 1982 to 47% in 1985), and most of that shift has come among those previously undecided on the issue. How far this conservative trend will go, no one can say. In the meantime, our enemies patrol the perimeter of remaining restrictions like puritans along a sexual Siegfried Line.[9]

Sodomy Laws vs. the U.S. Constitution. Where is the federal government in this battle for personal freedom? Where is the U.S. Supreme Court? Must the matter simply be left to the (in)discretion of states, or is there a higher right involved—say, a constitutional right to privacy—that warrants federal intervention to bring about more uniform tolerance for homosexuals?

Don't hold your breath. Regarding gay rights, the Supreme Court has shown malign neglect. After dodging the issue for many years, the Court finally addressed the constitutionality of state sodomy laws in 1986. In *Bowers* v. *Hardwick,* a bare majority (five to four) ruled that the Constitution does not protect homosexual relations between consenting adults, even in the privacy of their own bedrooms; therefore, they ruled, a Georgia law forbidding all people to engage in oral and anal sex may be used to prosecute such conduct between homosexuals. The majority laid groundwork for a double standard on sodomy: in a footnote, it observed that the constitutional right to privacy might indeed protect heterosexuals engaged in sodomy (that question was left undecided); nonetheless it could never apply to homosexuals engaged in the same conduct.

Why not? The four dissenting justices, in an opinion written by the Hon. Harry Blackmun, argued that the Constitution's implied right of privacy—the right to be left alone in such personal matters—should extend to homosexual conduct. Blackmun's reasoning was principled, his rhetoric impassioned: "The fact that individuals define themselves in a significant way through their intimate sexual relationships with others suggests, in a nation as diverse as ours, that there may be many 'right' ways of conducting those relationships . . ." If so, those relationships deserve respect from the state—the more so when conducted in the bedroom. Argued Blackmun, "The right of an individual to conduct intimate relationships in the intimacy of his or her own home seems . . . to be the heart of the Constitution's protection of privacy."

On the contrary, replied the majority, homosexuality should be excluded from the class of privacy-protected behaviors because . . . well . . . it has always been excluded in the past, and it has always been regarded with disgust. The criminality of homosexuality, you see, has "ancient roots" in English common law and in American history—why, even today it's criminalized in two dozen states—so the Court concluded that it *must* be constitutional.

The majority's decision in *Bowers* v. *Hardwick* was a disaster for gays, both in its reasoning and results. The historical reasoning was blatantly circular, enshrining prejudices of the past as just cause for oppression today. As legal scholars have noted, the majority opinion was lame and labored—a transparently awkward attempt to muddle through, willy-nilly, to the desired conclusion. It was also suspiciously similar to historical arguments the Court had heard before, and rightly dismissed, in defense of such venerable American institutions as slavery and miscegenation laws ('but our traditional community standards have *never* allowed black/white marriages in the past!').

The majority's reasoning in this case was so shallow, in fact, that it gives hope of eventual overturn by a more enlightened Supreme Court in future years. It also gives hope that Blackmun's powerful dissent will ultimately command the moral and legal authority that the majority's opinion failed to do. This has happened before. In 1896, Justice John Harlan issued a thundering dissent in *Plessy* v. *Ferguson* that eventually overshadowed and shamed the majority's "separate but equal" rationale for the segregation of Blacks. "The Constitution is color-blind," said Harlan, "and neither knows nor tolerates classes among citizens . . . The thin disguise [in the majority's rationale] . . . will not mislead anyone, nor atone for the wrong this day done." In *Bowers* v. *Hardwick,* the gay community has been handed its own *Plessy* decision; now the community must await real justice through a gay *Brown* v. *Board of Education.* Let us pray that another Warren Court is not too long in coming. (Alas, the increasingly rightward tilt of the Court during the Reagan and Bush years leaves us feeling, at times, as though we haven't even a prayer.)

Meanwhile, gays must live with the dismal results of the *Bowers* decision. It reinforces and legitimizes the nation's homohatred, implicitly solidifying grounds for discrimination against gays. It also means, of course, that for the time being, gays will get no relief from sodomy laws through the federal courts, and must now shift their efforts back to piecemeal attacks at state and local levels.

It is sad to think that the nation's highest court—historically the last resort and heroic protector of so many other maligned minorities—should turn its back on gays, thereby denying the intrinsic dignity and worth of one tenth of America's citizenry.

CLASS 2: DENYING GAYS THEIR FUNDAMENTAL CIVIL RIGHTS

On the surface, at least, Americans seem more willing to grant gay citizens their civil than their sexual rights. This ambivalence reflects tension between the nation's liberal civic culture, on the one hand, and its conservative religious values, on the other. As Americans—rather than as Christians and Jews—our citizens pay lip service to a kind of 'live and let live' individualism demanding respect and fair treatment for those with whom they may disagree.

It's not surprising, therefore, that while roughly three in four Americans believe homosexuality is always wrong, far fewer say they'd actually infringe on the civil liberties of homosexuals, especially if the liberties in question were those explicitly set forth in the Bill of Rights. Heterosexuals are more fond of those legal rights, and of their self-image as good Americans, than they are of queerbashing.[10]

That's the good news. Now, the bad: many straights feel that homosexuals should receive the minimal rights bestowed on all citizens by the Bill of Rights, *and nothing more*. This is a problem, for two reasons. First, the Bill of Rights has done little to protect gays against other Jim Crow laws or policies at state and local levels, which serve to promote discrimination against gays in housing, employment, parental rights, and so forth. Second, the equal treatment of citizens is regulated only in small part by the nation's laws, still less by the Constitution; the rest is left up to each citizen's sense of fairness. Yet it is within this unregulated domain of private and semiprivate action that the sharp teeth of bigotry clamp down most tightly on gays.

So long as there's no law against it—and Americans generally resist the enactment of special laws to protect bedeviled minorities —our citizens think it their right to abuse and discriminate against others, as an act of self-expression. A bare majority may feel bound to let gays have their own say and (in some states, at least) their own sex, but this doesn't mean that they have to pretend they like what's going on.

Instead, straights find a thousand extralegal ways to express their dislike, collectively exerting an oppressive social control that brings as much misery to gays as any law could. "Protection, therefore, against the tyranny of the magistrate is not enough," argued John Stuart Mill, a century ago:

> there needs protection also against the tyranny of the prevailing opinion and feeling; against the tendency of society to impose, by other means than civil penalties, its own ideas and practices as rules of conduct on those who dissent from them; to fetter the development, and, if possible, prevent the formation, of any individuality not in harmony with its ways.

Gay 'individuality' in America today has precious little protection against 'the prevailing opinion.' The malevolent manifestations of that opinion—or at least *some* of them, since the full list is as long as the roll call in hell—will be our subject for the remainder of this chapter.

Denial of Rights: Free Speech and Assembly. To begin our review on an upbeat note, let's start where the infringement of civil rights seems slightest, and seek to understand why. No other minority group in America today enjoys, and depends upon, free speech and public assembly more than the gay community does. In most large cities, it is now so easy for homosexuality to dare speak its name, and for gays to gather at their own watering holes, that those who are young or forgetful may suppose that gays have always enjoyed these liberties without much fear of arrest.

Yet the freedoms of public expression and association did not exist for gays at all until early in this century, and have come to be enjoyed as *de facto* rights only during the last twenty years. The delay in granting freedom of assembly to gays came, in part, from the persistence of sodomy and prostitution laws, which mark all homosexual conclaves, by definition, as potential sites for criminal activity.

Thus, as recently as the 1960s, even in Greenwich Village—the gay Vatican City—suspected fairies were routinely harassed or arrested by police for 'loitering' in groups on street corners. Likewise, until a crowd of queens at the Stonewall Inn actually fought back for the first time (on June 27, 1969), the Village's gay and lesbian bars were periodically raided by police, who typically charged that prostitution or drug traffic was conducted on the premises. Such raids still occur in cities across the nation, but their frequency has declined. (We don't mean to suggest, by the way, that raid-free gay bars are all there is to gays' right of free assembly: the right of gay social groups to gather on church, college, and public properties, for example, has also been challenged through the courts, with only mixed results.)[11]

Gays have also come to enjoy greater freedom of speech, as well as assembly. Until the second half of this century, the mainstream would not stomach the faintest whiff of homosexuality in public (just ask Oscar Wilde and Bill Tilden). Only since the 1960s has the solitary and subdued voice of the gay community burst forth in a brash Tabernacle Choir of novelists, musicians, artists, pornographers, and pundits whose works explicitly extol homosexuality and whose audience is the general gay public.

This increase in gay self-expression has met with expanded tolerance. Granted, nearly one-third of Americans, in a 1985 poll, said they would not allow an "admitted homosexual . . . to make a speech in [their] community"; still worse, roughly 40% of the public would not permit a book "in favor of homosexuality" (such as this one) to become available in public libraries, nor would they allow a homosexual to "teach in a college or university." But the exciting fact remains nonetheless that these stiflers were outnumbered, for once, by those who would preserve free speech for gays.[12]

Accordingly, homosexuals speak out through several media, and above all in print—in newsletters, novels, and countless magazines; in well-established vehicles such as the *Advocate*, the *Sentinel, Christopher Street*, and the *Gay Community News*; in hundreds of more obscure publications ranging from *Gay Alaska* to the *Brazen Hussy Rag*. (And the larger gay periodicals receive advertising from the likes of Levi Strauss, Bank of America, Perrier, Dean Witter Reynolds, and Seagrams.) Gays also write lots of books: New York's largest gay bookshop offers more than seven thousand gay-related titles, a great many of them published by mainstream houses seeking to tap into the large market of prosperous gay consumers.

The very abundance of gay writings, in fact, teaches us two things about the outer boundaries of straight tolerance. First, in civil rights as in all other matters, money talks. "Business is business," as one straight columnist optimistically remarked. "The dollar bill has no prejudice." We could even call it the unwritten Right of Gay Consumption: *Straights are most inclined to preserve and promote those gay liberties that create a gay consumer demand.* Thus, gays are allowed their own books, pornography, fashion wear, vacation resorts, and bars (which are, not infrequently, owned by straights, bankrolled by organized crime, and shaken down by the police for payoffs). America best earns its reputation as the proverbial 'free marketplace of ideas' when those ideas are converted into profitable merchandise for the not-so-free marketplace of things.

Second, we learn that *the primary communication medium allowed to gays is print, rather than broadcast,* a fact of enormous social significance. In America, a television picture *is* worth ten thousand words. TV and, to a lesser extent, radio are mass media; but this is not necessarily true of print. Except for a few urban newspapers and a handful of national magazines, print vehicles in the United States have narrow audiences, each numbering in the hundreds of thousands rather than the millions. In contrast, a single half-hour television show (or, for that matter, a single thirty-second commercial) can command an audience of 20 million or more.

Print, then, is the forum left over for minorities whose views and interests are not deemed 'ready' or 'appropriate' or 'newsworthy enough' for primetime television. Naturally, it takes more effort to find free speech in print than it does to turn on the tube: you must seek it out and, ordinarily, pay for it. Since the general public is, at best, semiliterate and intellectually lazy, it does not seek out minority viewpoints in print. Consequently, most citizens are utterly unaware of the intense clamor of 'free speech' actually taking place in America's communication byways, and know virtually nothing about the thriving gay press. One wonders: if a tree falls in the forest, to be used in the printing of progay speeches that no straights hear, does it make a sound? For heterosexual America, the answer is no.

This silent free speech, then, is precisely what the mainstream will tolerate, and not much more. Gays are free to sit together in their darkened closet—with their crude romance novels, political screeds, and dirty pictures—and talk to themselves; this does not disrupt the Big Lie. Generally speaking, they are *not* free to air gay news and views in mainstream broadcast media:

- Newscasters who consider it their civic and professional duty to cover, routinely, news items from America's black, Hispanic, Asian, and Jewish communities, feel no such responsibility toward the gay community, which is as large as any of these. What gays get instead is sporadic reporting on exposed celebrities, sadistic crimes, and gay diseases—that is, news that makes gays look bad.

- TV and radio stations will not, as a rule, permit gay organizations to announce upcoming local events or meetings, thereby contributing to an information blackout that impedes freedom of assembly by gays.

- Beyond reporting mere news, broadcast networks have shown almost no willingness to allow gays to *promote* their cause through commercials or public service announcements (PSAs) that plead for a more tolerant, caring society, even though blacks, Mormons, and others have been permitted to do so.

Gay activists who request better access to the broadcast media discover quickly that TV and radio function as *public* forums *privately* owned and are usually controlled by straights. The impresarios who own the major networks get to decide what appears in their broadcasts and what does not; and, by and large, they refuse to accept what they call 'issues advertising'—persuasive advertising on controversial subjects. Such advertising can provoke a storm of resentment from the public and from corporate sponsors, which is bad for business.

What exactly constitutes 'issues advertising'? It evidently does *not* include platitudinous appeals for the virtues of family unity (courtesy of the Mormons); nor does it include tirades against perfidious Albion (courtesy of self-appointed presidential candidate and national kook, Lyndon LaRouche); nor reminders that a mind is a terrible thing to waste (courtesy of the United Negro College Fund); nor religious shows that condemn gay 'sinners'; nor paeans to nuclear energy; nor pious condemnations of nuclear war and racism. All these messages have appeared, as paid advertisements, on national TV or radio over the last ten years and apparently have not crossed over the line into the forbidden zone of controversial, persuasive 'issues advertising.' Some guys get all the breaks.

What issues advertising does include these days is almost any communiqué presented openly by or for homosexuals. In a rigid reinforcement of the Big Lie, the words 'gay' and 'homosexual' are considered controversial *whenever they appear!* Those salacious words, and more abusive ones, are sometimes inserted by the network's own writers and producers in order to spice up nighttime soap operas and made-for-television movies, of course; but homosexuals are seldom permitted simply to represent themselves on the air. Such free speech would be unthinkable, because it would turn the fictionalized, TV-land existence of gays into a concrete reality: no, straights would much rather put words in our mouths via contrived dramatizations.

The courts and the Federal Communications Commission (which licenses operators) have been rightly concerned about the danger that private ownership of public forums poses to free speech and have provided some remedies that we'll review in detail in Chapter 4. To break TV stations' extraordinary stranglehold on civic discourse, the FCC began, many years ago, to require that broadcasters observe the Fairness Doctrine, which requires that stations give equal time to proponents of opposing viewpoints on important public issues.

To date, however, the doctrine has been of little use to gay activists. After all, it's difficult to demand *equal* time to defend the gay lifestyle when broadcasters won't give the subject any time at all, save here and there in uncountable, bloody little jabs and stabs so quick that the gay community barely has time to demand an apology, let alone prepare a counterassault. This state of affairs could change for the better, and in later chapters we'll explain how.

Denial of Rights: Work and Shelter. The rights of gays to work as they please, live where they wish, and enjoy equal access to public accommodations all concern an underlying right of association, the freedom to rub shoulders with whomever one must in order to get along in life. But this right of association flies in the face of straights' desire to distance themselves from homosexuals as much as possible. We'll discuss the resulting tensions by focusing primarily on employment discrimination.

"Purple is a poor idea, regardless of the shade," warns John Molloy in his career climber's classic, *Dress for Success.* An expert on appearance and prejudice, Molloy has more in mind than one's choice of shirt color: he bluntly advises gays that they must choose between, on the one hand, expressing their gayness (and thereby advancing the liberation movement) and, on the other, seeking personal success in the workaday world. Gay men, in particular, can expect to encounter job interviewers who will scrutinize their attire for any suggestion of effeminacy; as Molloy comments tartly *vis-à-vis* men and jewelry, "the only completely acceptable ring is the wedding band. Period." *Capisci?*

The choice between gay and A-OK is not as drastic as Molloy suggests. There are fields in which the color purple is welcome: one critic cites tolerance for gays in the "theater, music, letters, dance, design, architecture, the visual arts, fashion at every level . . . the list could go on." She's right: we could add careers in retail sales, library science, nursing, antiques, advertising, and other areas. Not by accident, gay men are least unwelcome in certain service-sector careers that, in our male-dominated commercial world, have traditionally been more open to women. Much the same goes for lesbians, who—unless they stomp to work in male drag—face discrimination first and foremost because they *are* women.

The problem, of course, is that 'tolerant' fields are only a fraction of all occupations; most gays prefer to work in less accepting fields. They expect equal opportunity to advance in the career of their choice, which is, after all, the guts of the American Dream.

What holds gays back is homohatred, expressed through a system of hiring and promotion whose machinery is ordinarily beyond the regulating grasp of the law. Employment prejudice is hard enough to prove when a blue-collar job is involved (to which rigid union contracts on hiring and promotion procedures may apply); with a white-collar job it is virtually impossible. Most personnel decisions in business, government, and academe cannot be effectively monitored and controlled from outside, since those decisions depend less on quotas, résumés, and other formal criteria than on judgment of a candidate's social skills and 'chemistry' with co-workers. Defined as outsiders, minorities of any kind— black, Hispanic, gay, et al.—are presumed by bigots to make for unstable chemistry within the company's homogenized workforce. So they are not hired.

The hookworm of prejudice has ample opportunity to bore into the heel of promotion, as well as hiring, decisions. At promotion time, an applicant's leadership and managerial qualities must be considered yet cannot be objectively measured. The homohater faced with promoting a homosexual builds his own contempt into a pseudo-valid reservation: can an effeminate man or 'odd' woman command authority and respect from subordinates? He thinks: not if the subordinate were me.

Worse, the higher paid or more prestigious a job, the more vague its qualifications become; and the more vital it is that the jobholder represent the organization 'appropriately' to—that is, make a winning impression on—the outside world. Given the diversity of bigots roaming the world, 'general acceptability' becomes an elastic excuse for refusing to promote into prominent positions *anyone* who seems unconventional in any way.

Those who refuse marriage and family are among the least conventional—'queer old ducks,' they used to be called—and often their careers grind to a halt once they have risen to the level where further advancement requires their frequent appearance, comely spouse in tow, at the company's social functions. The senior management of more than one corporation still uses the informal Thirty Rule: any junior executive not married by age thirty is 'not promotion material,' because he manifestly lacks either stability, maturity, minimal social skill, or 'normal sexual drive.'

Such grounds for refusing a job or promotion are almost never admitted directly, so there is little concrete evidence of discrimination. Once in a great while, one hears about a gay person who is told, point-blank, that he's been fired because his lifestyle offends co-workers (as reportedly happened recently to an employee of a major long-distance telephone company). Far more often, however, 'They just said I wasn't right for the position.' Anyone might see malignant intent behind the use of lie-detector tests to screen the sex lives of applicants for entry-level positions, as the Coors brewery reportedly used to do; but who can prove that bigotry has influenced the selection of a new foreman, supervisor, or CEO?

While employed during the mid-'80s in a large corporate office in New York, one of the authors met a somewhat effeminate middle-aged bachelor and a fortyish spinster (who clearly had been a beauty in her maiden days). Both were respected for their expertise and dedication; the woman, in fact, had been with the company for nearly twenty years. But recently, behind their backs, a homohater in top management had begun to call them "the Fudgepacker" and "Lisa Lesbo." When a decline in business led to layoffs, Lisa and the Fudgepacker were among the few to be fired from middle management. Had the homohater's name-calling stuck? Had his malevolence influenced the firing decisions?

Indeed, job discrimination against gays is harder to confirm than that against any other disadvantaged group. At least with female, black, or disabled applicants, there are objective physical characteristics to cite, quantify, and track—essential in building a legal case against systematic discrimination. But when it comes to sexual orientation, there are no valid external markers, just a passel of informal stereotypes, applied indiscriminately to both gays and those who merely 'look gay.'

There exist, therefore, no hard numbers on the exact extent of job discrimination against gays. (This lack of firm data, incidentally, gives our enemies room to protest—as a Maine gubernatorial candidate did in 1986—that "I'm not convinced [homophobia translates directly into housing and employment discrimination. Therefore, I do not support the 'gay rights' bill.") What we do have, instead, are four clues.

The first clue comes from the few statistics available, drawn from recent national opinion polls, which tell us how eager Americans are to work alongside gays, particularly in the AIDS era:[13]

- 52% of those polled prefer not to work with gays, including 25% who "strongly object."

- 22% believe it should be completely legal "to keep people out of jobs and housing if they are homosexuals." (This and other polls suggest that about two-thirds of the public support fair employment and housing rights for gays, the remainder being either opposed or undecided.)

- 35% admit that they are "uncomfortable around gays," and 33% avoid places "where homosexuals may be present."

- 49% say they have reason to believe that "AIDS is causing unfair discrimination against all homosexuals," and we must suppose that much of that discrimination concerns employment and housing practices. (Further, of the 43% who claim to see no "unfair" discrimination, at least some, no doubt, do perceive discrimination but think that it is perfectly fair.)

The second clue to the extent of employment discrimination is, paradoxically, the very extent to which authorities have sought to protect gays from such discrimination. To rework an old saw: where there's smoke, there's a gay under fire. Thus, since 1975, homosexuals have been permitted to serve as federal employees per special ruling of the Civil Service Commission. Likewise, as of 1987, a dozen states, as many counties, and forty-five municipalities had made special provisions to allow homosexuals in government. In addition, two states, three counties, and twenty-eight cities had adopted measures to illegalize employment discrimination against gays in the private sector, as well. Indeed, no other civil right of our community has been shielded by more special legal provisions and executive orders. Unfortunately, these protections have jurisdiction over only a small proportion of the country's gay employees; and the extreme difficulty of proving antigay discrimination in hiring and promotion limits their effectiveness.

The third clue to antigay job discrimination is the public's hostile reaction to government efforts to stop it. After Houston's mayor added protection of gay government employees to the city's antidiscrimination ordinance, angry opponents mounted a public referendum in 1985 that forced withdrawal of such protection by a stunning vote margin of four to one. No surfeit of brotherly love in that town; nor in Miami and half a dozen other major cities that have repealed gay civil rights ordinances since the late '70s.

When, in 1986, the New York City Council finally succeeded in passing a law against antigay discrimination in jobs, housing, and public accommodations, it did so over widespread and bitter opposition. Councilman Noach Dear protested, "We shouldn't make any special laws to protect individuals who practice a deviant behavior . . . Their claim that hundreds of people are being discriminated against is hogwash." (Mr. Dear, in his very next malicious breath, showed why such special protection was needed: "The law sends the wrong message to our youths while they are growing and dealing with their sexuality." In other words, everyone should be 'scared straight,' and those youngsters who would dare to grow up as homosexuals anyway should know in advance that society will punish them.)

The fourth clue to antigay job discrimination is the concerted attempt by homohaters to make such discrimination explicitly legal. It is not enough, for some, that the careers of gays be constantly imperiled by private prejudice, nor that ordinances to protect them be voted down: no, a sizable minority (perhaps one in five) will be content only when the laws explicitly enshrine job discrimination. This is one goal of the Family Protection Act, submitted to Congress by right-wingers in 1981 and defeated, but whose components have reappeared in other forms and other places. The FPA's "Homosexuality and Unlawful Employment Practices" clause would amend the 1964 Civil Rights Act to make sure that the term "unlawful employment practice"

> shall not be deemed to include any action or measure taken by an employer, labor organization, joint labor-management committee, or employment agency with respect to an individual who is a homosexual or proclaims homosexual tendencies. No agency, bureau, commission, or other instrumentality of the Government of the United States shall seek to enforce nondiscrimination with respect to individuals who are homosexual or who proclaim homosexual tendencies.[14]

Other, more direct efforts to codify denial of employment to gays are built upon the pretext that homosexuality carries some inherent flaw which should automatically disqualify a gay job applicant on *functional,* rather than moral, grounds. The supposed flaws are invariably derived from one or another of the seven myths about gays.

There is, for example, a standing rule in the intelligence and defense communities against hiring gays for jobs requiring high-security clearance, on grounds that their promiscuous lifestyle leads to too much, and too intimate, contact with strangers (remember, loose lips sink ships) and also makes them vulnerable to blackmail. Because gays are furtive sex addicts, they are also untrustworthy Americans. This security-clearance rule seems to be collapsing slowly under the weight of its own illogic: monogamous gays who are completely open about their sexuality are no more vulnerable in these regards than are married heterosexuals. We know of one openly gay man, living in a stable relationship, who applied for security clearance in the early 1980s and, after several years of careful investigation and foot-dragging in Washington, was finally granted limited clearance. This is a small victory, but a victory just the same: better that homohaters drag their feet than simply put them down.

In contrast, straights have been trying for decades to put their feet down against gay public-school teachers, and for reasons even less logical. According to a 1987 Gallup poll, two thirds of the public believes gays should never be hired as elementary school teachers.[15]

Some fear that gay teachers, degenerate sex maniacs by definition, will seduce their pupils. Even if they don't, gay teachers— whether 'avowedly' or only 'apparently' homosexual—are believed to exert an unwholesome influence: presumably they will, as role models, turn their previously straight students into limp-wristed pansies and coarsened tomboys. (Never mind that this presumptive role-model dynamic seems to have produced no countervailing effect upon the gay pupils of straight teachers.)

At the very least, straights fear, 'respectable' gay teachers will contradict one of the key social lessons of American schooling— reinforced with fists during lunch recess—about the value of conformity, of looking and acting like everyone else. (In social studies classes, America the Great Melting Pot is extolled, but the metaphor's subtext depicts the melting down of human diversity into a single all-American alloy.) In particular, straights are afraid that gay teachers will stand as living refutations of society's worst myths about homosexuals; this might soften homohatred in the next generation and enable gay children to come out earlier and better adjusted, with less shame and self-hatred. Wouldn't that be awful?

These fears in mind, Oklahoma attempted to enforce a law authorizing dismissal of any teachers "advocating, soliciting, imposing, encouraging or promoting public or private homosexual activity in a manner that creates a substantial risk that such conduct will come to the attention of school children *or school employees."* [Stress added.] (Fortunately, the U.S. Supreme Court declared that law unconstitutional in 1985, thanks partly to the law's artlessly blatant oppressiveness, and partly to a well-argued brief from the National Gay and Lesbian Task Force.)

Such witch hunts are futile and cruel. The hunt is futile because it would—as with the clergy—turn up such an astonishingly high proportion of homosexuals among schoolteachers that we think the persecutors would regret ever having got themselves into such a mess; the Big Lie would be undermined. Although we have no firm statistics on the number of gays in lower education, that number is probably high; not because gays are out to seduce little boys or girls, but because the loving, nurturing—dare we say 'parental'?—side of adult gays seeks an outlet and is not infrequently channeled into teaching. Only now do the authors recognize that many of their best and most widely admired elementary- and secondary-school teachers were probably gay. One is reminded of a letter to the *New York Times* several years ago:

> Two of my high school teachers . . . were male homosexuals . . . and both had a great effect on my life. Because of their intellectual interest in me, they encouraged me to develop my writing talents . . . [N]ot one faint hint . . . of improper conduct was made to me by either of those teachers. I was, however, seduced by a 30-year-old lady . . .

Teaching is not the only profession from which straights seek to exclude gays *en masse:* they are also rejected by the armed forces because, as an Army spokesman explained in the *Boston Globe,* "homosexuality is incompatible with military service." Polls reveal that four out of ten citizens believe gays should never be inducted, and virtually all military officers agree.[16] The excuse one hears in the barracks for excluding homosexuals has something to do with their reputed pusillanimity and/or sexual rapacity, the first making them unaccomplished on the battlefield, the second making them *too* accomplished for the sweaty confines of same-sex quarters. Military officers suspect the motives of any gay person seeking access to their crowded bunkrooms, bad food, and showers filled with naked men or women. The gay person's mixed motives for enlistment were celebrated in a '70s pop music hit, "In the Navy (You Can Join Your Fellow Men)," performed with a leer by the campy disco group, the Village People. In any case, rampant barracks sex won't do at all, since the military's vitality depends upon sublimation—its ability to harness and divert to military purposes the roiling libido of young males and females consigned to those barracks.

But such excuses for excluding gays are superficial: the real reasons pertain to what organizational psychologists call 'associational attractiveness.' Despite the low-grade pay and lifestyle, unsophisticated young men are drawn to a military career by the macho thrill of being associated with an icon of masculinity, a fearsome all-male club, a disciplined and lethal gang of bullyboys. (We admit we haven't the faintest idea what attracts straight women to the armed services—perhaps the same things?)

Thus, if the military were to roll out the welcome mat for homosexuals, it could easily develop a reputation as a haven for 'boys who like to be close to other boys.' It could become a laughingstock, thus devastating its associational attractiveness to straight males. The military's ever-erect phallus of tribal pride would shrivel instantly and disastrously. (It seems unimaginable now that officers in ancient Greece actually encouraged gay love among their troops in the conviction that it would make them more fierce and loyal to one another in battle.) Indeed, if the Big Lie—'we have no homosexuals here'—is essential to the survival of any American institution, it is the military.

Thus, the armed forces refuse to make any formal accommodation for gays, though the Navy and Air Force have begun, in some cases, to let exposed homosexuals depart quietly with honorable discharges. Only recently have federal courts shown any willingness to challenge military bigotry. In 1988, a U.S. Court of Appeals stunned the Army by declaring that its policy of excluding gays is a violation of the Fourteenth Amendment's equal protection clause and "illegitimately caters to private biases." Then, responding to the consequent uproar, the appellate court nullified its own ruling and decided to rehear the case, with the issue remaining unresolved at the time of writing.

In the end, the tough line taken against gays by the armed forces is mostly for show, to reassure straight recruits. Certainly, the military does a far poorer job of identifying gays than of outlawing them: according to one study, its screening techniques have provided no real obstacle to the enlistment of gay men and women.[17] Lesbians, in fact, are overrepresented. Just don't tell anyone.

Gays, like women, are also unwelcome in many other miserable occupations that depend upon macho esprit to make them attractive. As the fire chief of San Jose declared testily in 1986, "If some guy comes prancing into my office in a pink leisure suit saying, 'I just *love* truck men,' I'm not going to hire him"; one gets the impression that an openly gay applicant would fare poorly, no matter what his apparel. "I don't have anything against gays personally," explained a New York police sergeant to the *Boston Globe* in 1987, "I just don't want to work with one." What the sergeant, and many other straights, have something against, is association with homosexuals, and how this association might rub off on their reputations and job status.

The same motives can be seen behind denial of housing and public accommodations to gays. The landlord and hotel manager advise apparently gay couples that they have no more vacancies, when what they really mean is that they do not welcome gays, lest their establishments develop a 'bad' reputation. While more than half the states have decriminalized homosexual behavior, only Wisconsin and Pennsylvania have sought to include gays under laws or ordinances ensuring fair housing and equal access to public accommodations for minorities.

Protection is still less if one is a *minor*. No laws stop the cruelest denial of shelter: the child abuse perpetrated by parents who discover that their kid is gay and respond by throwing him or her out of their home, onto the streets. There are no firm statistics on the frequency of these family disasters, though they may account for a good share of the many thousands of runaways reported across America each year; 'castaway' or 'throwaway' might be a more appropriate term for unwanted gay kids. Unless promptly lured into foster care, or with an older, financially secure lover on hand to pick up the pieces (seldom the case), the gay teen castaway too often drifts helplessly into urban centers, seeking shelter and cash, and securing both, by the hour, through prostitution and the sale of drugs.

These Dickensian stories abound, so depressingly similar, one to the next, that a single illustration, drawn from a personal acquaintance of ours, will suffice.

> 'Ted' comes from a poor family in southern Vermont. When he was sixteen, a local sex scandal involving a high school gym teacher led to the exposure of Ted's homosexuality to his parents. The young man confessed to his parents in the family room of their modest home. His father began to weep, shakily pouring himself a drink and then dropping the glass. While Ted stood frozen in horror before them, his furious mother demanded to know, "What's the matter with you? Can't a girl suck your cock as good?" They ordered him to move out. Ted traveled to Boston, failed to pull himself together and, at last report, was drinking too much and hustling tricks to survive.

There is a refuge called Covenant House, for teen prostitutes and runaways, in the heart of New York City's red-light district, and its caretakers can detail thousands more cases whose essentials do not differ from Ted's story: they begin with gay children losing the shelter every family should provide. They end, at best, with lonely gays entering adulthood, estranged from their families yet cursed by the pious for being, of all things, 'antifamily.'

Society, of course, suggests a solution to all this discrimination against homosexuals, young and old, in work and shelter: there can be no discrimination if there are no gays, so stay in the closet and keep the door tightly shut. Let the Big Lie beget little lies. If you're a gay male teen, keep your hands to yourself and take a nice girl to the senior prom; or, if lesbian, get a boyfriend who won't paw you too much. At your job interview, wear a gold wedding band. Once employed, get an opposite-sex stand-in for social functions; or fake a spouse, then announce a divorce. When you and your lover go hunting for a condominium, split up and apply for adjoining suites, one at a time. When you move in to-gether, get separate telephone lines to avoid suspicion. Hotel ac-commodations can easily be had for your vacation together: sim-ply settle for a room with twin beds, or let one of you hide in the car while the other rents a full-sized. And so on.

As a cure, deception of this sort is as bad as the disease, for both patient and society; worse, in fact, since it obscures the symptoms and darkens the prognosis. But for gays who cannot bear to jeop-ardize career, home, and mobility for gay liberation, deception seems the only option. Gays are permitted to embrace the Ameri-can Dream only by entering into an endless social nightmare.

A final note: these days, antigay employment and housing dis-crimination is exacerbated by fear of AIDS, the virus all gays are presumed to carry. Some employers are reluctant to hire recogniz-able gays, out of fear that they might pass AIDS on to co-workers or might become a health liability to the company. Likewise, landlords avoid or eject gay tenants out of fear that they may carry AIDS. Antigay discrimination by health insurance compa-nies is a growing problem. The Congressional Office of Technology Assessment released a study in 1988, showing that 86% of com-mercial insurers admitted that they try to identify applicants who have been infected with the virus, and 30% sometimes consider sexual orientation as a factor in underwriting decisions.

The Justice Department under the Reagan-Bush administration further reinforced the climate of panic and discrimination when, in 1986, it announced that laws protecting the handicapped from discrimination did not apply to victims of communicable diseases; and that workers who carried the AIDS virus might, therefore, be summarily fired both when there was a serious risk of AIDS transmission and when there existed the mere *fear,* reasonable or not, that an employee might transmit AIDS to others. Considering the large proportion of homosexuals who have been exposed to the virus—perhaps one in three in New York, and one in two in San Francisco—the Justice Department was sanctioning an open hunting season against gay employees. True, there is *some* progress at the federal level: in March 1987, the U.S. Supreme Court explicitly extended antidiscrimination protection to people with contagious diseases. But, according to the *Advocate,* that ruling specifically left unresolved the question whether those who have merely been exposed to the HIV virus, rather than sufferers of full-blown AIDS infection, should be afforded similar protection.[18]

Nearly half the states have moved to counteract the federal administration's neglect, explicitly including persons with AIDS under laws protecting the handicapped from discrimination in jobs, housing, and public accommodations. How cruelly ironic that infection with AIDS will offer many homosexuals the first explicit protection they have ever had against such discrimination. Only while dying—with AIDS fluttering over them like a white banner of surrender, an admission of degeneracy—are gays received with a modicum of mercy and justice by the mainstream.

Heterosexuals applaud themselves for this last-minute compassion, like kindly executioners granting a final wish to a condemned man. Yet only when confronted by the blank enormity of death itself do straights sense vaguely—many for the first time— that sexual orientation is not such a great and terrible issue in the larger scheme of things; only then is there an inkling that it should be extraneous to all the most important rights and joys of life. Too late.

Denial of Rights: Marriage and Parenthood

He: *"Celeste will never eat that: you* know *she hates liver."*
Spouse: *"You're spoiling her, Tom. She's two years old now: stop treating her like a baby."*

—MIDDLE-AGED GAY COUPLE,
OVERHEARD IN THE WELL-STOCKED PET FOOD AISLE
OF A GREENWICH VILLAGE GROCERY

Straight or gay, a great many adults sooner or later get the urge to settle down with a mate and raise a family. On the right to marry and parent, however, more than on any other, straights make sure that gays lose out, and lose big. No state legally recognizes gay marriages. As for gay parents, they had best hope the state does *not* recognize them.

Gay marriages are not given legal sanction because, of course, this would appear to condone homosexuality and suggest that society respects and values stable gay relationships—which, in fact, it does not. Moreover, if millions of gay marriages were to begin dotting the legal landscape, society would have no choice but to take official notice of them, thereby unmasking the Big Lie.

Legalized gay marriage would be significant chiefly because of the mutual property and inheritance rights it would create. These rights are among the primary yardsticks by which social relations are measured and attested in Western societies: the more coextensive the property and inheritance rights shared by two persons, the more significant their social relationship is seen to be. These rights reflect and shape our social order. As Tocqueville first observed, in his critique of Jacksonian America, "The laws of inheritance . . . should head the list of all political institutions, for they have an unbelievable influence on the social state of peoples . . . By their means man is armed with almost supernatural power over the future of his fellows."

Refusing to recognize gay marriage, the state does worse than merely debase and undermine the durability of gay relationships: it actually renders their legacy invisible by striking them from society's written record of coupled properties; it deliberately erases all lasting tangible signs that a gay family structure ever existed and prospered, or ever could do so. The tactic bears a disturbing resemblance to that of ancient armies that sought to obliterate their enemies by slaughtering them, then burning their villages to the ground and scattering the ashes to the winds, so that history would never know they had lived.

There are a few hopeful signs in recent years that this tactic for erasing social history may eventually be abandoned: even absent legal marriages, a few liberal courts across the country are beginning, on their own, to recognize the shared property rights of long-lasting gay relationships, evaluating them in much the same way as they assess heterosexual common law marriages. But we are still many moons away from recognizing gay relationships *as* marriages, whether by common law or license.

Straights determined to preserve the Big Lie have coldly Machiavellian motives for preventing marriages between homosexuals. But they also have deeply emotional reasons. First, the prospect of gay marriage and parenthood offends their sentimentalized notions of *family*, notions critical to the heterosexual self-image. Marrying and rearing children—creating one's own family—are milestone decisions that reassure straights of their normalcy and worth, and of their fidelity to the elementary conventions of their society. Of necessity, straights tolerate much diversity among those who conform to the basic, heterosexual notion of the family. (Even the Munsters and the Addams Family were warmly welcomed in TV-land.) But if marriage and parenthood are to continue reassuring straights of their normalcy, these rights must be forbidden to a few beyond the pale. And so, gays are impaled.

At the same time, straights eagerly cite the fact that gays neither marry nor produce offspring with one another as the ultimate evidence that homosexuality is a bankrupt lifestyle, inherently promiscuous, unstable, superficial, and worthless to society.

Straights even feel that gays—who purportedly live only to indulge their own appetites—do not *deserve* spouses and children: a
family is seen as a reward reserved to straights for having
foresworn the carefree, self-indulgent, more promiscuous lifestyle
of their youth.

Beyond all this, there is one more reason why straights are scandalized by the prospect of gay matrimony: marriage assuages their
sexual guilt. Most Americans, without realizing it, hide in their
bosom the traditional Christian feeling that sex is naughty and
vulgar—profane. Sex can be rendered pure only when treated as a
ritual of holy matrimony bonding a man and woman until death,
or when justified by the 'higher purpose' of procreation. Religion
has devised elaborate nuptial ceremonies—and the state, specific
legal procedures—that signal the exact point at which a couple's
heterosexual acts become godly and legitimate. But how can marriage possibly work this purification of heterosexuality if also permitted among those whose sexual proclivities seem irredeemably
unclean and an 'abomination before God'? That would confuse
everything: either ceremonial marriage would have no purifying
magic and straight sex would remain profane, or else gay sex
within marriage would become pure, a concept as oxymoronic as
dry water or a square circle.

Both the sacred-family and sexual-purification motives for opposing gay marriage can be seen behind a pamphlet on homosexuality issued by the Catholic Archdiocese of New York:

> Homosexual practice is essentially anti-family. It undermines
> the institution of heterosexual marriage as the exclusive
> home of responsible human sexuality. It is inescapably sterile
> and contributes significantly to the disdain of the procreative
> power and purpose of human sexuality upon which depends
> the future of society in its children.

Most straights are only dimly conscious of their reasons for opposing gay marriage—why ponder the preposterous?—yet they
dredge up quite conscious arguments against *gay parenting*. They

do so because, whereas gay marriage is hypothetical, gay parenting is an occasional fact. Newspapers crackle with stories of divorced lesbian mothers fighting to keep their children, and of gay men seeking to foster or adopt. Joy Schulenburg, author of *Gay Parenting*, estimates that 1.5 million American families are headed by gay parents. These families have come under heated attack in recent years. "We'd been coasting along unnoticed and there was actually a lot of [gay] parenting going on," one lesbian mother told the *New York Times* in 1987. "It was a real shock when we realized there was this deep-seated homophobia."

The rise in hostility toward gay parents has corresponded directly to their increased visibility, the result of bitter public disputes over child custody and foster placement policies. In the past, such policies were often administered so as to preserve the Big Lie while discreetly delivering children into responsible gay homes. "The truth about adoption is that social workers have been placing kids with gay people for a long time," observed Roberta Achtenberg, directing attorney of the San Francisco Lesbian Rights Project, in 1987. "In some cases, they're the only people who want the child. In any case, if you don't bring up the fact that you're gay, nobody asks."

Unfortunately, more placement services *do* ask, now that conservative forces have been made aware of the practice and are on patrol. "One of the greatest urges in life is to parent," a gay father in Boston has remarked. "Why should we be any different?" But his question strikes homohaters as bizarre and suspicious: if gays are so interested in procreation, why aren't they also interested in heterosexuality, which is pretty much the same thing? Why are gays more eager to lay their hands on kids than on the opposite sex? You can see where this argument is heading.

The public is generally opposed to gay moms and dads for the same formal reasons it is opposed to gay teachers. As the Massachusetts legislature charged in 1985, gay parents are a threat to "the psychological or physical well-being of the child." Put more directly, homosexuals are child-molesters or, at the very least, a 'bad influence.' The fear persists that, as warped role models, gay

parents will raise confused little bisexuals or transvestites (hor-
rors!).

This fear is apparently groundless. In February 1988, the *New
York Times* summarized a recent professional report on gay-
parented households; based on the results of seventeen separate
clinical studies, the report found "nothing unusual in gender identity development, no greater preference for homosexuality and no
serious social and emotional maladjustments" among the children
of gay parents. The last finding is remarkably encouraging, since
children of gays must somehow learn to deal with the bigotry
visited upon their parents. Perhaps it is true, as some child psychologists have claimed, that kids in gay households ultimately
receive *better*-than-average parenting precisely because their parents know the family faces special challenges and therefore try
harder.

In any case, homohaters have pinned gay parenting upon the
horns of a false dilemma: as a New Hampshire legislator put it, the
question is "whose rights are we going to protect—the rights of the
children or the rights of the homosexual?" The prey or the
predator? The lamb or the wolf? In 1987, to no one's surprise,
New Hampshire became the second state, after Florida, to explicitly outlaw adoptions by homosexuals. Indeed, the Granite State
did the Sunshine State one better, banning gay foster homes too.
Homohaters have been encouraged by similar measures in states
as politically diverse as Massachusetts and Arizona.

This is not to say that public authorities systematically and aggressively deny the rights of gay parents: the vast majority, and
their children, live quiet lives unmolested. But this is only because
the state is too preoccupied to notice them and, in any event, not
fond of home-wrecking (an appetite peculiar to 'pro-family' conservatives).

Nonetheless, when ugly divorces degenerate into accusations of
homosexuality, the courts either lean toward the more 'wholesome'—read: heterosexual—parent, or extract stringent promises
from the gay parent. In *Mothers on Trial: The Battle for Children and
Custody,* Phyllis Chesler locates several cases in which lesbian

mothers were adjudged "good enough" to keep their children, provided they (a) didn't live with their mates, (b) didn't allow their mates or any other female lover to spend the night, (c) didn't make any economic demands on their ex-husbands, and (d) didn't oppose their husband's visitation preferences. No doubt these judges considered themselves of courageous heart and open mind. We'll look the other way, they ruled primly, as long as you abandon all demands on your 'normal' spouse and conceal your homosexuality from your children and neighbors. As appointed conservators of mainstream sensibility, then, these judges made lesbian mothers 'an offer they could not refuse': either collude in the Big Lie or else . . . or else we know when your kids get out of school.

○　○　○

There are, we said, three classes of actions by which straights express homohatred. The first, actions that outlaw homosexual behavior *per se,* serves less to prevent gay lovemaking than to brand it with the State's disapproval. It's left to bureaucracies and straight citizens to apply the State's prejudice in specific, 'civilized' ways, including denial of the right to speak and gather, reside and work, and marry and parent. There is no more serious impediment to gay advancement over the long run than the denial of these rights.

As bad as Class 2 is, however, there *are* more immediately frightful and uncivil ways to say 'I hate homosexuals.' We've saved public taunting, harassment, and violence for Class 3.

CLASS 3: VENTING PUBLIC DISAPPROVAL OF GAYS

Though your tissues gel,
And you rot in hell,
Don't feel gloomy, friend—
It will never end.
Happy Death, Faggot Fool.

—FROM "DEATH THREAT CHRISTMAS CARDS"
SENT TO GAYS IN 1987 BY THE IRON FIST,
A HATE GROUP AT THE
UNIVERSITY OF CHICAGO

The Kellogg Company launched a cereal named Nut and Honey Crunch in 1987, with the help of a TV advertising campaign. The commercials played off the social mischief that might arise when one fellow asks another what's for breakfast, and he seems to reply, "Nuttin', honey." In one vignette, a sheepish soldier is compelled to reply "Nuttin', honey" to a sneering sergeant. In another, a chuckwagon cook finds himself making the same reply to a surrounding gang of cowpokes, who react with displeasure and immediately draw their pistols.

This is supposed to be harmless and funny. Yet, while TV viewers, young and old, are entertained, they are also conditioned as homohaters. The ad's humor turns upon a not-so-subtle lesson concerning the proper way to react to apparent homosexuals— with contempt and, if necessary, violence. The cowboys' menacing response only makes sense if the public understands it as the 'natural' reaction to being called 'honey' by someone of the same sex. Address in this intimate manner offends male honor, implying that one is gay, perhaps a lover. So of course the offended fellow should make clear where he stands, by threatening to kill the other.

Some advertising fans homohatred in even less subtle ways: for example, a Schmidt's beer campaign in 1986, as described in *Advertising Age,* was proud to exclude from among its drinkers "prissy women, men who want to be prissy women, hairdressers, most interior decorators, guys who drink beer out of a glass, and guys who say they'll just have one beer and mean it."

Taken alone, these ads may seem a trivial annoyance. But they cannot be taken alone. Single clods in a mudslide, their message combines with countless other homohating media messages, which all work together to crush gays by venting and encouraging public bigotry. When TV ads, screenplays, comedians, talk-show hosts, novels, televangelists, and politicians all let their contempt show, the grand lesson learned is that gays should be taunted, harassed, and brutalized.

They are. In 1987, a federally commissioned report concluded that "[h]omosexuals are probably the most frequent victims" of hate-motivated violence in America. Who are the most frequent perpetrators? The statistics point to teen and young adult males. But the real perpetrators are those who taught them to hate.

Learn Stereotyping the Easy Way: Hunt and Peck, Taunt and Harass. To teach hatred, the tactic favored by society's leaders is not so much the direct attack as the taunt. The word conjures the school-yard bully, the big boy who torments little boys, provoking and humiliating them before their classmates. Sometimes the bully gets his classmates worked up too, then slips away as the victim is pummeled. Thus with adults: homohaters in command of public opinion, be they politicians, preachers, or entertainers, love to taunt homosexuals. Youthful audiences note this, then go out to do likewise, usually with malevolence less restrained. The taunts of their elders are *incitements* to violence.

Politicians, for example, have real trouble addressing the concerns of homosexuals—"them lollipops," as a Connecticut legislator described them—without a public snigger or slur. Anyone doubting this should examine the minutes of legislative debates, such as those leading to the defeat of recent efforts to include gays under state laws penalizing hate crimes in Illinois, Minnesota, Oregon, and Washington. (At press, specific penalties for harassment of gays have been accepted into law in only one state, California—further indication that many straights look benignly upon queerbashing.)

Some politicians drag gays into contempt whenever they can. President Reagan often amused his entourage with an imitation of a lisping faggot. Officials of the Reagan-Bush administration reportedly derided Title IX, a federal law that guarantees equal educational opportunity for women, as the "lesbians' bill of rights." On a more vindictive note, Senator Jesse Helms of North Carolina and other conservatives have deliberately confused homosexual conduct with the pandemic, exhorting "Americans who don't want to risk being killed by AIDS" to take immediate action: "reject sodomy and practice morality."

As we have seen, the church does its bit to taunt gays and incite backlash. The Vatican's much-criticized October 1986 letter on "The Pastoral Care of Homosexual Persons," for example, never mentions AIDS, but brands the practice of homosexuality, and its "advocates," as a serious threat to the "lives and well-being of a large number of people." Does this serious threat then justify a violent rebuff from the righteous? The Vatican replies with an artful ambiguity that reserves at least as much sympathy for homohaters as for homosexuals: "when civil legislation is introduced to protect behaviour to which no one has any conceivable right, neither the Church nor society at large should be surprised when . . . irrational and violent reactions increase." It is simply a law of social physics, says the Vatican, that action leads to reaction: one wrong provokes another wrong, and two wrongs don't make a (gay) right.

Nobody having religious authority goes further to taunt gays than the Christian conservative fringe: "You are not gay, you are miserable," declares one flyer. "You are not gay, you are polluted and filthy. You are not gay, you are snared in a world of lust . . . You will not be gay in hell, but tormented far worse than in this life." One gets the feeling that the flyer's authors would like to be there too, in hell, watching gays roast slowly over an open fire. (And maybe they will be: from the vantage of a nearby spit.)

At least they recognize that gays *are* tormented "in this life." The only regret of some fundamentalists is that the harassment doesn't go far enough. "To reduce prison overcrowding, execute all convicted murders [sic], rapists, homosexuals, child-molesters and etc.," recommends one pastor from Michigan, "[and] re-enact all sodomy laws." A representative of Santa Clara's Moral Majority agrees that "homosexuality should be coupled with murder . . ." In a more lovely and perfect world, "it would be the government that sits on this land that would be executing homosexuals." For now at least, fundamentalists must settle for the extra-governmental handiwork of thugs.

Not to mention the handiwork of homohating entertainers. Comedians/film stars Eddie Murphy and Rodney Dangerfield tell fag jokes of the old-fashioned nigger-and-kike variety, to the uproarious delight of their largely white, gentile audiences. Howard Stern, celebrated East Coast radio sleaze jockey, "spends his mornings bashing gays, dwarfs, and AIDS victims with equal abandon," according to *Newsweek*. Out West, listeners to KTKS radio get their daily dose of mean chuckles from the parody soap opera, "Gays of Our Lives." And so on, and so forth.

All this gay-taunting via mass media is defended as a rightful exercise of free speech, however cruel and abusive. But protecting such behavior preserves free speech no better than an election in a one-party state preserves democracy, since gays are allowed no opportunity to reply. Moreover, this bigoted expression crosses over the line into brutal action. It is, we say, a direct incitement to violence, a clear and present danger to public order, like a man (to borrow the Holmesian example) falsely shouting "Fire!" in a crowded theater, or a man (to borrow the Millite example) standing before a corn dealer's house and telling a hungry, torch-wielding mob that corn dealers are starvers of the poor. Burn, baby, burn.

The excitable masses are listening, of course, torches in hand, and pick up the taunting chant themselves. "Kill a Queer for Christ," reads a bumper sticker. "AIDS = America's Ideal Death Sentence," reads a graffito. Such hatred literally ignited in Jacksonville, Florida, in 1985: arsonists twice set fire to the local gay church, which was attacked so often that bulletproof windows had to be installed. In Wilmington, North Carolina, the gay helpline receives a thousand hate calls and bomb threats a year.

The excitable masses, by the way, include the college crowd as well as their blue-collar brethren—a sobering warning to any gay person who thinks that superior education, by itself, produces superior tolerance. George Segal's sculpture "Gay Liberation" is repeatedly vandalized on the Stanford campus. An enterprising student at the University of Kansas recently silkscreened and sold four hundred "FAGBUSTERS" T-shirts within just a few days. Back East, a scandal erupted after a *Wall Street Journal* article declared, "Yale has a reputation as a gay school," prompting the university's president, alumni, and students to repudiate the dastardly charge. The only serious problem with Yale, complained straight students in one article, is that "people are afraid to express [negative] views about gays." At Dartmouth, at least, the bigots are less abashed: in 1985, a sorority beer fest maliciously toasted Rock Hudson's impending demise. On another occasion, we hear, the conservative gentlemen of Dartmouth tanked up on beer to pee it under the dormitory doors of suspected gay students. Ah, the high jinks of youth.

"What astonished me," said Sara Davidson after touring the country to promote her Rock Hudson biography, "was that people felt free to express their distaste for homosexuals in a way that no one today would publicly express a dislike of Jews or blacks." In her recounting of the tour for the *New York Times Magazine,* Davidson recalled:

> In Cleveland a reporter told me he thought homosexuals were a "menace" and should be "locked up in camps." A radio interviewer in Detroit said: "I find the whole gay life-style repulsive. They've ruined one of our most beautiful cities—San Francisco. Now they're going to ruin the country."

One sees reflected everywhere ominous little glimmerings of the persecution gays endure each day. In 1987, for example, the unrelenting jibes against their children became so trying for the residents of a street named Gay Drive that, sensibly enough, they got the town board of West Seneca, New York, to change the name to Fawn Trail instead. At about the same time, down in Florida, a paranoid man became so upset by his belief that others thought him homosexual and were laughing at him, that, less sensibly, he went on a retaliatory rampage of mass mayhem and slaughter. To some homosexuals, these two outcomes represent, in an odd way, the only remaining avenues of response to gay harassment: either drop your gay identity altogether, if you can, or else declare war on America.

Monster Mash: When Homohatred Turns Violent

Sooner or later, of course, the escalating harassment ends in physical assault and murder. On rare occasions, the tormentors are felled. In small-town Lewiston, Maine, in 1985, a gay man was set upon in his own home by a rabid gang of youths screaming "Faggot! Faggot!" and was forced to shoot one of them in self-defense. One of the surviving attackers later explained why he had gone after the gay man: "I'd smash any homo . . . because they are gay. Weird. Sick. I'd like to smash this guy."

Far more often, however, it is gays who are butchered. In another part of Maine, for example, one year earlier, three homohating high school students assaulted an effeminate young man named Charlie Howard and threw him off a bridge to his death. (The state courts punished the murderers with wrist-slap sentences and later enforced a cancellation of Tolerance Day at an Augusta high school—on grounds that the lesbian guest speaker would be "too controversial.")

It's the same sickening story over and over again.[19]

- While witnesses look on, a young man—a gardener for the city of San Francisco—is stabbed to death by four youths shouting "Faggot! Faggot!" In the same city, a lesbian is beaten in the face, knocked to the ground and kicked repeatedly while attackers scream "dyke" and "bitch."

- In New Jersey, three college-aged men are charged with entrapping a twenty-year-old gay at midnight in a shopping mall; after working him over and burning cigarettes in his face, they allegedly tied him by the ankles to their truck and dragged him down the road.

- In Los Angeles, a group of men screaming "Die AIDS faggot!" throw a flesh-scorching beaker of acid at a lesbian employee of the L.A. Gay and Lesbian Community Services Center.

- In Winston-Salem, the killer of a gay man is released on probation, then murders another by cutting his throat and planting a butcher knife in his chest. (Prosecutors reportedly let the killer plea-bargain after concluding that jurors won't impose a stiff sentence for cutting a gay man's throat.)

- In Boston, a patron in line outside a gay bar is stabbed in the eyes by a band of attackers wielding broken bottles and lead pipes. Outside a disco in that city, another man pulverized by a group of drunken youths receives no help from a watching security guard—who shrugs his shoulders and says, "A guy who dresses like that should expect some trouble." (The guard only intervenes when the victim drags himself back to his car and attempts to run his attackers down).

- In New York City, a gay couple steps out of a taxi and, before they can reach the front door of their Greenwich Village apartment, have received broken ribs, concussions, and severe internal injuries.

- A statistical report of antigay violence in the Bay Area catalogs the following 'favorite' implements of assault: knives, guns, baseball bats, bottles, crowbars, large boards without nails, large boards with nails, and chains.

But these are isolated cases, retort those intent on preventing special legislation to protect gays. Where are your hard statistics? They know that statistics on antigay violence are very hard to come by, for three reasons. First, gay victims are understandably reluctant to admit to authorities the reason why they were attacked; an estimated 80% of all attacks go unreported. How many of the thousands of unprovoked, unexplained public assaults upon strangers year after year—assault cases that never find their way into the courtroom—are actually instances of queerbashing? Perhaps most of them, but we'll never know for certain.

Second, the term 'faggot' and its cognomens are so commonly

hurled in challenge during street fights that it is often hard to determine whether they are central or merely peripheral to the violence.

Third, and unforgivably, we lack firm statistics because our legislators and law enforcement agencies have, over the years, deliberately discouraged the collection of such statistics. The former director of a crime-monitoring organization in North Carolina recently explained, for example, that she was reluctant to keep a record of antigay violence because she didn't want to "encourage homosexuality." In 1987, fully one third of the House Judiciary Committee voted for an amendment *removing* sexual orientation from a bill mandating the Justice Department to collect national statistics concerning hate crimes based on race, religion, sexual orientation, and ethnicity.

We can take heart that that particular amendment failed, probably because its very introduction convinced the majority that selective prejudice against gays is obviously a serious problem. But it's less heartening to realize that only recently—since the AIDS crisis produced a marked efflorescence of queerbaiting and -bashing—have serious efforts been made to track the pattern of American cruelty against homosexuals.

Now, at last, violence statistics—such as can be collected, anyway—are being tracked by the gay communities, city governments, and police in certain urban areas. The Violence Project of the NGLTF now issues an annual report of its findings. The results over the last few years confirm what anyone with eyes and ears already knew: that attacks on gays are commonplace, and that AIDS is provoking more frequent and more serious outbreaks of gaybashing than ever before.

What does this endless barrage—these public taunts, insults, and brutal attacks—do to gays, body and soul? It robs them of the sense of security that every citizen should have. It dampens or breaks their natural confidence, their social ease. Depending, of course, upon demeanor and experience, many become gun-shy—never completely off guard in public. This is usually a subtle nervous tic, not an obvious one: we don't mean that gays cower and cringe whenever they step outside (though we do know of one gay man who, for two years, found himself haranged so frequently by youths on the streets of Boston that he no longer left his home, except for short trips during restricted hours of the day).

What we mean is that gays, like physically deformed or otherwise stigmatized citizens, are constantly conscious of their stigma, and learn to circumvent abuse in public with an everpresent wariness. Even those not obviously gay nonetheless live their lives like spies, a life of wearying vigilance, of precisely calculated behavior, nagged always by the fear that some slip or betrayal will leave them suddenly exposed and attacked. A suppressed but chronic anxiety results. It is a daily corrosive to the spirit, something we've found to be unimaginable and unexplainable to straights.[20]

o

OUR FIELD TRIP CONCLUDES: AN AGENDA FOR CHANGE

Discouraged? So are we. Yet we've systematically uncovered many things that homohating straights believe and feel, as well as hardships they visit upon gays. What we have discovered is, in fact, an agenda of heterosexual thoughts and actions that we must somehow change, and which therefore become the guiding agenda of the Waging Peace Campaign that we'll propose in Part II. The list looks like this:

○　○　○　○　○　○　○　○　○　○　○　○　○

BELIEFS

Current	*Preferred*
1. Gays don't warrant or deserve much attention from straights.	*Gays are a valuable part of American society: we should be familiar with their nature, culture, news, and heroes.*
2. Gays are few in number; I don't know any gays.	*Gays constitute a large minority of our society; and some of my friends/family are gay.*
3. Gays are easy to spot.	*They are not: most of them look just like anyone else.*
4. Gays become gay because of sin, insanity, and seduction.	*Sexual feelings are not really chosen by anybody: homosexuality is just as healthy and natural for some persons as heterosexuality is for others.*
5. Gays are kinky sex addicts.	*The sex and love lives of most gays and straights today are both similar and conventional.*
6. Gays are unproductive, untrustworthy members of society.	*Gays are hardworking, patriotic Americans.*
7. Gays are suicidally unhappy.	*Gays would be as happy as anyone else, if we'd just treat them fairly.*

ACTIONS

Current

8. Homosexual acts, and intimate public contact, are outlawed across roughly one half the nation.

9. Freedoms of speech and assembly by gays are impeded by public intolerance.

10. Rights of gays to work, shelter, and public accommodations are limited by public intolerance.

11. Gay couples cannot legally marry (nor enjoy property rights therefrom); nor are their rights to parent natural or adoptive children secure.

12. Gays are often taunted, harassed, and brutalized.

Preferred

All sex acts among consenting adults are decriminalized; no discrimination is permitted between straights and gays in content and application of laws.

Gays are provided, by special law if necessary, the same opportunity to speak (including access to mass media) and gather as straights currently enjoy.

Gays are assured, by affirmative action if necessary, equal opportunity in these regards.

Gays are permitted all the standard rights of marriage and parenthood.

The public no longer sanctions this behavior, which becomes as socially incorrect, discreditable, and repugnant as overt racism or anti-Semitism.

In important ways, this agenda is like those awful before-and-after photographs for weight-reducing plans. As with an obese person, a heterosexual America burdened down with homohatred must necessarily do most of the bigotry reduction by itself. Our duty, on the other hand, is to prod the body politic with a plan of deliberate stimuli, to hurry the change along.

The list above also resembles a pair of before-and-after photographs in what it reveals and conceals. Nothing in the photographs themselves reveals *how* to get from one condition to the other. Indeed, what is concealed by this picture is the *physiology of prejudice:* how our citizenry developed its excessive homohatred in the first place, why it persists, and how to melt its bulk away. Essential questions about that physiology must be answered, or no plan to turn America from beast to beauty will work.

The answer cannot be found in the seven homohating *beliefs* themselves, since these beliefs are generally a symptom—a rationalization—of prejudice, not its cause. Homohatred is rooted in strong, inward feelings, not outward beliefs. To understand those feelings, sorry to say, requires one more excursion to the straight world. The trip will be more like a covert reconnaissance mission across battle lines: prepare to navigate the gutters and sewage ducts of sheer hatred in Chapter 2.

2

○   ○   ○   ○   ○

THE ROOTS OF
HOMOPHOBIA
AND
HOMOHATRED

'Let me tell you, Mary, if you've met one low-class, mongoloid, rednecked, hairy-backed, pot-bellied, stereotyping bigot, you've met them all.'
—OFTEN OVERHEARD IN BOSTON-AREA
GAY BARS.

One of us had a Jewish professor who, courting the Gentile girl he later married, was invited to dinner with her family, including an anti-Semitic Aunt Thelma nearly one hundred years old. After the meal—during which, as the quiet and mannered gentleman he is, he behaved impeccably—his fiancée drew Aunt Thelma aside.

'There, Aunt Thelma!' she said. 'Didn't I tell you that he's not at all the way you thought he'd be? Not loud or pushy or obnoxious in the least!'

Aunt Thelma grunted malevolently. 'Y-e-e-sss,' she rasped; 'he's one of the silent, sly, scheming ones!'

Although scenes like the above are, depending on your sense of humor, either wryly amusing or damned depressing, they are too abundant for illustration to be really necessary. You've no doubt embroiled yourself in many such. Superficially varied, they have a haunting family resemblance—they contain the same essential elements, and, in fact, follow the same script: (1) X says he hates Y. (2) You ask *why* X hates Y. (3) X explains that he hates Y because

Y is a Thuringian—or whatever—and cites several reasons why Thuringians are hateful. (4) Flashing brilliantly, you prove that all of X's reasons for hating Thuringians are false, and that none of them apply to Y, anyway. (5) To your amazement, although you may have disproven every one of X's assertions, his attitude is unchanged—he still hates Y . . . because Y is a Thuringian . . . and Thuringians are hateful. The reasons cited by X weren't reasons at all. X doesn't *have* any reasons—just hate.

This, of course, is 'prejudice.' Lest you feel, smugly, that you, at least, are free from such foibles, remember that prejudice is part of human nature—a basic part, serving a basic purpose—from which none of us is free. We have reason to analyze prejudice in detail. There's a naive notion among folks in general—especially among gays—that you can argue a person out of a prejudice (such as homohatred) by overwhelming him with facts and logic about the group he hates. This is untrue. Many careful studies have demonstrated the complete uselessness of chopping logic with a bigot—even a fairly intelligent one—but reeling them off would be tedious and unnecessary. Prejudice is deep, automatic, and prelogical, the product of an emotional conditioning unassailable by any appeal to the intellect. It follows that homohatred is also impervious to argument, and that gays who, by raising the consciousness of the prejudiced, think to alter the oppressive circumstances under which we live, are simply urinating into the wind. Though laudably sincere, they're wasting their efforts and throwing away our hopes.

We cannot make this point strongly enough: to solve a problem, you must first understand it through and through. If your car breaks down by night in a countryside packed with wolves and ax-murderers, you had better find out what's wrong with it. If the problem is the alternator, but you spend the night doggedly cleaning and recleaning the spark plugs, you've had it. People who refuse to face reality sooner or later get clobbered.

LOOKING FOR THE MEANING OF PREJUDICE

One of our recurrent themes is the great difficulty of seeing that certain parts of everyday life are quite arbitrary, and need not have developed in the same way at all. The goldfish, continuously surrounded by the water of its fishbowl, never dreams of dry land; similarly, we humans take the verities of life—if we think about them at all—as givens, fixed and unalterable, and it seldom occurs to us that they're no such thing.

So it is with prejudice. We only think about it when we witness an extreme case. Then it's anomalous, exceptional; we really see it. What we don't see, even then, is that we're constantly surrounded by the same pernicious habit of thought in a milder form —that it's characteristic of our neighbors and our friends—and ourselves. And when something's always around you and in you, you tend to accept it as one of the necessary vagaries of existence, and never inquire *why*.

But there *is* a why. Attitudes and behaviors only become universal when they serve some evolutionary purpose. Attributes characteristic only of some people may be the product of random variation, and have no deeper evolutionary meaning; attributes characteristic of most or all humans reflect some original function, something carrying a survival advantage. Thus, prejudice. In the remainder of this chapter, we'll seek a better understanding of the meaning of prejudice, in the hope that such understanding will give us some clues as to how to deal with homophobia and homohatred.

WHAT PREJUDICE ISN'T

Implicit in telling you what prejudice is, is spelling out what it is not:

• Not misinformation; since people are not misinformed or misargued into it, you can't inform or argue them out of it.

- Not 'evil'; while we don't like prejudice, calling it names doesn't help to cure it. We can neither burn our enemies at the stake nor exorcise them.
- Not 'illness'; and so can't be 'cured' by psychotherapy, either (hardly an option for mass populations, in any event).
- Not, by and large, the result of the conspiracy of a sick or wicked few. Although there *are* such conspiratorial individuals, who knowingly lie to the masses, they really aren't the major problem; the masses hate already, and would hate even if they had never heard the mouthings of these conspirators. Although conspirators make our lives more difficult, and should be attacked and silenced, we will never solve our problem once and for all until we have deafened the masses to their malevolent appeal.

Understanding what prejudice *isn't* will help us to understand why certain ways of fighting prejudice won't work, including:

- Consciousness-raising, insofar as it boils down to mere argument, or ethical/intellectual attempts to persuade.
- Gay pride marches featuring men in tutus, dykes on bikes, and other shock tactics.
- Learning to love and respect ourselves, so that others 'must' love and respect us, too.
- Storming the barricades (violently) or even picketing (annoyingly).
- Blatantly sucking and fucking in the parks and on the streets— as though you could, eventually, *shove* your homosexuality down 'Amerika''s throat.

. . . and so forth.

With patience and respect for the careful thinking enabled by science, let us begin to explore the Mechanism of Prejudice.

○
PREJUDICE: WHY IT EXISTS IN SOCIAL MAMMALS, ESPECIALLY PRIMATES LIKE MAN

Prejudice combines thought and emotion; before we can understand prejudice, specifically, we must understand emotion, generally.

EMOTION IN MAMMALS: SOME GROSS BUT USEFUL OVERSIMPLIFICATION

The brain isn't a big, undifferentiated blob (except on certain mornings; but the less said of these the better). It has a large number of sharply differentiated substructures, or organs; the electrochemical activation of a given organ corresponds to the subjective experience of a given mental state. Among the broad classes of mental states are thought and emotion.

The 'seat of emotion' is the *limbic system,* a set of six or eight organs located in the center of the brain. Although the organs of the limbic system are tightly interconnected, they can be individually activated with an electric probe. When this is done to a conscious patient undergoing brain surgery, he reports a single, specific, and very unmixed emotion. Thus, activation of the *septal region* causes pure pleasure; of the *locus ceruleus,* pure fear; of the *amygdala,* pure anger. Without doing excessive violence to the facts, you can conceive of these organs as 'radio transmitters,' each broadcasting its special, licensed emotional frequency.

Although it may sometimes seem hard to believe, everything in and of the brain evolved for a good reason and serves some function. What, therefore, is the function of emotion?

Put simply, emotions serve as internal drive states that motivate a mammal to do the right thing, at the right time, in order to survive and reproduce. Appropriate emotions, appropriately timed, motivate appropriate behavior. Mammals that behave appropriately live long enough to have lots of little mammals, which inherit the genes for the brain-organs that broadcast the appropriate emotions . . . and so forth. Eventually, the world is full of little mammals with appropriate emotions. Absurdly simple though it may seem, that's pretty much the sort of thing that evolution is all about.

Now, emotions all fall into one or the other of two major classes. These are (a) *trophic* emotions, which are pleasant, feel good, and induce an animal to *approach* that which elicits them, and (b) *countertrophic* emotions, which are unpleasant, feel bad, and induce an animal to *avoid* that which elicits them. The trophic emotions are, essentially, driven by certain dopamine-containing nerve fibers—call them 'pleasure circuits'—of the mid-brain, which have much to do with activation of the septal region. Activation of the septal region just plain feels good.

The countertrophic emotions, however, are more complex: although all of them are driven by norepinephrine-containing nerve fibers—for consistency's sake, call them 'pain circuits'—of the mid-brain, they subdivide into two further categories, located in separate brain-organs, and motivating two separate behavioral functions. (Both of these subcategories, however, just plain feel *bad.*)

First is anxiety, or fear. This unpleasant emotion corresponds to activation of the locus ceruleus and tends to cause an animal to run away. It is appropriately elicited by creatures or situations too dangerous to be dealt with by fighting. In evolution, as in human axiology, discretion is the better part of valor.

Second is anger, or rage, or hate. Corresponding to activation of the amygdala, anger, though quite as disagreeable as fear, has a different subjective quality and, rather than inducing flight, drives the animal to attack and attempt to kill. It is appropriately elicited by creatures (rather than situations) that, though dangerous, are weaker, and more feasibly dealt with by aggression than by flight.

In order to appreciate the flavor of this scheme of things, apply it to your cat, or to yourself. When your cat sees a fire, she feels fear, and runs away; she doesn't attack it in a rage, still less leap into it with pleasure. When a straight person sees a reproductively viable mate, she feels pleasure and approaches; she doesn't flee in terror or attempt to kill him. (If you're gay, of course, affairs sort themselves out otherwise. Yet, even here, evolution shows its hand: are you attracted to senile decay or gross illness? No; even in a mate of your own sex, you're attracted by youth and health: the signs, however irrelevant, of reproductive viability. Old age and sickness are seldom sexually exciting, and for good evolutionary reason.) In short, be we mice or men, our feelings induce us to do the right thing for our species (though not necessarily for ourselves), and that's why we have them.

LISTEN UP, YOU BIG APE: THIS APPLIES TO YOU!

What applies to mammals, in general, applies to Man, specifically—the most highly evolved of the primates. However, primitive feelings and behaviors are more clearly seen and analyzed in the lower primates than in Man, because there they aren't obscured by the clutter of Man's higher functions, which complicate the picture. An excellent lower primate to study if one wishes to understand Man's primitive feelings and behaviors is the baboon, an ape with a moderately developed social structure analogous in many respects to our own, although simpler. To the scientist, this simplicity is not a drawback, but an advantage. It is to the baboon that we turn.

LIFE ON THE VELDT, 1,000,000 B.C.

We can now begin to consider the evolutionary function of a specific emotional pattern, prejudice: the survival and reproduction advantages it confers.

Baboons, like all higher primates, tend to band together into tribes, the members of which feel (a) desire for acceptance by members of their own tribe, and (b) hostility toward the members of all other tribes. (Which is what humans like President Bush mean when they use the word 'Patriotism.') These feelings are biologically built in: baboons don't learn them, they're born with them.

Such emotions serve an evolutionary function called *agnatic selection.* You've no doubt heard the phrase 'survival of the fittest.' This means that strong, clever animals survive and reproduce, passing on to their offspring the genes for strength and cleverness, thus, over time, making their species as a whole stronger and more clever. Agnatic selection is like this, except that here it isn't the strongest and cleverest individual animals that survive and reproduce, but the strongest and cleverest tribes, the strongest and cleverest societies. All baboon tribes are hostile to one another, and fight viciously upon contact; the 'best tribe' wins, gains greater land-space and food, and so reproduces in greater numbers. This process concentrates 'successful' genes. (You may not like this—neither, really, do we—but there's nothing to be done about it. Reality isn't politically correct.) Among human societies, the impulse toward agnatic selection is the origin of warfare. From the sociobiologist's point of view, there is little to choose between two baboon tribes slugging it out with sticks and stones on the African veldt in 1,000,000 B.C., and the colossal mechanized armies of the Second Reich and the Third Republic slaughtering each other on the Somme in A.D. 1916. Though the terminology used to describe them differs, the phenomena are, at bottom, identical.

In order for agnatic selection to work, individual baboons come equipped with the ability to *discriminate* at a glance—or, perhaps, a sniff—between members of their own tribe and members of other tribes. Since baboons have neither the brains nor the social skills nor the time to conduct careful interviews with unfamiliar baboons, they must make snap judgments on the basis of superficial characteristics—knee-jerk rejections—without thinking. Here we see prejudice unfolding!

Having discerned the stranger at a glance, our baboon must then react immediately, so as to jump the gun on his enemy. This automatic reaction has two stages: (1) an unpleasant emotion—countertrophic fear and/or anger, as described above—which motivates (2) a behavior, either (a) *fleeing*, if there are too many stranger-baboons, and fear predominates, or (b) *fighting*, if the strangers are outnumbered, or weaker, in which case hate and rage predominate.

Someone once summed this up as 'the baboon reaction: see the stranger, fear the stranger, hate the stranger, kill the stranger!' The actual sequence of events, feelings, and behaviors is more complicated, but not much. It's blind, unthinking, emotional, and, though subhuman, found also *in* humans. The entire pattern survives today on battlefield, street corner, and playground. It's prettied up, called by other—and more academically pompous— names, but it comes down to the same old baboon reaction. Could anyone familiar with the panorama of human history possibly doubt this?

But there's more to prejudice than fear and hate, as we hinted earlier when we mentioned the desire for acceptance. As a general rule, the behavior of higher mammals is controlled by both unpleasant and pleasant emotions. A baboon flees or fights so as to relieve the unpleasant fear and anger he feels toward stranger-baboons; the relief he feels from these unpleasant emotions is, of course, rewarding. But when a baboon flees from or fights with strangers, he's also behaving in the 'right' way—the way baboons of his tribe are supposed to behave—and he experiences a second reward: a pleasant feeling, which humans call solidarity, or pride, or even self-righteousness. Humans feel, in connection with the experience of prejudice, exactly the same sorts of things as baboons do: a rewarding sense of relief from fear and anger when they avoid or destroy outsiders, and an equally rewarding sense of pride, self-righteousness, and the respect and approval of their own 'tribe'—their parents, their family, their neighborhood, their 'set', their class, their nation, and their race.

○
THE INTELLECTUAL BABOON:
HOW HOMOHATRED ARISES IN MAN

Although humans retain the emotions, motivations, and patterns of behavior of their (comparatively) primitive primate forebears, they are not, of course, exactly the same as those forebears: they've had, as it were, stuff added on top. This stuff is intellectual, and comprises two new, or at least far more highly developed, abilities: (a) the ability to *learn* patterns of behavior, instead of being limited to those instinctive patterns with which one is born; and (b) the ability to form mental patterns, or *concepts*—like little models of things inside the head.

Consequently, although humans retain the baboonish mechanism of prejudicial discrimination, it is somewhat altered—and, in some respects, greatly and dangerously aggravated—by the so-called higher intellectual functions. Whereas prejudice among the baboon-tribes is a knee-jerk reaction to obvious differences in visual appearance (size, body and facial proportions, and especially patterns of coloration) and smell, prejudice among humans is just as frequently touched off by abstract concepts, that may have no hard-and-fast relation to the way people look. For example, Saltonstall may have learned in the nursery to hate what he calls Jews. He has a very vague idea of what a Jew is; ultimately, the concept reduces—as we shall see—to little more than a label attached to raw hate. If Saltonstall meets Rosenbloom, he may like Rosenbloom very well until he hears his surname—at which point he'll say, 'Why, isn't that a *Jewish* name?' and turn from Rosenbloom in disgust. In short, baboons are prejudiced against things in the real world; humans, by defect of their intelligence, are also prejudiced against things existing purely as concepts and labels inside their own heads, which they *attach* to things—and people—in the real world. It is Man's great difficulty, as well as his blessing, that the spooks and hobgoblins inside his head often seem as real as the furniture on his front lawn. His intellect allows him to create concepts, and to respond to them as well as to the external world. His knee jerks to both.

Moreover, because humans associate and conceptualize so easily, they tend to learn to hate more and more things and classes of people, as they come to notice—or dream up—not-so-obvious ways in which others differ from themselves.*

Now, the role of learning in human prejudice gives us cause for hope in the matter of fighting homophobia and homohatred. What can be learned can be unlearned; connections made can be broken; failing that, new connections can be learned that will counteract and nullify the effects of the old. It would be impossible to train a baboon to like a hated enemy baboon; it's comparatively easy to train a relatively flexible human being if not to like, then to feel and react neutrally to previously hated minority groups. If we choose, this can include gays.

1. BENDING THE TWIG: HOW THE MECHANISM OF PREJUDICE DEVELOPS IN THE CHILD

And now, to get to the nub of the matter—how does a child learn a prejudice like homophobia?

To answer this question, we must make a few points. First, it's clear that, although human children are—as remarked above—evolutionarily primed to learn hatred, they do, indeed, *learn* it. No child comes into the world genetically equipped with the capacity to recognize and hate a specific class—e.g., 'fags.' Second, when we speak of prejudice or homohatred, what is being learned is an emotional reaction to an arbitrary stimulus—in this case, anger and/or fear in response to an arbitrarily defined outgroup: fags. Third, children learn this emotional reaction, as they do all emotional reactions, not by direct instruction or appeal to the mind,

* Please note that when we say that a human can 'learn' to hate more and more things, we mean only that he isn't limited to built-in hatreds, but can be conditioned into hating almost any concept that anyone cares to put into his head. Appeal to the rational mind isn't entailed.

but in accord with certain fundamental laws of behavioral conditioning—specifically, two rules asserted here:

Rule 1: Associative Conditioning. When a person experiences, either by direct sensory perception, or in the form of a thought or emotion, two things either simultaneously or in immediate succession (such as a plate of Baked Alaska, and a bellyache), an Associative Link is formed between the two so that, in the future, experiencing one of the things will tend to evoke the other thing (e.g., eating Baked Alaska, or even thinking about it, will tend to cause nausea).

Rule 2: Direct Emotional Modeling. Very young children tend to feel, quite automatically and with no choice in the matter, whatever they perceive their parent(s) as feeling. For example, it's notoriously true that when parents are badly scared, even if they try to hide it, their children also will tend to become frightened. (Similarly, the children of parents who crack up in laughter over an adult joke will also tend to crack up in laughter, feeling a genuine merriment, although they haven't the foggiest idea of what the laughter is all about.) Obviously, children don't *reason* that if their parents are scared there must be cause for them to become scared also; rather, they automatically take fright as the result of a basic mechanism that all normal human beings seem to come equipped with.

Direct Emotional Modeling developed—as have all mechanisms of human thought, emotion, and behavior—in accord with basic evolutionary principles. Emotions motivate biologically necessary behaviors, including fight or flight; when social mammals, living in herds, are confronted by enemies of their own or other species, it is most unlikely that all or even many of the herd will become aware of the presence of the enemy at the same time. Rather, one or two members will become aware of the presence of the enemy *before* all the other members do. They will experience an immediate kindling of xenophobic, prejudicial fear and anger. Direct Emotional Modeling will result in a rapid, automatic kindling of the same, presumably appropriate, emotion(s) in the rest of the herd, far faster than would be the case if the other members had to detect the enemy by themselves, or, worse, had to be *told* enemies had arrived. The entire herd will become angry and/or frightened without the delay inherent in independent observation, thinking, or communication, and will either attack or run away, *en masse*. An excellent example with which you are quite familiar is the cattle stampede. Although this looks unbelievably stupid—and is!—it carries with it an obvious survival advantage. Nature is, indeed, red in tooth and claw, and the devil does, indeed, take the hindmost!

Now, let's see how these two rules work together to prejudice the child.

The normal child spends a great deal of time in the presence of his parents (or, failing that, other adult caretakers). He observes their actions, statements, and apparent emotions with a good deal of acuity, taking them in and reacting to them quite automatically. In the course of a typical day, the following chain of events occurs over and over.

Something happens. A person appears at the door or on TV, or arises in conversation; the topic of communism is raised; a Cadillac rolls down the street. The parents, owing to their own previous conditioning, react prejudicially: they experience countertrophic emotion. Although they may attempt to conceal or play down their prejudicial reaction in the child's presence, they inevitably manifest outward signs of their emotion—altered volume or tone of speech, tightening of facial muscles, and so on. The child, a naturally acute observer of such minute signs, perceives his parents' emotion—and may, in a very vague way, even though such things are usually over his head, perceive the event, thing, or person that evokes it.

Two things then happen. First, Direct Emotional Modeling: the child automatically experiences the same emotional state as his parents. Second, Associative Conditioning: to the extent that the child has, even vaguely, perceived the cause of his parents' emotion, he automatically forms a *link* between that cause, and his own Directly Modeled emotional reaction. With repeated exposure to instances of his parents' prejudice, he responds, at first slightly, then more and more strongly, with that very same preju-dicial emotion. Eventually, the parents, having mediated the child's learning, are unnecessary; the child has learned, as a condi-tioned emotional reaction, to hate the things his parents hate—and all this entirely without a word of instruction, or a second of reasoned reflection.

Voilà—the child is now prejudiced!

Everyday experience abounds with examples—e.g., phobias, which have been much studied, from the standpoints of both the-ory and practical therapy, and as such provide an excellent test-tube model of the nature and treatability of prejudices in general. Phobias are formed in exactly the same way as prejudices, but usually by fewer exposures to the feared thing, in far more aver-sive settings. In extreme form, a common phobia, such as that of spiders, can develop from a single, intense experience of being present, as a small child, when Mother comes upon a spider and screams in disgust and fear—resulting in a lifelong, inordinate horror of crawling insects.

But suppose we take an example of *homo*phobia (more properly, homo*hatred)* itself. The Bigots are at home watching prime-time television, as Billy Bigot, age five, crawls about de-winging flies, and keeping a weather eye on parents and TV both. Suddenly, who should appear on screen but A Big Movie Critic—a posturing, gesturing, lah-di-dah, superannuated prettyboy embalmed in Max Factor cosmetics. The elder Bigots, pegging the Critic (correctly or incorrectly) as a homosexual, feel a horrid mixture of embarrass-ment and contempt. Their faces stiffen; their lips twist; they ex-change a surreptitious, significant glance with raised eyebrows; perhaps Mr. Bigot, thinking (incorrectly) that Billy Bigot is too absorbed by his current hapless fly to notice, nastily mutters some epithet, such as 'Fag!' Billy, of course, *has* noticed—the Critic, who, as even he can detect, talks in a somewhat distinctive tone of voice; his parents' reaction of embarrassment and contempt; and their choice epithet. He doesn't know what a 'fag' is; but he auto-matically feels a degree of the same unpleasant emotions. In the future, the sight of the Critic, or of anyone reminiscent of him, or even hearing 'fag!' will evoke the same negative emotions. As his parents, the mass media, and, later, his chums, run through this routine over and over and over—and you have to be gay to perceive just how constantly this really does happen—Billy's conditioning will grow ever stronger, his prejudicial emotional response ever greater. By puberty at the latest, Billy will have a hatred and fear of the very subject of effeminacy and homosexuality, impervious to the most cogent facts and logic. What's worse, there may eventually be a Billy Jr. in the picture, in which case the whole miserable, senseless cycle starts all over again.

Where the Child Is, in Fact, Gay: Reaction Formation, Self-Loathing, and Gay Flame

Let's add one more twist to this mess. According to the Kinsey studies, one in three males has homosexual tendencies; what if Billy, Jr. should be so inclined? In that case, his response to the above process will include new, and even uglier, aspects. He will undergo exactly the same process of Direct Emotional Modeling; he will associate effeminacy in males with his own fear and anger; he will develop a *bona fide* prejudice against gays—and then, probably at puberty, he will, to his lasting horror, discover that *he himself* is one of the people he's been conditioned to loathe.

What happens then? Well, one thing is clear: in most cases, neither the homosexual desires nor the homohatred gives way without years of bitter struggle, internal conflict, and psychological abnormality.

How this struggle resolves itself (if it does at all) depends, largely, on how strongly developed the homosexual desires are. Three distinct patterns of response emerge; any one boy may abruptly shift from one pattern to another, rather like certain unstable, 'pleomorphic' chemical substances in nature, which can exist in any one of several distinctly different physical states, and will pop from one to another virtually without warning. (Although data are lacking, this model probably applies to budding lesbians as well, except for the overt queerbashing of Pattern One

—girls simply aren't as prone to extreme violence as boys; a matter of the enraging effect of testosterone.)

Pattern One: Rage. When the boy becomes aware, at puberty, of relatively weak homosexual desires, he will indulge in a psychological game called *repression and reaction formation.* Horrified at his emotional and physical yearning for other boys, he will, fairly immediately, repress this awareness, squeezing it into the subconscious. The external sign of his repression is reaction formation: a constant, insistent, terribly uneasy, and belligerent preoccupation with 'queers,' and loud expressions of his loathing for them. Such a boy has a subconscious need to seek out and destroy in others— if necessary, via mutilation and/or murder—what he cannot tolerate in himself. Superficially quite heterosexual, the boy's motivations are seen through by the psychologically sophisticated: his homohating smoke conceals a homosexual fire. The tragedy is that these walking time bombs, programmed for hatred, impelled by a queasy mixture of disgust, dread, and desire, so often do take their self-loathing on safari to gay cruising grounds, where they can satisfy both sides of their conflicted state with a program of lewd voyeurism and self-righteous rage and assault.

Pattern Two: Terror. Where the homosexual desires are too strong to repress, quite a different pattern develops. Such a boy is conscious of his homosexuality, but hates it, and himself. He also hates effeminate gays, because they draw attention to the subject, which—unlike the more repressed boy—he doesn't want raised at all, lest others start probing into *his* sex life. By the same token, therefore, he won't discuss gays as much, let alone assault them. This is the boy who'll strive mightily to appear straight, whose ads in the personals sections of newspapers—should he ever get up the guts to submit them—will lay heavy emphasis on 'straight acting and appearing,' and who will, in day-to-day life, avoid being seen near the 'Ho' drawer of the library card-file. Unlike the reaction-former, he's too conscious of the truth about himself to take it out of other gays' hides, and may experience a lifelong wretchedness and misery. Always betwixt and between, these are, in their way, the most pitiable cases.

Pattern Three: Wretched Excess. Where homosexual desires and a naturally feminine appearance and effeminate comportment are too strong to be concealed from others, let alone himself, the boy is likely to throw his hat over the windmill and let the flames rise. In essence, these 'fairies' simply don't have the option of hiding, and, rather often, translate their conditioned self-hatred into a hatred of all conventions, and of society in general. They fill the ranks of the full-time drag queens, the marchers in tutus, the gender-benders and sexual shockers. Although, in an odd way, they're the most psychologically well adjusted of the three groups —having, so to speak, lost the world to gain their souls—they still have—and constitute—problems. We will have much to say about them and the long-term effects of their shock tactics.

This effect of inducing homohatred in children who may themselves later turn out to be gay is of no small import to the mess in which we currently find ourselves. One of our most serious—and most seriously galling—afflictions is the gay homophobe: the Joe McCarthys and Roy Cohns, who, falling (in our opinion) into Pattern One, take their internal conflicts all the way to the halls of power, and launch a paranoiac vendetta against what they cannot admit is their own kind. It's natural to despise such latter-day Quislings, the more so as some of them—moral lepers on a grand scale—actually fall into Pattern Two, doing what they do with full consciousness of its massively pernicious effects, placing the needs of their own cowardice above the reputations and even the lives of millions of others, a failing of the ethical test of life so great that if the fundamentalists are even half right they'll go straight to hell. However, many others are genuinely sad cases, such as the Rev. Rose Mary Denman, a United Methodist minister, formerly strongly opposed to the ordination of gays as pastors, who one day awakened to her lesbianism, declared it, and was promptly defrocked. According to the *New York Times,* "In retrospect, she attributed her previous vehement stand against ordaining homosexuals to the effects of denying her unacknowledged lesbian feelings." Such people are, in their way, as much victims as the rest of us.

Coalescence: The Formation of the Picture-Label Pair

Of course, Billy, like all small children, doesn't know a hawk from a handsaw; he has no real notion of what a homosexual is, or to what, exactly, his parents are objecting. Nor, except in grotesque circumstances, is he likely to receive explicit instruction. Rather, Billy associates his parents' annoyance with whatever it is about the original stimulus that, for him, stood out from the usual. If nothing stood out, he may simply zero in on a random element in the situation. Consequently, the Billies of the world are gradually conditioned to fear and hate vast and ill-defined clouds of quite unrelated things, unified in their minds only by the fact that Mom and Dad apparently detest them. These nebulae of protoprejudice slowly coalesce around verbal labels, and then, like newborn suns, take flame with hatred.

Thus, the elder Bigots may, for years, express amusement, disdain, contempt, or outright loathing for what they consider 'inappropriate behavior for one's gender.' Without having a specific word for such behavior, Billy will, very early on, absorb a general set of nasty attitudes toward those who violate gender norms. Only later will he pick up the labels 'faggot' and 'queer.' These he'll apply to everyone who's a little bit different, without knowing what the hell he's talking about. Like youngsters we've known, he'll sneer not only at prissy boys but at prissy girls as 'you fag!' Under 'fag,' he'll mentally file all sorts of extraneous and mistaken information as to what goes along with being a queer, and will draw into his burgeoning hurricane of prejudice the idea that wristwatches, raincoats, rubber boots in winter, and sweaters that button up the front are all earmarks of the pansy. He may even reach adulthood with these notions intact, and peck out a book informing scared and contemptuous rabbits that Real Men Don't Eat Quiche.

Verbal labels are, therefore, of great importance. Human memory stores immense masses of data in many disparate forms— pictorial, emotional, propositional (that is, in the form of verbal statements), and so forth. These heterogeneous data require 'tying together' in some way around 'mental landmarks,' so that one can find one's way about in one's own memory. It so happens that most people organize broad classes of data around the convenient landmarks of *words,* or verbal labels. Early in a child's development, single words—like 'fag'—become associated with the masses of primarily visual data that flesh out a stereotype; after this point, all further data are attracted to the same label, and are, in a sense, mentally filed under that heading. Associative Conditioning assures that the accumulated emotional charge associated with all the pictures and ideas and experiences in the stereotypic grab bag will become attached to the label itself. This goes a long way toward explaining why words like 'faggot'—which mean nothing more than 'Mommy and Daddy hate that'—arouse such intense feeling; the intensity is nothing more than an indicator of how many emotionally charged data are organized behind that label.

All this said, the verbal label is not, itself, an element of the stereotypic 'picture,' only a label *referring* to that picture, as its caption does to a caricature or a cartoon. To one extent or another, the separability—and manipulability—of the verbal label is the basis for all the abstract principles underlying our proposed campaign.

2. BLUEPRINTING THE GEARBOX: HOW THE 'ENGINE OF HOMOHATRED' FUNCTIONS IN THE ADULT

We've now seen how kids learn homohatred. But what happens when Billy Bigot grows up? Let's explore, step by step, how an entrenched homohatred functions in a typical adult. Our analysis will isolate and lay bare those gears, pistons, and ratchets of the engine of homohatred most open to effective counterattack by a psychologically informed program of counterpropaganda.

In the abstract, prejudice comprises a seven-step sequence of stimuli and responses:

STEP 1: The bigot either sees and hears, or thinks about, an instance of the picture/label pair.

STEP 2: His sighting, or thinking about, the instance evokes, from his limbic system, a conditioned response of *countertrophic emotion*—that is, fear and/or hate. If the emotion is sufficiently intense, he may

STEP 3: run away (by trying to ignore the instance, or by crossing the street), or attack (verbally or physically)—which discharges the fear and/or hate, and thus

STEP 4: rewards the behavior.

STEP 5: Steps 2 and—if present—3 are interpreted (perhaps automatically and unconsciously) by the rest of the brain as 'being like Mom and Dad'—meaning, 'those from whom I get my love and respect.' This notion evokes

STEP 6: a conditioned response of *trophic emotion*—felt subjectively as 'being loved,' and labeled 'pride and solidarity.' This, once again,

STEP 7: rewards the whole sequence.

Note well that *reward* occurs in two places:

First, under 3 and 4, in which fighting or fleeing from the source of the fear and/or anger provides rewarding relief from punishing countertrophic emotion, and

Second, under 6 and 7, in which the adult feels, once again, the sense of pride and solidarity, of belonging, of being loved and respected, that he was conditioned to feel in childhood when he felt or did as his parents felt or did.

For most adults, we can, eventually, add to this sequence Step 8 —Rationalization. Unlike the lower animals, humans who are alarmed—and have a minute to spare—tend to Rationalize. A sense of fear or hate automatically induces them to explain these sensations to themselves by evoking a hodgepodge of *beliefs*—usually picked up *post hoc* and added to the *propter hoc* of the hatred itself—that would seem to support such a negative reaction: e.g., 'I hate gays because . . . they're child molesters, diseased, good for nothing,' etc. These are, of course, the myths about gays outlined in Chapter 1.

Rationalization is the tribute that irrational bigotry pays to logic —the pathetic effort by a bigot's cortex to run a quick reality check on the reasonableness of his feelings. Since the bigot accumulates, along the way, quite a shoal of such beliefs, his momentary pause for reflection can only confirm and validate his homohatred—and, as below, his impulse to attack. All systems go!

Please note, however, that, just as a bigot learns his rationales *after* he learns his hatred, Rationalization occurs last in the above sequence of prejudice. It supports hatred, but doesn't cause it; if deprived of Rationalization, hatred will usually live on. For this very reason, Rationalization isn't an especially fruitful target for attack by argument ('consciousness raising'), nor by propaganda, and our campaign won't lay heavy emphasis on it.

A Ghastly Illustration: Don't Leave West Hollywood Without It!

And now, suppose we flesh out our bloodless, abstract analysis with an illustration from everyday life.

Conveniently enough, we revert to Billy Bigot; now forty-two; a resident of Redd's Neck, Arkansas; partially employed; mean as a rattlesnake with kidney stones; and known as 'Bubba' Bigot to his beer-swilling cronies.

What does Bubba, beneficiary as he is of an early conditioning into homohatred, think of gays now? Six words: 'Stomp the piss out of 'em!'—which, from time to time, he has, in fact, done. (To the delight and kudos of said cronies—to whom Bubba's a Good Ole Boy.)

Let us peer into the crude inner workings of what we shall call Bubba's 'brain'—it being, at any rate, the largest organ inside his tiny head.

One evening, while sousing with the boys at the local bar, Bubba spies, with his little red eyes, a 'city feller'—a hapless wretch, let's call him Sid, from El Lay, who, en route to Florida on a cross-country car trip, has lost his way at the Dubuque off-ramp on I-440, turned left where he should have turned right, and ended up, not unlike Dante in the *Inferno*, in Bubba's smoky lair. Why has Bubba spied him as a city feller, and worse? Let's just say that Sid should have dressed down to the occasion—the worthies of Redd's Neck don't know *haute couture* from hot pants.

Sid—whose ass will soon be grass—pirouettes to the bar and orders a Shirley Temple, Bubba criticizing the ballet meanly through a haze of cigarette smoke and pre-cirrhotic inebriation. Suddenly, a thousand things about Sid click into place. 'Why!' says Bubba, perceiving Sid's close fit to the stereotype, 'that's a queer!'

What exactly has happened? There exists in Bubba's mind a sort of grab-bag of logically discrete, but experientially associated, sensory elements of appearance of body structure and face, dress and accessories, physical movement, and tone, style, and content of speech, all gathered together under (a) a single *stereotypic picture* —you may conceive of this as a sort of horrid, cruel cartoon incorporating a host of exaggerated characteristics—and (b) a single *verbal label*, or very small group of roughly synonymous labels, here rendered as 'queer!' These constitute the *picture/label pair*. When we write that the elements are 'associated,' we mean *neurologically* associated, such that Bubba's seeing or hearing—or, for that matter, thinking about—any one of these elements tends to activate not only some or all of the others, but the stereotypic picture and the verbal label. Had Sid possessed just one or two of the elements in Bubba's grab-bag, Bubba's picture/label pair might or might not have been activated into full consciousness. (Although Bubba's sensitivity to any other possible elements would be increased, quite unconsciously, even if the picture/label pair were not so activated.) However, as the number of Sid's relevant elements increases, their synergy greatly augments the likelihood that the picture/label pair will, in fact, become conscious, and Bubba will make the identification. As he has!

Given the above scenario, the unfolding of further events is as readily predictable and comprehensible as though Bubba and Sid were wind-up dolls enacting a pre-written tragedy (which, in a real sense, they *are*.)

Growling 'Queer!', Bubba feels a surge of very unpleasant emotion—a commingling of anxiety and hate. Neither sensation is pleasant; each demands relief in the form of an 'appropriate' action—either flight or fight. The two wrestle; aggression wins out.

Accompanied by six or eight cronies, Bubba pops from his seat like a jack-in-the-box, strides across the room, grabs Sid by the collar, frog-marches him out to the alleyway behind the bar, grins evilly, and, accompanied by expressions of the audience's visceral appreciation and Sid's squeaks of protest, proceeds to rearrange his face.

As he rearranges, Bubba feels relief from his unpleasant emotions, which is, of course, highly rewarding; and the more rewarding his activity, the more inclined he is to continue it—in this case, to its logical conclusion: he destroys the object of his countertrophic response via the simple and irresistable expedient of removing Sid from the land of the living. In due course, the police arrive; Bubba is carted away to the pokey, Sid to the morgue. *Exeunt omnes!*

Nevertheless, however relevantly, we've anticipated our story. We must also point out that Bubba felt something further, and something very important, as he pounded away at Sid. He felt self-righteous: that this is what his Daddy would have done; that he would have been right to do it; and that he, Bubba, is right too! He felt, in fact, a warm glow of pride, and the sense that he's one helluva Good Ole Boy—a profound sense of *reward*.

WHERE DOES THIS LEAVE US? A TRANSITION

We've plowed a long furrow to reach the point at which we can claim some detailed understanding of what prejudice is, why and how it develops, and how it functions. And now, the harvest: we will use our knowledge to consider, first, why the tactics used so far by the gay community to combat homophobia and homohatred have proven either weakly effective, ineffective, or disastrously counterproductive, and second, what the implications of our knowledge are for the structuring of a truly *effective* plan of action against antigay bigotry.

○

PUSHING THE WRONG BUTTONS: SENSELESS ATTEMPTS TO DERAIL THE ENGINE OF PREJUDICE

What follows wasn't easy to write, and, for many, won't be easy to read. Nevertheless, we must make a first pass at an unpleasant, but inescapable, topic: why it is that practically everything so far done by gays to better their lot, though done with honesty and dedication, has been done incorrectly.

You might retort, 'Hold on now—you're going entirely too far— we've made tremendous strides toward legal and social acceptance,' and, as evidence, cite the twenty-six states that have revoked or nullified their sodomy laws since 1960, as well as the concurrent emergence of the gay *demimonde* into the light of day. Surely this proves that we've been doing *something* right?

Actually, the answer is still no—we've haven't done anything right. Yet we have made advances. Paradox? Hardly. Success— complete, or, in our case, very partial—doesn't argue that one's *tactics* are successful, let alone sensible; one can succeed for silly, extraneous reasons. In almost any endeavor, there occasionally pop up special circumstances, in which the protagonist can make all the wrong moves, yet still wind up ahead. Thus, even the most idiotic stockbrokers, buying and selling in accord with perfectly dreadful judgment, nevertheless made pots of money in the 'pit bull' market of the 1980s—because just about *everything* went up!

The point is, although the stockbroker 'succeeds' despite bad tactics, he'd be a great deal more successful if he used good tactics. Just so with the gay community. It came out in the midst of the most socially and sexually liberal decade the world has seen since the days of Julio-Claudian Rome. From 1967 to 1976, a liberal, even radical, chic prevailed in this country, making it fashionable to oppose the establishment in all things, and to reject all traditional values as 'old-fashioned' and 'puritanical.' This went very far, even having a certain political and legislative impact. Against this backdrop, almost any small and socially oppressed minority, especially if regarded by the establishment as dubious or marginal, was eagerly courted by the Brie and Chablis set. Hence the Black Panthers' status and, to a lesser extent, our own. We were exotic, and won victories.

But we won them *despite* our tactics, not because of them. Indeed, given the sexiness of oppressed groups in general in that decade, and the gigantic strides made by, say, blacks, what's really striking about gay progress is how limited it was. The real question is, why didn't we do better? Yes, twenty-six states agreed to stop rounding us up and hustling us off to jail; but in twenty-four we're still criminals. Yes, our lifestyle is now 'public'—in highly restricted urban areas—but, taking it coast to coast, hatred and contempt for gays isn't far from where it was twenty-five years ago. The situation remains an outrage.

In short, our partial success has been a credit less to our tactics than to a freak of social and political history. Now that the United States has returned to business as usual—what William Burroughs, in *The Ticket That Exploded,* called "the Ugly Spirit" of conservative hatred—we will no longer be protected by 'special circumstances' from the natural consequences of our continued use of ill-considered tactics. In the '60s and '70s, we sowed the wind; in an era of renewed conservatism, we will most certainly reap the whirlwind.

This discussion will offend many people. Some are 'career homosexuals,' professional agitators and attention-seekers, with a vested interest in the Old Ways. Others, though driven by the understandable need to do *something,* however ineffective, have adopted mistaken tactics by default. They have actually acted on behalf of others, not of their own celebrity. We don't wish to anger them, or hurt their feelings; we wish to show them a better, more effective way.

o   o   o

Past tactics, though superficially extremely various, tend to simplify into three main approaches. Considered in light of our new understanding of how prejudice functions, each approach is formally defective. We will consider them separately.

1. ARGUMENT—A.K.A. CONSCIOUSNESS RAISING

Argument takes many forms, including lobbying of legislators and lawyers, public debate with homohaters high and low, informational leafleting of student dormitories, and the like. Historically, very large proportions of the meager funds collected by gay organizations and designated for 'serious purposes' have been expended on one form or another of argument.

Trying to argue people out of their homohatred is, however, founded on a completely false assumption—namely, that prejudice is a belief. But prejudice is not a belief; it's a feeling. Argument *can* change beliefs, but not feelings. It's not very useful in the treatment of homohatred.

Consider why this is so. Beliefs play a role in prejudice only insofar as they support Rationalization—which comes last. Homohatred is supported by antigay myths, but not caused by them; even if, by argument, you dispel all myths and thereby amputate Rationalization from the end of the sequence, homohatred still exists. Why? Because the rest of the mechanism is intact, and continues to reward actions of withdrawal or aggression, even if they're 'taken' purely in the imagination—and what continues to be rewarded continues to occur.

Let's revert, for a moment, to phobias. Have you ever, like some two thirds of Americans, had an irrational fear? And did others infuriate you by trying to prove that there was 'no reason' for your fear? Didn't work, did it? You probably thought, 'What a jackass! I'm not afraid for any *reason*, I'm just afraid!' And if you 'outgrew' your fear, it wasn't in response to facts and logic, but action: *forcing* yourself to experience the feared thing in small but increasing doses, thus short-circuiting the withdrawal-reward, and allowing the fear to peter out.

Just so for all phobias, and for all prejudices: argument doesn't work. This is terribly difficult for some people to grasp and/or believe—especially those who've devoted their lives to the attempt to persuade others by reasoned debate—but it isn't just a consequence of the theoretical model set forth in this chapter: it's empirically true, as well. One can argue with a theory, but arguing with fact is a waste of everybody's time.

None of this is to say that argument has *no* place in propaganda; it can sometimes serve as an effective adjuvant to an essentially emotional appeal. Understand, however, that, even where argument seems effective, one rarely, if ever, actually persuades intellectually: rather, the appeal succeeds for emotional reasons. Although people like to believe that their thoughts determine their emotions, it's actually vice versa: strong prejudices motivate and direct a search for beliefs that seem to justify the prejudice. Knocking over all the beliefs accomplishes little.

What an apparently effective argument amounts to is this. You try to argue X out of hating Ys. X's hatred of Ys may indeed lessen, in which case you congratulate yourself that you've swayed X with facts and logic. Actually, however, X's hatred has lessened not because of the dissonance between her hatred and your facts and logic, but because of the dissonance between her hatred and her love . . . for you. You've quarreled with her; she cares what you think of her. If she loves you more than she hates Ys, her hatred may lessen. This is no result of the form or content of the argument, but of the very fact that there *was* an argument. The appeal is emotional. Two emotions have been brought into dissonance: the dissonance is resolved in favor of the stronger of the two. As we shall see, this basic principle—which parallels that of Leon Festinger's "cognitive dissonance"—underlies much of our thinking and recommendations.

It should go without saying, of course, that for an argument to be effective in such a way, there must exist an emotional relationship between the arguers. The selfsame argument printed up and published in a magazine would have no effect whatever on a perfect stranger reading it.

The *appearance* of an argument can often aid an emotional appeal for other reasons. (Arguments against homohatred, or any other prejudice, cannot be true arguments, in the Aristotelian sense; nobody can prove that a person 'shouldn't' hate gays, because that's a matter, literally, of opinion.) Where the target of an emotional appeal is aware of the attempt at manipulation, he will tend to resist it; where he is distracted from the true nature of the appeal by a 'cover argument,' the emotional effect, paradoxically, will be all the greater. Thus, an argument can function as a distractor.

Our remarks apply primarily to the (intellectually) lower 90% or so of the general population, whose beliefs more or less never alter their emotions. This is largely true of the upper 10%, as well, but, fortunately, not entirely. The highly intelligent sometimes display the capacity, although less often the inclination, to step outside themselves and analyze their feelings, and the causes of their feelings, dispassionately, and this sometimes modulates the feelings themselves. Of course, the 10% are not our primary problem, anyway. However, arguments directed at the 10% sometimes trickle down to the 90%. If one can spread arguments based on facts and logic among the intelligentsia, these will tend to form the nucleus of a general consensus, spread in turn through magazines, newspapers, and television broadcasts, as to what it is politically correct to believe. As the 90% become aware of the position of the intelligentsia, two things tend to happen: first, some *weak* bigots, though emotionally unswayed, shut themselves up out of fear of being thought Neanderthals. Keeping quiet out of embarrassment makes these bigots feel hypocritical; in some cases, this weakens the prejudice; they tell themselves, 'I'm not keeping quiet because I'm a coward, but because I don't really hate those people, anyway.' Even where the prejudice fails to weaken, shutting up its overt expression is an excellent thing, as it tends to prevent the transmission and reinforcement of prejudice, and so tempers the general ideological climate. Second, other weak bigots, who *have* been swayed by separate, purely emotional appeals, will now have 'reasons' to feel comfortable with their new opinions.

Nevertheless, outside of a small minority of the population, who aren't as strongly prejudiced to begin with, any apparent appeal to the mind will succeed only as the result of an actual, simultaneous appeal to the emotions. Argument doesn't work because it convinces people that they're wrong; it works as a weapon, an emotional bludgeon.

As though all these caveats against reliance upon argument were not enough, there is, too, the danger of achieving not just no effect, but an effect actually the opposite of your intentions. It's a truism among salesmen that you should never try to argue a customer out of a strongly held belief or feeling; what generally happens is that, rather than convincing the customer of the validity of your argument, you simply encourage him to marshal not only his old but also new and better arguments in favor of his position —which actually reinforces his conviction of correctness. This is, of course, trebly so where the arguments concern matters of opinions and values. Here, facts can rarely be brought to bear to any good effect, and even where facts can be advanced, they can rarely be proven to be true. (We're sure, for example, that it's a fact that the oft-heard imputation of coprophagia—eating feces— to the majority of gays is false, but can we *prove* its falsity? Hardly.)

Finally, there is yet another reason why argument can be dangerous to gay rights. Insofar as our opponents advance reasons for their homohatred, these tend to center around assertions like 'Homosexuality is disgusting,' or 'Homosexuality is sinful.' While phrased as apparently legitimate statements about an aspect of the world, they are actually statements about the one making the assertions. Logically speaking, nothing whatever is either disgusting or sinful, except as one feels it to be so—which is to say, such assertions mean nothing more than 'I *really* dislike that.' Our opponents' arguments have nothing to do with reason, and cannot be refuted by reason. Moreover, we cannot *disprove* the validity of the Bible, or of other authoritative sources of moral judgment, nor even attempt to do so without arousing tremendous antagonism. For us to attempt to argue with homohaters is to risk carrying the argument onto their turf, which gives attention and, implicitly, credence to many of their basic assumptions. Thus, if we're going to enter into arguments with them, we'd better have a strong emotional appeal in our back pocket.

Of the three major classes of tactics, argument is merely largely useless. We turn now to the other two, which are dangerously self-destructive.

2. FIGHTING—A.K.A. STORMING THE BARRICADES

Serving, day in and day out, as a target for scorn and abuse is no fun, and only a saint could stand it without feeling, sooner or later, an entirely healthy desire to retaliate with physical force, if not mayhem. Most gays are no more saints than we are, and it isn't surprising that when the Stonewall finally erupted into violence in 1969, it was to a sizable chorus of hurrahs and hopes that the cavalry, as it were, was coming.

Unfortunately, solving your problems with your fists, though exhilarating, is ill advised unless your fists are awfully big indeed. An eight-hundred-pound gorilla sits wherever it wants; we, however, are not seen as eight-hundred-pound gorillas. Rather, we're seen by straights as a submicroscopic population of puny freaks, and for us to raise our fists on TV and shout, 'You'd better give us our rights, or else!' can elicit only amusement and disgust. Indeed, the rejoinder has usually been, 'The hell you say, little freak,' followed by the weighty descent of a bug-squashing legislative or judicial foot, most memorably that of the Supreme Court in the Bowers v. Hardwick case, in which five of the nine Justices decided that they wouldn't presume to judge whether *straights* have a right to privacy in the boudoir, but that gays definitely don't . . . because they're hated . . . which is right and proper . . . because they've *always* been hated. (Yep, that was the 'reasoning.' Should we call them *In*justices?)

Consequently, it gets a little tiresome to keep seeing and hearing, at this late date, calls for insurrection, and to keep encountering a mind-set that damns all proposals as politically incorrect to precisely the degree that they rely upon cunning manipulation rather than pugnacity. Some people develop ideological tunnel vision so narrow that they can no longer contemplate the problem of gay-straight relations save in terms of thrown stones, shouting matches, and stormed barricades. One individual, addressing a meeting of Harvard's Gay Students Association, deprecated any approach entailing voluntary toning down of our gay image, and informed the enthusiastic students that the tremendous Washington, D.C. gay rally then slated for the summer of 1987 would very likely involve 'nonpeaceful' activities. If the idea displeased him, he gave no indication of it.

The trouble with threats and acts of violence, beyond the fact that we gays don't have the wherewithal to put our fists where our mouth is, is that they not only do nothing whatever to improve straight America's picture of us, but actually confirm and aggravate that picture! Straights already see us as mentally unbalanced or willfully perverse; how much more moral obloquy would they heap upon our heads if we were to stand up and declare that we are willing to burn down cities in order to force America to allow us to practice our despicable sins untrammeled? There's such a thing as putting people's backs up, and if you do, you'd best be prepared to stand off a wicked backlash.

It's often argued that 'If blacks could do it [i.e., intimidate white America, by dint of riot and Molotov cocktail, into guaranteeing black civil rights], then we can, too!' A lot of people buy this fatuous comparison. But consider these points. (1) What makes you so sure that the threat, and reality, of physical force *advanced* the cause of black civil rights? There was a big difference between Martin Luther King's peaceful marches, and the riots in Watts and elsewhere; we suspect that the latter actually hurt black interests. (2) Shout and burn though the disaffected denizens of the ghetto might, the mass of white Americans never doubted that blacks had just cause to be angry. There was never any widespread belief that blacks *deserved* oppression, as punishment for some intrinsic evil. But gays *are* thought to be evil. In the view of many, our oppressors are performing God's work, and our mere requests that they give it a rest are considered the height of insolence piled atop infamy—as though mass murderers were to form a union and express outrage that the laws should dare to immure their kind in prisons. (3) Although there are roughly as many black Americans as there are gay, in the 1960s blacks gave the impression of being more numerous—and therefore more powerful—than they actually were, quite probably because of their extreme concentration into the biggest cities, whence so much news originates. Gays, on the other hand, are thought to be relatively rare—rarer, certainly, than they actually are—and in any event are 'invisible' in most cases. (4) For whatever reasons, a lot of white Americans find blacks scarier than they do gays. In fact, they find gays laughably weak. Thus, militant blacks had an easier time intimidating the country than gays ever could.

It's been argued that gay demonstrations *would* be a good thing if conducted peaceably and soberly. The idea, we suppose, is to achieve the massive numbers, the somber dignity, of the great black civil rights marches of the early 1960s. Straights, or so the argument goes, cannot but be favorably impressed by the integrity entailed in such an obvious act of conscience by a very large group of dignified people. Alas, it can easily be demonstrated that this line of thinking doesn't hold water; we need go no further than the lack of public response to one of the most immense demonstrations in American history—the October 1987 gay march on Washington, in which some five hundred thousand people participated.

Can you conceive of half a million members of *any* other minority marching on the nation's capital and *not* receiving massive, in-depth media coverage? We can't. Had the marchers identified themselves as women, blacks, Asians, Jews, Catholics, fundamentalists, or the physically, mentally, or emotionally handicapped—had they marched as anything whatever except gays—then, ah, then, we'd have been treated to on-the-spot coverage and instant analyses by Dan Rather (or even a hastily resurrected Walter Cronkite), ten-page Focus pieces in every major newspaper, and cover stories in *Newsweek.* The story would have been hashed and rehashed from every conceivable angle, the media salivating over it like Pavlov's dogs for a solid month.

Not so the Great Gay March on Washington! From where we sat in Boston and New York, all we could see on the media horizon were two or three clouds a great deal smaller than a man's hand—a twentieth-page newspaper squib here, thirty seconds on the evening news there (devoted, by-the-bye, to the few incidents of civil disobedience—usually described, less charitably, as 'disorderly conduct'—that occurred, and only obliquely to the demonstration itself!), and scarcely a word of evaluation. Needless to say, this negated most of the hoped-for effect. The march may have made its participants feel good, but from a public-relations standpoint it was a fiasco. The news heard by the mass of Americans is restricted to what the media choose to spoon-feed them, and, in this case, they refused to dirty the spoon: to have given the story the coverage it deserved would have undermined the Big Lie. And that, friends, is why the argument for sober demonstrations is specious: even the most peaceful, dignified demonstration imaginable will achieve zip *if no one hears about it.*

Our focus, in this section, has been on actual physical force, as a useless and dangerous tactic. Physical force need not be actual—smashing, burning, or killing—to damage our p.r. Insofar as rallies or marches are conducted in such a way as to be physically intimidating or obstructive—angry placard-waving and sit-ins—they garner, though in lesser degree, the same sort of emotional response as a full-blown riot. Insofar as they are absolutely peaceful and unobtrusive, they fall into the black hole of the Big Lie, achieving little beyond local irritation. And insofar as they become celebrations of gay individuality, they become the worst advertisement imaginable—and it is to the latter case that we turn next.

3. SHOCK TACTICS—A.K.A. GENDER-BENDING

We don't really know whether Shakespeare meant the line sarcastically, but, whenever we see a really gaudy gay pride march, we think, "O brave new world, that hath such people in it!"

Really, if you think about it, it's enough to make you cry. Here we are, a community painted from end to end with one broad brush—laughed to scorn, vilified, as a collection of perverted freaks, evil or insane—in any case *disgustingly* different—and incapable ever of fitting in with the mentally healthy and morally upright. We're assumed to consist entirely of extreme stereotypes: men ultraswishy and ultraviolet, Frankensteinian thug-women with bolts on their necks, mustachio'd Dolly Parton wanna-bes, leather-men in boots and whips, ombudsmen of pederasty squiring their ombudsboys—all ridiculous, deranged, or criminal. And when we are *finally* allowed to rally and march, to lay our case before the cameras of the straight American public, what do we do? We call out of the woodwork as our ambassadors of bad will all the screamers, stompers, gender-benders, sadomasochists, and pederasts, and confirm America's worst fears and hates. You can call it gay liberation if you like: we say it's spinach, and we say the hell with it!

The reasoning of the engineers of these embarrassing displays runs roughly thus: we're different; we've been shut out of the majority culture; we've been made to feel worthless and wicked. We'll show America that we don't need their heterosexist culture at all—we can do just fine without it: we've got our own culture. We'll *celebrate* our difference. If we do it openly, loudly, and proudly, straight America will eventually get used to it. They'll see that even complete weirdness, let alone mere homosexual orientation, is acceptable. Besides, in dressing and acting as we want, we're striking a blow for what should be everyone's basic right: to celebrate one's individuality, unconstrained by conformitarianism.

This reasoning is a compote of vague notions, irrelevancies, non sequiturs, and wishful thinking, garnished with just enough truth to render it savory and seductive. In short, it's wrong; here's why:

The effect of presenting a bigot with an extreme instance of his stereotypic picture/label pair is to augment the strength of the bigotry. Just as the prejudice is originally formed by repeated pairing of the picture and label with a negative parental or societal reaction, so encountering an *extreme* instance of the stereotype reinforces the pattern of stereotypic thinking, and arouses correspondingly extreme anxiety and hostility. When these negative emotions are intense, they nearly always motivate either avoidance—which alleviates the anxiety, and thereby rewards the prejudice—or else jeering—which discharges hostility, bolsters the self-image, and so also rewards the prejudice. However you slice it, the prejudice is rewarded, and what is rewarded prospers exceedingly.

It would be great if we lived in an Ideal World, where everyone could do his thing and be what he wanted to be, and be judged only on the essentials of his personality, not mere externals and window-dressing—but we don't. Such wishful thinking is reminiscent of the plaints of the 1960s hippies, who, like spoiled toddlers, whined, 'But *why* can't I wear dirty jeans and a T-shirt to work? *Why* should Ogilvy and Mather expect me to be washed and suited?' The answer's obvious: You live in a world of stereotypes and rapid, merciless judgments—which, for gays, can be lethal. Like it or not, you—and the groups you represent—are instantly approved or condemned, by those you seek to impress, on the basis of your appearance. Nobody else in this busy world is interested in your glorious individuality; they only wish to determine —quickly!—whether they'd like to deal with you or not. If you conform, visibly, to a bizarre or irritating stereotype, they won't want to listen to you—and, because they're calling the shots, they *won't* listen. You both lose. That's the reality. People who persist in closing their eyes to reality usually end up getting belted in the chops by it.

We, the authors, long for that Ideal World just as much as the drag queens et al. do. In the meantime, we all have to live in the

Real World, in which their behavior, when indulged in publicly, is self-destructive, and destructive to the gay community as a whole.

When you're very different, and people hate you for it, this is what you do: *first* you get your foot in the door, by being as *similar* as possible; then, and only then—when your one little difference is finally accepted—can you start dragging in your other peculiarities, one by one. **You hammer in the wedge narrow end first.** As the saying goes, Allow the camel's nose beneath your tent, and his whole body will soon follow.

By the same token, allowing advocates of legalized 'love' between men and boys to participate in gay pride marches is, from the standpoint of public relations, an unalloyed disaster. For the purposes of our argument, it is irrelevant whether pederasty is good or bad; what *is* relevant is that arguments against it, not easily refutable, can be made, and are associated with widespread abhorrence, not to mention universal—and severe—legal sanctions. Even if we were to grant to the advocates of pederasty an ethical dispensation to go about their child-rearing with our blessing—and the authors grant nothing of the sort—it would remain the direst folly to invite them to rain on our parade. Gays are already assumed to be child molesters; participation in gay pride marches by would-be pederasts seems, to the straight community, to prove it. As a purely practical matter, we cannot ameliorate straight America's abhorrence of homosexuality, per se, by wrapping ourselves in the far more—and possibly justifiably—abhorred flag of 'man-boy love!'

'Fringe' gay groups ought to have the tact to withdraw voluntarily from public appearance at gay parades, marches, and rallies, but they don't seem to care whether they fatally compromise the rest of us. Like fretful valetudinarians drowning at sea who frantically grab the younger and heartier about the waist and refuse to let go, bearing their hapless victims to Davy Jones' Locker, they seem elementally selfish. If unencumbered, the gay community would have an excellent chance of swimming ashore. Its line must be, 'We're not judging you, but others do, and very harshly;

please keep a low profile. You offend the public more than other gays.' Others would seem to share our grave disquiet. We have been informed by participants in New York's annual gay pride march that when NAMBLA marches by, the cheering abruptly stops.

What it boils down to is that this community isn't the personal turf of drag queens and pederasts. We greatly outnumber them, and they have no right to set themselves up as spokespersons for the rest of us—especially when the rest of us are working our butts off to convince straights that, in all respects other than what we like to do in bed, we're exactly like folks. The actions of the gay pride marchers don't take place in a vacuum, and, as long as their disastrous tactics drag us down with them, we have a just cause for complaint.

o   o   o

How can it be that gays have almost invariably done exactly the opposite of what they should—as though they couldn't have been more fully aware of the structure of the mechanism of prejudice, but were perversely bent on wrenching its levers the wrong way? Perhaps because human beings are dimly aware of what makes their clockwork tick, but have a terrible tendency, in whatever they do, to try to insert the winding-key backward—with results far worse than if they'd been completely ignorant. In psychology, as elsewhere, a little knowledge is a dangerous thing.

o

PUSHING THE *RIGHT* BUTTONS: HALTING, DERAILING, OR REVERSING THE 'ENGINE OF PREJUDICE'

In the past, gays have tinkered ineptly with the engine of prejudice. Is it possible to tinker more favorably? We present (in order of increasing vigor and desirability) three general approaches— very nearly the opposites of the three tactics described above.

These approaches, once understood, will lead us directly to the principles upon which a viable campaign can be erected.

1. DESENSITIZATION

From the point of view of evolution, prejudice is an alerting signal, warning tribal mammals that a potentially dangerous alien mammal is in the vicinity, and should be fought or fled. Alerting mechanisms respond to *novelties* in the environment, because novelties represent change from the usual, and are, therefore, potentially important.

One of two things can happen: (1) If the alerting mechanism is very strongly activated, it will produce an unendurable emotional state, forcing the tribal mammal to fight the novelty or flee it. (2) If, however, the novelty is either low-grade, or simply odd without being threatening, the alerting mechanism will be mildly activated, producing an emotional state that, if other environmental circumstances militate against it, will be too weak to motivate any actual behavioral response. In the latter case, the mammal may peer curiously at the novelty for quite some time, but will not do anything about it, or to it.

As a general physio-psychological rule, novelties cease to be novel if they just stick around long enough; they also cease to activate alerting mechanisms. There are excellent evolutionary reasons for this: if the mammal either has no good reason to respond, or is for some reason incapable of doing so, it is actually hindered in its normal activities if its attention continues to be taken up by an irrelevancy. You'll have noted this in your own life: if you hear a protracted, earsplitting mechanical screech, you'll either be so alarmed, or so annoyed, that you'll be forced to take action; if you hear a softer—though, perhaps, nonetheless annoying—sound, like the ticking of a clock, and can't shut it off, you will, eventually, shut it out, and may cease to hear it altogether. Similarly with a rank odor, smelled upon entering a room; if you can't get rid of it, you eventually cease to smell it.

Franz Kafka wrote a delightful fable ("The Animal in the Synagogue") that might almost have had Desensitization in mind. His story—never finished—deals with a peculiar animal, the only one of its kind, which has been living, since time immemorial, in a synagogue. The elders take a dim view of this state of affairs; though quiet, the animal emerges from its nook during services and distracts the women (who sit at the back) from their devotions. Moreover, there is no telling, with so very odd an animal, what its habits might eventually prove to be. Suppose it bites? There is talk of mounting an expedition to catch and kill it. But the synagogue is very large and very old, with a thousand bolt-holes in which the animal might hide, and it is capable of climbing high and running fast. Any such expedition would be difficult, and would run the risk not only of failure, but of damaging irreplaceable artwork. The upshot is that the elders call the whole thing off; and, as the animal never gives anyone the least trouble, they get used to its presence, and eventually cease to think about it at all.

Apply this to the problem of homohatred. If gays present themselves—or allow themselves to be presented—as overwhelmingly different and threatening, they will put straights on a triple-red alert, driving them to overt acts of political oppression or physical violence. If, however, gays can live alongside straights, visibly but as inoffensively as possible, they will arouse a low-grade alert only, which, though annoying to straights, will eventually diminish for purely physiological reasons. Straights will be desensitized. Put more simply, if you go out of your way to be unendurable, people will try to destroy you; otherwise, they might eventually get used to you. This commonsense axiom should make it clear that living down to the stereotype, à la Gender-Bending, is a very bad idea.

We can extract the following principle for our campaign: to desensitize straights to gays and gayness, inundate them in a continuous flood of gay-related advertising, presented in the least offensive fashion possible. If straights can't shut off the shower, they may at least eventually get used to being wet.

Of course, while sheer indifference is, itself, vastly preferable to hatred and threats, we would like to do better than that. We turn next to more difficult, but also more vigorous and rewarding, tactics.

2. JAMMING

The engine of prejudice can be made to grind to a halt not only by Desensitization, in which it is simply allowed to run out of steam, but also by the more active process of Jamming. As the name implies, Jamming involves the insertion into the engine of a pre-existing, *incompatible* emotional response, gridlocking its mechanism as thoroughly as though one had sprinkled fine sand into the workings of an old-fashioned pocket watch. Jamming, as an approach, is more active and aggressive than Desensitization; by the same token, it is also more enjoyable and heartening.

Jamming makes use of the rules of Associative Conditioning (the psychological process whereby, when two things are repeatedly juxtaposed, one's feelings about one thing are transferred to the other) and Direct Emotional Modeling (the inborn tendency of human beings to feel what they perceive others to be feeling).

Turning Associative Conditioning and Direct Emotional Modeling against themselves, we Jam by forging a fresh link between, on the one hand, some part of the mechanism, and, on the other, a pre-existing, external, opposed, and therefore incompatible emotional response. Ideally, the bigot subjected to such counterconditioning will ultimately experience *two* emotional responses to the hated object, opposed and competing. The consequent internal confusion has two effects: first, it is unpleasant—we can call it 'emotional dissonance,' after Festinger—and will tend to result in an alteration of previous beliefs and feelings so as to resolve the internal conflict. Since the weaker of the clashing emotional associations is the more likely to give way, we can achieve optimal results by linking the prejudicial response to a stronger and more fundamental structure of belief and emotion. (Naturally, in some people this will be impossible, as prejudicial hatred *is* the strongest element in their beliefs, emotions, and motivations. Without resorting to prefrontal lobotomy—ah! sweet dreams!—these people are more or less unsalvageable.) Second, even where an optimal resolution does not occur, the internal dissonance will tend to inhibit overt expression of the prejudicial emotion—which is, in itself, useful and relieving.

The 'incompatible emotional response' is directed primarily against the emotional rewards of prejudicial solidarity. All normal people feel *shame* when they perceive that they are not thinking, feeling, or acting like one of the pack. And, these days, all but the stupidest and most unregenerate of bigots perceive that prejudice against all other minority groups—e.g., blacks, Jews, Catholics, women, et al.—has long since ceased to be approved, let alone fashionable, and that to express such prejudices, if not to hold them, makes one decidedly *not* one of the pack. It was permissible, some forty years ago, to tell the vilest ethnic jokes at the average party, and, if the joke was reasonably well told, the joker could expect to receive applause and approval from his or her roistering confrères. (Should you find this hard to believe, read *2500 Jokes for All Occasions,* a popular 1942 compilation by Powers Moulton, which will surely stand your hair on end.) With the exception of certain benighted social classes and backward areas of the country, this is quite generally no longer the case.

The trick is to get the bigot into the position of feeling a conflicting twinge of shame, along with his reward, whenever his homohatred surfaces, so that his reward will be diluted or spoiled. This can be accomplished in a variety of ways, all making use of repeated exposure to pictorial images or verbal statements that are incompatible with his self-image as a well-liked person, one who fits in with the rest of the crowd. Thus, propagandistic advertisement can depict homophobic and homohating bigots as crude loudmouths and assholes—people who say not only 'faggot' but 'nigger,' 'kike,' and other shameful epithets—who are 'not Christian.' It can show them being criticized, hated, shunned. It can depict gays experiencing horrific suffering as the direct result of homohatred—suffering of which even most bigots would be ashamed to be the cause. It can, in short, link homohating bigotry with all sorts of attributes the bigot would be ashamed to possess, and with social consequences he would find unpleasant and scary. The attack, therefore, is on self-image and on the pleasure in hating.

When our ads show a bigot—just like the members of the target audience—being criticized, hated, and shunned, we make use of Direct Emotional Modeling as well. Remember, a bigot seeks approval and liking from 'his crowd.' When he sees someone like himself being *dis*approved of and *dis*liked by ordinary Joes, Direct Emotional Modeling ensures that he will feel just what they feel —and transfer it to himself. This wrinkle effectively elicits shame and doubt, Jamming any pleasure he might normally feel. In a very real sense, every time a bigot sees such a thing, he is unlearning a little bit of the lesson of prejudice taught him by his parents and peers.

Such an approach may seem much too weak to work, yet bear these thoughts in mind: (a) the procedure is exactly that which formed the prejudicial complex to begin with; (b) the majority of casual bigots do not, in fact, see themselves as unpleasant people and would hate to think that others see them as such, let alone that their hatred has caused suffering and death; (c) there has, in fact, been a major turnaround in the acceptability, in this country, of prejudice against other minority groups, due, in our opinion, in no small part to exactly such counterconditioning and linking; and (d) such an approach has actually been used in TV advertisements, most memorably in an antidrinking ad showing a teenage boy drinking at a party, but *not* meeting with approval: indeed, as he gets more and more drunk, his behavior becomes more and more obnoxious, and he is regarded by the other partiers with disgust; ultimately, his head turns into that of a heehawing jackass. One can readily see how this sort of thing could be adapted to our own purposes.

Note that the bigot need not actually be made to *believe* that he is such a heinous creature, that others will now despise him, and that he has been the immoral agent of suffering. It would be impossible to make him believe any such thing. Rather, our effect is achieved without reference to facts, logic, or proof. Just as the bigot became such, without any say in the matter, through repeated infralogical emotional conditioning, his bigotry can be alloyed in exactly the same way, whether he is conscious of the attack or not. Indeed, the more he is distracted by any incidental, even specious, surface arguments, the less conscious he'll be of the true nature of the process—which is all to the good.

In short, Jamming succeeds insofar as it inserts even a slight *frisson* of doubt and shame into the previously unalloyed, self-righteous pleasure. The approach can be quite useful and effective —*if* our message can get the massive exposure upon which all else depends.

3. CONVERSION

Desensitization aims at lowering the intensity of antigay emotional reactions to a level approximating sheer indifference; Jamming attempts to blockade or counteract the rewarding 'pride in prejudice' (peace, Jane Austen!) by attaching to homohatred a pre-existing, and punishing, sense of shame in being a bigot, a horse's ass, and a beater and murderer. Both Desensitization and Jamming, though extremely useful, are mere preludes to our highest —though necessarily very long-range—goal, which is Conversion.

It isn't enough that antigay bigots should become confused about us, or even indifferent to us—we are safest, in the long run, if we can actually make them like us. Conversion aims at just this.

Please don't confuse *Con*version with political *Sub*version. The word 'subversion' has a nasty ring, of which the American people are inordinately afraid—and on their guard against. Yet, ironically, by Conversion we actually mean something far more profoundly threatening to the American Way of Life, without which no truly sweeping social change can occur. We mean conversion of the average American's emotions, mind, and will, through a planned psychological attack, in the form of propaganda fed to the nation via the media. We mean 'subverting' the mechanism of prejudice to our own ends—using the very processes that made

America hate us to turn their hatred into warm regard—whether they like it or not.

Put briefly, if Desensitization lets the watch run down, and Jamming throws sand in the works, Conversion reverses the spring so that the hands run backward.

Conversion makes use of Associative Conditioning, much as Jamming does—indeed, in practice the two processes overlap— but far more ambitiously. In Conversion, the bigot, who holds a very negative stereotypic picture, is repeatedly exposed to literal picture/label pairs, in magazines, and on billboards and TV, of gays—explicitly labeled as such!—who not only don't look like his picture of a homosexual, but are carefully selected to look either like the bigot and his friends, or like any one of his other stereo- types of all-right guys—the kind of people he already likes and admires. This image must, of necessity, be carefully tailored to be free of absolutely every element of the widely held stereotypes of how 'faggots' look, dress, and sound. He—or she—must not be too well or fashionably dressed; must not be too handsome—that is, mustn't look like a model—or well groomed. The image must be that of an icon of normality—a good beginning would be to take a long look at Coors beer and Three Musketeers candy commercials. Subsequent ads can branch out from that solid basis to include really adorable, athletic teenagers, kindly grandmothers, avuncu- lar policemen, *ad infinitem.*

The objection will be raised—and raised, and raised—that we would 'Uncle Tommify' the gay community; that we are exchang- ing one false stereotype for another equally false; that our ads are lies; that that is *not* how *all* gays actually look; that gays know it, and bigots know it. Yes, of course—we know it, too. But it makes no difference that the ads are lies; not to us, because we're using them to ethically good effect, to counter negative stereotypes that are every bit as much lies, and far more wicked ones; not to big- ots, because the ads will have their effect on them whether they believe them or not.

When a bigot is presented with an image of the sort of person of whom he already has a positive stereotype, he experiences an involuntary rush of positive emotion, of good feeling; he's been conditioned to experience it. But, here, the good picture has the bad label—gay! (The ad may say something rather like 'Beauregard Smith—beer drinker, Good Ole Boy, pillar of the community, 100% American, and gay as a mongoose.') The bigot will feel two incompatible emotions: a good response to the picture, a bad response to the label. At worst, the two will cancel one another, and we will have successfully Jammed, as above. At best, Associative Conditioning will, to however small an extent, transfer the positive emotion associated with the picture to the label itself, not immediately replacing the negative response, but definitely weakening it.

You may wonder why the transfer wouldn't proceed in the opposite direction. The reason is simple: pictures are stronger than words and evoke emotional responses more powerfully. The bigot is presented with an *actual* picture; its label will evoke in his mind his own stereotypic picture, but what he sees in his mind's eye will be weaker than what he actually sees in front of him with the eyes in his face. The more carefully selected the advertised image is to reflect his ideal of the sort of person who just couldn't be gay, the more effective it will be. Moreover, he will, by virtue of logical necessity, see the positive picture in the ad *before* it can arouse his negative 'picture,' and first impressions have an advantage over second.

In Conversion, we mimic the natural process of stereotype-learning, with the following effect: we take the bigot's good feelings about all-right guys, and attach them to the label 'gay,' either weakening or, eventually, replacing his bad feelings toward the label and the prior stereotype.

Understanding Direct Emotional Modeling, you'll readily foresee its application to Conversion: whereas in Jamming the target is shown a bigot being rejected by his crowd for his prejudice against gays, in Conversion the target is shown his crowd actually associating with gays in good fellowship. Once again, it's very difficult for the average person, who, by nature and training, almost invariably feels what he sees his fellows feeling, not to respond in this knee-jerk fashion to a sufficiently calculated advertisement. In a way, most advertisement is founded upon an answer of Yes, definitely! to Mother's sarcastic question: I suppose if all the other kids jumped off a bridge and killed themselves, you would, too?

o   o   o

We've now outlined three major modes by which we can alter the itinerary of the engine of prejudice in our favor. Desensitization lets the engine run out of steam, causing it to halt on the tracks indefinitely. Jamming, in essence, derails it. Conversion— our ambitious long-range goal—puts the engine into reverse gear and sends it back whence it came.

These modes are abstract—we've only hinted, here and there, at how they can be harnessed and put to work for us in a practical propaganda campaign. In Chapters 3 and 4, we shall unfold, in detail, exactly how this can be done.

o

BUT *CAN* IT BE DONE?

> It will be said that such a scheme . . . is un
> practical . . . This is perfectly true . . . This
> is why it is worth carrying out . . . For what
> is a practical scheme? . . . either a scheme
> . . . already in existence, or a scheme that
> could be carried out under existing conditions.
> But it is exactly the existing conditions that one
> objects to; and any scheme that could accept
> these conditions is wrong and foolish.
>
> —OSCAR WILDE, THE SOUL OF MAN
> UNDER SOCIALISM

Our goal, being high, is also difficult. The bottleneck in reaching it, however, isn't lack of knowledge of the psychological principles involved, nor lack of efficacy in the methods available; the principles are known, and the methods work. The bottleneck is purely and simply achieving a sufficient scope for the dissemination of our propaganda. Success depends, as always, on flooding the media. And that, in turn, means money, which means man-hours, which means unifying the gay community for a concerted effort. Let's be blunt: those who aren't with us in this effort, either because they have better ways of wasting their time, or because they think we're politically incorrect, are most decidedly against us, against unification, and against the best interests of the gay community as a whole.

MOVING RIGHT ALONG

As we approach the end of Chapter 2, and therefore of Part I, so, also, we approach a turning point in our book. We have seen what is, and why; in Part II, we will see what must be. It is an exciting prospect. *Avanti!*

PART II

SOLUTIONS:
DRIVING
T H E
WEDGE

3

STRATEGY:
PERSUASION,
NOT INVASION

Groups are subject to the truly magical power of words.

—SIGMUND FREUD

○ ○ ○
GOOD PROPAGANDA:
THE IDEA BEHIND 'WAGING PEACE'

G ay life in America is hard, and promises little improvement unless something is done, and promptly, to transform society's antigay attitudes. If this isn't clear by now, you must be reading our book from the wrong end: we closed Chapter 1 with a daunting checklist of the myths and injustices which grow out of homohatred learned in childhood.

What's to be done about this checklist? Many solutions could be proposed, ranging from the idealistic and fanciful to the necessary but insufficient. Such solutions will be noted (and castigated!) briefly below. But from here on, this book is devoted to the one scheme that would, if correctly administered, radically hasten and broaden the spread of tolerance for gays in straight society.

We have in mind a strategy as calculated and powerful as that which gays are *accused* of pursuing by their enemies—or, if you prefer, a plan as manipulative as that which our enemies themselves employ. It's time to learn from Madison Avenue, to roll out the big guns. *Gays must launch a large-scale campaign—we've called it the Waging Peace campaign—to reach straights through the mainstream media.* We're talking about propaganda.

To most people, the word 'propaganda' has the worst connotations. Propaganda is supposed to be what Communists and Fascists (and certain TV weathermen) are up to—gross distortion and fraud perpetrated for evil ends. This is a misconception. *The term 'propaganda' applies to any deliberate attempt to persuade the masses via public communications media.* Such communication is everywhere, of course, being a mainstay of modern societies. Its function is not to perpetrate, but to *propagate;* that is, to spread new ideas and feelings (or reinforce old ones) which may themselves be either evil or good depending on their purpose and effect. The purpose and effect of progay propaganda is to promote a climate of increased tolerance for homosexuals. And that, we say, is good.

Three characteristics distinguish propaganda from other modes of communication and contribute to its sinister reputation. First, propaganda relies more upon emotional manipulation than upon logic, since its goal is, in fact, to bring about a change in the public's feelings. Bertrand Russell once asked, "Why is propaganda so much more successful when it stirs up hatred than when it tries to stir up friendly feelings?" The answer is that the public is more eager to hate than to love, especially where outgroups are concerned; and that, knowing this, propagandists have seldom attempted to elicit friendly feelings or dampen hatred. This time, however, we gays will attempt precisely that. And we'll be more successful than before because we can base our efforts on techniques (desensitization, jamming, and conversion) derived directly from a solid understanding of the psychology of homohatred.

The second sinister characteristic of propaganda is its frequent use of outright lies, a tactic we neither need nor condone. In the long run, big fat lies work only for the propagandists of totalitarian states, who can make them stick by exercising almost complete control over public information. But in pluralistic societies, such as ours, chronic liars on controversial subjects are invariably found out and discredited in the press by their opponents. (There is, alas, an exception: certain lies become hallowed public myths, persisting for as long as the public *chooses* to believe them. Need we mention the Big Lie?)

Third, even when it sticks to the facts, propaganda can be unabashedly subjective and one-sided. There is nothing necessarily wrong with this. Propaganda tells its own side of the story as movingly (and credibly) as possible, since it can count on its enemies to tell the other side with a vengeance. In the battle for hearts and minds, effective propaganda knows enough to put its best foot forward. This is what our own media campaign must do.

When, in a 1985 *Christopher Street* article, we presented a blueprint for a national propaganda effort, doubters derided the proposal as irrelevant or impotent, the methods as demeaning and fraudulent, and our intent as reactionary. In February 1988, however, a "war conference" of 175 leading gay activists, representing organizations from across the land, convened in Warrenton, Virginia, to establish a four-point agenda for the gay movement. The conference gave first priority to "a nation-wide media campaign to promote a positive image of gays and lesbians," and its final statement concluded:

> We must consider the media in every project we undertake. We must, in addition, take every advantage we can to include public service announcements and paid advertisements, and to cultivate reporters and editors of newspapers, radio, and television. To help facilitate this we need national media workshops to train our leaders . . . Our media efforts are fundamental to the full acceptance of us in American life.

Since the war conference, local gay advertising efforts have sprung up across the nation—in California, Ohio, Virginia, and other states—and GLAAD and the Fund for Human Dignity for a time, even co-sponsored the beginnings of a national "Positive Images Campaign." Clearly, something is afoot. Recognition is dawning that antigay discrimination begins, like war, in the minds of men, and must be stopped there with the help of propaganda. Recognition is likewise dawning that certain other strategies, touted in earlier days by idealistic activists, cannot accomplish the task on their own. Several of these strategies deserve mention.

○

OUTREACH STRATEGIES OF THE PAST: WHY ONLY A MEDIA CAMPAIGN WILL DO

Those oft are stratagems which errors seem.
—ALEXANDER POPE, 1738

Pope's got it backwards."
—ERASTES PILL, 1989

FIRST STRATEGY: COME THOU, MOUNTAIN, TO MOHAMMED.

As discussed earlier, some gays believe we shouldn't reach out at all to heterosexuals in order to dispel discrimination. Some stalwart revolutionaries feel strongly that appealing for acceptance bespeaks groveling capitulation and conformitarianism. Instead, the radicals demand that straights simply accept us entirely on our own terms, or not at all. They point out that gays have spent their lives trying to force-fit themselves into a straight mold, so now it is the straights' turn to adjust.

In this scenario, it is the public's job to disburden itself magically, on its own, of its massive sexual hang-ups; the homosexual's only duty is to 'learn how to love' himself or herself. Who needs respect from others when he has self-respect? If 'they' don't like homosexuality, they can just lump it; 'liberated' gays will form their own proud nation—imagined as a sort of urban Navaho reservation—and ignore the larger world. Sooner or later, straights will be impressed by our gay pride, and come around.

As you might guess by now, we think this radical argument is rubbish (which has been sitting rankly on the sidewalk ever since the early '70s, waiting for someone to haul it away). There can be no reservation-like enclave, no sailing off on the good ship Sodom to colonize new lands of our own. We are Americans, going nowhere, living cheek-by-jowl with our persecutors.

In this unyielding predicament, to gain straight tolerance and acceptance is not just a legitimate goal of gay activism, it must be the *principal* goal. Certainly, helping gays to see themselves more positively is important too, but this in no way suffices. It's just as preposterous to argue, as one of our critics did recently, that "gay pride makes [straight] acceptance," as it is to pretend that gays could safely turn their backs on the straight world. The heterosexual majority's hostility is real, brutal, and largely indifferent to whether its victims have gay pride or not. Bigotry mauls gays, so our aim must be to muzzle and tame it. There's no point pretending to be Mohammed and waiting for straights to come around: left to itself, the mountain won't budge an inch.

SECOND STRATEGY: I'D LIKE TO TEACH THE WORLD TO SING.

Why not simply appeal to straights and gays to learn to love one another and give peace a chance; to be nice, for a change, on their own recognizance? After all, people are really good inside; one need only appeal to that universal goodness, and hard feelings will peel away like a dried old husk. Every man a saint, and a world of Leo Buscaglias!

There is, in fact, much to be said for efforts at self-improvement. Some social reform, like charity, does begin at home. Straights who have read this far will wish hereafter to challenge their own bigoted feelings, and those of their society, with renewed determination, while they reassess their stereotypic beliefs about gays.

Gays, on the other hand—particularly the men—can take greater responsibility, and refuse to live down to the gay stereotype. As the authors will argue strenuously in Chapter 6 (so strenuously, in fact, that everyone is guaranteed a sharp pain in the neck before we leave off), we gays can establish for ourselves a sturdier code of ethics stressing maturity in love relationships, moderation in the pursuit of sex and other entertainments, sincerity and loving-kindness—that venerable Old Testament notion—toward all our fellows, and restraint in our public deportment. In sum, we can and should assert more control over our own actions, rather than let ourselves be shoved back and forth as abused playthings between the puerile dictates of our own undisciplined impulses, on the one hand, and society's unreasonable demands for mindless conformity on the other. Self-mastery is freedom. Fidelity to an ethical code of one's own construction is independence, not conformity. Gays must know what they will live by and then live by it. Period.

If gays could, further, agree upon the general outlines of a code and begin to regulate themselves *as a community*, this would be better still. To date, our movement has been so fixated upon the attainment of what the philosopher Isaiah Berlin calls "negative liberty"—being left alone—that it has utterly failed to appreciate the value of "positive liberty"—being encouraged and helped by one's companions to achieve the good.

Admittedly, our campaign espouses, in part, this idealistic strategy for transforming social relations through self-conscious effort. *We'd* like to teach the world to sing, too; who wouldn't? But that strategy will be most effective for improving relations *within* the gay community, and only secondarily in reaching bigoted straights. After all, most heterosexuals dislike homosexuals on fundamentally emotional, not intellectual, grounds, and are, therefore, unwilling and unable to abolish their own prejudices through a change of principles and beliefs. Nor would the miraculous transformation of the gay *demimonde* into a province of virtue —though plenty nice for its own members—automatically win over straights, since their hostility is guided more by caricatures in their heads than by the gay reality that unfolds right under their noses.

THIRD STRATEGY: COME OUT, COME OUT, WHEREVER YOU ARE.

This is another scheme we heartily recommend but have faint hope of implementing until more fundamental changes have first occurred: *wherever possible, come out.* Naturally, coming out is a grave and dangerous step for anyone. Only a few will proclaim their sexuality all at once to everybody they know; most prefer to be more selective, to inform intimates one by one over time, on a 'need-to-know' basis. It's like the difference between ripping a bandage off all at once or bit by bit. But whatever the approach, coming out makes an enormous contribution to the fight against homohatred, since it generally provides an ideal opportunity to activate the psychological mechanisms we have called desensitization, jamming, and conversion. Here's how it works:

First, coming out helps desensitize straights. As more and more gays emerge into everyday life, gays *as a group* will begin to seem more familiar and unexceptional to straights, hence less alarming and objectionable. (Remember that most gays *are* otherwise unexceptional—or else straights would recognize them.) The more gays come out, the more the Big Lie will crumble, and with it the irrational foundation for moral condemnation and mistreatment.

Second, coming out allows more jamming of the reward system for homohatred. Jamming, you'll recall, means interrupting the smooth workings of bigotry by inducing inconsistent feelings in the bigot. One jams, for example, by displacing with shame and guilt the satisfying sense of social approval and self-righteousness that a homohater would otherwise feel when he attacks homosexuals. As gays come out, they and their friends will be free to play a more vigorous role in jamming, openly showing their disapproval of homohatred. Jamming can work, even if open gays merely stand around homohaters without saying a word: in their presence, extreme bigots become less confident that their incitements will generate applause, and are further inhibited by the majority of 'mild' bigots, who now become uneasy that a fag slur might provoke an unpleasant scene. Once these dynamics get going, displays of homohatred suddenly become off-color and boorish. Thus, when gays come out, they help transform the social climate from one that supports prejudice to one that shuts homohaters up. And when bigots fall silent, they cannot as easily pass their social disease on to the next generation.

Third, coming out is a critical catalyst for the all-important 'conversion' process, as well. Conversion is more than merely desensitizing straights or jamming their homohatred: it entails making them actually like and accept homosexuals as a group, enabling straights to *identify* with them. This becomes possible when a heterosexual learns that someone he already likes and admires, such as a friend or family member, is homosexual. The discovery leads to an internal showdown between the straight's personal affection on the one hand and his bigotry on the other. When the gunsmoke finally clears—and it can take years to do so—the stronger sentiment emerges more or less victorious. If it *is* the stronger, affection for the friend wins out and subdues bigotry, the straight's concept of gays is modified for the better, and a favorable conversion takes place. Imagine: all that, just because you decided to come out.

Finally, in addition to making desensitization, jamming, and conversion possible, coming out is the key to sociopolitical empowerment, the ability of the gay community to control its own destiny. The more gay individuals who stand up to be counted, the more voting and spending power the gay community will be recognized to have. As an inevitable result, politics and business will woo us, the press will publicize our concerns and report our news, and our community will enjoy enhanced prestige.

If coming out does such positive things to combat bigotry, why even bother with a national media campaign? Why not just wait for everyone to come out? Because *gay America is coming out too slowly.* The way things are going—and there are no firm statistics on this, only impressions—no more than a fraction of the gay population is likely to come out over the next thirty years, and that's not sufficient to transform public attitudes at a satisfactory pace. (Perhaps others have the patience of Job, but the authors, at least, are unwilling to be worried still in the year 2020 about receiving their basic civil rights, at an age when they should be worrying instead about receiving their first social security checks and hair transplants.)

The percentage of gays who are out remains low because so many still feel, with some justification, that any benefits of coming out that might redound to themselves or to the gay movement do not outweigh the personal penalties of self-exposure. Indeed, with AIDS reinforcing their pariah status, it appears that gays who might otherwise have come out completely—particularly among the younger generation—are now electing to dangle no more than a hand or a foot outside the closet. Because these gays go unrecognized, their homohating straight acquaintances may never be desensitized, jammed, or converted.

All this means that the long-term strategy of Everyone Comes Out must be supplemented and prepped by a media campaign, which will help in several ways. For starters, it will go some distance in compensating for the public's lack of direct personal contact with openly homosexual Americans. After 'meeting' enough likable gays on television, Jane Doe may begin to feel she knows gays as a group, even if none has ever introduced himself to her personally. Although it operates less quickly and effectively to thwart bigotry than does a personal confrontation with a gay loved one, familiarization with gays through the media nonetheless prepares the public for the gradual desensitization, jamming, and conversion that will take place during our community's slow-motion coming-out party.

Furthermore, carefully crafted, repeatedly displayed mass-media images of gays could conceivably do even *more* to reverse negative stereotypes than could the incremental coming-out of one person to another. One of the peculiarities of bigotry is that its carriers have a tendency to exceptionalize the few minority friends they have, retaining their dislike of the minority group as a whole. They accomplish this neat mental contortion by perceiving their minority friends as somehow different from, unrepresentative of, the rest. ('Ah, yes, Herr Himmler—Rosenbloom's *nose* is all Jew, but his *heart* is pure Aryan!') Homohaters would find it harder to get away with such selective prejudice if a media campaign were to expose them to an unending series of 'positive' gay images.

Indeed, the wide range of favorably sanitized images that might be shown in the media could eventually have a more positive impact on the homosexual stereotype than could exposure to gay friends, since straights will otherwise generalize a suboptimal impression of gays from the idiosyncratic admixture of good and bad traits possessed by their one or two gay acquaintances. (One of the special advantages of a media campaign is that it can—and should —portray only the most *favorable* side of gays, thereby counterbalancing the already unfairly negative stereotype in the public's mind. When this is done, the picture labeled 'queer' is aggressively painted over; prior images of dirty old queens or coarsened dykes are overlaid with pleasing new images of all-American and Miss American types.)

Lastly, the media campaign will work well in tandem with the Everyone Comes Out strategy because *it is actually a catalyst to coming out*. As mass-media advertising legitimizes homosexuality, enhancing public receptiveness and sensitivity, the balance between the costs and benefits of coming out will shift decisively toward the latter, prompting more and more gays to declare themselves. A media campaign, then, becomes an iron pickax driving at a widening crack in the dam of gay secrecy until, sooner or later, everybody comes rushing forth. The sooner, the better.

FOURTH STRATEGY: POLITICAL CONSPIRACIES.

As most activists see it, there are two different avenues to gay liberation: Education (i.e., propaganda) and Politics. The dissemination of propaganda is enormously expensive and difficult, however, so little has been done to date. Instead, activists have concentrated their efforts on politics, meaning efforts to secure gay rights by conspiring with liberal elites within the legal and legislative systems.

Gay activists first tried to manipulate the American judicial system via the Bill of Rights but, as noted in an earlier chapter, most courts have provided cold comfort, especially recently. Many activists turned, therefore, to the tactic of urgent whispering into the ears of liberal and moderate public servants at all levels of government. Given the generally conservative climate of recent years, our lobbyists have worked extra hard to present themselves as terribly polite, dignified, and respectful ladies and gentlemen; they have had to cut their suit to fit the available political cloth—a suit that is tailored with the utmost discretion and dresses to the right. The goal here has been to forge a little *entente* or conspiracy with the power elite, to jump ahead of public sentiment or ignore it altogether.

Sometimes the tactic works: many executive orders (which sidestep the democratic process) and ordinances passed by city councils now protect certain limited civil rights for gays in selected cities. Many of these victories constitute political payoffs by elected officials whose candidacy the organized gay community has supported, and demonstrate both our electoral muscle and savvy backroom politicking.

Yet the scheme to build elite conspiracies often proves impractical in the short run and imprudent in the long. In the short run, politicians must be responsive to public sentiment on sensational issues if they value their careers. A sympathetic straight politico can be a co-conspirator, perhaps, but only up to a point, after which he is unreliable and immobilized: one of his feet is nailed to the floor. (No wonder gays find themselves being danced around in circles.)

In the long run, even if a conspiracy is formed and some legislative deal is struck, the agreement is built on beach sand so long as the public is left out of the bargain. Time and again, religious conservatives have washed away our gains with a frothy tide of public outcry and backlash. The classic example was cited in Chapter 1: after their mayor had, in 1984, slipped a clause protecting gay government employees into the city's antidiscrimination ordinance, a referendum was called and Houston's more reactionary citizens were mobilized to defeat the clause by a four-to-one margin. (This lopsided plebiscite didn't necessarily reflect the general public's attitudes: the conservative fringe mobbed the voting booths, while many moderates stayed home. But this often happens in politics, especially on the gay issue where, as Yeats would say, "the best lack all conviction, while the worst are full of passionate intensity.")

The solution is not for activists to abandon Politics for Education, of course. All things considered, legal and political efforts have come along slowly but surely—at least until AIDS threw the brakes. Yet, with the first gust of direct opposition, elite conspiracies blow apart like a house of cards, unless fortified by a significant shift in public attitudes. Like the other partial solutions discussed above, our political success could be greatly advanced by a media campaign conducted prior to, or simultaneously with, political initiatives.

o

THE STRATEGY OF 'WAGING PEACE': EIGHT PRACTICAL PRINCIPLES FOR THE PERSUASION OF STRAIGHTS

> *Those who have supreme skill use Strategy to bend others without coming to conflict.*
> —SUN TZU, THE ART OF WAR

After gleefully pitching stones at other strategies (always an invigorating aerobic exercise), it's time to examine the recommended alternative in detail. Any effective media campaign to 'educate' straights must be guided by what we now know about the origins and workings of homohatred.

Generally speaking, the most effective propaganda for our cause must succeed in doing three things at once.

- Employ images that desensitize, jam, and/or convert bigots on an *emotional* level. This is, by far, the most important task.
- Challenge homohating beliefs and actions on a (not too) *intellectual* level. Remember, the rational message serves to camouflage our underlying emotional appeal, even as it pares away the surrounding latticework of beliefs that rationalize bigotry.
- Gain access to the kinds of public media that would automatically confer legitimacy upon these messages and, therefore, upon their gay sponsors. To be accepted by the most prestigious media, such as network TV, our messages themselves will have to be—at least initially—both subtle in purpose and crafty in construction.

Guided by these several objectives, we offer eight practical principles for the persuasion of straights via the mass media.

PRINCIPLE 1. DON'T JUST EXPRESS YOURSELF: COMMUNICATE!

Although gay activists regularly confuse the two, self-expression and communication are different processes motivated by different objectives. The first can be done in isolation, like singing in the shower—*sans* audience—whereas the second cannot. Self-expression is usually its own reward, but communication is not rewarding unless one has 'reached' (i.e., persuaded or moved) the listener.

To date, most public acts by the gay community have accomplished self-expression without communication (at least, without communication to the general public). These acts, ranging from modes of dress to mass demonstrations, have typically been enacted for the sake of self-affirmation, an effort to cast off shame by standing tall in the crowd and crowing, 'I gotta be me: either accept me as I am, or to hell with you.' (To say this in a spectacular way, as you know, certain gay, men who would not otherwise be caught dead out of doors without their Brooks Brothers sack suits, metamorphose into bespangled drag queens one day each year and sashay through town in gay pride marches.) It may be psychologically liberating and therefore healthy for some *individuals* to do things of this sort. But, you must always remember, what is healthy for the individual isn't necessarily healthy for his community. Don't mistake these acts of self-expression for public outreach.

Genuine public outreach requires careful communication. If it helps, think of yourself as an explorer cautiously approaching a spear-wielding tribe of suspicious, belligerent natives in New Guinea. Suddenly you're caught in a deadly game of sheer strategy, in which, as political economist Thomas Schelling defines it, "the best course of action for each player depends on what the other players do." The natives are debating whether to treat you as a dinner guest or as a dinner. Somehow, you must win them over—*quickly*. This is no time to burst out singing 'I gotta be me.' Each word, each gesture, is watched, stereotyped, interpreted by them *in native terms*. You must help them relate to you and your humanity, to recognize that you and they share many good things in common, and that they can like and accept you on their own terms. (Rest assured, they won't go to the trouble of accepting you on your terms.) To win them over will require your finest skills at communication.

Communication, then, not self-expression, is the basis of a mass-media campaign. To achieve it, every public message in the campaign should be the direct result of gays having put themselves in the public's binding high-button shoes and asked: If I were straight and felt the hostility most straights feel toward gays, *what would it take to get me to change my antigay feelings?* In other words, don't start by deciding what you most ardently wish to tell straights: start by determining what they most *need* to hear from you.

An essential corollary of this communication rule is that *straights must be helped to believe that you and they speak the same language.* They must become convinced that, despite a key difference—sexual orientation—you and they nevertheless share enough ideas and values so that dialogue can proceed in a meaningful and fruitful way. Straights won't even stop to listen to your message unless reassured by certain obvious surface cues—dressing and speaking 'like them,' for example—that you and they transmit on the same wavelength.

PRINCIPLE 2. SEEK YE NOT THE SAVED NOR THE DAMNED: APPEAL TO THE SKEPTICS

Once gays are ready and willing to communicate, the next question is: with whom? Our media strategists must know their target audiences; know which are ripe for persuasion, which not. On gay rights, the public is of several minds. There are, in this sense, several different publics to consider, each comprising, very roughly, one third of the populace.

As noted during our field trip to straight America, at one end of the spectrum there is already a wing—perhaps 25–30% of the public (including most gays)—that tells pollsters it doesn't seriously disapprove of homosexuality per se and is ready to defend equal treatment of gays. At the other extreme prowl the denizens of bigotry's darkest realm—say, 30–35% of the citizenry—so vehemently opposed to homosexuality that they would not permit one of its adherents to utter a single word in their community. Between our professed friends and our implacable foes—between the saved and the damned (or damnable)—are found the ambivalent remainder (35–45%), those who are basically skeptical about homosexuality but unwilling to nail gays to the wall.

Intransigents	Ambivalent Skeptics	Friends
←———————	←————————→	——————→
30–35%	35–45%	25–30%

Toward which audience, then, should gay media efforts be directed? Should we seek to protect ourselves by going after our most dangerous persecutors and taming them? Or should we merely preach to our own choir of supporters, as political advertising textbooks recommend, on the premise that you can only inflame the opinions people already hold, not change those opinions?

In our view, the campaign shouldn't set out to do either. It would make little headway against Intransigents, for whom homohatred serves essential emotional functions. Some Intransigents fight desperately to suppress their own homosexual proclivities; others, for complicated reasons, feel compelled to adhere rigidly to an authoritarian belief structure (e.g., an orthodox religion) that condemns homosexuality. Our primary objective regarding diehard homohaters of this sort is to cow and *silence* them as far as possible, not to convert or even desensitize them.

As for our handful of Friends, they must be agitated and mobilized for our cause. But this should not be the primary goal of a national media campaign, for two reasons. First, such a minority can accomplish little while it remains steadfastly opposed by three fourths of the citizenry. Second, our supporters will receive ample encouragement and reinforcement from *whatever* campaign we might undertake to reach the rest of the nation.

We conclude, therefore, that Ambivalent Skeptics are our most promising target. If we can win them over, produce a major realignment solidly in favor of gay rights, the Intransigents (like the racists twenty years ago) will eventually be effectively silenced by both law and polite society. Our Friends, on the other hand, will be emboldened to support our interests more aggressively.

Now, Ambivalent Skeptics are, themselves, anything but homogeneous. They number, on the one hand, those more or less *passively negative* about homosexuality, who display automatic, unthinking opposition without getting very worked up over the subject. They also include citizens more *ambivalently positive,* who have strong convictions in favor of civil rights for all, but a weak stomach when it comes to the issue of homosexuality (rather like gourmets who profess a love of shellfish but cannot bear the look of oysters).

Every Skeptic is a candidate for desensitization. It may turn out, however, that passive-negatives can be reached *only* by desensitization (further sedating those who already don't care much either way); whereas ambivalent-positives (those already emotionally torn) may respond more favorably to jamming and conversion techniques, in addition to desensitization. If this reasoning is correct, then we can assign different propaganda objectives to specific target segments of the population. Mind you, all these objectives could be achieved by a campaign focused on Ambivalent Skeptics:

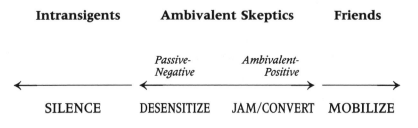

Intransigents	Ambivalent Skeptics		Friends
	Passive-Negative	Ambivalent-Positive	
SILENCE	DESENSITIZE	JAM/CONVERT	MOBILIZE

PRINCIPLE 3. KEEP TALKING

> *The mind of the bigot is like the pupil of the eye: the more light you pour on it, the more it will contract.*
>
> —O. W. HOLMES, JR.

The third principle is our recipe for desensitizing Ambivalent Skeptics; that is, for helping straights view homosexuality with neutrality rather than keen hostility. At least at the outset, we seek desensitization *and nothing more.* You can forget about trying right up front to persuade folks that homosexuality is a *good* thing. But if you can get them to think it is just *another* thing—meriting no more than a shrug of the shoulders—then your battle for legal and social rights is virtually won.

Application of the keep-talking principle can get people to the shoulder-shrug stage. The free and frequent discussion of gay rights by a variety of persons in a variety of places gives the impression that homosexuality is commonplace. That impression is essential, because, as noted in the previous chapter, the acceptability of any new behavior ultimately hinges on the proportion of one's fellows accepting or doing it. One may be offended by its novelty at first. Many, in decades past, were initially scandalized by goldfish swallowing, high hemlines, premarital sex, and 'streaking.' But as long as the behavior remains popular and Joe Sixpack feels neither physically nor financially threatened by it (and the gay lifestyle posed little threat in either regard until AIDS came along), he soon gets used to it, and life goes on. The conservative may still shake his head and think, 'People are crazy these days,' but in time his objections will become more reflective, more philosophical, less emotional.

The fastest way to convince straights that homosexuality is commonplace is to get a lot of people talking about the subject in a neutral or supportive way. Open, frank talk makes gayness seem less furtive, alien, and sinful; more aboveboard. Constant talk builds the impression that public opinion is at least divided on the subject, and that a sizable bloc—the most modern, up-to-date citizens—accept or even practice homosexuality. Though risky (because it can keenly arouse, and thereby reinforce, the homohatred ingrained in listeners), even serious debate between opponents and defenders can serve the purpose of desensitization so long as appealing gays are front and center to make their own pitch. The main thing is to *talk about gayness until the issue becomes thoroughly tiresome.*

And when we say *talk* about homosexuality, we mean just that. In the early stages of the campaign, the public should not be shocked and repelled by premature exposure to homo*sexual* behavior itself. Instead, the imagery of sex per se should be downplayed, and the issue of gay rights reduced, as far as possible, to an abstract social question. As it happens, the AIDS epidemic—ever a curse and boon for the gay movement—provides ample opportunity to emphasize the civil rights/discrimination side of things, but unfortunately it also permits our enemies to draw attention to gay sex habits that provoke public revulsion.

Would a campaign of open, sustained talk about gay issues be enough? Could talk alone, for example, quell the religious heebie-jeebies felt by many Ambivalent Skeptics and played upon by Intransigents? Not completely, and this remains a grave tactical difficulty. While public opinion is one important source of mainstream values, religious training in childhood is another. Yet two things *can* be done to confound the homohatred of the moderately religious.

First, gays can use talk to muddy the moral waters, that is, to undercut the rationalizations that 'justify' religious bigotry and to jam some of its psychic rewards. This entails publicizing support by moderate churches and raising serious theological objections to conservative biblical teachings. It also means exposing the inconsistency and hatred underlying antigay doctrines. Conservative churches, which pay as much lip service to Christian charity as anybody else, are rendered particularly vulnerable by their callous hypocrisy regarding AIDS sufferers.

Second, gays can undermine the moral authority of homohating churches over less fervent adherents by portraying such institutions as antiquated backwaters, badly out of step with the times and with the latest findings of psychology. Against the atavistic tug of Old Time Religion one must set the mightier pull of Science and Public Opinion (the shield and sword of that accursed 'secular humanism'). Such an 'unholy' alliance has already worked well in America against churches, on such topics as divorce and abortion. With enough open talk about the prevalence and acceptability of homosexuality, that alliance can work for gays.

Where we talk is critical. We'll discuss specific media tactics shortly. It suffices here to recall that the visual media—television, films, magazines—are the most powerful image makers in Western civilization. For example, in the average American household, the TV screen radiates its embracing bluish glow for more than fifty hours every week, bringing films, sitcoms, talk shows, and news reports right into the living room. These hours are a gateway into the private world of straights, through which a Trojan horse might be passed. For once, Marshall McLuhan is right: where desensitization is concerned, the medium *is* the message . . . of normalcy.

PRINCIPLE 4. KEEP THE MESSAGE FOCUSED: YOU'RE A HOMOSEXUAL, NOT A WHALE

If desensitization is to work, it mustn't be weakened by admixture with superfluous issues that might further upset or distract ordinary Americans. So when we say 'talk about homosexuality,' we mean *talk about gay rights issues and nothing more: be single-minded.* The gay community must explode a multitude of nasty stereotypes of itself, and must accomplish this Augean task with a painfully limited fund of dollars and credibility. We literally cannot afford to introduce additional prejudices into the picture by allying our movement with that of every other righteous cause in the political universe.

Yet this is exactly what our leaders have long done. Those drawn to gay activism seem inclined to regard themselves less as hardboiled lobbyists for a particular interest group than as philosophical crusaders for a grand panoptic program to inaugurate the Age of Aquarius—with harmony and understanding for all. In this, the American gay movement shows its 1969 vintage and its predilection for wishful thinking all too plainly. (Or perhaps its schemes for radical social reform trace their inspiration back to the lesbian dual agenda, mixing gay rights with desiderata for the root-and-branch transformation of our male chauvinist society.)

Typically, Wayne Olson exhorts fellow activists, in a 1986 *Christopher Street* article, with the following bad advice:

> Show throughout [public debates on gay rights] that you identify with all those who are persecuted unjustly, that you advocate rights for all human beings, not just homosexuals. Talk about racism, sexism, militarism, poverty, and all the conditions that oppress the unempowered. A victory for any oppressed group is a victory for all.

Because of such thinking, any and all fellow outcasts are embraced as political partners, and the gay community has filled its dance card with a 'rainbow coalition' of society's underdogs and benevolent but offbeat causes. Our activists have waltzed from one political issue to the next, publicly committing our movement to solidarity with the Sandinistas, animal protection leagues, migrant farm workers, Trotskyite revolutionaries, the Fat Persons' Liberation Front, the anti-apartheid movement, the antinuclear movement, and the Greenpeace Save-the-Whales campaign, to name a very few. They speak at our rallies, we speak at their rallies (though less frequently), and everyone has a delightfully militant time.

While some of these causes may indeed be noble, not one of them is directly concerned with the issue of homosexuality. Not one of them is even a "natural ally" of gays, if by that term is meant "someone who is happy we [gays] are here, rather than someone who is unhappy at the way we are being treated." As Michael Denneny has rightly perceived, "We have no natural allies and therefore cannot rely on the assistance of any group. We have only tactical allies—people who do not want barbarous things done to us because they fear the same thing may someday be done to them."

Not surprisingly, our motley little crew of foul-weather friends appreciates our support but is generally restrained in reciprocation on behalf of the gay cause. In any case, none of them has much clout or good will with the American public. On the contrary, even though gays constitute a far larger and broader constituency than any of these, association with other marginal groups only reinforces the mainstream's suspicion that gays are another microfaction on the lunatic fringe.

How can straights be expected to take gay rights seriously, when gay activists seem just as passionately devoted to a bulging grab-bag of utterly extraneous causes as they are to their own? What are straights to make of the following cobbled-together chants, all shouted vigorously during the 1988 Gay Pride March in New York City? "Cruise men, not missiles;" "The people fight back from Stonewall to South Africa;" "Gays yes, Contras no;" "Gay lib through atheist lib;" "End racism, sexism, and war/ Money for

AIDS/ We won't take no more;" "First dogs and monkeys too/Next time they'll cut into you." From what we could see, straight on-lookers at the march were variously bewildered, bemused, or annoyed by these *non sequitur* protests. One of them reacted with eloquent simplicity: "I don't get it." Clearly, while it might be comforting and kind to link arms with the wider losers' circle in American society, we do little thereby to advance our cause.

As a practical rule of thumb, then, gay organizations (and their media strategists) are advised to think twice about public association with any group that is:

- generally unpopular;
- smaller than the gay community; and/or
- concerned with issues remote from, and more ephemeral than, those that must permanently concern the gay community.

Because our movement must first grow stronger before it can help its still weaker friends, we recommend a rule for public alliance that is tough and selfish. But that rule doesn't favor insularity: the movement should eagerly ally itself with large, mainstream groups that can actually advance our interests (e.g., the Democratic Party, the National Organization for Women, or the Presbyterian Church). But even then, we should demand to see some major public demonstration of their commitment to our cause before we rush to commit to theirs.

Unless and until such bold alliances materialize, however, the bottom line remains: be *focused* in your efforts to reach the public via mass media. In the minds of straights, we must be gay people, not leftists or whales. So talk, talk, talk about gay rights, and leave it at that. (Feel free to agitate for any other cause you like, of course, but do so while wearing another hat.) And downplay any support from outgroups whose very names are likely to arouse suspicion and antipathy. Otherwise, desensitization will be all the harder to achieve.

PRINCIPLE 5. PORTRAY GAYS AS VICTIMS OF CIRCUMSTANCE AND OPPRESSION, NOT AS AGGRESSIVE CHALLENGERS

In any campaign to win over the public, gays must be portrayed as victims in need of protection so that straights will be inclined by reflex to adopt the role of protector. If gays present themselves, instead, as a strong and arrogant tribe promoting a defiantly nonconformist lifestyle, they are more likely to be seen as a public menace that warrants resistance and oppression. For that reason, we must forego the temptation to strut our gay pride publicly to such an extent that we undermine our victim image. And we must walk the fine line between impressing straights with our great numbers, on the one hand, and igniting their hostile paranoia—'They're all around us!'—on the other.

The purpose of victim imagery is to make straights feel very uncomfortable; that is, to jam with shame the self-righteous pride that would ordinarily accompany and reward their antigay belligerence, and to lay groundwork for the process of conversion by helping straights identify with gays and sympathize with their underdog status.

To this end, an effective media campaign would make use of symbols and spokespersons that reduce the straight majority's sense of threat and induce it to lower its guard. Mr. and Mrs. Public must be given no extra excuses to say, 'They are not like us (so they deserve to be punished).' Persons featured in the media campaign should be wholesome and admirable by straight standards, and completely unexceptional in appearance; in a word, they should be indistinguishable from the straights we'd like to reach.

In practical terms, this means that cocky mustachioed leathermen, drag queens, and bull dykes would not appear in gay commercials and other public presentations. Conventional young people, middle-aged women, and older folks of all races would be featured, not to mention the parents and straight friends of gays.

One could also argue that lesbians should be featured more promi-
nently than gay men in the early stages of the media campaign.
Straights generally have fewer and cloudier preconceptions about
lesbians and may feel less hostile toward them. And *as women*
(generally seen as less threatening and more vulnerable than
men), lesbians may be more credible objects of sympathy.

It cannot go without saying, incidentally, that groups on the
farthest margins of acceptability, such as NAMBLA, must play no
part at all in such a campaign. Suspected child molesters will
never look like victims.

Now, two different messages about the Gay Victim are worth
communicating. First, the public should be persuaded that gays
are *victims of circumstance,* that they no more chose their sexual
orientation than they did, say, their height, skin color, talents, or
limitations. (We argue that, for all practical purposes, gays should
be considered to have been *born gay*—even though sexual orientation, for most humans, seems to be the product of a complex
interaction between innate predispositions and environmental
factors during childhood and early adolescence.) To suggest in
public that homosexuality might be *chosen* is to open the can of
worms labeled 'moral choice and sin' and give the religious Intransigents a stick to beat us with. Straights must be taught that it
is as natural for some persons to be homosexual as it is for others
to be heterosexual: wickedness and seduction have nothing to do
with it. *And since no choice is involved, gayness can be no more blame-
worthy than straightness.* In fact, it is simply a matter of the odds—
one in ten—as to who turns out gay, and who straight. Each heterosexual must be led to realize that he might easily have been
born homosexual himself.

Second, gays should be portrayed as *victims of prejudice.* Straights
don't fully realize the suffering they bring upon gays, and must be
shown: graphic pictures of brutalized gays, dramatizations of job
and housing insecurity, loss of child custody, public humiliation,
etc. (For the complete and dismal list, see our Agenda for Change
at the end of Chapter 1.)

Bear in mind that these arguments are no more than an appeal to rationality and as such would scarcely make a dent in an emotional condition like homohatred. What arguments can do, however, is suspend the straight viewer's rush to judgment just long enough to slip in front of her visual images that either arouse shame over her homohatred or else build favorable emotions toward gays.

More than any other single element of our blueprint for a media campaign, this principle of Victim Imagery has been criticized by the gay community. Few have questioned whether it will have the desired effect on straights; we are convinced it will. But some are offended, even so, by the proposition that gays should be portrayed as victims. They fear that this will make our community look weak, miserable, and self-hating, equating homosexuality with some dreadful disease that strikes fated 'victims.' If gays point out that they never chose to be gay, it is claimed, this implies they would rather not be gay, and so suggests that gays themselves view homosexuality as a bad thing. All very negative for the community's self-image.

We can only reply that gays indisputably *are* victims of circumstance, regardless of whether their leaders pretend otherwise. A victim of circumstance is someone thrust by events into a tough spot—like a black child who happens upon a gang of racists. The child has every reason to be proud of his identity but also has good cause to remind his persecutors that there is no sense or justice in condemning him for his skin color. The campaign can and should make this distinction clear.

It's nonsense to claim, as some do, that a person who acknowledges himself in any way a victim thereby accepts that condition and *becomes* a victim; such is merely magical thinking. Nor is it true that straights will look down on gays more than they already do, simply because we have managed to arouse in them feelings of shame for past bigotry and a new protectiveness toward the gay community. This has not happened to the Jews, who have effectively leveraged widespread sympathy for themselves as past victims of circumstance. The plain fact is that the gay community, like the Jewish, is a permanent minority: it is weak and must deploy the special powers of the weak, including the play for sympathy and tolerance. The arousal of protective instincts doesn't require that homosexuality be cast in a negative light.

Others worry that, by our techniques, gays will gain the world but lose their souls. They fear that victim imagery will mean that homosexuals, who have struggled so long to get beyond guilt and self-hatred, must now forego self-affirmation and smother their gay pride. After all, gay pride parades can be wonderfully positive exercises for their participants, even if their excesses disturb straight onlookers.

We recommend a compromise: *march, if you must, but don't parade.* Drop the Mardi Gras foolishness and assemble yourselves into a proud, dedicated legion of freedom fighters, like the civil rights marchers of the '60s. Such marches would certainly enable gay self-affirmation yet would be taken more seriously by straights. Don't expect too much, though.

For some critics, it isn't so much the idea of victim imagery that offends, but *whom* we will present as victims: all-American types so starchily conformist in appearance that they can barely bend their knees, let alone stoop to fellatio. Some fear that a media campaign featuring only 'ordinary-looking' gays would disdain-fully disenfranchise drag queens, bull dykes, and other exotic elements of the gay community. This is not our goal, and it is painful to think that such people might begin to feel like second-class members of their own outgroup.

Our ultimate objective is to expand straight tolerance so much that even gays who look unconventional can feel safe and accepted. But like it or not, by the very nature of the psychological mechanism, desensitization works gradually or not at all. For the moment, therefore, unconventional-looking gays are encouraged to live their lives as usual, but out of the limelight. Drag queens must understand that the gay stereotype is already heavily skewed in their direction, and that more balance should be achieved by leaning in the opposite direction for a while. In time, as hostilities subside and stereotypes weaken, we see no reason why more and more diversity should not be introduced into the projected image. This would be healthy for society as well as for gays.

PRINCIPLE 6. GIVE POTENTIAL PROTECTORS A JUST CAUSE

The Waging Peace media campaign will reach straights on an emotional level, casting gays as society's victims and inviting straights to be their protectors. For this to work, however, we must make it easier for responsive straights to assert and explain their new protective feelings. Few straight women, and fewer straight men, will be bold enough to defend homosexuality per se. Most would rather attach their awakened protective impulse to some principle of justice or law, some general desire for consistent and fair treatment in society.

Thus, our campaign should not demand explicit support for ho*mosexual* practices, but should instead take *antidiscrimination* as its theme. Fundamental freedoms, constitutional rights, due process and equal protection of laws, basic fairness and decency toward all of humanity—these should be the concerns brought to mind by our campaign.

It's especially important for the gay movement to hitch its cause to pre-existing standards of law and justice, because its straight supporters must have at hand a cogent reply to the moralistic arguments of its enemies. Homohaters cloak their emotional revulsion in the daunting robes of religious dogma, so defenders of gay rights must be ready to counter dogma with principle. Thrice armed is he who hath his quarrel just.

PRINCIPLE 7. MAKE GAYS LOOK GOOD

In order to make a Gay Victim sympathetic to straights, you have to portray him as Everyman. But an additional theme of the campaign will be more aggressive and upbeat. To confound bigoted stereotypes and hasten the conversion of straights, strongly favorable images of gays must be set before the public. The campaign should paint gay men and lesbians as *superior*—veritable pillars of society.

Yes, yes, we know, this trick is so old it creaks. Other minorities have used it often, in ads that proudly exclaim, 'Did you know that this Great Man was Thuringian (or whatever)?' But the message is vital for all those straights who still picture gays as 'queer' losers—shadowy, lonesome, frail, drunken, suicidal, child-snatching misfits.

The honor roll of prominent gay or bisexual men and women is truly eye-popping. From Socrates to Eleanor Roosevelt, Tchaikovsky to Bessie Smith, Alexander the Great to Alexander Hamilton, and Leonardo da Vinci to Walt Whitman, the list of suspected 'inverts' is old hat to us but surprising news to heterosexual America. Famous historical figures are especially useful to us for two reasons: first, they are invariably dead as a doornail, hence in no position to deny the truth and sue for libel. Second, and more serious, the virtues and accomplishments that make these historic gay figures admirable cannot be gainsaid or dismissed by the public, since high school history textbooks have already set them in incontrovertible cement. By casting its violet spotlight on such revered heroes, in no time a skillful media campaign could have the gay community looking like the veritable fairy godmother to Western civilization.

Along the same lines, our campaign should not overlook the Celebrity Endorsement. The celebrities in question can, of course, be either straight or gay (and alive, for a change), but must always be well liked and respected by the public. If homosexual, the celebrity jams homohatred by presenting a favorable gay image at odds with the stereotype. If straight, the spokesperson (who deserves the Medal of Valor) provides the public with an impressive role model of social tolerance to emulate. In either case, the psychological response among straights is the same, and lays the groundwork for conversion:

I like and admire Mr. Celeb;
Mr. Celeb is queer and/or respects queers;

so either I must stop liking and admiring Mr. Celeb, or else it must be all right for me to respect queers.

PRINCIPLE 8. MAKE VICTIMIZERS LOOK BAD

The real target here is not victimizers themselves but the homohatred that impels them. Understand this point clearly: while it will be a sheer delight to besmirch our tormentors, we cannot waste resources or media access on revenge alone (indeed, the media will not *allow* us to do so). The objective is to make homohating beliefs and actions look so nasty that average Americans will want to dissociate themselves from them. This, of course, is a variant on the process of jamming. We also intend, by this tactic, to make the very expression of homohatred so discreditable that even Intransigents will eventually be silenced in public— much as rabid racists and anti-Semites are today.

The best way to make homohatred look bad is to vilify those who victimize gays. The public should be shown images of ranting homohaters whose associated traits and attitudes appall and anger Middle America. The images might include:

- Klansmen demanding that gays be slaughtered or castrated;
- Hysterical backwoods preachers, drooling with hate to a degree that looks both comical and deranged;
- Menacing punks, thugs, and convicts who speak coolly about the 'fags' they have bashed or would like to bash;
- A tour of Nazi concentration camps where homosexuals were tortured and gassed.

In TV and print, images of victimizers can be combined with those of their gay victims by a method propagandists call the 'bracket technique.' For example, for several seconds an unctuous beady-eyed Southern preacher is shown pounding the pulpit in rage against 'those perverted, abominable creatures.' While his tirade continues over the soundtrack, the picture switches to heart-rending photos of badly beaten persons, or of gays who look decent, harmless, and likable; and then we cut back to the poisonous face of the preacher. The contrast speaks for itself. The effect is devastating.

The viewer will ordinarily recoil from these images of victimizers, thinking automatically: 'I don't like those maniacs, don't want to be like them, and would be ashamed if others thought I was like them. Surely I'm more compassionate and sophisticated, because I don't share their irrational hatred of gays.' Every time a viewer runs through this comparative self-appraisal, he reinforces a self-definition that consciously rejects homohatred and validates sympathy for gay victims. Exactly what we want.

A campaign to vilify victimizers will only enrage our most fervid enemies, of course. Yet the shoe surely fits, and we should make them try it on for size, with all America watching. Gay media strategists must, however, try to slide the slipper on very gradually. At least at the beginning, the broadcast media—which have not yet permitted gays even to say nice things about themselves on the air—certainly will not allow any direct attacks on archconservatives. On the other hand, they just might permit some mention of Nazi atrocities, the pink triangle as a symbol of victimization, and so forth. If so, the Nazi story alone will be a sufficient opening wedge into the vilification of our enemies. After all, who on earth would choose to be associated with the Nazis? (Argentina doesn't count.)

SUMMARY: STRATEGIC PRINCIPLES FOR THE PERSUASION OF STRAIGHTS

We have reviewed the range of public-outreach strategies commonly touted by gays. Like zealous prosecutors, we've rounded up all the usual suspects, studied their trial records, and concluded with disappointment that none of the most popular strategies can be promptly, effectively executed.

So, instead, we propose our own strategy for a large-scale media campaign, whose objectives and reasoning are expressed in terms of eight practical principles for persuading straights:

1. Don't just express yourself: communicate!
2. Appeal to the Ambivalent Skeptics.
3. Keep talking about gayness.
4. Keep your message focused: the issue is homosexuality.
5. Portray gays as victims, not as aggressive challengers.
6. Give potential protectors a just cause.
7. Make gays look good.
8. Make victimizers look bad.

Do these strategic principles seem straightforward, even a bit bland? Perhaps, but just try—as we do in the next chapter—to develop p.r. events and TV commercials that obey all the rules, and you'll see what a challenge they present. Any ten-year-old can balance a spinning plate on her finger; it takes a preternaturally clever Chinese acrobat to balance eight of them at once.

4

○　　　○　　　○　　　○　　　○

TACTICS FOR
EATING
THE MEDIA ALIVE:
A SOUND BITE
HERE,
A SOUND BITE
THERE

Strategy is a series of makeshifts.
—VON MOLTKE, *ESSAY ON STRATEGY,* 1871

I n the last chapter, to make a point, we abandoned you to a
tribe of cannibals. This time, we've reached into our old
cedar chest of hackneyed metaphors and, *voilà!:* you find
yourself stranded on a desert island . . . *with* the cannibals. (As
your hosts, we realize that this is rather shabby treatment, but we
want to teach you a lesson you'll never forget.) Stuck in this predicament, you have doubtless chosen a Strategy: survival. But it's
hardly enough: you also need Tactics. As your dining companions
chase you down the beach, inevitably you come across a bottle
(with pen and paper), and then, coincidentally, espy a ship steam-
ing along the horizon. Looking, in turn, at the natives, bottle, and
ship, you suddenly develop a keen practical interest in the fine
points of Public Relations, News Reporting, and Advertising—
three media tactics whose arcane details interest only those in
desperate need. But that includes you, and it also includes the gay
community, which must master its public image in order to survive. Peruse this chapter, therefore, as though your (gay) life de-

pended on it; conquer the media, and you'll soon have the savages on the run.

The Waging Peace Campaign uses all three basic routes to public outreach: newsmaking and reporting, p.r. tactics, and paid or unpaid advertising. Because they permit gays to reach the broadest audience with the most carefully controlled message, advertising tactics are of greatest interest to us—indeed, we end the chapter with a portfolio of possible ads. But we'll briefly discuss the other tactics first, as they're generally less expensive and easier to initiate than advertising. No wonder gay activists come back to them again and again.

o

MAKING NEWS AND IMPROVING PUBLIC RELATIONS

GAY NEWS MAKES LOUD NOISE! READ ALL ABOUT IT!

Americans have an insatiable appetite for whatever public events the press sets before them—"newspaper gossip," as Thoreau liked to call it—the more scandalous, the better; and this has given our activists their opening. At both the national and the local level, gay organizations have quietly begun to cultivate liaisons with broadcast companies and newsrooms in the hope of seeing issues important to the gay community receive some coverage.

This has not been easy; society would still rather look in almost any other direction than at homosexuality. Even so, gays have learned to assemble press lists, issue news releases, circulate background reports, and hold press conferences. They have trained spokesmen and offered their services to news-analysis programs. Local gay organizations have begun to set up annual meetings with station heads and issue 'report cards' on their good or not-so-good performance. (For a primer on these tactics, see *Talk Back! The Gay Person's Guide to Media Action,* by Boston's Lesbian and Gay Media Advocates.) Correspondingly, the sensation-hungry press has learned, bit by bit, to use the information resources our community offers. Interaction between activists and the straight press has, of course, been strengthened by the persistence of AIDS as a newsworthy item.

But that such increased interaction had to await a crisis like AIDS reveals two inherent drawbacks to news reporting. First, reliance on crises means that the gay community's image is controlled by the latest news event instead of by careful design—and most gay-related stories are deemed newsworthy by the straight press only when sensationally negative (AIDS, sex scandals, etc.). Such stories can hardly be said to desensitize the public. Second, most news services (including both straight broadcasters and the gay information outlets that supply them) do not see progay propaganda as a top priority or even a responsibility. Some gay news services are actually trying to reach other gays, not straights, via public broadcast (e.g., to give them helpful information on AIDS prevention). Others limit their function to that of a watchdog, monitoring the straight press for homophobic distortions or slurs.

WHAT DISTURBS US ABOUT PUBLIC DISTURBANCES.

Impatient with straight neglect and indifference, some activists have gone a step further by making their own news through staged media events, mainly marches, rallies, boycotts, and demonstrations. Although such events can, in theory, provide propagandistic benefits, they seldom live up to their potential. If reported by the straight press, these events do help combat the Big Lie by showing hundreds or thousands of homosexuals coming out of the woodwork. But activists repeatedly violate Persuasion Principle 1 by trying to accomplish two things at once: unbridled self-expression *and* public outreach. Thus, gay pride marches for self-affirmation tend to degenerate before the TV cameras into ghastly freak shows, courtesy of newsmen seeking 'human interest material' and gender benders who think the mental health of uptight straight viewers is improved by visual shock therapy. Because such therapy is far and away the favorite approach of many activists, we've gone to lengths to explain why it fails in psychological terms (Chapter 2) and strategic terms (Chapter 3); now we'll review its pitfalls in tactical terms.

Even orderly acts of symbolic civil disobedience are often misread by the straight press and its audience, who tend to construe the most peaceful events disagreeably, as antisocial, troublesome, and implicitly violent. For example, in March 1988 New York City's AIDS Coalition To Unleash Power (ACT UP) sought to draw attention to the plight of the disease's sufferers. ACT UP held a spirited demonstration that blocked traffic in the Wall Street district of Manhattan. But the headline carried that evening on local news shows was that a number of gay protesters had been arrested for "disturbing the peace" and "disorderly conduct."

Because they're almost always viewed negatively by outsiders, we remain skeptical of the ultimate value of protest marches and the like. Still, it's *conceivable* that carefully organized public displays of civil disobedience could be a useful part of gay outreach to the straight community. As Bayard Rustin has argued, "You have to get people to believe that you are sincere, . . . and that you are willing to pay a price—even willing to go to jail—to get your rights." Civil disobedience might help convince the public of our seriousness, *if* conducted under a number of strict guidelines (many of them set forth in a thoughtful 1987 essay by *Advocate* writer Mark Vandervelden).

First, it must look enough like a *mass event* to warrant media attention. Without sufficiently numerous participants, the impression conveyed is of a few cranky eccentrics—exactly what we *don't* want.

Second, the behavior of gays must be completely *nonviolent;* participants must hope that onlookers are not. As explained by one trainer in civil disobedience tactics, "When the other side reacts [violently], it becomes clear to the public at large which side the problem is with. But if you come to a demonstration with clenched fists, yelling and screaming . . . and swinging at cops, then it is unclear where the problem is." If the press correctly reports an attack on gay protesters, this reinforces 'gay victim' imagery (Persuasion Principle 4).

Third, the disobedient act must be portrayed as a *last resort,* undertaken by aggrieved gay citizens who have exhausted all other remedies. (Otherwise, these citizens will be viewed as mere troublemakers.)

Fourth, the viewing public must somehow be helped to understand that gay protesters—as a measure of their ethical convictions—accept and *expect arrest;* they're not just out to break laws and be disruptive.

Fifth, and related, the public must understand the *logical connection* between the gay right at issue and the particular act of civil disobedience adopted.

Perhaps you can see now why we're so nervous about civil disobedience as a persuasive tool. It's hard enough to make others understand your actions when they're standing right there on the sidelines; it's almost impossible to convey all this information accurately to the public when the message must be relayed and edited by (straight) television news teams, and then presented as a 'news bite' lasting one minute or less. Not surprisingly, the takeaway is usually just 'more disorderly conduct.'

LET ME ENTERTAIN YOU: PUBLIC-RELATIONS TACTICS.

Mass demonstrations are merely one type of p.r. tactic. There are many other ways to get attention and, for that matter, to manufacture news. Some gays start small, like the folks who—evidently intent upon undercutting the Big Lie—posted shiny round stickers declaring "A Homosexual Was Here" across greater metropolitan Boston . . . but posted them *in public toilet stalls,* of all stereotypic places (an example of a good idea misapplied). Other stout-hearted gays stand in shopping malls and distribute booklets, brochures, and flyers by hand.

Still others aim to get their message onto local or nationally syndicated TV and radio talk shows, which thrive on controversial subjects such as homosexuality and AIDS. Indeed, the three topics that shows such as *Donahue* and *Oprah* cover with the greatest regularity are sex, health, and money; so gay activists begin with one foot (or perhaps two out of three) in the door. Public-relations experts suggest a range of generic get-on techniques that publicists for the gay cause may as well keep in mind:

- *Creative Formatting.* Face it: as 'perversions' go these days, homosexuality is old hat on the talk-show circuit. It's no longer enough that you're gay, and willing to admit it before 20 million housewives; surely the program producer and host have heard it all before. To be invited onto a show, therefore, gay spokespersons need a fresh angle, a way to make their gay-rights argument more topical.

- *Use News to Make News.* For instance, gay spokespersons can offer to respond to a new law, court case, death, or scandal. They may announce or discuss the results of a recent opinion survey or study (e.g., on antigay violence). They can schedule their TV appearance around another gay media event, such as National Coming Out Day, or some public anniversary of symbolic importance to gays (Stonewall, the *Hardwick* decision, etc.). They can give awards that make good publicity.

- *Human Interest.* Although you'll appear on a talk show ostensibly to discuss some public issue, hosts and their audiences are usually more interested in the human, personal side of your story, so be prepared. Relate your own encounters with bigotry and discrimination. But watch out for hosts who try to spice things up, luring gays into explicit sexual tattle to titillate and scandalize their audience. (Indeed, certain circuses of ridicule, such as the *Morton Downey Jr. Show,* exist only to spill the malodorous guts of their guests before a colosseum of whooping yahoos. Unless you're determined to disgrace your cause, avoid such shows.)

- *Celebrity Spokespersons.* Because a celebrity does not simply make news—she *is* news—she can get on the air and tout the gay cause relatively easily, without further pretext. *Finding* credible straight or gay celebrities to speak about homosexual rights, however, is the problem. (Ed Asner? Marlo Thomas? Barney Frank? The list of forthright liberals peters out rapidly thereafter.)

In addition to these pointers, our own eight principles for persuading straights apply in full to talk show appearances and similar p.r. tactics. It's especially important that gay spokespersons look fundamentally indistinguishable from the straights they'd like to reach, so that there is a greater sense of common ground between speaker and listeners. This advice was recently ignored by a lesbian who chose to debate with a vociferous antigay minister on a public-television program, *Tony Brown's Journal.* The host, his house audience, and the minister were black; the show was a black-oriented public-affairs program. The lesbian, on the other hand, a white yuppie, looked strikingly out of place. Although she held her own on discussion points, she was very coolly received by an audience that could not easily relate to her. *Caveat vendor.*

In sum, newsmaking and public-relations tactics can make vital contributions to public outreach if they follow the suggested guidelines. Unfortunately, these tactics are inadequate, by themselves, to reverse straight prejudices. News events and talk shows are too sporadic and leave too much to chance; they don't give us our best shot at positive-image management. To attack homohatred directly via desensitization, jamming, and conversion, we need a gay advertising campaign.

○

ADVERTISING TACTICS FOR THE CAMPAIGN

> *I cannot think of any circumstances in which advertising would not be an evil.*
> —ARNOLD TOYNBEE

> *The general raising of the standards of modern civilization . . . during the past half century would have been impossible without . . . advertising.*
> —FRANKLIN D. ROOSEVELT

Until they think carefully about it, people invariably agree with Toynbee, not Roosevelt. Anyone with any intellectual pride hates advertising on principle. Advertising is patently commercial; it stoops to conquer; it panders to our lowest instincts; it treats us like idiots. No wonder we've seen more than a few activists roll their eyes at the notion of a gay ad campaign. But we've also found, upon inquiry, that persons who claim to be morally offended by the crass practice of advertising good causes—shilling them like toothpaste or laxatives—are usually mistaken. What actually offends them is not the *tactic* of advertising, but the particular message being conveyed.

By now you know our message and either do or don't accept it. All that remains is to show you how this message can be most effectively conveyed through paid and unpaid advertising. Let's start with two fundamental, and related, objectives: (1) getting into the mass media, and (2) desensitizing the public about gay issues. Accomplishing the first with any frequency will contribute mightily to the second, because gay advertising in mainstream media suggests that gay issues themselves are becoming mainstream. For our purposes, however, not all mass media are created equal, so we provide you, below, with a concise consumer's guide to the alternatives.

THE BIG FIVE MEDIA: WHICH ARE RIGHT FOR US?

You can count the basic media on one hand: television, radio, magazines, newspapers, and 'outdoor,' which means billboards, subway posters, et al. (We're tempted to add a sixth medium, 'direct mail'—a.k.a. junk mail—but that expensive technique is usually reserved for fundraising appeals to Friends, not Ambivalent Skeptics.) Which media are right for gay advertising?

Television. You probably already suspect that television is our first choice, but may wonder why. First, its breadth of audience is unparalleled. Because virtually every household owns a TV set and watches it daily, television reaches more of the public than any other medium. (On an average day, one fourth of all American households tune in by 9 A.M., and nearly two thirds are watching by 9 P.M.) So long as you stay away from PBS and other upper-crust programming, the audience is a thorough mixture of lower- and middle-class Americans, of all ages, races, and creeds. Plenty of Ambivalent Skeptics are watching.

We like television, second, because it's the most graphic and *intrusive* medium for our message. In everyday life, intrusiveness is considered impolite; but not in public communications, where nine tenths of the challenge is simply getting people's attention. If one hears a lot of yowling about bad TV commercials, it is because, like a poke in the eye with a sharp stick, they have a way of getting to even the most resistant viewers. Remember that we need to change the picture in the picture/label pair that represents us in the public's mind. To this end, television is the most cogent medium, combining sight, sound, and motion to make new pictures so vivid that they can displace the old.

The main limitation of the medium is its sky's-the-limit cost to advertisers. Sixty seconds of Super Bowl airtime, for example, can cost sponsors more than $1 million. (And some spend as much or more just to *produce* their commercial, before it even gets on the air.) About 60% of all TV viewing goes to the networks. ABC, NBC, CBS, and Fox represent most of the thousand or so commercial stations in the country, and buying time on these networks is painfully expensive. Either gay activists will have to develop a war chest of many millions each year or they will have to scale down their targeted audience. Starting with a less opulent budget, gay advertisers may wish to consider sponsoring only local spot-TV airtime, cable channels, or syndicated shows.

Radio. Often neglected, this is the 'other broadcast medium.' There are nearly nine thousand radio stations in operation, reaching four out of five Americans over age twelve every day. What we like about radio is that it is an *intimate* medium. People usually listen to the radio at bedside, puttering around the house, or driving to work—times when they're alone with their thoughts. In these settings, with nobody else watching them, listeners may not feel compelled to dismiss out of hand a message for gay rights. Furthermore, the cost of airing each radio commercial is quite low (relative to TV time) on any given station. This means that if gays can settle upon a few radio stations or networks, they can afford to expose listeners repeatedly to their message.

But there are several things we don't like about radio. Obviously, it is not a visual medium (though it can sometimes evoke mental pictures quite effectively). And it's primarily a passive, background medium; it rarely has the listener's full attention—hasn't had it, in fact, since the days of FDR's Fireside Chats. Moreover, the medium is extremely narrow. Each station reaches only a tiny fraction of the public—the fraction that happens to like a particular programming format (rock, classical, country, talk radio, etc.). Thus, while using radio makes it easier to screen out certain types (e.g., Intransigents listening to religious stations), gay advertisers would have to use a great many stations of various kinds to reach the broad target we have in mind. Trying to build a big audience through radio is like trying to get elected president by telephoning American voters one by one: better start your campaign ten years in advance and have an awesome roll of quarters.

Magazines. The same would be true of magazines, were it not for what advertisers call 'mass-reach books.' Each month, 95% of American adults read one or more of over fifteen hundred consumer-oriented magazines. Most magazines, however, are designed to interest only a small segment of the public. Gay activists may rightly wonder whether their dollars would be spent wisely in the likes of *Fly Fisherman, Air Combat,* or *Country Living.* One could go mad just trying to keep track of ad placement in so many small periodicals. The alternative is to concentrate gay media dollars in a handful of mass-circulation publications, such as *Time, People, Sports Illustrated, Reader's Digest,* and—hold your nose—the *National Enquirer.* For example, in 1986, a single issue of (alas, editorially conservative) *Reader's Digest* could reach about 40 million adults, almost one quarter of the adult population.

Magazines are good vehicles for the gay message, for several reasons. Magazine reading is a solitary pastime: the reader is generally paying attention and in a thoughtful frame of mind. Furthermore, a magazine ad provides what the pros call 'depth of sale': it lets gays tell their story to straights in more detail than is possible on TV or radio. And gays can ask to have their ad shown next to editorial columns that build interest or avoid uncomplimentary associations. (In *Newsweek,* for example, we may advertise in the "National Affairs" section, rather than in "Medicine" or "Lifestyle.")

A magazine campaign, you'll be relieved to learn, is generally more affordable than a TV blitz. On the other hand, the medium is less intrusive and packs less punch than television; its impact builds more slowly over time. Moreover, their affordability makes magazines the preferred vehicle for numerous public-service ads and cause-related appeals. The clutter and competition can be severe, and readers have become adept at focusing on editorial columns while screening out advertisements. Finally, many diverse (and patently wacko) groups are permitted to publish ads, so appearing in magazines does less to confer legitimacy upon one's cause than appearing on television can.

Newspapers. Newspapers do even less to build legitimacy than magazines. But gay strategists should consider newspapers anyway, because they're often more willing to accept political or controversial ads such as ours, and don't mind long, detailed advertising copy. Indeed, the daily paper is a natural medium for our issues-oriented ads, because readers are in a news-hungry, public-affairs-oriented frame of mind. Readers are plentiful, too: nearly two out of three adults examine a newspaper every day. And papers are browsed more thoroughly than magazines (although they aren't kept around as long).

The roughly seventeen hundred dailies offer geographic flexibility: their ad space can be purchased city by city, an important advantage if our media campaign is undertaken on a region-by-region basis, or administered piecemeal by local gay groups. But the sheer multitude of newspapers also makes a national campaign through this medium more pricey. For example, the cost in 1988 dollars for placing a single half-page black-and-white ad in the top three hundred newspapers, reaching 60% of U.S. homes, would add up to roughly $1 million. (And one may *need* to buy a half or full page just to be visible, since newspaper pages are densely cluttered.) It's almost enough to make one resort to sky-writing instead.

Outdoor. Which brings us to so-called outdoor advertising (i.e., advertising displayed to large groups in public areas). If you think billboards and subway placards are as cheap and worthless as they look, you're wrong. Outdoor advertising is actually expensive because it does such an excellent job of reaching a broad audience —everyone who commutes—over and over again, within a specific city or region. In just one month, for example, a well-placed series of billboards in a given community can reach 90% of its adult residents up to thirty times each.

The utility of outdoor ads depends on the advertiser's message: it must be very simple and benefit from being seen over and over. Gays have such a message. If the goal is to desensitize straights to homosexuality, this can be done in part by repeated exposure to billboards presenting an agreeable statement, plus the tag: A Message from Your National Gay and Lesbian Community. Driving to and from work each day, the average Joe or Jane will quickly get used to seeing the reassuring statement and the name of its sponsor. At current advertising rates, you could expose about half of all Americans to this message for one month, at a cost of roughly $4 million. For that kind of money, however, gays could blanket the biggest national magazines with ads, and see fewer of them defaced by spray-painted graffiti.

Which Medium? Our Conclusions. Over the long term, *television and magazines* are probably the two media of choice, the first for its persuasive power, the second for its greater affordability. Over the short term, we must choose any medium that will accept our ads, and that we can manage to pay for (except matchbook covers; there *are* limits). The regular appearance of gay advertisements in any one of the mass media will gradually break down the resistance of the rest. It's cash and carry in the ad biz, and sooner or later TV networks and magazine publishers will realize that gays, like everyone else, come to their doorstep dressed in green, not lavender.

GETTING INTO THE MAJOR MEDIA: CAN'T GET THERE FROM HERE

Even cash in hand, our community will find getting on air far from easy. We noted in Chapter 1 that broadcast (and, to a lesser extent, print) media are public resources privately owned. Broadcasting networks reserve the right to refuse any so-called controversy advertising they happen to dislike, including ours.

Government Rules. But what about freedom of speech, the right to equal time, and all that? Sorry, folks: you'll get little help from Uncle Sam in securing media access for gays. Congress created the Federal Communications Commission in the 1930s to regulate the use of scarce broadcasting bands in the "public interest, convenience and necessity." Evidently, it's proven convenient, even necessary, to the public interest to keep gays and other annoying, unempowered minorities off the airwaves. (Out of sight, out of mind.) Courts have decided that the First Amendment's protection of free speech, for the most part, protects broadcasters themselves from censorship or manipulation from outside; it doesn't guarantee that citizens such as ourselves will be given access to express themselves via broadcast.

True, there is a *Fairness Doctrine,* adopted by the FCC in 1959, under which the broadcaster is obliged to "afford reasonable opportunities for the discussion of conflicting views on issues of public importance." But the doctrine—which has, in any case, been regulated with increasing laxness in recent years—is a two-edged sword for our purposes. It lets broadcasters themselves choose which issues of "public importance" they'd like to handle. Not surprisingly, most would rather steer clear of sensitive subjects like homosexuality, where they'll be damned if they do and damned if they don't take a position.

Craig Davidson, executive director of the Gay and Lesbian Alliance Against Defamation, tells us that the current weakening of the Fairness Doctrine might actually work to the movement's advantage, since now broadcasters cannot as easily refuse giving airtime to gays on the pretext that, were they to do so, the doctrine would also require giving equal airtime to rabid homohaters.

Even if the broadcaster decides to enter the fray, the Fairness Doctrine leaves him in control of communications. He may decide which of several contrasting viewpoints to present, and may present all of them himself, if he wishes. The bottom line is that the broadcaster is under no obligation to let anyone else use his facilities for cause-related advertising or programming purposes.

Then there is the *Personal Attack Rule,* adopted by the FCC in 1967 to apply the Fairness Doctrine explicitly to certain circumstances. Whenever an identifiable person or organization has been attacked on air, the Personal Attack Rule requires that the station notify the attacked party, provide a tape or summary of the accusations, and give that party a reasonable opportunity to respond. The rule does not apply to political candidates, or to attacks launched during a news program.

The Personal Attack Rule could, in theory, provide gays with the needed leverage to get on air (though not via advertising). After all, homosexuals are continually under siege in the media. Yet, in practice, the rule has seldom been of use to us because gay individuals and groups are almost never specified outside news-type programs. It is far safer, and more to the purpose of general bigotry, to malign homosexuals in the aggregate, as a type. This is the practice among, for example, televangelists.

Finally, the federal government gives us the *Equal Time Rule.* It requires stations to provide equal time to all declared candidates for public office; if the station gives time to one, it must to all. (Once again, the rule doesn't apply to news-type programs.) Thus, the Equal Time Rule will only be helpful if gay activists are running for office . . . which gives us a provocative idea we'll discuss presently.

The upshot is that no federal communications regulation or constitutional protection guarantees the gay community the right to reach the public through advertisements, because ads must be placed in media vehicles (TV and radio channels, magazines, billboards) owned privately by others. With no Uncle Sam to hold the door open, gays will have to employ their own wiles to wedge it open, one foot at a time. We can proceed in several steps.

Step 1: A Loaf of White Bread, a Jug of Ink, and Thou.

It will be easiest to approach the print media first, encouraging magazines and newspapers to accept gay money by showing them ads whose messages are pure white bread—that is, completely unobjectionable and only obliquely concerned with homosexuality. At the same time, however, these ads must manage to get the word 'gay' into the headline or tagline. Ideally, straight Americans will begin to see them everywhere: small print ads (and, if we have the money, large highway billboards) that earnestly propound appealing truisms, the safer and more platitudinous, the better.

IN RUSSIA, THEY TELL YOU WHAT TO BE. IN AMERICA, WE HAVE THE FREEDOM TO BE OURSELVES . . . AND TO BE THE BEST

—*The* National Gay & Lesbian Community *proudly joins America in celebrating July 4.*

THREE THINGS MAKE AMERICA GREAT: DIVERSITY, FREEDOM, AND COMMUNITY
America, You Make *Us* Proud Too
—*Your National Gay and Lesbian Community*

PEOPLE HELPING INSTEAD OF
    HATING—
THAT'S WHAT AMERICA IS ALL
    ABOUT.

—*Your National Gay and Lesbian Community*

And so forth. Turns the stomach, doesn't it? But remember, mainstream Americans have been raised on a diet of precisely this sort of corn, to which they have the fondest of associations—so corn is what we'll feed them. In so doing, we not only desensitize them but transfer these fond associations to the gay label as well, with a fair prospect of converting a few Ambivalent Skeptics.

Long copy isn't necessary. But each brief message should tap public sentiment, patriotic or otherwise, and drill an unimpeachably agreeable proposition into mainstream heads—'a public service message' suited to our purposes. In this way, the public becomes accustomed to gay sponsorship in the media.

If these bland ads are refused by major magazines at the start, gays should try instead to place them in the 'prestige' news dailies

(New York Times, Los Angeles Times, Washington Post, and so forth), from which lesser publications take their cue as to "all the news that's fit to print," and all the ads, too. These newspaper ads can then be clipped out for presentation to hesitant magazines.

Whether advertising in magazines or newspapers, the idea here is to *go after middlebrow or upper-middlebrow publications and then work your way down.* You may skip the intellectual, the obscure, the highbrow: don't bother with the *New Republic, Dissent,* and the *Financial Times of London.* Instead, place ads in *Newsweek,* then approach the *Star, Us,* and the *National Enquirer.* While we might wish it otherwise, only the latter really qualify as mass media. It could take anywhere from two to ten years to break into these forums, so patience and persistence are essential.

Step 2: We Interrupt This Program to Announce . . . PSAs.

Quick, tell us: What's the media activist's favorite four-letter word that begins with *f?*—Free. While storming the barricades with salvos of ink, we should explore opportunities for *free* TV and radio advertising. The FCC requires that station licensees devote a small part of their airtime to unpaid public-service announcements (PSAs) for causes and nonprofit organizations the station deems worthy. The PSAs they air are produced by dedicated public-interest groups, the Ad Council, or the stations themselves. PSAs are like your aunt Helga, always dispensing good advice that nobody takes: they encourage citizens to stop smoking and drinking, start voting, pay their taxes on time, consider family counseling, help the needy, and check their blood pressure regularly.

But if you turn on the TV in Philadelphia, you may also encounter PSAs deploring discrimination against homosexuals. If you spin the dial on a radio near that city, you might, on any of several channels, hear a one-minute gay-history segment or the phone number of an antigay violence hotline. Likewise in New York City, you'll see PSAs trumpeting the number to call if you've been attacked for being gay.

Surprised? So are straights who see these spots for the first time.

But surprise soon passes as these modest PSAs begin to desensitize viewers toward homosexuality, even as they seek to *sensitize* them to the dangers of homohatred. These New York and Philadelphia PSAs are an entering wedge in several respects. The major TV stations that air them gradually commit themselves to more open support for gay rights. Meanwhile, the very appearance of these PSAs on a regular basis heartens gay viewers and suggests to millions of others that the protection of gay civil rights is now a valid and generally accepted goal of society.

How did local activists pull this off? The Philadelphia Lesbian and Gay Task Force started making thirty-second spots for the City of Brotherly Love in the early 1980s. It took several years of persistent appeals, but the PLGTF eventually convinced the city's half-dozen TV stations—reaching some 15 million viewers in Pennsylvania, New Jersey, and Delaware—to air a few of these ads. Which spots have been aired and which not? The two most widely accepted ads stress a single theme, antigay discrimination. One shows a varied group of men and women emerging from a closet into an adjoining room. The narrator remarks, "Someday, no one will have to live in a closet." The other PSA shows bright-eyed, eager college graduates receiving their diplomas. The narrator asks, "What could stop them? Discrimination." The spot ends by showing PLGTF's name, phone number and address. While the Philadelphia PSAs are primitively produced and lack emotional punch, they nevertheless do what it takes to get on air *and* desensitize the public.

Significantly, the two gay PSAs that *no* Philadelphia station has yet agreed to run commit obvious violations of our Persuasion Principles 1 and 3 (which recommend that you talk about antigay discrimination, but don't show even the mildest homo*eroticism*). According to the *Advocate,* "One [of the rejected ads] is an excerpt from the movie *Word Is Out,* in which a young gay man tells how ecstatic he felt when he first fell in love; the other is a bucolic picnic scene in which lesbian and gay male couples are shown with arms around each other." Gay advertisers are expressing themselves splendidly here but doing a lousy job of communicating with straights (including most broadcasters), who still find homoeroticism scary and repellent.

We can't expect stations in many other cities to adopt gay-sponsored PSAs as readily as liberal Philadelphia and New York. So it may be necessary to try a more oblique approach, one that makes refusal to air our PSAs look unreasonable, possibly illegal, and patently bigoted. Gay-sponsored ads could be patterned exactly after those currently aired by the Church of Latter-Day Saints and others. A recent Mormon spot, for example, extols the wonderfulness of being different and the value of social diversity to the nation—a spot virtually made to order for the gay cause. In our versions, viewers would be treated as usual to squeaky-clean skits on the theme—but this time the narrator would end by saying, "This message was brought to you by . . . Your National Gay and Lesbian Community." These ads would both desensitize and subtly jam homohatred. If stations refuse to air them as unpaid PSAs, gays must quickly offer to pay for the airtime (just as the Mormons do). Watch broadcasters squirm.

The next move, once such 'neutral' ads are on the air, is to advertise, either locally or nationally, on behalf of support groups *ancillary* to the gay community. AIDS-related support groups may be the first to win airtime. For our money, however, we'd rather see ads for gay antiviolence projects, hotlines, counseling groups, senior citizens' homes, runaway-shelters, and organizations such as PFLAG—Parents and Friends of Lesbians and Gays. With the last of these, for example, viewers would be treated to frowsy but upbeat moms and dads announcing telephone numbers and meeting times. Can't you just see such ads now, presented during the late movie, sandwiched between messages from the Disabled Vets and the Postal Workers' Union?

Although these harmless ads sound no different from the Mormon-style spots that went before, they differ markedly, because of their implicit but unmistakable support for homosexuals and homosexuality—not just general encomium for family harmony or opposition to violence. To place such ads on the airwaves across the nation for the period of, say, one year would create a turning point in gay American history, an elevation of public awareness and gay legitimacy, from which there could be no turning back. Don't think for an instant that broadcasters and Intransigent viewers would fail to see what was up at this point (if not much sooner), and try to head us off at the pass.

Step 3: When All Else Fails, Homosexuality for President.

What if Intransigents kick up such a fuss from the outset that broadcasters and publishers adamantly refuse to play ball? Gays will then have to consider a bold stratagem to seize media attention forcibly, without full media cooperation. The scheme we have in mind would require careful preparation, yet would save expense even as it elevated the visibility and dignity of the gay movement overnight.

Well before the next national election, we might lay contingency plans to run symbolic gay candidates for every high political office. (We would have to deal with the problem of inducing gays and straights to sign enough petitions to get us on the ballot. We'd start by demanding the support of our 'friends' in the 'rainbow coalition' and in the Democratic Party.) Our candidates would participate responsibly in such public debates as they could, run progay advertisements coordinated by our national headquarters, and demand media access under—you guessed it— the Equal Time Rule. (And here, of course, it could *not* be refused.)

Candidates running on a gay slate probably couldn't win a single government seat, unless West Hollywood were suddenly declared the fifty-first state. (In a national poll taken by Roper in 1985, more than half the public stated categorically that it would not vote "for a generally well-qualified person for president if that person happened to be a homosexual.") But electability is not our concern. Indeed, we think the slate definitely should *not* ask the public to vote yea or nay on the gay issue at this early stage: that would only end up committing most to the nay position, and tally huge and visible defeats for our cause. So we recommend that gay candidates, having broken the ice, graciously pull out of the race before the actual elections, while formally endorsing more viable straight contenders.

Through such a political campaign, the mainstream would get over the initial shock of seeing gay ads, the acceptability of which would be fortified by the most creditable context possible. Yet we're reluctant to try the political gambit. Indeed, it should be undertaken only as an act of desperation, fraught with as much risk as promise. Our enemies would brew a thunderstorm of vitriol and violence, of character assassination—and even, perhaps, the other kind. Broadcasters might balk, Equal Time Rule or no, and the whole mess end up in the federal courts. Our efforts would backfire if the public resented our exploitation of the electoral process to promote our special interests. On the other hand, it's just conceivable that a courageous and respectable performance by gay candidates in the face of savagery from the far right could win them a new measure of legitimacy, and even become a *cause célèbre.*

Now, the payoff: at the election's close, we must be ready, without skipping a beat, to ask broadcasters to replace our political ads with mild gay-sponsored PSAs. After all, the network will have been running gay ads for the previous six to eight months, so what's to complain about now? If this maneuver won't work to keep us on the air, perhaps nothing will.

Step 4: The Gloves Come Off: A Portfolio of Progay Ads.

By now—several years down the road—our salami tactics will have carved out, slice by slice, a large portion of access to mainstream media. What next? It will finally be time to bring the Waging Peace campaign out of the closet. We will launch media messages of open support for the civil rights of gay people, in ads that work directly to jam homohatred and convert straights to feelings of greater tolerance.

We present here a small portfolio of possible ads, for print and television. Most are presented as magazine ads yet could easily be adapted to TV or radio. Nearly all have been developed by us; a few have been created by others; and some have already appeared in major media. We'll explain which mechanisms—desensitization, jamming, conversion—each ad is expected to activate. And we'll give our assessment of each ad's strengths and weaknesses *vis-à-vis* the eight practical principles for the persuasion of straights. Likewise, you should subject every gay ad you create or promote to a close strategic analysis (if not a systematic effectiveness-test with straight media-viewers). Our community cannot afford to spend one red cent on ads that merely entertain or, far worse, misfire with regard to our objectives.

Finally, we emphasize that these examples are presented in rough form, assembled from readily available—but not the very best—photographs and drawings, and as such fall short of the full impact they might have if properly produced. Even so, with a bit of imagination, you should be able to see what we have in mind.

A PORTFOLIO OF
PRO-GAY ADVERTISING

```
┌─────────────────────────────────────────────────────────┐
│                 STRATEGIC EVALUATION                    │
│                                                         │
│  Key principles                              Key        │
│  behind ad(s):                               violations:│
│                                                         │
│    X    1. Communicate; don't just express yourself.  __│
│    X    2. Appeal to ambivalent skeptics.             __│
│    X    3. Keep talking (desensitize, don't shock).   __│
│    X    4. Keep message single-minded: gay rights.    __│
│    __   5. Portray gays as victims, not aggressors.   __│
│    __   6. Give potential protectors a just cause.    __│
│    __   7. Make gays look good.                       __│
│    __   8. Make victimizers look bad.                 __│
└─────────────────────────────────────────────────────────┘
```

STRATEGY: *Desensitization.* Remind straights repeatedly that homosexuality is commonplace and perfectly natural for some people, so don't be disturbed by it. This strategy assumes that the more people there are who appear to practice homosexuality, and the more innate it appears to be, the less abnormal and objectionable—and the more legitimate—it will seem to straights.

COMMENT: This simple ad is humorous and striking because it compares the 'popularity' of homosexuality directly to that of mundane and harmless middle-class pastimes—and finds that gay sex is *more* popular. How creepy can this vice really be when 'everybody's doing it'? (The homosexuality/sports comparison may not always work, however, since, though valid, the results of the comparison are *so* surprising that many straights may not believe them.) The ad concludes with a pitch for anti-discrimination.

MEETING PLANNED:
PARENTS AND FRIENDS OF LESBIANS
AND GAYS

PFLAG is a self-help group for those who are coming to terms with the orientation of their loved ones. Everyone is welcome. Come talk with us.

Call 123-555-1212 for next meeting date.

GAY AND LESBIAN REPUBLICANS
OF BLANDVILLE, OHIO

Next meeting: June 3, 8:00 P.M.
Location: VFW Bldg., Main Street
Topic: Referendum on Pet Leash Law

DEMOCRAT OR REPUBLICAN,
BLACK OR WHITE,
STRAIGHT OR GAY . . .
REGISTER TO VOTE!

—A Message From
*Gays and Lesbians
for a Strong America*

GAY ALLIANCE
FOR THE HEARING AND SIGHT
IMPAIRED

We meet every month for social support and fun! All gays with disabilities are welcome. Call 123-555-1212 for next meeting time.

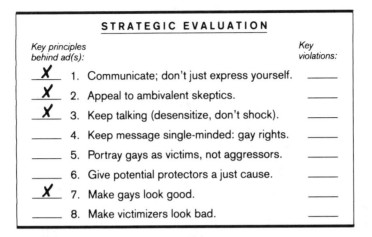

STRATEGIC EVALUATION

Key principles behind ad(s):		Key violations:
X	1. Communicate; don't just express yourself.	_____
X	2. Appeal to ambivalent skeptics.	_____
X	3. Keep talking (desensitize, don't shock).	_____
_____	4. Keep message single-minded: gay rights.	_____
_____	5. Portray gays as victims, not aggressors.	_____
_____	6. Give potential protectors a just cause.	_____
X	7. Make gays look good.	_____
_____	8. Make victimizers look bad.	_____

S T R A T E G Y: *Desensitize* straights by exposing them to the words 'gay' and 'lesbian' in neutral or favorable contexts. Gays are linked to good causes, non-controversial activities.

C O M M E N T: They needn't be long or clever, but to be effective, these modest ads must appear *repeatedly* in mainstream media. And the word 'gay' or 'lesbian'—which sounds less negative than 'homosexual'— should be readable at a glance, in the headline or tagline.

Neutral or positive associations are key here: these ads would be far more upsetting (i.e., just the opposite of desensitizing) for straights if they instead announced meetings of the Gay Man/Boy Sex Syndicate, Radical Fairies Club, Lesbian Anarchists League, or Gay Sadomasochist Society. Such ads would violate Principles 3, 4, and 5.

ADOLF HITLER

MADMAN.
MURDERER.
HOMOPHOBE.

THE OTHER HOLOCAUST:
When Hitler seized power in 1933,
he immediately launched a campaign to
persecute gay people.

Every year for ten years, Hitler sent
thousands to wear the *pink triangle*
in Nazi concentration camps.

Young gay people were beaten to death.
Starved to death. Worked to death.
Frozen to death.

At one camp, SS guards forced gay
prisoners to construct an earthwork
firing range, and then used them as
living targets.

TODAY, GAYS ARE STILL TARGETS FOR BIGOTRY,
BY ATTACKERS WHO FEEL NO SHAME.

A Reminder From
YOUR NATIONAL
GAY AND LESBIAN
COMMUNITY

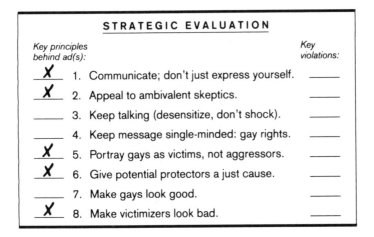

STRATEGIC EVALUATION

Key principles behind ad(s):		*Key violations:*
X	1. Communicate; don't just express yourself.	_____
X	2. Appeal to ambivalent skeptics.	_____
_____	3. Keep talking (desensitize, don't shock).	_____
_____	4. Keep message single-minded: gay rights.	_____
X	5. Portray gays as victims, not aggressors.	_____
X	6. Give potential protectors a just cause.	_____
_____	7. Make gays look good.	_____
X	8. Make victimizers look bad.	_____

S T R A T E G Y: *Jam* homohatred by linking it to Nazi horror. Make victimizers look bad, while helping straights to see gays as victims and feel protective toward them.

C O M M E N T: The Nazi/pink triangle story makes for powerful media communication, for four reasons:

1. Hitler and his Nazis are endlessly interesting to readers, and indisputably evil.

2. Gays in concentration camps were undoubtedly victims deserving sympathy and protection.

3. The media might more readily accept emotional ads of this sort when they deplore dead Nazis than when they attack contemporary hate groups such as the KKK.

4. Most contemporary hate groups on the Religious Right will bitterly resent the implied connection between homohatred and Nazi fascism. But since they can't defend the latter, they'll end up having to distance themselves by insisting that *they* would never go to such extremes. Such declarations of civility toward gays, of course, set our worst detractors on the slippery slope toward recognition of fundamental gay rights.

Incidentally, note that this ad and others in our portfolio use the term 'homophobia,' not 'homohatred.' While the latter term might be more accurate, '-phobia' works better as rhetoric because it's less offensive to straights and suggests, in quasi-clinical terms, that anti-gay feelings stem exclusively from the bigot's own unhealthy psychological hang-ups and insecurities.

Would Walt Whitman Be Allowed to Teach English in Virginia?

Walt Whitman was Gay.

He was also one of America's greatest poets.

If he were alive today, some people would not let him be a teacher.

That isn't right.

Photo: N.Y. Public Library

ADVICE FROM AN OLD SOLDIER

ALEXANDER THE GREAT

W/P

A Message From
YOUR NATIONAL GAY AND LESBIAN COMMUNITY

They say I was the most brilliant general in history.

Before my thirtieth birthday, I conquered virtually all of the ancient world. I led one hundred battalions into battle, and the loyalty of my troops was legendary.

But if I were alive today, the U.S. Army wouldn't even let me enlist, *just because I was gay.*

Before they lose more good soldiers, someone should tell them—they're fighting the wrong war.

Stop Anti-Gay Discrimination in the Military.

LEONARDO DA VINCI

Artist,
scientist,
inventor,
philosopher.

Probably gay, too.

That would make this gentle genius a criminal across much of the United States, if he lived today.

Homophobia could keep him out of the classroom, the laboratory, even the art studio.

That's not genius. That's just bigotry.

W/P

A Message From
YOUR NATIONAL GAY AND
LESBIAN COMMUNITY

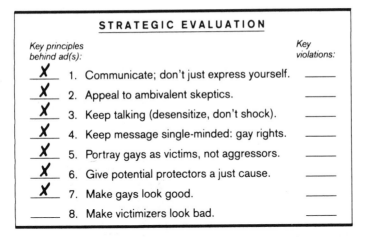

Key principles behind ad(s):		Key violations:
X	1. Communicate; don't just express yourself.	___
X	2. Appeal to ambivalent skeptics.	___
X	3. Keep talking (desensitize, don't shock).	___
X	4. Keep message single-minded: gay rights.	___
X	5. Portray gays as victims, not aggressors.	___
X	6. Give potential protectors a just cause.	___
X	7. Make gays look good.	___
___	8. Make victimizers look bad.	___

S T R A T E G Y: *Conversion / Jamming.* Create a more favorable attitude toward gays by making them look good, and discrimination look bad. Evoke the admiration that straight readers feel for legendary historical figures, then arouse indignation that modern-day homohatred would hold them back.

C O M M E N T: There are many ways to present famous gays, of course. But the Whitman, Alexander, and Leonardo ads are exemplary, since each provides: (1) a visual image of the Great Man, to which readers can relate; (2) the startling and prominent announcement of his homosexuality; and (3) explicit linking of the Great Man to contemporary discrimination issues—directly posing a relevant dilemma which the reader must confront.

By the way, the A.G.C.A.'s Whitman ad was patterned closely after a concept we'd sketched out some years earlier, to show how the persuasion principles might be put into practice. Encouragingly, when the Alexandria group placed the Whitman ad in the *Washington Post* in February 1988, it generated both favorable public reaction and donations.

In picking famous American and world figures believed to be gay or bisexual, there are literally scores to choose from. But expect editors and broadcasters to demand documentation supporting your claim—they don't relish a libel suit any more than you do.

THE FACE OF BIGOTRY

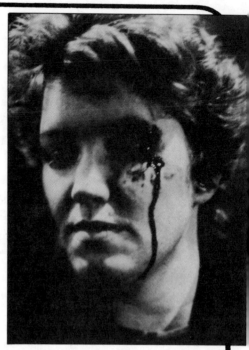

Another victim of anti-gay violence

Sooner or later,
you'll have to face up to a choice—

Either you think this picture is okay or
you don't.

Either you make fun of 'fags' and 'dykes' or
you refuse to.

Either you hate gays, the same as bigots do,
or you say 'live and let live.'

So choose now.
Which kind of person do you want to be?

***Helping instead of hating—that's what
America is all about.***

A Message From
YOUR NATIONAL GAY AND LESBIAN COMMUNITY

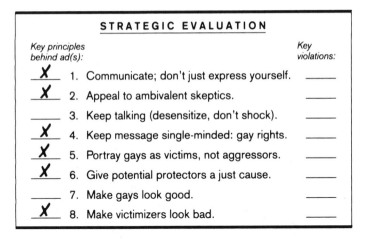

STRATEGIC EVALUATION

Key principles
behind ad(s):

Key
violations:

_X_ 1. Communicate; don't just express yourself. ____

_X_ 2. Appeal to ambivalent skeptics. ____

____ 3. Keep talking (desensitize, don't shock). ____

_X_ 4. Keep message single-minded: gay rights. ____

_X_ 5. Portray gays as victims, not aggressors. ____

_X_ 6. Give potential protectors a just cause. ____

____ 7. Make gays look good. ____

_X_ 8. Make victimizers look bad. ____

S T R A T E G Y: *Jam* the self-righteous pride of homohatred by showing its grisly consequences: victimization of gays. Seize the moment to make readers pick sides—demand that readers identify themselves with either social tolerance or gruesome cruelty.

C O M M E N T: This ad is a shocker of the right kind, a deliberate play to humane emotions—so graphic and disturbing, in fact, that some media may well balk at running it (protesting that it's in 'poor taste'). The brutalized face is a haunting rebuke to all of bigotry's pieties and rationalizations. Probably no ad could do a better job of jamming, or of giving straights a 'just cause' to defend and protect gays.

IF YOU GO OUT OF YOUR WAY TO PICK ON GAYS, PSYCHIATRISTS HAVE A NAME FOR YOU.

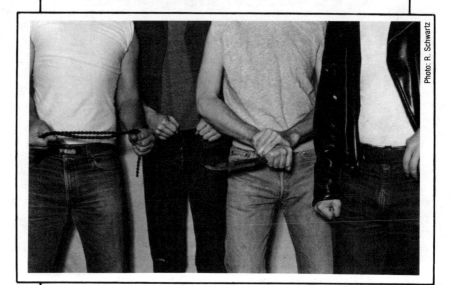

Photo: R. Schwartz

. . . *LATENT HOMOSEXUAL.*

There was a time, years ago, when people
could hide their own homosexual tendencies
by loudly attacking other gays in public.

But not anymore.
These days, when you harass gay people,
it just puts the spotlight of suspicion on *you.*

So maybe you'd better mind your own business,
unless you want others to think that
homosexuality *is* your business!

WAGING PEACE · W/P

A Message From
YOUR NATIONAL GAY AND LESBIAN COMMUNITY

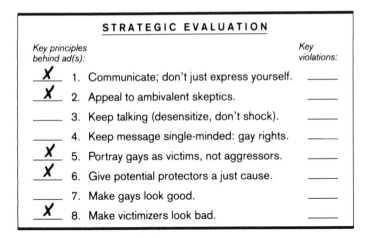

S T R A T E G Y: *Jam* homohatred and discourage anti-gay harassment by linking them to latent homosexuality. Get readers to silently question their own motives for homohatred. And get them to believe that displaying homohatred may not lead to social approval, but to personal embarrassment and loss of status.

C O M M E N T: You may think this ad is directed to bashers and baiters from the Intransigent camp—a violation of Principle 2. Such ads will, with time, silence Intransigents, but the principal target is Ambivalent Skeptics. If ads such as this one take effect, Skeptics will begin to censor their own homohatred. Moreover, the ad's visual further blackens homohatred by associating it with menacing thugs—another disliked outgroup.

HOW TO STOP CHILD ABUSE

IT WILL HAPPEN TO ONE IN EVERY TEN KIDS . . .

As he grows up, he'll realize that he feels different than his friends.

He'll discover that he's *gay*.

If he lets it show, they'll cut him off, humiliate him, even attack him.

If he confides in his parents, they may throw him out of the house, onto the streets. And say that *he* is 'anti-family.'

Nobody will let him be himself. So he hides. From his friends, his folks. Alone.

It's tough enough just being a kid these days. But to be the one in ten!

HELP STOP CHILD ABUSE— TREAT GAY TEENS WITH THE LOVE AND RESPECT THEY DESERVE.

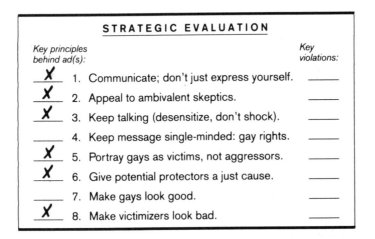

STRATEGY: *Jamming / Conversion / Desensitization.* Build straight sympathy and protectiveness toward gays by portraying them as innocent victims of circumstance and bigotry. Teach readers that homosexuality is extremely common.

COMMENT: The headline catches the eye, and trades on the perennial public hysteria about child abuse (which is, of course, often blamed on gays). Then the copy turns the tables on straights: by focusing on teens, the ad portrays gays as innocent and vulnerable, victimized and misunderstood, surprisingly numerous yet not menacing. It also renders the 'anti-family' charge absurd and hypocritical. Bull's-eye.

READ MY LIPS

KISS IN

Friday, April 29:
- 9:00 pm March from Christopher & West Sts.
- 10:00 pm Rally at Sheridan Square
- 10:30 pm Kiss In at 6th Avenue & 8th St.
- 11:30 pm Tracks—ACT UP/ACT NOW Fundraiser

FIGHT HOMOPHOBIA: FIGHT AIDS

SPRING AIDS ACTION '88: Nine days of nationwide AIDS related actions & protests.

Gran Fury

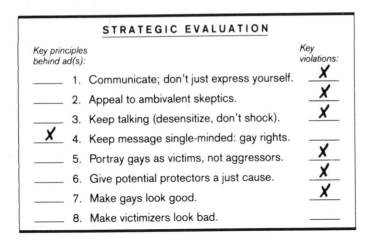

STRATEGIC EVALUATION

*Key principles
behind ad(s):*

       1. Communicate; don't just express yourself.

       2. Appeal to ambivalent skeptics.

       3. Keep talking (desensitize, don't shock).

   X 4. Keep message single-minded: gay rights.

       5. Portray gays as victims, not aggressors.

       6. Give potential protectors a just cause.

       7. Make gays look good.

       8. Make victimizers look bad.

*Key
violations:*

1. **X**
2. **X**
3. **X**
5. **X**
6. **X**
7. **X**

STRATEGY: On behalf of the AIDS Coalition to Unleash Power (ACT UP), a group of activists calling themselves Gran Fury designed and posted this ad throughout Manhattan in April 1988 (and, since then, has sold T-shirts emblazoned with the visual/headline). The piece announced a public "Kiss In" as "an aggressive demonstration of affection." The back of the ad declared a mixed list of objectives:

> "We kiss to protest the cruel and painful bigotry that affects the lives of lesbians and gay men. We kiss so that all who see us will be forced to confront their homophobia. We kiss to challenge repressive conventions that prohibit displays of love between persons of the same sex. We kiss as an affirmation of our feelings, our desires, ourselves."

COMMENT: Though their intentions may be good, Gran Fury and ACT UP have produced and promoted an ad that is defiant self-expression, *not* persuasive communication. As an effort to reach skeptical straights—or, as Gran Fury puts it, "to inform a broad public"—it's a disaster. Visual deliberately shocks and antagonizes by displaying homosexual foreplay between soldiers, accompanied by a taunting headline, "Read My Lips" (implicitly: "So fuck you!"). Rather than offering potential friends the ideal of Love as a just cause worth defending, this ad offers the ideal of Gay Lust, which isn't half so compelling or, legitimate to straights. Overall, the ad's effect is not to desensitize, jam, or convert: it merely reinforces revulsion and inflames homohatred. Not recommended.

Is it a Crime to Love?

In 25 states and the District of Columbia it can be a
crime for two women to love each other.

That isn't right.

There's too much hate in the world without making
love a crime.

**Alexandria Gay Community
Association**

People Helping Instead of Hating

Enclosed is my contribution.
I want to help AGCA increase understanding about
homosexuality.

□ $25 □ $50 □ $100 □ $250 □ _____
□ Tell me how I can help.

AGCA
P.O. Box 19401, Alexandria, VA 22320

S T R A T E G Y: *Jamming / Conversion.* Jam homohatred by pointing out that it's inconsistent with the reader's belief in the value of love between individuals. (*Love* becomes the 'just cause' for straights to protect gays.) At the same time, convert Ambivalent Skeptics into Friends by showing them a lesbian couple they can like.

C O M M E N T: Sound strategy spoiled by the wrong picture. This ad is one of several assembled by the Alexandria Gay Community Association, and the series ran in the *Washington Post* during 1987–88. The A.G.C.A. tells us that it deliberately created the series with our principles in mind—even lifted some copy verbatim from our previously published ad ideas.

Even so, the "Crime to Love?" ad violates important rules. First, it inflames the reader's smoldering fear of homoeroticism by showing gay lovers together in intimate contact, even if the contact is not coarsely impassioned or taunting like that in the "Read My Lips" ad.

Second, it showcases a couple that reinforces an unappealing stereotype—suggesting, perhaps, two leathery old dykes from tobacco road who bark at each other with gin-cracked voices, and who first met at a motorcycle roundup. Not surprisingly, this ad, when it appeared in print, generated the fewest donations for A.G.C.A. and the greatest hostility (with one irate fellow even mailing back an envelope of dog dung).

SOME GUYS HAVE TROUBLE ACCEPTING GAY PEOPLE.

. . . They think we're crazy and we dress funny.

Underneath those foolish costumes is sheer bigotry. Dangerous homophobic bigotry. The Ku Klux Klan is waging a campaign of fear and hate against gay people, just as it has against blacks. And now they want *you* on their side.

Will you join them?
Or are you like millions of other decent Americans who believe they should 'live and let live'?

We hope so, because our civil rights depend on you. Help us fight bigotry

. . . and tell *them* you only wear silly costumes on Halloween.

A Reminder From
YOUR NATIONAL GAY AND LESBIAN COMMUNITY

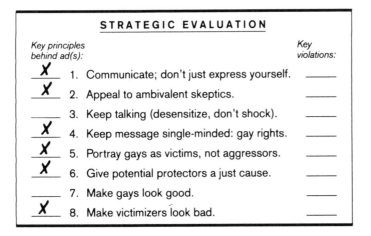

STRATEGY: *Jam* the self-righteous pride that homohaters feel, by linking it to a disreputable hate group. Portray gays as victims of bigotry, and build a feeling of protectiveness toward them.

COMMENT: Few Skeptics would willingly liken themselves to the Ku Klux Klan, so this ad should jam homohatred nicely. But everybody, including editors and broadcasters, is rather afraid of Klan retaliation, so we may have some trouble placing this emotional ad until later in our media campaign. When the time comes, gays must be prepared to document KKK anti-gay bigotry in detail—which will prove as easy as rolling off a log.

MR. THORNBUG'S REVENGE
SCENARIO FOR A TV/RADIO COMMERCIAL

The camera approaches the mighty oak door of the Boss's office. The door swings open, and the camera (which represents you, the viewer) enters the room.

Behind the oversized desk sits the Boss, a scowling curmudgeon chomping on a cigar. He looks up at the camera and snarls, "So it's you, Smithers. Well, you're fired!"

The voice of a younger man is heard to reply, with astonishment, "But . . . but . . . Mr. Thornbug, I've been with your company for ten years. I thought you liked my work."

The Boss responds, with disgust, "Yes, yes, Smithers, your *work* is quite adequate. But I hear you've been seen around town with some kind of *girl*friend. A girlfriend! Frankly, I'm shocked. We're not about to start hiring any *hetero*sexuals in this company. Now get out."

The younger man speaks once more: "But, Boss, that's not fair! What if it were you?"

The Boss glowers back as the camera pulls quickly out of the room and the big door slams shut. Printed on the door:

**A MESSAGE FROM
YOUR NATIONAL GAY AND LESBIAN COMMUNITY.**

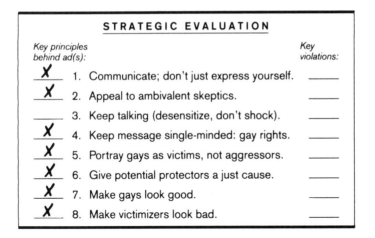

STRATEGY: *Jamming / Conversion.* Educate about civil rights discrimination, and build identification with and sympathy for, the plight of gays through role-reversal. Portray gay persons as hardworking, all-American types, and bigots as unpleasant bullies.

COMMENT: Although merely a cartoonish morality play (indeed, the TV ad might be irresistible if animated like a comic 1940s cartoon), this old switcheroo would be entertaining and surprising to straights—indeed, how would *they* feel if subjected to job and other discrimination for no good reason?

This ad concept may be weaker than others, however, because it is, to some degree, substituting humorous entertainment for hard-hitting emotional impact. As a rule, we would use humor sparingly in the campaign, not because we don't enjoy it, but because we don't need it. Commercial advertisers use humor primarily to get the viewer's attention—hardly a difficulty of gay ads, whose subject matter is automatically sensational.

COULD A SHRINK MAKE YOU GAY?

Could hours of psychotherapy turn you into a homosexual?

You'd say, "Of course not!"
Most people understand what's natural for themselves, and nothing's going to change that.

Millions of gay Americans feel the same way.
For them, it's just plain natural to be gay.

So you can either go on pretending that gays can "see a shrink and straighten out."

Or you can do something healthier:
learn to live and let live.
It's just what the doctor ordered.

A Message From
YOUR GAY AND LESBIAN COMMUNITY

YOU PROBABLY NEVER CHOSE TO BE . . .
Straight or Gay

BUT YOU *CAN* CHOOSE TO BE FAIR OR UNFAIR.

It takes all kinds.
Psychologists now believe it's as natural and normal for some folks to be gay as it is for others to be straight.

Gays don't really *choose* their sexuality, any more than you chose yours.

The only *real* choice, then, is whether you'll treat everyone with the same dignity and respect.

After all, what if it were you?

A Message From
YOUR NATIONAL GAY AND LESBIAN COMMUNITY

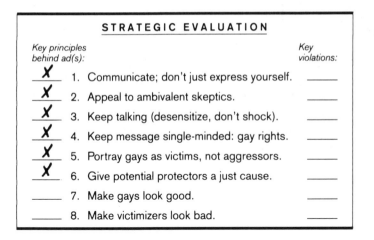

STRATEGIC EVALUATION

Key principles behind ad(s):		Key violations:
X	1. Communicate; don't just express yourself.	___
X	2. Appeal to ambivalent skeptics.	___
X	3. Keep talking (desensitize, don't shock).	___
X	4. Keep message single-minded: gay rights.	___
X	5. Portray gays as victims, not aggressors.	___
X	6. Give potential protectors a just cause.	___
___	7. Make gays look good.	___
___	8. Make victimizers look bad.	___

S T R A T E G Y: *Desensitization / Jamming.* Convince straights that homosexuality is healthy and natural for some people. Remind them that sex orientation is not a choice, so it's unfair to condemn gays.

C O M M E N T: These ads address the reader directly, calling him or her to a higher standard of fairness. They obliquely challenge Judeo-Christianity's moralistic slant against homosexuality, suggesting that Science now tells us that gayness is perfectly natural. Secular humanism rides again!

The ad "Could a Shrink . . . ?" takes a humorous approach, inviting straights to view gays' sexuality as they view their own. But there is a measure of risk that the ad may be off-putting to some, who will shudder at the scary prospect of becoming gay, and reaffirm their rejection of gayness all the more strongly.

The same might be said of the ad "Straight or Gay." Its mirror-image pictures suggest that gays and straights are like identical twins who resemble each other in all respects but one: their sexual perspective. At the same time, however, the reversed photos remind viewers that—but for fate—they might have found themselves in the same predicament as gays do. The psychological impact of such reminders should be copy-tested thoroughly before they're used in ads.

Photo Credit: Valerie Snyder

"I'M PROUD OF MY LESBIAN DAUGHTER"

"It's been twelve years since we at home were responding to Lynn's 'I'm gay' letter mailed from college. Reading it to the family, I suddenly knew I'd had a plan for Lynn, and this was off course.

She had had to put miles between us before making her announcement and I was feeling her courage. How terrible for her to have worried: "Will they love me after they know . . . love me with restrictions . . . check me off?"

The process of my adjustment wasn't instant or without fluctuation, but I asked myself, what of real importance had changed? Lynn was still my pretty and winsome daughter, still the young woman, a crusader, bent on correcting every social and political shortcoming. Surely, she was entitled to her own life.

Twelve busy years have passed. My 'Lynn' file bulges with her writings, causes, and activities. It seems that her calling has always been political so that is where she works. She has established, with a perfect companion, a remarkable, loving home full of trust and respect.

Yes, I not only love my daughter, I am filled with a sense of pride and completion as her life unfolds."

— Lamonta Pierson

LESBIAN AND GAY PUBLIC AWARENESS PROJECT

People United To End Homophobia

Enclosed is my tax deductible contribution non-profit 501(c)3.
I want to help LGPAP increase understanding about homosexuality.
☐ $25 ☐ $50 ☐ $100 ☐ _____
☐ Tell me how I can help.

LGPAP
P.O. Box 65603, Los Angeles, CA 90065
© 1988 Lesbian and Gay Public Awareness Project.

```
┌─────────────────────────────────────────────────────────────┐
│              S T R A T E G I C   E V A L U A T I O N          │
│              ─────────────────────────────────────           │
│  Key principles                                    Key        │
│  behind ad(s):                                     violations:│
│    _X__  1. Communicate; don't just express yourself.  ____   │
│    _X__  2. Appeal to ambivalent skeptics.             ____   │
│    _X__  3. Keep talking (desensitize, don't shock).   ____   │
│    ____  4. Keep message single-minded: gay rights.    ____   │
│    ____  5. Portray gays as victims, not aggressors.   ____   │
│    ____  6. Give potential protectors a just cause.    ____   │
│    _X__  7. Make gays look good.                       ____   │
│    ____  8. Make victimizers look bad.                 ____   │
└─────────────────────────────────────────────────────────────┘
```

S T R A T E G Y: *Conversion.* Build liking for gays among straights, by presenting the personal lives of appealing and successful gay individuals. Also, reassure readers that it's 'all right' to accept and like gays, by showing them other straights who do.

C O M M E N T: One in a series produced by a Los Angeles-based group called the Lesbian and Gay Public Awareness Project, this straightforward ad offers much to admire. First, the headline summarizes the main message at a glance, shouting "lesbian" in a boldly positive way that will seize the attention of straights.

Second, the visual presents a friendly gay couple arm in arm (ordinarily off-putting to straights), but defuses any erotic overtones by showing a beaming mother in the same frame. The resulting impression is one of family bliss.

Third, the ad's conversion strategy resembles that for our own ad about 'Steve Henson,' but goes about it differently. Instead of meeting the gay subject through a personal interview, you meet her through a statement by her mother. Reading about the daughter through the affectionate voice of her parent, helps straights identify with the situation, and provides a role-model of tolerance and love.

CAN YOU FIND 3 THINGS WRONG
WITH THIS PICTURE?

ANSWER: If you picked the giraffe, the cannon, and the upside-down door, give yourself a gold star—those things *are* wrong here.

But if you picked out the three gay couples dancing together, then go straight to your room and think about the difference between right and wrong.

Millions of decent, hardworking Americans happen to be gay, and they deserve to fit into the picture too. Still puzzled? Here's a simple clue: *Different things are natural for different people.*

Now, study the drawing again.
Be fair.
And draw your own conclusion.

A Message From
YOUR NATIONAL GAY AND LESBIAN COMMUNITY

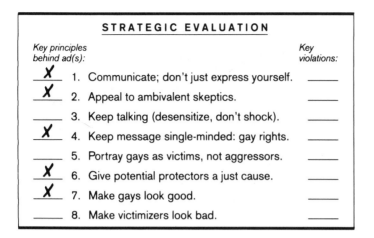

S T R A T E G Y: *Desensitization.* Reinforce two points: (1) gays are everywhere in great numbers, and (2) "different things are natural for different people."

C O M M E N T: This ad should prove amusing and involving, since even grown-ups are usually intrigued by 'mixed-up picture' puzzles. Moreover, the headline's challenge puts readers in an attentive, 'discovering' frame of mind. The puzzle rewards those who get the answer 'right'— many of whom will be surprised to realize, tellingly, that they never even *noticed* the gay couples. Whereas those who saw the gay couples but missed the real oddities will feel suitably foolish.

The ads tone is friendly and civilized, even sophisticated. The underlying message is 'everybody's different, and so what?' This is well and good. Even so, the ad is a soft-sell approach appropriate only to better-educated readers. The ad is so genteel, in fact, that it may do less for us than more blunt tacks.

Photo: R. Schwartz

SOMEONE YOU'D LIKE TO KNOW

INTERVIEWER: Steve is an electrical engineer who lives in Minneapolis. He's talking to us today about his life as a gay American.

STEVE [*chuckling*]: Well, you make it sound like my life is totally different, but it's really the standard stuff. I work pretty hard, have a bunch of friends—some straight, some gay. We get together and shoot baskets once a week, until it gets too cold. I love to ski too. Also I try to help each year on the local food drive—that's important. Oh yeah, and I've got your typical beagle who's addicted to corn chips.

INTERVIEWER: What?

STEVE: Her name is Tashi. David and I got her from an animal shelter about six years ago. She's stayed with us ever since.

INTERVIEWER: Have you always been gay, Steve?

STEVE: Yes. I just grew up that way, and I'm proud of it. To me, different things are natural for different people, that's all.

INTERVIEWER: Are you still close to your family?

STEVE: Very. My folks are terrific—they helped David and me afford our first apartment. Now they drop by a lot. [*Laughs*] Except, of course, that our ferocious guard dog Tashi won't let them in without a bag of corn chips.

ANNOUNCER: Steve Henson—someone we thought you'd like to know.

SUPER: A MESSAGE FROM YOUR GAY AND LESBIAN COMMUNITY.

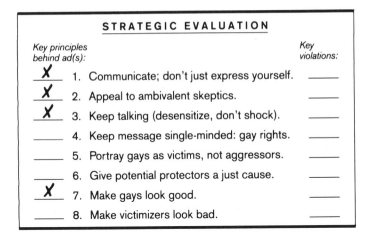

S T R A T E G Y: *Conversion.* Compensate straights' lack of familiarity with gay people by presenting them with 'solid citizens'—likable individuals who defy uncomplimentary stereotypes. The interviewee talks about his conventional gay life in a relaxed, low-key, matter-of-fact way, undercutting several myths as he talks.

C O M M E N T: Staged 'candid' interviews, such as this one, are especially compelling because they humanize homosexuality—that is, give straights a real gay person they can like and relate to. Notice, too, that the interview introduces three important social facts:

(1) There is someone special in Steve's life, a long-term relationship (to stress gay stability, monogamy, commitment);
(2) Steve's family is important to him, and supports him (to stress that gays aren't anti-family, and that families needn't be anti-gay);
(3) As far as he can recall, he was born gay, and he certainly didn't *choose* his preference one way or the other, so people should simply learn to accept such natural differences.

Subjects in these commercials should be interviewed alone, *not* with their lovers or children, since to include others in the picture would raise disturbing questions about the complexities of gay social relations, questions that these commercials could not, by themselves, explain.

This interview format will also work well to showcase any gay/straight *celebrities* we can convince to speak up for the gay cause. One could easily imagine David Kopay, for instance, beginning the interview by discussing his football career, only at the end surprising viewers with the casual admission that he's gay.

The principal drawback of ads like these is that to be effective, they must last thirty seconds or longer—it takes that long for the viewer to warm to the subject. Whether produced for radio (which would work quite well) or TV (even better), this means these ads will be quite expensive to air—expensive, indeed, but worth every penny.

245

5

○   ○   ○   ○   ○

GETTING OUR ACT(IVISTS) TOGETHER: UNITY, ORGANIZATION, FUNDRAISING

This day is a day of trouble . . . for the children are come to the birth, and there is not strength to bring forth.

—ISAIAH 37:3

W hen first framing our proposal for a national media campaign, we blithely assumed that the gay movement would have the wherewithal to implement it. When we actually examined the *anatomy* of the movement, however, what we found was a headless horseman; and, frankly, the sight has scared us half to death.

There's no point mincing words: the current condition of organization and fundraising in gay America is deplorable, and makes a pipe dream of our plans for an effective campaign. Without a unified national movement, led by an organization with sufficient resources to produce and guide the campaign, gay America hasn't nearly the "strength to bring forth."

o

WHY THE GAY KINGDOM IS DISORGANIZED

TOO MANY FIEFDOMS.

The throne of national leadership is not without its many pretenders, both individual and organizational: that much is plain. Anyone asking a gay hotline to connect him with 'the national gay organization' will be directed, depending on the locale, to any of the following: the National Gay and Lesbian Task Force, the Fund for Human Dignity (which split from NGLTF in 1986), the Human Rights Campaign Fund (which swallowed the insolvent Gay Rights National Lobby that same year), the National Gay Rights Advocates, the Lambda Legal Defense and Education Fund, the National Coalition of Black Lesbians and Gays, and, in recent years, the new AIDS empires of GMHC (Gay Men's Health Crisis), the AIDS Action Council, and others.

Some of these 'national' organizations acknowledge the specificity of their missions in their names. Yet even those groups with general-sounding names turn out, upon inquiry, to concern themselves chiefly with some particular aspect of gay advocacy—political lobbying, legal defense, public education, gay health protection, advancement of women's rights, etc.—and not with the guidance of the movement as a whole. There is *no* central institution, no gay equivalent of the National Association for the Advancement of Colored People.

Certainly, the talented and ambitious leaders of the quasi-national gay groups might each *like* to be Queen of the Realm (or perhaps Pope of Greenwich Village), but none has been allowed to accede by the rest. Indeed, our organizations are locked in a fratricidal struggle for members and dollars—that is, for their very survival. They take frequent swipes at one another in the gay press. The movement's leaders are inclined to trace this bureaucratic caterwauling, like everything else, back to "internalized homophobia," because—explains Jeff Levi, the executive director of NGLTF—"We're more willing to attack one another than to go after our common enemy." But a more plausible motive is old-fashioned *Realpolitik*. As Humpty Dumpty observed, "The only question is, which is to be master—that's all." Hearing a dozen different answers to Humpty's question is no answer at all.

Given the diffuseness of gay power and the chaotic state of gay organization, it's no wonder that our meager advances have come primarily in scattered localities, and that our community's stature on the national political stage has been abysmally low.

This must change. There should be *one* national gay organization, universally known as such. That organization should have coordinated task forces dedicated to political lobbying, legal action, gay life (i.e., the protection and enrichment of gay society and culture), health issues, and public education. It should represent gay men and women, young and old, of every race and religion. The organization should link up local branches in every city and hamlet in the country and be able to direct its national resources at specific regional targets as needed. Membership and regular donations should be strongly encouraged by local branches.

As trade unions (pointedly, the AFL-CIO) learned many years ago, there is tremendous strength in unification under a single, well-run organization. The need for such is obvious to everyone in the gay community except those activists with a personal stake in the status quo. Yet activists remain entrenched in their fiefdoms. Consequently, we're left with a movement that resembles the United Nations without a General Assembly: a loose handful of weak specialized agencies, claiming as members many hundreds of local 'grass roots' groups that never come together to caucus. Or, to put it another way, gay organization in this country is a wagon wheel with an extensive rim, a snaggle-toothed arrangement of frail national spokes, and no hub at all.

IF PARTS WERE GREATER THAN THE WHOLE.

Now, although a unified national organization would benefit the gay movement enormously in several ways, the current toothless wagon-wheel arrangement is not *ipso facto* unworkable for the limited purposes of our media campaign. It may not be necessary to reinvent the wheel, if only we can find some way to use it as is.

Perhaps we only need the rim: fully decentralized management. In this scenario, a patchwork media campaign would spread around the country a bit at a time, guided by a uniform persuasion strategy such as ours, as a growing number of local organizations in selected cities gathered funds to launch their own public-outreach programs. After all, local groups best understand local communications needs. Besides, many activities of the media campaign (e.g., supplying spokespersons for local talk shows, orchestrating media events, monitoring local news) are best handled at the metropolitan level in any case.

The trouble with this option is that it makes the advertising component of the campaign considerably more difficult to pull off. Probably no more than a few local groups in a few major cities— already more liberal on gay issues—have the sophisticated skills, infrastructure, and finances to produce effective ads and place them in high-visibility media. Moreover, they would be buying only local, not national, media time, which has two key drawbacks. First, of course, these efforts wouldn't reach the vast majority of straights in the remainder of the nation. Second, even in targeted localities, gay ads would have less impact if placed in local media than if seen in bona fide national media (such as network television and major magazines). As Lambda's executive director, Thomas Stoddard, has argued in the *Advocate,* "Most people derive their impressions of the world through the *national* media . . . That's the reason we need national organizations that will get the gay story across to the national media." Clearly, *some* central coordination of the design and placement of nationwide advertising is needed.

ALL FOR ONE, ONE FOR ALL.

So consider an alternative scenario: perhaps we need only the spindly spokes of the wheel to get things rolling. Under this scheme, the various national gay organizations would survive as separate entities but throw their combined support and funding behind a joint effort.

We favor this second option over the first, but it, too, is problematic. A national media campaign collectively administered by competing bureaucracies is like a ham bone 'shared' among hounds: it isn't for long. After a brief round of nuzzling and snarling, the most determined national group would inevitably pull away with its jaw clamped firmly on the campaign, leaving the rest to decide what to do next.

If most of them followed and supported the leader, in hope of getting a few scraps for themselves from the venture, then the scores of gay groups would, in effect, have picked a national umbrella organization at last. We say this because, undoubtedly, the group that presides over the nation's first gay media campaign will fix the spotlight upon itself as no gay organization has yet been able to do, and will be taken automatically as *the* national gay organization by both straight and gay publics. For the future of gay politics, such a consolidation of power would be all to the good, and we would have the launching of the media effort itself to thank for it.

If, on the other hand, gay organizations stormed off in all directions to launch their own national ad campaigns simultaneously, based on different strategies, the resulting cacophony would hurt our cause. Not only would the various media campaigns confuse the public, they would give broadcasters an additional excuse for refusing airtime to all gay groups (If we give time to one of you we'll have to give time to all of you, and that would be overdoing it.)

NO SPARE CHANGE MEANS NO CHANGE.

Even if they could settle the leadership issue, could our pack of self-appointed quasi-national organizations *afford* to do the job right? Probably not: they are too poor. Naturally, our enemies are fond of arguing the contrary, as Reverend Rueda does in his elaborate exposé, *The Homosexual Network:*

> There is no question that the homosexual movement has relatively large sums of money at its disposal. Homosexuals tend to be wealthier than the rest of the population . . . Moreover, the homosexual movement is an integral part of the American left . . . [resulting] in the availability of substantial funds for homosexual organizations . . . The gross annual income of the homosexual movement—exclusive of profit-making organizations (businesses)—[is estimated] to be $245,625,000.

Just imagine: $246 million to underwrite a media campaign! And mind you, Rueda was spinning out this lovely speculation in 1982; following his reasoning, the gay movement should be as posh as the Pentagon by now, and more than able to buy commercial airtime. Alas, back on planet Earth we learn that Rueda's grand estimate—though grounded in plausible assumptions about how rich the movement *ought* to be, given its constituency—is off by a factor of ten or more.

The movement's financial realities are depressing. Not only are there numerous 'national' organizations with functions both narrow and redundant, the memberships and budgets of those organizations are shamefully small because they all draw from the same shallow well. When we last checked, in 1988, none could claim more than thirty thousand members or so, and almost all created their measly budgets out of donations from the same forty to fifty thousand big donors (working off mailing lists that, if combined, probably wouldn't total more than three hundred thousand names). This tiny platoon of saints constitutes *half of one percent* of the estimated ten million American adults who admit to themselves that they're gay. The very largest political organizations—HRCF, NGLTF, Lambda—reportedly each take in a few of million dollars per annum, which barely meets current expenses. This is, of course, a far cry from $246 million in discretionary cash, or even from the $10 million to $20 million that is minimally needed to bankroll an effective national media campaign.

So even if a unified organization existed with the authority to lead a nationwide media campaign—an organization that could scrape together every last piaster and peseta donated—*there still would not be enough money to launch a serious campaign* unless that organization abandoned every other service to the gay community and concentrated all funds on advertising. Clearly, our community could not afford such a sacrifice.

○

PAYING OUR DUES: WHY NOBODY DOES IT

Why is the community's program for national activism—taking its several organizations together—so pathetically strapped for cash? What's going on here? Why are gays so unwilling to support their own advocates? Are they as feckless, selfish, uncommitted, and short-sighted as some critics claim?

Gays are all these things to some degree, we fear, but the picture is complicated. At its center are three rather uncomfortable truths:

- Gays don't feel an urgent need to liberate themselves and transform their society by eradicating homohatred.
- Gays don't see themselves as members of a valuable and cohesive cultural group worth fighting for.
- Gays don't believe that national gay organizations do much good in any case.

Let's stop right here and think, for a few minutes, about these problems, for they are profound obstacles both to our media campaign and to the viability of the gay movement in coming years.

GAYS DON'T FEEL AN URGENT NEED TO LIBERATE THEMSELVES AND TRANSFORM THEIR SOCIETY BY ERADICATING HOMOHATRED.

Gay people are not particularly agitated about their lot in life; they feel no pressing need for change. A shocking admission, no? Yet it hardly confirms the claim made by our enemies, that anti-gay discrimination is exaggerated. A child beaten with regularity comes to expect abuse, takes it without protest, and finds ways to accept the battering. For their part, gays have become like the proverbial 'good nigger' who frowns on emancipation, so thoroughly reconciled to his condition that he no longer recognizes it as oppression, can envision nothing better, and fears that abolitionists will only make more trouble for him. Gay youths grow up knowing the abuse they'll suffer for having been born homosexual; most simply learn to put up with mistreatment as an inevitability. The yoke of our nation's soft sexual despotism—as Tocqueville might have called it—does not seem as heavy to gays as it would have, had they ever, for even a minute, been without it.

Moreover, despite mistreatment, gays do prosper. Life in America is not, on the whole, economically or culturally oppressive (compared to the misery elsewhere in the world); gay life here is likewise tolerably comfortable for those who keep their heads down and oblige the Big Lie. Our life is, in fact, a bargain—a devil's bargain. Who really needs to come out of the closet, anyway? Gays are quite used to the secrecy and the dark. And the richer and more established the gay person (i.e., the more he could assist the cause with cash and influence) the more he has to lose if he openly agitates for social change. Thus, the prevailing gay attitude is: 'Let others risk their own comfort, if they like, to make things better for me. God bless them. But I'm getting along just fine, thank you, without signing my good name to any checks for any national gay organizations.'

This *laissez-faire* attitude toward oppression is only encouraged by the myth to which many gays cling: that homohatred will, in any case, deliquesce on its own, like a snowbank in springtime, naturally, inevitably, because our sunny modern world is wise and good, whereas homohatred is anachronistic, foolish, and bad. Surely folks are waking up to this fact even now. So let's lie low and wait.

GAYS DON'T SEE THEMSELVES AS MEMBERS OF A VALUABLE AND COHESIVE CULTURAL GROUP WORTH FIGHTING FOR

A Permanent Identity Crisis. Whereas American blacks, Asians, and other minorities typically define themselves first in terms of their ethnicity, and take pride in it, many, if not most, gays do not. Indeed, in a society that deprives them of dignity, many spend a lifetime struggling just to accept their sexuality and get past self-condemnation and guilt; genuine gay pride is far rarer than we'd like.

As a way of denying their gay identity to themselves, it is common, instead, for homosexuals to *compartmentalize* their notion of self into two halves, like a split personality—part gay and part non-gay—and hold that the latter part is really more representative.

This bifurcated identity is made easier by childhood socialization, and by the dual lives that most gays lead as adults. Whereas the gay identity has little chance to develop until the mid-teens or later, the non-gay identity is rooted in basic positive affiliations—racial, religious, class, national, provincial, cultural, recreational—that form during childhood, long before it ever occurs to the homosexual to define himself as a Gay Person. Then, typically, as he grows up, he'll spend most of every day assiduously projecting himself to the world as something other than homosexual. (Indeed, the very ability to hide one's stigma from others is what makes the gay identity particularly easy to deny to oneself; this is not an option for more recognizable minorities.) For the deeply closeted gay, in fact, the resulting disjuncture between the two parts can seem so absolute, it's as though his sexual preference were not a fundamental trait but rather a specific *place*—a particular gay disco, a cruising block—that he visits voluntarily and returns from once a week.

Few choose to make public scorn part of their self-image, preferring instead to preserve a certain feeling of detachment, if not from homosexuality per se, then from gayness (i.e., membership in the subculture). But this detachment poses a terrific obstacle to gay organizing. For most, the act of donating openly *or even anonymously* to a national gay organization would signify excessive commitment to their gay identity. They'd rather give the United Way.

Sex Is Not Politic. Then, too, many cannot relate to the very idea of a national homosexual movement. Just as the topic of sex makes the general public titter anxiously, the idea of rallying militantly around homosexual politics seems slightly ridiculous. "My sex life should be a bedroom thing—private," complained a friend, some years ago, "but 'gay lib' wants us to march up and down the streets with pink triangles and our dicks hanging out. I can't get into that." (Could this tittering factor be one reason why activists try so hard to dignify their cause by linking it to every other liberal one under the sun?) The root of such discomfort about the national movement is probably lingering shame over sex in general and homosexuality in particular.

Not One Big Happy Family. These factors are motive enough for homosexuals to distance themselves from the gay movement. But there is an even more central reason: *the gay ghetto does not cohere.* It offers *Gesellschaft* without true *Gemeinschaft.* That is, it offers society without the 'we-feeling' or solidarity that holds a true community together.

And why should it be otherwise? As sociologists would say, 'gay' signifies not a social *group* but a *category.* 'Homosexual' is merely a descriptive classification—like 'homo sapiens' or 'all people driving brown cars.' The so-called gay community is artificial, imposed upon its members by nonmembers, like a leper colony or prison. Why should captives naturally love associating with one another? If free to do so, most would go their separate ways.

It's the same with gays, who are as diverse a group as could be imagined. There are, of course, the usual divisors of class, education, and race—even though our world is often touted for the egalitarian way it captures and commingles all types, sifting only through the sieve of sheer beauty. This is partly true, partly wishful thinking. Precisely because gay watering holes press people of every ilk into one another's company, they actually create opportunities to exploit differences of class, attainment, and race as weapons in the battle to attract or deflect suitors.

But none of this is really unusual in American society. There are more extraordinary—indeed, unique—factors that discourage we-feeling among gays.

Battle of the (Third) Sexes. One giant factor is the social chasm between homosexual males and females (who, you will note, insist upon separate names: 'gay men' and 'lesbians'). The two differ markedly in lifestyle and social circumstance. Indeed, all that gays and lesbians really share in common is their oppression at the hands of straights and their relative sexual indifference toward each other. Paradoxically, *gay men and women are forced into political intimacy with one another precisely because they don't wish to be sexually intimate;* and what situation could possibly be more awkward than that? Try one in which this house of political intimates stands divided against itself, because the agenda of radical feminism shared by many (but not all) lesbians is intrinsically hostile to the machismo-worshipping chauvinism of many gay men.

This tension can be seen or sensed within the amorphous national gay organizations, and as a result many gays and lesbians prefer to support all-male and all-female groups, respectively, at the local level. After all, how can anyone be expected to donate heavily to a national association s/he suspects has been 'coopted' by the 'other half' for its own purposes? As a male friend of ours complained (with unintended pun), "Ever notice how you never see the rad dykes around, except in gay organizations? It's like, for them, politics is a substitute for sex, and our interests always get screwed by their anti-male thing."

We've heard a corresponding mutter from certain lesbians, who resent that the efforts of the national movement have been diverted, since 1982, by the 'gay *men's* health crisis.' While many lesbians have demonstrated remarkable solidarity with gay men during this time—through AIDS fundraising, organizing blood drives, etc.—others have recoiled. As separatist Yolanda Retter bitterly reminded *Advocate* readers in October 1988, "AIDS, once again, is asking women to take care of boys because they weren't able to control themselves." Obviously, such feelings make wholehearted support for unified national organizations more difficult to muster.

In sum, gay men and lesbians are apples and oranges; they happen to find themselves in the same barrel only because their society treats all fruits alike. Were it otherwise, these two probably would not socialize with each other, much less unite in organizations.

The Male Camp: Q's vs. R's. Unfortunately, male versus female is neither the only nor the worst rift in the gay community. As it happens, homosexual men are themselves divided bitterly into apples and oranges, undercutting the feeling that they belong to a cohesive group worth supporting.

On one side are what we call *'R-types.'* R's prefer to see themselves as 'straight gays'; they think their conventional, manly appearance lets them pass as straight on the street. R's, though not necessarily closeted, choose not to emphasize their homosexuality because they value highly their acceptance in general society. By keeping their heads down, R's reinforce the Big Lie.

On the other side are *'Q-types'*—homosexuals on display. Q's don't *wish* to be seen as straight (indeed, many couldn't pass if they tried). Instead, they jauntily assume any one of several recognizable public personas: the long-haired androgyne or permed 'fem,' the titanic leather master, the dude-ranch cowboy, the clipped clone, the Bruce Weber hyperboy, and others. (Manliness, you see, is troublesome to Q's and must be deflated by burlesque.) Whereas R's were just 'one of the guys' during childhood and grew up to like it that way, we suspect that Q's are men who somehow couldn't fit in during their youth (too passive, pretty, homely, effeminate, or otherwise unpopular). So they became rebels with a cause, making a lodestar virtue out of individualism. Because looking different entails risks and isolation, Q's tend to camp together—in both senses—in gay ghettos. The most vocal among them have involved themselves in gay politics and organization, and have played a key role in shaping the agenda and defining the sensibility of the entire gay movement.

The tableau of Q's and R's, then, resembles the battle between black "Jigaboos" and "Wanna-Be's" in Spike Lee's controversial film *School Daze:* Q's affect nonconformity, while R's 'wanna be' conventional, and accepted into the mainstream. As you might imagine, Q's and R's neither sympathize with nor understand one another, with fascinating but horrendous results for gay life and organization.

In a nutshell, R's dominate the sexual hierarchy of the gay male world, while Q's dominate its political hierarchy. All-American R's look down on flamboyant Q's as sexual and social inferiors, attack their effeminacy, and openly resent them for giving all gays a bad reputation. (As John Reid, the R-type author of *The Best Little Boy in the World,* has written of Q's: "Those people I saw on the streets with their pocketbooks and their swish and their pink hair disgusted me at least as much as they disgusted everyone else, probably more.") Yet R's decline to join organizations and work to change gays' public image, in part because these organizations are too 'radically gayified' (read: Q-oriented) for their tastes, but largely because R's are loath to be identified as gay activists.

Q's, for their part, find macho R's sexy on the dance floor but, once spurned, dismiss them as maladjusted closet cases, afraid to reveal their 'true androgynous nature.' (A misunderstanding: many R's may indeed be maladjusted, but their masculine demeanor is natural, not put on.) Not surprisingly, then, the conformist values of R's—being reviled as politically incorrect, unliberated, and self-loathing—have generally been unwelcome to the movement over the past twenty years. As a result, our national organizations have alienated millions of potential R-type members, who probably constitute a majority of the gay male community. And if a Q-R split likewise exists in the lesbian camp

—we're told that it does—then the membership loss has been further compounded.

Having said this, however, it's also worth noting that the balance of power within some gay organizations seems to be shifting
back to center in recent days, what with more R's fronting as
public spokespersons for these groups, more R's prompted to become members during the AIDS era, and more conservatism generally among gays (as among straights) during these times. But the
truce between Q's and R's remains uneasy.

We see only one permanent solution to the Q-R cold war (and,
to a lesser extent, to the battle of the third sexes): eliminate internal tensions by making the movement itself obsolete. In other
words, gays as a whole must make so much progress toward social
acceptance in the straight world that gays whose sensibilities are
mutually irreconcilable will no longer feel compelled to mingle
socially or align politically just because they happen to share a
sexual preference.

Until that glorious day, however, the short-term solution is for
activists deliberately to strike a better balance between the values
and imagery of Q's and R's in public. This will help teach straights
that a great many nonstereotypic gays do, in fact, exist. At the
same time, it will build support for the movement among R's. Our
proposed media campaign is designed to do precisely that.

GAYS DON'T BELIEVE THAT NATIONAL GAY ORGANIZATIONS DO MUCH GOOD IN ANY CASE

National gay organizations get little support from their constituency because it is both complacent and internally divided, as
we've said; but also because they do not appear to offer much to
their members. It's a vicious circle: lacking concrete support
(votes, funds), gay activists can't accomplish much; failing to accomplish much, activists receive tepid support. To an extent, the
problem is one of appearances. The Task Force, for example, can
cite a score of notable advances toward gay rights since 1973 in
which NGLTF played a role, *but it has nobody to tell!* The straight

press seldom indicates which gay groups could take credit for such advances, and most homosexuals have no other way to find out, since relatively few read the gay press.

Not that most would jump to join national organizations, even if they knew of their good works. Although the same may not be true of lesbians, it is our impression that gay males are often loners, not joiners. Early on in life, they adopt the chary perspective of outsiders and don't cotton to sustained teamwork and community. Since affiliation is not its own reward with them, gay men seem more inclined to ask, 'What's in membership for me?'

Local organizations are fairly popular; membership can serve selfish private, as well as selfless public, ends. (All voluntary public organizations necessarily serve both to some degree.) Local groups can mix political activism with fun and schmoozing. The meeting places of local gay groups are regarded favorably as 'secure spaces'—just like the bars—where gay people can relax, hang out with their friends, and meet new ones, even as they man hotlines and stuff envelopes for a good cause. Indeed, local groups invariably become happy hunting grounds for romance, and it is the veiled hope of this, as much as anything else, that lures new members in. Finally, one of the nice things about local groups is that you can just show up in person; you needn't give anyone your mailing address or even your full name, if you'd rather not.

In contrast, what can national gay organizations offer members on the private front? Not much. Not even privacy: a national group is a mailing list. It's cold, remote, and abstract. Its 'secure space' is in some other city. Gays may view local organizations as auxiliary cruising zones, but what practical use could they have for a cruising zone that spans the entire nation? Not surprisingly, then, enthusiasm for our national gay institutions is lukewarm and highly intellectualized. Less involving than local groups, it's no wonder they have far fewer members.

o

FUNDRAISING FOR THE MEDIA CAMPAIGN: THE BUCK STARTS HERE

SEEING AND BELIEVING.

So we have a problem: the gay media campaign will require leadership and finance on the national level, yet our national organizations generate precious little commitment and commensurate funding. What can be done to bring more gays into the national effort? What will ignite their enthusiasm and support?

Vic Basile, executive director of the Human Rights Campaign Fund, observes, "Once you convince them that what you're doing is worthwhile, gay people do contribute. The difficulty is finding them and telling the story. The person who figures out how to find this community will be able to raise millions of dollars."

For the most part, Basile is right. And the best way to find and inspire the majority of gay people is to reach them where they live: tucked away at home—shoes off, feet on the coffee table—watching TV or reading the paper. In other words, we can and must *build enthusiasm and financial support through the very process of presenting homosexuals (and the rest of the world) with gay ads that move them, make them proud, stir them up.* *

Gays will give money in response to national gay advertising because, at last, their cash is going to support a specific program or crusade, not 'just another organization.' Gays will give money because they will be able to see where the money they mail is actually going: to public media. Whereas the drudgery of lobbying and legal defense are done out of sight and with uncertain result, for media consumers—both straight and gay—the proof of our pudding will be in the eating.

---

* We are grandly assuming, for the rest of this chapter, that this is a team effort; that the various national organizations have, in a miraculous outbreak of enlightened self-interest, successfully collaborated in designing such a program, and that a myriad of local organizations are helping to implement it.

PREACHING TO THE CHOIR: THE NEW GAY TELEVANGELISM.

Let's get religious for a minute. A gay media campaign can do wondrous spiritual—and then financial—things for our torpid community. It may be only a fundraiser's leap of faith, but we dare to believe that national gay advertising can pull itself up financially by its own bootstraps. Its effect upon the minds and motivations of gay Americans can prove so catalytic that, once gay advertising gets on the air, it will be held aloft by voluntary contributions. (Reverend Oral Roberts, move over: if the authors are wrong about this, the Lord might just have to call *us* home.)

True, the majority of closeted gays, at least at the outset, will lack the courage to contribute to the campaign, even anonymously. Moreover, the divisions that alienate many homosexuals from the putative gay community will remain. Yet, in an important sense, the campaign itself will soon redress the deficit in natural solidarity and organization among gays. It will give all of them —whether they like one another or not, live in the gay ghetto or not, are closeted or not—something to focus on, and contribute to, with proud enthusiasm. If the ads project a new, resolutely positive, all-American image with which most gays can identify, we think that, in no time, millions will be so eager to perpetuate these good works that they'll begin to donate money to our appeals on TV as though their social salvation depended on it. Which it does.

When one thinks about it, this process *does* resemble a religious conversion of sorts. He who, upon seeing our gay ads, believes enough to mail in cash will build his own sense of legitimacy, militancy, and political involvement. First he'll feel proud; later he'll come out, redefining himself and his commitments in the process. For gays, coming out in public is like being "born again to a living hope," as St. Peter says. A legion of gays who have hope, who are finally awakened—from shame, from resignation, from powerlessness—will pound the Big Lie into dust. "Who has heard such a thing?" asked Isaiah. "Can a land be born in one day? Can a nation be brought forth all at once?" If anything can empower and mobilize gays quickly, it is a national media campaign.

NOW, THE BORING STUFF ABOUT FUNDRAISING.

What we've said so far may sound inspirational, but it raises a dilemma. Here, as elsewhere, it takes money to make money, and it will take a committed few to arouse commitment in the rest. If the only way to get gays to support a national media campaign is actually to mount one, how do we obtain the initial scratch, the investment capital, to put a campaign on the air in the first place?

Clearly, fundraising must proceed in two steps. *Phase I,* before the campaign, solicits funds from gays through gay channels. In *Phase II,* we solicit additional funds from gays and straights via straight media, through the ads themselves. All tactics employed in Phase I must be continued even after the campaign is launched.

First Steps: Name, Mission, Tax Deductibility, and a Good Ladder. To raise money, the campaign's organizers—and that, we hope, includes you—must agree upon a single, pungent 'trademark' name for the campaign, to appear on all campaign materials and gradually become recognizable to both gays and straights. (Though there are many worthy candidates, we've recommended calling it the Waging Peace campaign.)

Organizers must also settle upon a *statement of mission,* the basic purposes of the campaign. This book itself, obviously, suggests many purposes, but the campaign board and staff must formally agree to accept those they consider most central to their work. Then they must *prioritize objectives,* and set specific, measurable milestone goals along the path toward each objective. Until this is done, our fundraisers will never be able to make a clear case to potential contributors as to what the campaign will accomplish. Professional fundraiser Fisher Howe, writing in the *Harvard Business Review* in the spring of 1985, proposed a sensible test that we think gay campaign organizers must be able to pass before going one step further:

> What would you and your board do with a million dollars if you had it tomorrow? Or just one hundred thousand? It isn't good enough to respond, "Just let us have the money; we can spend it all right." Agreement about how to apportion the money to program, facilities, and staff, and the work you do to reach that agreement will strengthen immeasurably your ability to raise the money.

Once mission and working plan are hammered out, it's time to make two cases. We make one case to the government, presenting the campaign, truthfully, as a benevolent *not-for-profit program* whose goal is public education and whose donations should receive *tax-deductible* status. We make the other case to prospective donors themselves, requesting advance funding for the campaign. Explanatory materials, showing how the advertisements might actually look, should be prepared and circulated. But to which donors? Unless they earn their own revenue—by selling greeting cards, Girl Scout cookies, or the like—all not-for-profit organizations must turn to four standard funding sources:

1. Government grants
2. Foundation grants
3. Business contributions
4. Individual contributions

Government and foundation grants to educate the public about gays and gay life are still quite hard to come by—though the Fund for Human Dignity has already won a few. But extreme skittishness about the H-word remains: it caused many foundations to hold off for years on funding for AIDS research and education. As the art and science of winning grants would make a tedious book in itself, let's put it aside for now, and consider instead how to win business and individual contributions in advance of the campaign.

This is where the ladder comes in. Professional fundraisers have a general rule, which we'd like to pass on to you: *the more directly personal your contact with donors, the more funds you will raise.* Consequently, the ladder of communication effectiveness, again adapted from Fisher Howe's article, looks something like this:

Figure 1.

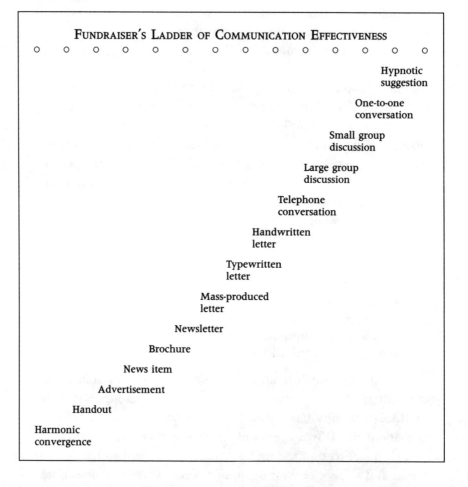

FUNDRAISER'S LADDER OF COMMUNICATION EFFECTIVENESS

Hypnotic
suggestion

One-to-one
conversation

Small group
discussion

Large group
discussion

Telephone
conversation

Handwritten
letter

Typewritten
letter

Mass-produced
letter

Newsletter

Brochure

News item

Advertisement

Handout

Harmonic
convergence

O.K., we're joking about its highest and lowest rungs, but the rest of the ladder holds true. Note, however, that the personal-communication rule doesn't mean that indirect solicitations never produce donations. On the contrary, activities on the bottom half of the ladder necessarily provide most not-for-profit organizations with a large part of their operating budget. There is no alternative, since personal contact is the most costly thing any organization can dispense, and must be used sparingly. Besides, indirect contact will be unavoidably important in gay fundraising, since most prospective donors will wish to be anonymous. Even so, the lion's share of individual donations usually comes from a few wealthy individuals and business executives who must be wooed in person. As we review the range of fundraising techniques below, keep asking yourself whether each is best implemented indirectly or through personal contact.

What follows is not a fundraising plan in itself but a short list of basic fundraising ideas for Phase I, most of them to be continued into Phase II. We don't indicate who should take responsibility for implementing them, nor at what level—national, state, or local. (We must leave *something* for you to do!) Yet many, if not most, of these ideas seem best suited to local implementation.

The list distinguishes between *grass-roots appeals'* and *'exposed-roots appeals.'* Grass-roots appeals are made to individual donors. Exposed-roots appeals seek funding from publicly exposed representatives or servicers of the gay community—chiefly gay organizations and businesses that, in one sense or another, profit from the gay subculture.

A SHORT LIST OF FUNDRAISING IDEAS FOR PHASE I (AND THEREAFTER)

A. Grass-roots appeals

1. Cultivate the gay upper class. If this doesn't sound like grass roots to you, you're tilling the wrong soil. There exists a class of ultrasuccessful, ultra-discreet gay men and women in America —captains of industry and finance, or persons born into wealth —who have plenty to give.

These gentlemen and ladies also have plenty to lose to adverse publicity. They must be approached with intelligent caution (this is where person-to-person contacts come in) and assured of the greatest possible confidentiality; their large donations may even need 'laundering' through innocuous-sounding intermediary funds before entering the campaign's coffers.

2. *Conduct direct-mail appeals* to the members of as many gay organizations as will support the media campaign. (And follow up with phone calls, if possible.) Materials sent should build excitement, describing the upcoming campaign and what it can mean for the future of gay America.

To spur their involvement, point out that the gay community is under particularly sharp attack these days; the AIDS crisis has been like blood in the water to homohating, right-wing sharks like Jesse Helms & Co. (Be sure to cite Helms as bogeyman wherever possible, since polls show that much of the public—indeed, every human with a brain and heart above room temperature—already loathes him thoroughly.) Gays on mailing lists should be further invited to consider 'planned giving' to the campaign: monthly or semiannual contributions, bequests, stock, property, trusts.

3. *Place fundraising ads in the gay press,* to reach that broad outer circle of gays who have access (in bookstores and bars) to some gay literature but are not on any mailing lists. Given the importance of the cause, gay media should be asked to provide at least some of the ad space free or at a deep discount. We can't be picky at this stage: gays peruse glossy skin magazines as well as 'serious' gay newspapers, so our ads must appear in both places. (Ads should also appear in any available broadcast media, such as the handful of gay-format radio stations and cable TV programs.)

Neither can we be too finicky about our donors, for we need both the liberated and the closeted. To this end, our fundraising ads should explain how an anonymous contribution can be made (e.g., via money orders). They should also reassure those who identify themselves—by sending a check, for example—that they're not automatically assumed to be gay. (A clip-out coupon might even let donors designate themselves as 'Proud Member of the Gay Community' or just 'Friend of Gay Community, Not Member'; and it could also let donors indicate whether or not they'd mind going onto a confidential campaign mailing list.) In sum, our ads must make reader response as easy and nonscary as possible.

4. Develop dedicated fundraising events, in cooperation with other gay national or local groups (sharing the proceeds with them, if necessary). The range of standard tactics is broad: benefits; raffles; movie screenings or gay film festivals; sports events and walkathons for cash; sponsored concerts, talks, debates, poetry and play readings; special once-a-year campaign drives; gay group-travel packages that include a donation; coin-collection cannisters in bars; and the sale of T-shirts, buttons, and posters emblazoned with the campaign's message.

5. Introduce an affinity credit card for the campaign. All sorts of benevolent groups (the Sierra Club, public TV stations, charities) are discovering a terrific way for supporters to contribute financially to their favorite cause without actually sacrificing much themselves (the best of both worlds—advancing one's principles without self-abnegation!). In cooperation with a friendly bank, the group co-sponsors the special offering of a major national credit card (e.g., Visa, Mastercard) from which the group receives a profit (from the membership fee, finance charges, and store subscription).

For the most part, only uncloseted gays will have the courage to admit their sexual preference tacitly, and traceably, in their choice of credit card, but the number of such gays is already sizable and growing. (Almost needless to say, the card itself should be subtle in appearance: few gays really want to come out to *everybody,* including the lout who pumps their gas and the blue-haired crone who works the cash register.)

B. Exposed-root Appeals

1. Let other gay organizations contribute directly to the campaign. Assuming grandly, once again, that cooperation can be achieved among the realm's principalities, each should be asked to pledge some modest fraction of its operating budget in support, or on a dollars-per-member basis; while also providing, where possible, both manpower and access to its mailing lists.

2. Persuade gay bars and other gay-patronized businesses to donate regularly to the campaign. This will take some doing. The biggest gay bars are astonishingly profitable enterprises that could well afford to donate, say, a couple of cents for each drink sold, or the proceeds of one benefit nightevery month or two.

But whether 'our' bars, whose owners are as penny-pinching as the next businessman, would dig so deep to help gays is doubtful. Yet if the campaign begins to catch on, further pressure might be applied: gays can be encouraged to patronize only those establishments whose annual donations have earned them an official Waging Peace campaign seal for their door. Uncooperative bars should be reminded gently that their furtive clientele will take a powder at the first sign of a noisy picket line and TV cameras.

Much the same goes for other businesses that profit from gays —hotels and resorts, clothing stores, travel and dating services, bath houses (if any remain), porn shops, haircutters, certain restaurants and gyms. Heretofore, many of these establishments have benefited from their captive audience. Now it's time for them to repay the favor with financial support for their captives' liberation.

These, then, are the various ways in which the movement should be able to gather enough Phase I cash—say, several million dollars—to launch a Phase II mass-media campaign. Thereafter, as we said, advertising will have to start pulling its own weight by appealing for support and announcing fundraising events of the sort discussed above.

You'll have noticed no great magic in this list of fundraising techniques—nothing with which the Cub Scouts haven't already beaten America senseless. Rather, the magic comes from those who implement these ideas, with craft and enthusiasm. And it comes from those who respond generously, seizing the opportunity of these raffles, walkathons, and credit cards to do what they've secretly always wanted to do anyway: help advance justice for gays in America.

Much the same goes for unifying the gay movement and coordinating the media campaign under one national organization. There is no secret to achieving this. There is no institutional super glue, apart from hard work and the subordination of bureaucratic egos: our leaders will either decide to join forces, or not. Like hanging together or hanging separately. May the gay community bring forth the strength it needs to survive.

PART III

NOT IN OUR STARS, BUT IN OURSELVES

6

THE STATE OF OUR COMMUNITY: GAY PRIDE GOETH BEFORE A FALL

The hungry sheep look up, and are not fed; but,
Swol'n with wind and the rank mist they
draw,
Rot inwardly, and foul contagion spread.

—JOHN MILTON, *LYCIDAS*

○   ○   ○

OUR PURPOSE IN WRITING THIS UNPLEASANT CHAPTER

In Chapter 1 we went to great lengths to shake you out of your complacency, by showing you just how bad things are for you—how intensely you are hated and despised by straights—and how great the danger is of the already unacceptable becoming, in the not-too-distant future, completely intolerable. We showed that affairs have reached a sorry pass, and threaten still worse.

In Chapter 2, we established that our problem is fundamentally one of a bad image with straights, which can, in theory, be helped —if not wholly corrected—by standard image-management techniques.

After the Ball has now detailed a comprehensive public-relations campaign that should go a long way toward sanitizing our very unsanitary image. But we can't hide forever beneath a coat of whitewash; we have to step out from behind the façade eventually, and unless we've made some real changes by the time we do, people will see that we're still the same old queers. Straights hate gays not just for what their myths and lies *say* we are, but also for what we *really* are; all the squeaky-clean media propaganda in the world won't sustain a positive image in the long run unless we start scrubbing to make ourselves a little squeakier and cleaner in reality. And as it happens, our noses (and other parts) are far from clean. In one major respect, America's homohaters have, like the proverbial blind pig, rooted up the truffle of truth: the gay lifestyle —not our sexuality, but our *lifestyle*—is the pits. This chapter will tell you what's wrong with a lot of gays, why it's wrong, and how you can dance the new steps . . . after the ball.

WHAT? AREN'T STRAIGHTS THE ONES WHO HAVE TO CHANGE?

Unfortunately, no. American straights are clearly at fault; they've done their best—or, should we say, their damnedest?—to herd us to this pass, imposing upon us a burden of deprivation and suffering deserved by no one, least of all us. Yet it would be, and indeed has been, a disastrous mistake to deny that we also are at fault in the matter—because we are. For twenty years, we've insisted that because straights treat us badly, and not vice versa, it's their responsibility to change, not ours. That was unrealistic. Straights aren't going to change on their own—at least not for the better—and this means that if we're to solve our problems, we must take action. And clever video spots and sound-bites won't go all the way. Out of sheer expedience, we must start doing a lot of what we don't want to do, and *stop* doing a lot of what we *do* want to do. The Great God of Reality helps those who help themselves; to help ourselves, we must change ourselves, not congregate in gay ghettos, cut ugly capers, and thumb our collective nose at the outside world.

This chapter's purpose, therefore, is Constructive Criticism. We outline ten categories of misbehavior—things that many gays do, or that are praised and idealized by the gay leadership as part of our 'lifestyle'—that can no longer be borne, and for two reasons: they make us look bad to straights, and they cause needless suffering, lowering the quality of life within the gay community. We are aware that criticizing gays is massively politically incorrect; that it has been decreed by the powers that be that Gay is Good, period; that anyone who would question our lifestyle is an enemy, to be summarily suppressed. This bad attitude, too, is a misbehavior, and must also come to a screeching halt, starting right now.

CAVEAT LECTOR: THE (NECESSARY) LIMITATIONS OF OUR CRITICISM

Compiling data for this chapter presented special difficulties. Gays are, understandably, more fond of documenting their mistreatment at the hands of straights than they are of documenting their own misdeeds, failures, and follies. The material and impressions of this chapter are drawn largely from our own experiences, and necessarily so: there are no statistically reliable data from large-scale studies to validate our impressions of such imponderables, such hard-to-quantify attitudes, values, mind-sets, and behavior.

However, we've tried to buttress our impressions wherever possible with other people's impressions, which we've collected via wide reading and—probably more important—literally thousands of hours of conversation, over a period of years, with hundreds of other gays.

Our criticisms relate largely to gay *men*—admittedly a defect of the whole of this book. Some of the most negative aspects of the gay community are associated almost entirely with gay men, though, both in widespread perception and actual fact, so our somewhat one-sided view does little violence to reality. (Indeed, the gay community itself is a bit one-sided; it is at least two-thirds male.)[1] Lesbians may, in fact, consider it a compliment that we find less to fault in their behavior and values than we do in those of gay men.

What we describe as the ugly aspects of gay life may, in fact, simply be the ugly aspects of human nature in general, and by no means limited to gays. Although we don't believe for a second that this is true for every aspect we will discuss, it's possible that we've pilloried gays unfairly in some instances for misbehaviors equally characteristic of straights. Even where this is so, however, it matters not a whit to our argument. Suppose straights *are* just as guilty as gays of Misbehavior X; what of it? Gays, being oppressed, will nevertheless be punished more harshly for Misbehavior X than will straights. As Avis once said, "When you're number two, you have to try harder." We have to be, not *as good as* straights, but actually better than straights, to win acceptance.

And, after all, why should we set our personal standards as low as those of straight America? Think about it.

A real problem is that you may decide we simply don't like gays very much, and dismiss our work as the lucubrations of a pair of cranks. But the sad fact is, while we wish well to both gays and gayness as such, we have been disheartened and angered for many years by what we've seen of the blemished *behavior* of gays. A lot of it has looked immature, self-centered, destructive, silly, and creepy. We have too much pride invested in this community to sit back with our mouths taped shut and nod our heads in silent agreement with the theme song of the politically correct, 'If It's Gay It Must be Good.' Readers who have heard for too long only what's good about them must now sit up and pay attention to what's *bad* about them. Even if our critique goes overboard, it will still help to right the balance scale of self-perception.

Oh, and while we're at it—*we*, the authors, are every bit as guilty of a lot of the nastiness we describe as are other gays. This makes us not less qualified to inveigh against such evils but, if anything, even more so: "My heart showeth me the wickedness of the ungodly."

Finally, don't be alienated by our implicit assumption of a definite 'right and wrong'—a *morality* (that taboo term!) transcending merely human values—to which we appeal, and against which we judge the behavior of our peers. We think there is such a morality, but even if you don't—even if you're an utter materialist with no room in your thinking for metaphysical foofaraw—we can (and do) appeal to you still, on the grounds that presupposing and obeying a 'moral code' is an act of 'enlightened self-interest,' and for these reasons:

(1) In the long run, the Ten Misbehaviors all make life in the gay community less happy for everyone. A widely endorsed social code would smooth the rough edges of gay life and induce each of us to restrain his more hateful and selfish impulses. Voltaire said, "If there were no God, it would be necessary to invent him." *Gays* should invent a sensible, kindly code of ethics and manners, and live by it as though its prescriptions and proscriptions were backed by a compelling moral force.

(2) Like it or not, what straights think of our behavior affects our lives. If we have difficulty convincing them not to hate and oppress us for something as harmless as the physical love of members of our own sex, it's going to be a whole lot harder to get them to swallow gay misbehavior that almost anyone, of any sexual persuasion, would find harmful, reprehensible, and contemptible. For our own good, we have no choice but to *look* good; that means defending what's essential—our identity as gay men and women —and chucking what isn't: the bad, the indefensible, the throwaway parts of our character and lifestyle.

Enough preamble; into the courtroom!

○

READING YOU THE RIOT ACT: HOW GAYS MISBEHAVE

1. LIES, LIES, ALL LIES!

> *The world is naturally averse*
> *To all the truth it sees and hears,*
> *But swallows nonsense and a lie*
> *With greediness and gluttony.*
> —SAMUEL BUTLER, *HUDIBRAS*

As the Twig Is Bent

The first and most fundamental respect in which the gay experience differs from the straight is a nearly universal stage, lasting anywhere from a few months to a lifetime, in which the gay youth's dawning awareness that his feelings are different leads, almost inevitably, to pain, fear, and the need to lie. Although unusual family or community standards, or an unusually headstrong and rebellious temperament, may spare the occasional gay youth this need, massive deceit is otherwise ineluctable and universal.

Alternatively, of course, the gay teen may feel no especial pain or fear over his homosexuality, but regard it, instead, with a certain odd pleasure, as the one thing he knows about himself that no one else knows. Along these lines, one of our gay classmates at Harvard remarked that, as a teenager, he had taken pleasure in this dark secret, as though he were an undercover agent. Even in these cases, however, the result is the same: a commonsense regard for self-preservation makes lying the gay teen's constant companion.

Sometimes this phase of conscious concealment is preceded by a period of unconscious denial—refusing to recognize the true state of one's affairs and attempting to avert the painful task of honest self-appraisal by lying to oneself. This sad self-deception can last for years or decades, and may, in fact, never terminate in self-confrontation at all. Such unhappy gays rationalize that their feelings are 'just a phase,' or 'don't mean anything because I'm going out with girls,' and reflect an astounding ability to sequester unpleasant truths in hermetically sealed compartments of the mind. (We've seen amazing personal ads reading 'Straight white male seeks similar for hot times. No gays, bis' and letters to men's magazines asking, 'Is it normal for a totally straight young guy to enjoy getting oral sex from his best buddy?' In at least one case, the answer was 'Yes!') A conversation we had with one gay man of forty or so—who had decided, belatedly, to come out, now that, so to speak, the party was over and the chairs were being put up—is representative of a great many similar cases:

Q. But didn't you realize that you were gay many years ago?
A. No.
Q. But surely you had dreams or fantasies about other young guys, got embarrassing erections looking at them in the locker room, masturbated thinking about them, or something?
A. Well, yes, I did. In fact, I had a buddy in college that I fooled around with for years.
Q. Well—didn't this tip you to the fact that you were gay?
A. No; I didn't think it meant anything. I thought other guys had these feelings. I was afraid. And I always made sure I had a girlfriend.

Gay teens are driven by the intolerable fear of disgrace to lie more frequently, and about a far more serious matter, than the typical straight teen must. It's axiomatic that the repeated practice of any sin callouses the conscience, especially when the sinner realizes that, owing to unfair circumstances beyond his control, he has no practical choice but to sin. Lying is no exception to this rule.

Accordingly, it would be surprising indeed if the gay teen,

forced to lie seriously, constantly, and for a very long time, did not eventually experience a weakening of his pangs of conscience at lying and tend increasingly to resort to this expedient when confronted by difficulties in any sphere of living whatever.

'I'll Call You Thursday'—Lies Our Ad Respondents Told Us

Personal ads—where lovely fantasies founder on the rocky shores of cruel reality—are a veritable nonbreeding ground for gay liars.

We and our friends have placed many such ads over the years, with uniformly astounding and depressing results. We've learned that you can trust nothing—literally *nothing*—that an ad respondent says. Indeed, if a respondent specifies that he is a human being, we now assume that he is a gay Martian, hiding from the planetary immigration authorities.

Our mutual friend Kip, then nineteen and somewhat naïf, placed a roommate ad in a tabloid, stating his gayness—as is often done—to ward off homophobes. Predictably, this elicited a flood of jerkoff calls. Among these was John, who called many times over the next two months. John seemed pleasant, so curious Kip talked with him. John described himself as twenty-four, five-nine, blond and green-eyed, 140 pounds, muscular and athletic, clean-shaven and Ivy League-handsome. He asked if Kip were fat, as, he said, "I hate fat people." Feeling he now knew John—and as enticeable as the next fellow—Kip agreed to meet him at the Boston Aquarium.

Many readers will recognize the ensuing scenario with a wince. A man drove up in the agreed-upon Trans-Am. Kip thought, surely this can't be him. *Mais oui!* John proved to be forty, brown-haired and balding, five-eleven, carrying an immensely potbellied 210 pounds in a food-smeared T-shirt—in every way unlike his self-description. Kip said, "You are the biggest liar I ever met." John retorted, "Yeah—well—we all have to exaggerate a little to get some action!"

Pathological Liars and Con Men

In a sense, the pathological liar is just your garden-variety liar writ large. His lying is motivated by the same factors that give less flagrant liars their *raison d'être,* so it's revealing that, as the works of many students of the sociopathic personality assert, a surprisingly high percentage of pathological liars are, in fact, gay.

We first met 'Floyd' between innings at a meeting of the Framingham, Massachusetts Gay Men's Softball League. Off in the dugout, to a small audience palpitating with interest, Floyd—a local delivery boy—was disclosing the glittering facets of his recent job, working, so he said, with an "answering service for the stars" in Hollywood. As absorbing anecdotes of the foibles of the superstars poured from this raconteur—including his claim that he had been fired through the malice of the Princess von Thurn und Taxis—we began to smell the proverbial rat, and asked Floyd just how he had landed this glamorous position. "Oh," he said, blinking, "I answered a classified ad in a gay magazine."

To our way of thinking, this cockamamie story clinched the diagnosis. However, we later described Floyd and his implausible tale to a friend. "Oh, yes," snorted the friend, "I know him, Floyd McLloyd. He told *me* he'd been a *call-boy* in Hollywood. But then, he also told me his father was on the board of directors of Litton Industries." And, as it happened, our friend's father really had been on the board of Litton, and exploded the whole fable.

A mere fabulist like Floyd may be harmless, but the gay con man, endowed by nature with an uncanny talent for fleshing out his confabulations with more convincing—and usually unverifiable—detail, turns his lies to profit. Spuriously plausible and allergic to work, he simply finds it easier to lie his way through life, attaching himself like a parasite to the charitable or gullible. He finds older gay men, who are often lonely—and eager to believe in an attractive and personable young man—easy prey, and by his machinations, he breathes life into the cliché of the aging interior decorator who takes in the young 'hustler with the heart of gold,' and awakens one day to find his American Express Platinum Card, Rolex, cashmere sweaters, and five hundred in cash all gone with the wind.

A Message—for *Malcolm?*

Grotesque real-life examples are valuable, not because they're representative—thank God they aren't—but because they highlight, in memorable form, the principles underlying a point. One of the most memorable cases of callous mendacity we've ever encountered is well worth dissecting at length.

Some time ago, 'Wolf', a good (and straight) friend of one of the authors, called him, angry and upset. An unknown fellow named 'Rhett,' who had been leaving messages for months, had phoned again, and found Wolf in.

Rhett asked Wolf how he'd been since the previous summer, and how medical school was going. Confused, Wolf said that he wasn't in medical school, and couldn't recall ever having met Rhett. Rhett was skeptical: "Come on, Wolf, don't you live in Belmont, in a one-bedroom?" "Yes," answered Wolf. "Then you remember that I was at your house party last June." "I wasn't in town last June," Wolf replied. "My apartment was sublet to an acquaintance, Malcolm Y."

Rhett and Wolf then compared descriptions of Wolf's summer tenant and realized that Malcolm, during his stay, had been passing himself off at gay bars as Wolf and passing out Wolf's phone number to tricks. But there was more.

Malcolm was actually a twenty-three-year-old salesclerk, but the June evening he invited Rhett and several others over to Wolf's place he was claiming to be a thirty-one-year-old medical resident. At the party, Malcolm and his guests took drugs. Then Malcolm, assuring the others of his medical expertise, gave one of the visitors some sort of high-powered enema for sexual kicks while the others watched.

The unfortunate recipient of the enema, Rhett explained, subsequently developed a serious rectal infection, requiring expensive treatment for many months. His doctors wanted to locate 'Wolf' in order to have his medical license revoked. But the victim had been so drugged that he couldn't recall the exact location of Wolf's apartment, nor his surname. Rhett was now calling to warn Wolf that the injured party was out to get him, through legal action or violence, when next they met.

Wolf was deeply disturbed by Rhett's story. For years—since he'd learned of the authors' preference—Wolf had been struggling toward greater tolerance of gays. But now he felt a return of fear and disgust. When he learned that a group of gay men had conducted a perverse sex party in his own apartment—and had given one another enemas for thrills in his bathroom—he felt revolted and violated. He feared humiliating damage to his reputation should police officers invade his building with a warrant charging him with malpractice or sodomy.

When Wolf called Malcolm on the carpet, Malcolm blandly denied everything. "Perhaps somebody broke into your house and had the sex party while I was away," Malcolm purred helpfully. "Has your apartment ever been broken into?"

E Pluribus Unum: How a Great Many Little Lies Make One Big Lie

In the Introduction, we discussed the Big Lie: straights' comforting notion that gays are actually very rare, and that they, personally, don't know any. In fact, of course, they're usually quite wrong: anyone with six or seven adult male friends stands a better-than-even chance of knowing at least one gay person[2]; far from not knowing any gays, most adult Americans know a fair number—many of them close, valued friends. It's clear, therefore, that if every gay declared him or herself, the Big Lie would be exposed. Universal self-exposure alone would be sufficient to tip the balance against, and, ultimately, spell the end of, straight oppression.

But the gay friends of homohaters have excellent reason to keep them in the dark. After all, who wants to come out to, and court rejection from, someone so ignorant that he thinks gays are rare, dirty birds? Consequently, the vicious circle spins 'round and 'round: 'normal' gays lie and hide because they're afraid of straight ignorance and stereotyping; straight ignorance and stereotyping persist because 'normal' gays lie and hide. As long as all gays are thought to be obvious, flaming freaks, only obvious, flaming freaks will come out.

Although the gay real-estate market for roomy, solidly built, revelation-proof closets is, therefore, understandable, it is also exceedingly undesirable. When we take the self-protective action of hiding our homosexuality behind a mask of apparent heterosexuality, we simultaneously batten down our hatches against straight oppression, and ensure that it will continue, world without end, amen.

Now, although we disapprove of lying and hiding, we also feel sympathy for those compelled by circumstances and sanity to do so. It's all very well to talk of coming out for the good of the gay community as a whole, but that good will occur, if at all, in a future that the gay debutant may not see, and at the expense of making himself a martyr.

Nevertheless, many gays still prefer to lie and hide, out of cowardice and unrealistic paranoia. Many are sufficiently financially stable—self-employed or independently well-to-do—that coming out could not, reasonably speaking, be expected to entail fiscal hardship; many more have such good and broad-minded friends and family that coming out to them wouldn't entail the loss of friendship and love. (And of what value, by-the-bye, is friendship obtained under false pretenses, from people who don't like *you*, but what they falsely imagine you to be?)

But these 'secure' gays, too cowardly to take the plunge, exaggerate the adverse consequences of coming out into a vast, improbable bugaboo: querulously, they ask themselves, 'Ah, but *what if?* What if they hated me and said they never wanted to see me again? Or took out a full-page advertisement to precisely that effect in the *New York Times;* or flew into a frenzy of loathing and beat me with big sticks until I lost all kidney function; or notified the National Security Agency, who came in a dreadful black van with bars and flashing lights and Took Me Away?' Naturally, if one really tries, one can create all sorts of scary monsters which have very little likelihood of actually flying in one's window.

Nor does the reasonable expectation of *some* strain, *some* tension, and even some possibility of losing friendship free any of us from such an obligation. Integrity, by its very nature, isn't easy; if it were, we'd all be paragons of the quality. Only if you can reasonably anticipate, say, a serious, permanent loss of livelihood—or of a specific job in which you are currently doing great good for others—or of an absolutely essential relationship—can you plausibly claim that the evil done you by coming out is greater than the evil done your gay brothers and sisters by not coming out. For most of us, making any such claim would be hypocritical.

Although you must, ultimately, make the decision for yourself —and, be it noted, must never take it upon yourself to make it for another!—we'd like to suggest that too many who could come out choose to do the easy, selfish thing, and stay in the closet with the door nailed shut. Don't be one of these. And remember: you can choose who you come out to. You needn't take out that full-page advertisement in the *New York Times*.

Your friends will do that.

Thrice Before the Cock Crows Shalt Thou Deny Me

There is a zenith of cowardice beyond the mere refusal to stand up and be counted: there is the refusal, in all sorts of everyday circumstances, to stand up *for fear of being counted*. You know what we mean: the boardroom meeting or cocktail party at which a homohating coworker or friend tells a mean-spirited 'fag' joke, and you, writhing inside, play along, smiling and chuckling, lest your demurrer give your own secret away; the gay friend or stranger whom you allow to be insulted or attacked, for the same reasons. After all, who would defend a queer but another queer? And don't you dare say you haven't done it. Everyone has, including us.

Such self-serving cowardice is mean and dishonorable, and there isn't a shred of justification for it. So, no matter how much it may scare you to do so, stand up and speak out against expressions of prejudice. Worthwhile folk will think all the more of you for it. The opinions of worthless folk aren't worth a second thought.

You *Can* Take It with You: How to Remodel Your Closet as a Casket

No discussion of gay lying would be complete without a passing reference to the last, and saddest, manifestation of self-concealment: the refusal, even in one's obituary, to admit that one is—or, rather, *was*—gay.

We speak, of course, of that extraordinary epidemic, unremarked upon by the Centers for Disease Control, of 'liver cancer' (and related factitious ailments), that, since 1983 or so, has more than decimated the ranks of young, unmarried interior decorators and ballet dancers, at least in the greater metropolitan area of the City of New York. Although these lethal distempers used to be quite rare among men between twenty-five and fifty-five, scarcely a day now goes by that the death notices of the *New York Times* don't list one or two such medical curiosities. At the same time, and equally oddly, AIDS—currently the leading cause of death among such men—isn't featured in the death notices with a tenth of the frequency.

Simple arithmetic makes it clear that the majority of AIDS deaths are not being listed as such in the obituary columns; many are deliberately being listed as due to some other cause, and so covered up. Nor is it by any means always the family that is responsible for this cover-up; a friend, who recently died of AIDS after a three-year struggle, allegedly not only had unprotected sex with multiple partners—whom he failed to warn of his condition —up to within six months of his death, but left explicit instructions that any obituary notices were to ascribe his death to leukemia.

This sort of thing contributes to the Big Lie, and so unnecessarily. The great thing about being dead is that, regardless of your posthumous existential condition, you needn't fret yourself about how people remember you. Dying of AIDS at an early age is bad enough without robbing it of the little meaning and usefulness you might give it by speaking out, from beyond the grave, against the Big Lie, admitting that, yes, you were gay, and yes, you died of AIDS. Not to do so is to accord your enemies the ultimate victory —to have forced you not only to crawl quietly into your grave, but to pull the turf neatly up over yourself.

So, do be good to the last drop: leave behind, for your family and friends, explicit instructions that the cause of your death, should it—God forbid—be AIDS, is to be made known at your obsequies and via the newspaper.

o   o   o

The misbehavior of lying, in many guises, will weave itself insidiously into our other categories of misbehavior, like Sherlock Holmes's "scarlet thread of murder." Moreover, bear in mind that the effects of deceit can go well beyond the gay community, setting back our cause with straights by decades. This is not how we want to be advertised.

2. THE REJECTION OF MORALITY

> *I never came across anyone in whom the moral*
> *sense was dominant who was not heartless,*
> *cruel, vindictive, log-stupid and entirely lacking*
> *in the smallest sense of humanity.*
>
> —OSCAR WILDE, IN A LETTER TO
> LEONARD SMITHERS

But then, Mr. Wilde also said, "the only way to get rid of temptation is to yield to it." Throughout the gay community, his perverse moral sentiments have echoed down the decades to the present day, and are still staple ingredients of the half-baked political pronunciamentos of self-appointed gay 'spokespersons' and 'steer-ing committees.' The explicit, root-and-branch rejection of moral-ity by gays has been real, pervasive, and baleful in its effect on both the quality of life that we create for ourselves within the community, and our p.r. with straights. Specific examples of gay immorality will follow—indeed, will make up much of the rest of this chapter—but first we want you to understand clearly how an amoral mind-set develops among gays, and why it is illogical and unnecessary.

Dirty Bathwater, Dirty Baby?

Once a youth has confronted his gayness, he has two choices. He can (1) accept the received values of conventional morality and hate himself, or (2) step outside the conventional way of look-ing at things, begin to think for himself and form his own values, realize that the Judeo-Christian prejudice against homosexuality is arbitrary, absurd, and evil, and, by rejecting it, replace his self-hatred with self-esteem. In short, if others hate you because your hair is blond, you can either reject yourself ('They're right—I'm horrible—I guess I'd better roll over and die!') or, laughing in con-tempt and relief, reject *them* ('I *like* my hair—so go to hell!').

So much is understandable, necessary for mental and emotional health, mature, and, in a youth with any capacity for indepen-dent and critical thought, inevitable. Many—we hope most—gays eventually reach this stage of maturity.

Alas, for many gays the rethinking doesn't end there. When people defrauded of their self-respect finally see through the scam, they're understandably tempted to transfer their self-hatred to the fraud itself in the form of a scorching anger and contempt. Like all naïve youngsters, these gays first buy into their society's ideology completely; then, disillusioned by their realization that the ideol-ogy is partially arbitrary, they overreact: they decide that the whole thing is rubbish, and divest themselves of 100% of their holdings.

The necessity of lying is, for many, the first crack in the wall. It forces upon them the realization that morality isn't a take-it-or-leave-it monolith, but has parts, which are all more or less arbitrary. If you needn't accept the part forbidding lying, then why should you necessarily accept the parts forbidding anything else? If accepting or rejecting the parts of morality is up to you, then accepting or rejecting the whole is up to you. And if such decisions are up to you, why pay attention to anyone else's morality at all?

Even of those who don't throw in the moral towel altogether, many slip down the sleazy slope into 'situational ethics'—that system in which actions are judged not against absolute moral standards, but in terms of the unique aspects of the particular situation in which the actor finds himself. This is, of course, a valid basis for judging one's own behavior, but, unfortunately, all too often it's used as an excuse for demanding that one not be judged by others at all—because they 'can't know what my situation is *really* like.' Moreover, situational ethics lends itself to cheap rationalization. Most of us have had the experience of trying to argue a dishonest adherent of situational ethics out of taking or continuing some horrendously selfish course of action, and facing a blizzard of casuistic rationalization that would do justice to an Athenian Sophist. Situational ethics is like the little girl who, when she was good, was very, very good—and when she was bad, was horrid.

Some gays, of course, can't decide *what* to think or do and oscillate between vicious behavior and churchgoing guilt. Often given to genuine altruism, and prey to veritable convulsions of piety, they swing with equal ease to the opposite pole and lie and cheat with abandon. Rather as with Roman Catholic mafiosi, the link connecting these behaviors is habit and sentiment: their religiosity has nothing to do with considered ethical standards, it just makes them feel good. Sometimes.

However, it shouldn't go without saying that a great many gays —perhaps most—lead reasonably moral, caring lives . . . and have a helluva time adjusting to the hard-core gay community. To the extent that they do adjust, they tend to be corrupted themselves. It is against the corrupters and corrupted, and the misery they create for all who deal with them, that we inveigh.

'But That's a Value Judgment!'

In short, many gays reject morality, offering any one of a variety of reasons, rational and emotional, for doing so. But there's a simpler, darker reason why many gays choose to live without morality: as ideologies go, amorality is damned convenient. And the mortal enemy of that convenience is the value judgment.

When we first delved into the gay urban *demimonde*, we assumed that they held, if not our values, at least *some* values. We were quickly disabused of this notion. On several occasions, we were incautious enough to express, before a gay acquaintance, dismay at the selfish and hurtful behavior of third parties. Our friend's response was invariably the same: he'd clutch his drink, widen his eyes, flare his nostrils in grave disapproval, and exclaim, "But that's a value judgment! *You can't say that!*"

We were staggered but edified. It quickly became clear to us that urban gays assumed a general consensus to the effect that everyone has the right to behave just as he pleases, and that no one must judge anyone else's behavior—a sort of perversion of the injunction to "judge not, lest ye be judged." The exception to this rule, of course, was everyone's right to judge swiftly and harshly anyone else's appeal to any system of morality. We were thought to be 'beyond all that archaic thinking.' Everyone was to decide what was 'right for him'—in effect, to make up the rules as he went along.

Curiously enough, although gays talked as though this were a superior system, the rules they made up seemed remarkably self-serving. In fact, they boiled down to a single axiom: I can do whatever I want, and *you* can go to perdition. (If it feels good, I'll do it!)

The upshot was inevitable. Nature, which abhors moral vacuums as much as any other, quickly filled this one with a toxic vapor of uninhibited pernicious impulses. If a gay man felt like 'dishing' a homely fellow guest at a party, he could be as cruel and hateful as he liked, and pass it off as 'an amusing manifestation of the gay sensibility.' If he felt like seducing a trusting friend's lover —thus conspiring in old-fashioned 'adultery'—he'd do it, justifying it as an act of 'sexual freedom'—and the friend be damned. If he felt that his cash would be more pleasurably spent on an alligator belt than on the alleviation of other people's problems—like AIDS—then an alligator belt it would be. (Without morality, there can be no compelling basis for responsibility to others.) If, ultimately, he felt like destroying himself with drugs and alcohol for the sake of temporary thrills, why, then, down the hatch! All these misbehaviors, and many others equally endemic in the gay community, resulted in part from the rejection of morality, and will be discussed in their proper place.

We found that in the gay press this doctrine had hardened into stone. Any and every aspect of the gay lifestyle—defined, apparently, as the sum total of whatever is, in fact, being done by all people who happen to be gay—was to be accepted, even embraced with open arms, however questionable it might seem to a dispassionate outsider. The more outrageous the behavior, the more it was to be seen as 'celebrating our unique sensibility and culture'; the less ethically defensible, the less one was to feel entitled to speak out against it, lest one be accused of attempting to resurrect that bugbear, 'traditional morality.' Whatever objection one might make, and however well founded it might be, the counterattack was sure to be swift and stern, and to depend on the ready-made—and essentially unanswerable—*ad hominem* argument that gays who object to the gay lifestyle are actually incapable of accepting their own gayness and simply projecting their own self-hatred on the community around them.

The quintessential example of this phenomenon was the reception accorded Larry Kramer's *Faggots* in pre-AIDS 1978, when the head honchos of the gay press were still riding high in the saddle. The book was, of course, an absolutely scathing indictment of things abysmally wrong with the gay community, and with the gay lifestyle—which is to say, with the things that individual gay men and women actually did. Though satiric, *Faggots* was an honest report on how we were living our lives, how we were justifying ourselves, and why our self-justification was a lot of rot. But the P.C. gay response was, in Wilde's phrase, "the rage of Caliban seeing his own face in a glass." Kramer was, socially and editorially, crucified, as we'll discuss in Section 10.

I Have Everything I Want, Yet I Feel That Something Is Missing . . .

Ironically, many gays who abandon the traditional religions find that the religious impulse itself isn't so easily ignored. (What, after all, is the entire New Age phenomenon but urban humanity's response to the implosion of the organized religions?) Searching for something to fill the void left in their lives, they occasionally sail off into the wild blue yonder. Margot Adler, in *Drawing Down the Moon,* describes the "Spiritual Conference for Radical Faeries," held in Tucson, Arizona in 1979. The participants felt that the standard urban gay culture "didn't serve [their] needs." Several dozen gay men went into a desert park to indulge in "spontaneous and unplanned rituals" of a "Neo-pagan" bent. Naked and chanting, they lowered one another into a pool of ooze. "Joyously covered with mud . . . singing, dancing, shouting . . . ," one of the participants later recalled, "I [became] a true believer in the Fairy Spirit." "Tourists with Nikons" were observed taking photographs, perhaps as documentation of their opinion that gays really are nutbars.

Summing it up, one participant said, "We all wanted something that we didn't have and we desperately wanted it, but we didn't know what it was." What gay men want, without knowing it, is a return to a sense of the sacred, and a framework of ethics within which they can begin to trust and believe in one another.

So Where's Our Beef?

Oddly enough, we are as much adherents of Hedonism as those we decry—but (we hope) at a higher and kinder level. We judge actions by their effects: do they help people or hurt them?

Let's follow this reasoning. Rejecting morality leaves the apostate with no inarguable shoulds and shouldn'ts to constrain his behavior, and no guide to follow in controlling his own impulses but situational ethics. Situational ethics is undesirable because its adherents are tempted to rationalize their decision to do what they feel like doing anyway. What gays, like anyone else, feel like doing often includes lying; selfishness, self-indulgence, and self-destruction; cruelty; insult and injury; and adultery. We don't like these things because they hurt others, and make us look bad. So we look askance at the rejection of morality. It's just as simple as that.

Destruction without reconstruction won't go. Gays do the first part of their job, but not the second: using their newfound independence of thought and evaluation to construct their own system of morality. Without such a conscientious effort, self-centered behavior and self-indulgence become inevitable.

3. NARCISSISM AND SELF-CENTERED BEHAVIOR

> *My body is fantastic. A great, stunning, gorgeous body . . . [F]rom the mirror, I see a god looking back . . . He is exquisite . . . I am in love with him. . . . He will cum soon. I love myself. I'm going to cum.*
> —DAVID MITCHELL, "BALLS," IN
> BOYD MCDONALD'S *CUM*

Lying leads, for some, to the rejection of morality. Rejecting morality leads, in turn, to susceptibility to a personality disorder— with implications far more serious than merely not being invited to the right parties.

Personality Disorder and 'Evil'

Although in 'narcissism' we do include 'vanity,' we also mean something broader and more serious, of which physical vanity is merely a symptom—a pathological degree of self-absorption and inability to empathize with the concerns of others. For many, this is part of a very broad and deep-seated pattern of distorted attitudes, values, and behaviors, resulting in that chronic, lifelong inability to get along in the world that clinicians term 'personality disorder.'

The "histrionic" and "narcissistic" personality disorders—heavily overlapping clinical categories recognized by the American Psychiatric Association's *Diagnostic and Statistical Manual,* third edition (DSM-III)—have been described in the following phrases, which, even in condensed form, are telling:

> [Histrionic patients are] overly dramatic, always drawing attention to themselves . . . prone to exaggeration . . . act out a role, such as "princess," without being aware of it . . . excitability, irrational, angry outbursts . . . tantrums . . . crave novelty, stimulation, excitement . . . quickly bored . . . shallow . . . lack genuineness . . . superficially charming . . . quick to form friendships . . . demanding, egocentric, inconsiderate . . . manipulative . . . suicidal threats, gestures, or attempts . . . attractive, seductive . . . vain . . . flights into romantic fantasy . . . overt behavior often a caricature of femininity . . . promiscuous . . . little interest in . . . careful, analytic thinking, though creative and imaginative . . . influenced by fads . . . judgment not firmly rooted . . . *often associated with a homosexual arousal pattern.* [Emphasis added.] . . . common complication is Substance Use Disorder . . .
>
> [Narcissistic patients have, in addition to the above, a] grandiose sense of self-importance . . . need constant attention and admiration . . . relationships alternate between over-idealization and devaluation . . . lack of empathy . . . ex-

treme self-centeredness or self-absorption . . . fantasies of unlimited ability, power, wealth, brilliance, beauty, or ideal love . . . more concerned with appearances . . . than substance . . . being seen with the "right" people . . . exploitative . . . relations with others lack sustained positive regard . . . preoccupation with remaining youthful . . . outright lying . . .

Remind you of anyone you know?

Believe it or not, when we set out to write this chapter, we didn't have the above clinical description in mind as a hidden agendum. Rather, it worked the other way around: we started with a straightforward list of honest gripes, and, in ruminating over the problem of how to present the list in an orderly, organized fashion, found that we were driven insensibly back to clinical concepts. While reviewing such clinical concepts, we stumbled across the above description—which, in essence, is a brutal exaggeration of our list of complaints, precisely.

It's important that the reader understand what we and the DSM-III are *not* saying here. Although homosexuality was itself at one time considered a form of personality disorder, it is no longer, and the "histrionic" and "narcissistic" categories are not attempts to smuggle homosexuality back into the official listing of mental disorders under another name. In fact, these categories existed before homosexuality was 'taken off the books.'

Yet they seem to fit a certain sort of gay male like a condom. Why? Not because *homosexuality* is sick, but because certain *gays* are sick. An analogy: although homosexuality doesn't cause AIDS, old-fashioned gay sex is a good way to get AIDS. Similarly, although homosexuality isn't a personality disorder, the way gays are forced to live—by straights and by one another—lowers their resistance to personality disorders. Consequently, we find the gay community rife not only with AIDS but with histrionic and narcissistic behavior. If the shoe fits, eat it.

Psychologist M. Scott Peck, in *People of the Lie,* has characterized extreme, or "malignant," narcissism simply as "evil." "Evil" people, he says, have an unshakable will to be right, and will not consider the possibility that they are in the wrong. Consequently, they have a hardened heart, to which they do not listen, and will not accept criticism. Unable to submit their extraordinary willfulness to any value beyond and above the self, they put their own interests irrevocably before the interests and needs of others, readily inflicting any harm necessary to get what they want. Their main weapon, interestingly, is the lie, with which they distort reality to look good to themselves, and to confuse others.

While we wouldn't go to the idiotic extreme of calling all gay people histrionic and narcissistic, let alone evil, these terms represent extremes of a spectrum on which we all fall. The pathological and wicked do not differ from the rest of us in kind, only in degree. It seems to us that more gays than straights fall further out on this spectrum. This is not because homosexuality per se is 'worse' than heterosexuality; it isn't. Rather, the peculiar social position in which gays find themselves renders very many of them easy prey to the temptations of deceitfulness and narcissism —the easy way out of the hardships of gay life—and consequently to personality disorder.

This peculiar social position has two aspects. First, it's an exhilarating feeling to free yourself, at last, from years of guilt and shame over your homosexuality, and from the idea that you *must* live up to the expectations and standards of others—family and straight friends. It's very easy to go overboard, to say, 'From now on I'm going to live only for myself; I'm going to do what *I* want,' and, having rejected your guilt over being gay, to reject as nonsense all guilt, regardless of its origin. Second—and amplifying the first—concern for others is a sentiment requiring constant practice, and gay men just don't get enough. Unlike the majority of his straight counterparts, the stereotypical urban gay man has left his parents' family far behind, has no wife or family of his own to 'do' for, and, naturally enough, has an unusual amount of time, energy, and disposable pin money to devote all to himself. If you live like this, it takes the dedication of a saint not to become self-centered—and it's too much to ask that gay men be saints.

Indeed, they are not. While much of the misbehavior in this chapter comes back, in one way or another, to narcissism, we will discuss here two striking examples of self-centered behavior: the refusal to practice safe sex, and the refusal to contribute money for the good of the gay community as a whole.

Safe Sex, Schmafe Sex

What can we say of a man who places his desire to continue to have orgasms ahead of his partner's desire to continue to live? If we can trust Randy Shilts's journalism in *And the Band Played On,* that would certainly seem to describe the behavior of Gaetan Dugas, the "Patient Zero" who was apparently a main vector of the initial spread of the AIDS virus through North America. This handsome airline steward, with whom at least 40 of the first 240 reported cases were *traceably* sexually connected, was diagnosed with Kaposi's sarcoma in 1981. Although told repeatedly that his condition was terminal and almost certainly transmissible, he continued until his death in 1984 to have sex with anonymous strangers in dimly lit bathhouses. Numerous frightened gay men reported having had sex with this man—or a dead ringer—who then turned up the rheostat, revealed his lesions, and said "I'm going to die from this. Now you'll get it too." Excuses can be made —he was scared, bitter, resentful—but there is no excusing *away* such massive guilt.

While Dugas's case is extreme, the tendency illustrated is by no means isolated. Rock Hudson's biographies indicate a similar pattern of self-deception leading—potentially fatally—to the deception of others. (Roy Cohn seems to have done much the same, but in his case, this was entirely in character.) Also, we've been told of a clergyman, never tested for HIV despite thirty years of promiscuity, who allegedly assures young boys whom he seduces into unsafe sex practices that 'AIDS has been exaggerated,' 'it's almost over now,' and 'nobody's really worried anymore.'

None of this is to say that the gay community has made no changes in its sex practices. But, sweeping as such changes may

be, don't kid yourself: a very sizable proportion of gay men continue to show such callous disregard—and we think it's mon-
strous.

$$$s on the Soles of Our Running Shoes

Let's do a little arithmetic, using admittedly rough and ready
but fair and conservative figures[3]:

(1) As of 1988, there are 120 million males in the United States.
(2) Of these, 80 million are of working age—that is, between 18
and 65.
(3) Subtracting full-time students, the severely retarded, handicapped, and mentally ill, and the otherwise unemployed, 70
million are actually at *work*.
(4) Of these 70 million, at least 15%—or 10.5 million—are primarily gay.
(5) Of 10.5 million, at least two thirds—or 7 million—admit to
themselves, with a minimum of shilly-shallying, that they're
gay.

That's 7 million self-identified gay men at work in this country
(not to mention millions of lesbians for whom a similar calcula-
tion could be performed—but with a good deal more difficulty).
As a group, these men presumably do not earn much less than
their straight counterparts. Relatively few of them have the kind
of major financial commitments that tie down most straights—
supporting a wife and children, family health insurance, the children's education, a family-sized apartment or house, etc. Therefore, it stands to reason that, on average, gay men must have
many times the discretionary income of straight men—each of
whom himself disposes (at minimum) of several hundred dollars a
year on nonessentials.

Shall we say that the average employed gay man has at least
$1,000 a year to spend on pure luxury? If so, then gay men in this
country spend a good $7 *billion* per annum on themselves . . .
and that money is certainly in evidence. We don't have too many
gay friends who don't dress well, eat well, drink well, and live
well—a hefty share of them in apartments overdecorated to the

bursting point with the proverbial Marimekko, chintz, deep-pile carpeting, track lighting, and hi-tech iridium-plated electronic gewgaws.

Yet organizations like the National Gay and Lesbian Task Force, working for the benefit of such as these, and for the prevention of political catastrophes that could end the moveable feast once and for all, have difficulty scrounging up one 2,500th part of that $7 billion in contributions. Their constituency would rather convince itself that the problems are trumped up and the threats unreal, that the organizations are unnecessary, or full of self-serving cranks, or ineffectual, or doing so good a job that they don't *need* financial help. The dollar figures speak for themselves.

Gay bars, where so much gay money is turned into a liquid asset, could play a major role in ameliorating this niggardliness—say, by placing a 'voluntary' 10% surtax on each drink served and contributing it to the common good. So could other gay business establishments. However, that might (God forbid!) *cut into business* —and gay proprietors are just as greedy and selfish as their customers.

The fact is that gay bars and other businesses have a perfectly wretched record of failure to serve the community. Indeed, where not to do so would lose money, they've shown themselves willing to *harm* the community. It's hard to forget that when AIDS-related Kaposi's sarcoma was first rumored to be linked to the use of nitrite inhalants, the manufacturers of Hardware, Quicksilver, and Ram responded by taking out expensive magazine ads for their "Blueprint for Health"—in essence, exercise, eat right, keep a good thought, and "learn to ignore the prophets of doom"—when the moral thing to do would have been to take the loss and go into another line of business. It's hard to forget that, by and large, the gay bathhouses of New York and San Francisco shut down not as they should—voluntarily, as soon as it became evident to a reasonable person that what they were selling was death, and in abundance—but under legal duress, kicking and screaming in protest, and spewing out a sewer system of cheap rationales for their continued operation. Yes, it's hard to forget, and impossible to forgive.

So that leaves it up to rank-and-file gays themselves. Most of them think nothing of plunking down ten dollars for a cover charge and two drinks. If all 7 million of our 'liquid' members were to contribute that picayune sum once a year (and frankly, we have the right to expect a great deal more), we'd have a goodly war chest to start putting on line some of the plans to be discussed in the second half of this book. There's no excuse for not contributing. It sounds unpalatable, but it's true: if gay men don't make even this minimal effort to save themselves, they will have confirmed all that their worst enemies have said about them—and will deserve everything they get.

4. SELF-INDULGENCE, SELF-DESTRUCTION

There is maybe only one sin in life: when a hunky, blond, hard-muscled young man asks you to oil him up where his tan line stops, and you refuse to do it. Me? I'm no sinner; I'm a sprinter.
—JACK FRITSCHER, "BEACH BLANKET SURF-BOY BLUES," IN *WILLIAM HIGGINS' CALIFORNIA*

If the first consequence of the rejection of morality is narcissistic, self-centered behavior, then the second consequence, following hard on the heels of the first, is self-indulgence, leading, in extreme cases, to self-destruction.

'It's Our Orgy, and We'll Die If We Want To!'

Of all the misbehaviors we decry, self-indulgence is perhaps most characteristic of gays, and of the gay community as a whole. Indeed, it was institutionalized, long ago, by the gay media and arbiters of Political Correctness, as a central tenet of gay liberation. (Remember the "Sisters of Perpetual Indulgence"?) In a community in which every gay wants to be 'p.c.-er than thou,' any self-restraint is, itself, suspect of being a sign of self-hatred and bluenosery—so one virtually *must* act out one's most fleeting impulses in order to prove that one isn't a hung-up, judgmental old poop.

These attitudes, combined with youth, energy, spare cash, and lust, flowered, in the 1970s, into the so-called fast-lane gay lifestyle. For a supposedly creative community, the results were hardly anything to be artistically proud of. Primarily urban, and centered around discotheques, bathhouses, and condo shares on Fire Island, the fast-lane lifestyle, for most, meant dressing in eccentric and sexually titillating clothing, traveling 'round and 'round the world, buying very expensive personal possessions, staying up to party as late, as long, and with as many people as possible, having as much, and as varied, sex as possible, and seeking out every new experience one could possibly find in order to press ever harder upon the nerve of physical sensation. Except for the sex part, this is pretty much what one would expect if six-year-old boys were to take over the world.

The trouble with the self-indulgence of the fast-lane lifestyle, beyond the obvious fact that it looks—and is—selfish and immature, is that it's tiring and deadening, and cannot be sustained. As one gets older, one ceases to generate a superabundance of energy to squander on play; as one devours experiences in the search for sensation, one grows jaded, and needs ever more novel and intense experiences even to keep boredom at bay. By the age of twenty-five or so, the majority of fast-lane gays have burned out their lifestyle.

Far from seeing the fundamental unworkability of his approach to life, however, and rethinking the values that led to that approach, the typical fast-lane gay, once he's used up the energy and experiences that are healthy and legitimately his, begins to seek sources of energy and experience that are unhealthy and illegitimate: drugs and kinky sex.

At bottom, there are three reasons why gay men use drugs: (a) to anesthetize the fear and pain of being gay—a topic we'll discuss in Section 8, below; (b) to jack up failing energy supplies, in order to keep partying through the 36-hour night; (c) in pursuit of psychological and physical sensations beyond those the human mind and body are normally capable of feeling. Reasons (b) and (c) are expressions of self-indulgence, and tend, if kept up for long, to lead to self-destruction.

And Just What *Does* Love Have To Do With All This?

The course is much the same regarding sexual practices. When one is young and inexperienced, the tamest, most vanilla-flavored gay sex—mere cuddling and mutual masturbation—is more than enough to do the trick: it's new, forbidden, 'dirty,' and exciting. As one gains experience, vanilla sex with one partner becomes familiar, tame, and boring, and loses its capacity to arouse. At first, the increasingly jaded gay man seeks novelty in partners, rather than practices, and becomes massively promiscuous; eventually, all bodies become boring, and only new practices will thrill. Two major avenues diverge in this yellow wood, two nerves upon which to press: that of raunch, and that of aggression.

The pursuit of sexual happiness via raunch—fetishism, water sports and coprophilia, and so forth—seeks, essentially, to restore erectile thrills by restoring the 'dirty,' hence forbidden, aspect of sex—thereby providing, as C. A. Tripp called it in *The Homosexual Matrix,* a new barrier of "resistance" to be overcome. Unfortunately, this, as with all attempts to sustain the *furor sexualis* of youth by sheer intensification of some peripheral aspect of the experience, is doomed to failure: mere amplification of 'dirtiness' results, finally, in mere wallowing in filth—which, however far the ante is upped, eventually fails to satisfy, or even to arouse. (Next stop, impotence.) Not all sleaze addicts choose to advertise the fact in newspapers, but those who do simultaneously entertain, turn the stomach, and demonstrate the futility of the endeavor better than anything we could invent. Consider the following personal ad:

> *Feet First* Ripe dirty nasty feet. Hot muscular smelly feet. Toe Jam. Uncut cheesy meat. Stink . . . Heavy, funky male sweat. Who? Rex: unwashed, unshaven . . . dude, . . .

30's, . . . hung, filthy, uncut loaded with cheese, ripe pits sourballs, J/O games with nasty feet, pit sniffin' . . . Get dirty and check out the pigpen . . .

Aggressive sex is worse than a mere dead end: in extreme cases, it's dangerous. Typically, fast-lane gays who buy a (one-way) ticket on this express first get interested in bondage and discipline, then in sadomasochism, in their thirties and forties; the really jaded run rapidly through the milder versions (and perversions) of this scene and graduate to whips, executioner's masks, and fist-fucking. So much does it take to stay excited. By the age of fifty, these unfortunates are in real trouble.

Whatever its advocates may say, 'rough' sex isn't innocuous; nor is it, in the words of a common apologia, 'just another way of expressing love.' Its trappings, expressions, and emotions are those of pain and hate, and, say what you will, pain and hate are what it arouses. Alas, although pain and hate have nothing to do with love, they have plenty to do with lust; the brain-centers of sexual arousal and aggression are rather closely connected—an evolutionary relic of our extremely distant reptilian ancestry. Repeatedly exercising this connection strengthens it and leads, in our opinion, to an inability to experience arousal without aggression, and vice versa. This is a sinister development in almost anybody, and hardly to be encouraged.

But why do we oppose these practices, if this is the way people say they want to live? We oppose the fast-lane lifestyle, and the drugs and kink upon which it comes to depend, for exactly the same two principled reasons for which we oppose the other categories of misbehavior: because they diminish the quality of gay life, and make us look bad to straights. As a matter of straightforward, practical observation, the fast-lane lifestyle leads to exhaustion and dissatisfaction, loudly expressed, by gays who feel that 'something is missing,' that their lives are 'empty'—as indeed they are: of health; of peace of mind; of contentment; of love; of genuine interconnection with others. This lifestyle is unworkable, unnecessary, and devoid of the values that straight society, with such good reason, respects: moderation and service. Naturally, we look detestable to straights. If for no other reasons—and there are other reasons—the fast-lane lifestyle cries out for disposal in a general housecleaning.

We've talked primarily about the pernicious effects of self-indulgence on the individual, but those effects also extend to the profile of the community as a whole. Gays are aware that they cannot simultaneously indulge their own whims and censure those of others without appearing hypocritical; consequently, it's generally understood in the community that it's very bad form to criticize anything whatever that a fellow gay does to amuse himself.

Unfortunately, a man is known by the company he keeps—and the community feels compelled to keep company with any and all fringe elements whose sexual behavior involves partners of the same sex, and to condone and defend their activities in print and in public—which includes letting them march alongside us on Gay Pride Day. Since the world is full of the twisted and wicked who just happen to be gay as well, this puts us into some pretty questionable company. And when you lie down with toads, you get up with warts.

Although the men in tutus and dykes on bikes do little to burnish our reputation, things really fall apart when a group like the North American Man-Boy Love Association rains on our parade. Why, simply because we claim the right to make love to others of our own sex—an intrinsically harmless behavior in which society has no legitimate interest—must we welcome and defend men who clamor for the right to make love to small boys? NAMBLA lauds an inherently unequal, and therefore potentially exploitative and scarring, kind of relationship, with those not only too young to give informed consent but also legal wards of their parents, whose job it is to make decisions for them. The intervention, by a stranger, in a minor's sexual and psychological development is a legitimate focus of concern, indeed, for society. There's no connection between accepting ourselves and accepting NAMBLA, beyond a foolish belief that as long as we don't criticize anyone else, no one else can criticize us. For the sake of a self-serving mutual nonaggression pact, we condone harmful, exploitative activities—and still expect straight society to buy our ethical claims. This must cease.

5. INDULGING OUR PRIVATES IN PUBLIC

> [W]e have all the social skills we need. "Do you want a hot + wet blow job?" or "Come fuck me" or "Can I piss down your throat?" are always the correct ways to Meet New Friends.
> —JOHN MITZEL, IN BOYD MCDONALD'S *FLESH*

Talk about ambassadors of good will—with friends like these, we need never fear a shortage of enemies! Self-indulgent, self-destructive behavior is lamentable enough when it occurs, so to speak, 'within the family,' but when Brother Gay trots out his unsavory shenanigans for the consumption of the general public, the rest of us are dragged down with him.

Excuse Me, Sir . . . I Dare You to Knock This Taffeta Chip off My Padded Shoulder!

When surrounded by a powerful and hostile majority, it's advisable to tread lightly, but a certain kind of gay man is either too stupid or too insensitive to refrain from playing Bait the Bear with straights. On the streets and subways, eating in restaurants, he indulges in shameless stereotypy, camping it up, shrieking, making coarse, inappropriate jokes, twisting the straight community's tail for the (rationalized) purpose of 'shaking them up' and 'raising their consciousness.' His actual purpose, as one who feels devalued and angry, is attention-seeking and revenge. At the extreme, he may straddle the line between the crass and the arguably criminal, and make verbal or physical passes at attractive straight boys to 'call their bluff.' To him it's all a hoot.

But the straight community doesn't see it that way. They're angered and sickened by what looks, to them, like deliberate antagonism of a particularly vile sort. Such behavior neither wins friends nor influences political elections.

One of us, while living, years ago, in an undergraduate dormitory, affected considerable effeminacy of dress and comportment, wore cosmetics and arranged his hair in bleached ringlets, and baited the more attractive straight boys in the dining room with loud, calculatedly crude taunts and innuendos. Why? He was bored and maladjusted and thought that this behavior—which (Lord knows why!) he considered 'witty' and 'controversial'— made him more interesting, a 'personality.' Of course, nothing could have been further from the truth. His behavior was, in fact, distasteful and alienating and not only made strong enemies but lost the respect of the many friends he might otherwise have made had he not buried his real wit and charm beneath a rude pose. He came to regret his foolishness long ago.

Lords of the (Open) Flies?

Perhaps the most malignant form of gay misbehavior is public sex. Though grossly offensive, none of what follows is fictive, so let the viscera roil as they may.

It wasn't terribly long after arriving at Harvard that we became aware of some pretty blatant cavorting about in almost every one of the university's larger general-access men's rooms. Whenever we ourselves received the call of nature on line one or two, we were startled by the large numbers of men in the lavatory whose bladders and colons apparently achieved voidure only with glacial slowness, the seeming tardiness of their eliminative functions requiring that they either stand at a urinal for five and ten minutes at a time, or camp out in a stall for indefinite periods—typically as we hopped up and down in the urgency of our desire to perch upon the porcelain god. Being a bit thickheaded, however, it took us some time to realize just what the cavorting was all about.

But even we, naïfs though we were, couldn't fail to get the drift when, on one of the rare occasions that we succeeded in obtaining a bowl of our own, a scaly hand appeared beneath the interstall partition, proffering an explicit note written on toilet paper. Comparing it to similar stock offerings on the walls, the proverbial light dawned. Being, ourselves, all too human, we then spent some time observing the scene with closer attention. What we saw amazed us.

It apparently amazed a goodly number of others, as well—including staff and students who, less titillated than scandalized, left notes of their own ('Why can't a Harvard boy go to the john in this dump without being groped by a seedy queer!?') in library suggestion boxes, taking violent exception to the ongoing lavatorial passion play—because, reportedly, the Harvard Police, accompanied by maintenance personnel, eventually elbowed their way into the *dramatis personae.*

Abruptly—and to the great dismay of those who need privacy to do their business—the *doors* disappeared from every toilet stall in the main Harvard Science Center men's room, and uniformed policemen were periodically observed patrolling the premises for perverts. Predictably, a protest—at once sardonically amused and annoyed—by one Scott Long appeared in the *Harvard Gay and Lesbian Newsletter* mocking the straight staff, students, and police who had whipped up a "tempest in a tearoom."

Despite their high visibility, and attempts by authorities to squelch them, however, a coterie of gay men continues, daily and nightly, to perform the play before what is, all too often, an S.R.O. straight audience—in the men's rooms of Ivy League Colleges, and in the public lavatories, parks, and alleyways of every major city in the United States. Theirs is the wretchedest of all gay excesses.

Such men make no attempt to secure privacy for their intercourse, whether by locating a disused utility closet or waiting for a lull in the pedestrian traffic in and out of the lavatory; indeed, for many the dangerous possibility of being apprehended *entr'acte* is three fourths of the thrill. They masturbate at the urinals, wander totally naked up and down the length of the facility, and fellate one another in acrobatic positions in the open doorways of the stalls. When they ejaculate—and they do—on the seats, walls, or floors, they leave it there to congeal into a nasty, highly identifiable puddle. One can imagine the effect such a charming tableau has upon a young, sheltered, or uptight straight man, when he comes upon it suddenly and unexpectedly in a place in which he is accustomed to do his embarrassing but necessary business in peace and quiet.

The damage done to the gay image by these shady goings-on is, alas, calculable. Most Americans are trained by their parents to think of their genitals—and what is done with them—as 'nasty.' (No small part of the problem of homophobia, right there.) The pudendum is, after all, the same part of the body that mediates bathroom functions, themselves made 'filthy' by parents who shout 'Dirty, dirty!' and slap their toddlers when pants are messed at an untowardly late age. (Indeed, a good part of the appeal of bathroom sex is precisely that it *is* carried on in a place conceived of as filthy, making it all the more forbidden, illicit, taboo—and delightful.) When a straight male sees two men licking each other's genitals and anuses in a seedy rest room, it leaves an indelible image in his mind, confirming for all time what he already believes: that queers are filthy, diseased, furtive creatures practicing beastly acts right down there on the toilet floor, groveling in human waste. The new association with AIDS just adds, in Henry James's phrase, "one more turn of the screw."

The damage is redoubled when such creatures solicit straight boys—a prime example of the gay tendency to 'live down to the stereotype,' and with a double-barreled effect. On the one hand, such unwanted solicitation reinforces the old saw that gay men deliberately recruit innocent straight boys in order to replenish gay ranks; on the other hand, it makes apparent liars out of gays who protest that their sexual activities occur only in private and between consenting adults, and are therefore of no legitimate interest to the straight community or its legislative apparatus. Its ultimate effect, of course, is to ensure that each generation of more-or-less straight adults will be presided over by a leavening of homophobic male legislators and religious leaders who had the shit scared out of them by 'perverts' when they were just boys.

Although it seems incredible that gay men could be so reckless, many, driven more by their penises than by their brains, take their cue from William Burroughs, who, speaking through one of his characters in *Queer*, declared of a straight boy with whom he wished to have sex, "So he's not queer. People can be obliging. What is the obstacle?"

And we emphasize, such behavior isn't at all uncommon. We were once informed, by a cheery gay acquaintance, that, trapped in the crush of a recent rock concert audience, right behind a thirteen-year-old boy, he had taken advantage of the horrified youth's inability to move away by rubbing his crotch against the proffered but reluctant *derrière*. "I actually *creamed in my jeans*," he told us, laughing, "and there wasn't a *thing* he could do about it!"

This is *not* good public relations.

Amazingly, a certain sort of gay man comes to believe that he has a *right* to cut such didoes in public bathrooms and parks, as though these facilities were created for him expressly as a sexual playground. He may go so far as to express wrath when other patrons don't do in Rome as the Romans do, becoming a veritable arbitrager of the tearoom, like one of Boyd McDonald's correspondents in *cum*:

> I've had to scout a new [rest room, for sex] . . . Last week I was there from 12 noon until 5 P.M. . . . [T]he pain in the ass returned . . . He said, "I can't believe you're still here . . . Out of courtesy I left at least four times." I told him it is very bad manners to come in, stuff the [glory] hole [with toilet paper] and read a newspaper . . . The hole is too large to stuff so he draped it. I was about to set it alight . . . A couple of faggy teenyboppers . . . tried the stuffing trick. I just removed the wad . . . and said, "Don't try that again! It's bad manners. If you want it sucked stand up and put it through, if you don't then leave." I opened the door and said to his buddy, "That applies to you too." . . . Such assholes . . . need to be shown that their behavior is quite unacceptable.

One would imagine that gays would be anxious to discourage such antics as a blot on the communal escutcheon. In fact, they favor them with a wink of avuncular indulgence, tacitly or vocally encouraging them to continue. Not a few gays involve themselves in such activities; perhaps a third of all our gay friends have admitted—usually sheepishly—being drawn, at one time or another, past the taboo of tearoom trade. Perhaps the gay press falls into the same category, for it is quick to condemn any suggestion that such public frolics are a bad idea, and readily labels police efforts to put a stop to these activities as 'antigay harassment.' In fact, we don't consider this antigay at all—merely antinuisance. If a woman came into a public men's room, disrobed, and began masturbating before a mirror, she also would, no doubt, be carted away, however enthralling the male users of the facility might find the unexpected sexual windfall.

6. MISBEHAVIOR IN BARS

> [H]e saw Randy . . . coming toward him, hand outstretched, with a beaming and welcoming smile . . . "Go away, Crud Man!" he said . . .
>
> —LARRY KRAMER, FAGGOTS

How cruel we gays can be! And how richly we deserve it when it comes back and bites us in the ass!

By the millions, we flee the small-town homophobia of our adolescence to 'live among our own' in an urban ghetto where no one will shout 'Fag!' because everyone *is* a fag. But, unless we have a young, handsome face and tight body, and dress in fashionable clothing, the minute we step through the door of a gay bar we learn who the real queerbashers are: us. We might as well have put down roots in Mechanic Falls, Maine.

'*We're* Having A Party . . . and *You're* Not Invited!'

The gay bar is the arena of sexual competition, and it brings out all that is most loathsome in human nature. Here, stripped of the façade of wit and cheer, gays stand nakedly revealed as single-minded, selfish sexual predators . . . and enact vignettes of contempt and cruelty that make the Comte de Sade look like a Red Cross nurse.

Almost anyone can cite scores of examples, but the one that stands out in our memory occurred in a bar in Milwaukee, in which we heard one of a pair of supercilious young queens say, very audibly indeed, of a rather homely fat man standing in front of them, "God! Can you believe that he actually bothers to drag himself here!?" The implications are clear: the game is youth and beauty; the object is to score sexually; if you don't have a mallet, you've no business on the croquet ground, so drop dead.

Only those who've had the misfortune to be both gay and ugly will appreciate the full justice of the above remarks. Human nature takes personal credit for sheer good luck; those gay men lucky enough to have been born good-looking have, in our experience, disbelieved our arguments, almost to a man. 'There's nothing wrong with gay life,' they retort; 'we're having a *wonderful* time!' From these, too, we hear the most about how friendly and brotherly gay men are. Well, not always! While homely gays aren't exactly drowned in a sack by their attractive brothers, a night out in gayland may well make them wish they had been—at birth. Attributing their universally warm reception to their stellar personality, attractive gays haven't a clue as to just how far their looks have contributed to their social as well as their sexual success. Nor do they have any inkling of just how radically different things would have been for them had they been burdened with somewhat less Ralph Lauren-ish genes—nor for how little that stellar personality would have counted. But the ugly do know.

This cruel facet of gay life was succinctly expressed by Ethan

Mordden, writing in *Christopher Street* ("The Homogay") of a monstrously well muscled but facially unattractive—and justifiably bitter—acquaintance:

> Now let me tell you how to hold your beautiful gay lover. By being terrific in bed? No. That will guarantee a good premiere, but beautiful lovers by nature have already had much taste of fabulous carnal technique . . . By having pecs or thighs of death? No. Who doesn't, nowadays? . . . Cock of death, too, . . . is made for tricking, not love . . . Nor, I'm sorry to say, will wit or social grace avail you. No, there is only one way to hold a lover: by having a handsome face . . . I do not.

Andrew Holleran, in *Dancer*, has referred, approvingly, to the "democracy" of gay life, "whose only ticket of admission [is] physical beauty." That "democracy," we submit, is just as closed as the aristocracy of France before the arrival of Dr. Guillotin, and every bit as arrogant and cruel.

Looking for Bobby: Love and Death

But is this the way it has to be? There are other dreams, other goals, other ideals, of great beauty and compelling power—dreams we dreamed, and if we, then surely others. Indeed, one (perhaps oversensitive) fellow, now older, wiser, and sadder, delivered himself of this revealing bit of rueful autobiography.

> When I was thirteen, I started having these new feelings about a beautiful boy I knew, Bobby S. He was handsome, and athletic, and *so* nice—*everybody* liked him! He was just what *I* wanted to be. I didn't understand my feelings, but I knew they were the biggest thing in my life; the whole world looked bright and colorful, and the most beautiful things in it were his smile, and his eyes, and his hands. I didn't know whether I felt wonderful, or just awful—when I saw him,

my knees shook, and my stomach felt tense and jittery. I'd heard about puppy love, and thought this must be it, but it was more than I'd imagined. I daydreamed about Bobby all day, and drew his picture in my notebook, and thought about calling him, but I was scared. I wanted just to *be with him*, to hang around him. When I forced myself to walk up to him on the playground and meet him, my mouth was dry, and I got tongue-tied. I felt that I wanted him to touch me—maybe hug me. One day, in a friendly way, he put his hand on my shoulder—I almost fainted. That night, in bed, I had fantasies about him, but even then I was shy—even in my thoughts I didn't want to dirty him—my love was so much more important than my sexual feelings. I knew then that I was gay, and that I could never tell Bobby, or anyone else. For years I was terribly lonely, but knew I could never live for anything else but this beautiful, heartbreaking love. When I was seventeen, I read some articles, and realized that there must be other boys in the world who felt the way I did. I applied to college, mainly to get into the city. When I got to Providence, I went to bars. I found out what gay life is *really* all about: fucking.

Breathes there a gay man with soul so dead that he can't recall being in love with his own Bobby?

It's easy to sneer cynically at such naïve hopes, but cynicism is merely the smoke rising from scorched ideals. You can't be a cynic about love without disclosing your own needs, fears, and disappointments. Gay men are cynical about love precisely because they've been so disappointed by it, need it so badly, and are so afraid that now it's too late. Rather than end up with nothing, they sell their birthright for a mess of frottage!

And cynicism is a self-perpetuating thing. Every year, the ideals of countless naïve, fresh-faced youths are—metaphorically, if not literally—gang-raped in the bars by older, more cynical predators. Looking, as it were, for Bobby, these lonely youths think to recognize him in each new, and apparently kind and interested, face;

they *want* to believe that, finally, this is Love; the Boulder Dam of their emotions, so to speak, bursts, to their infinite relief; riding a gush of misplaced trust and affection, they hop into bed—only to discover, in the morning, as their bored, deflated, and suddenly uneasy paramour hustles them to the door (with a 'Yes, yes, I'll give you a buzz'—SLAM!), that it was all a fraud: it wasn't Bobby —just some guy who wanted to get his rocks off. Smarting, and seeking consolation, they return to the bars; the cycle is repeated; eventually, it dawns on them that this is all there is. The disillusionment is dreadful. Disillusioned idealists in a society of cynics quickly grow bitter. Wanting to retrieve *something* from the ruin of their hopes, and realizing with what contempt the cynics regard their ideals, such youths eventually highside their dreams, adopting the cynicism with which they're surrounded as a form of protective armor against further disappointment, and their ticket of admission to the Smart Set. And, sooner or later, there they are —at the Greyhound bus station, waiting to greet the next busload of farm boys from Peoria.

It's all summed up in the first gay experience of our lonely friend Wyeth, who went to a bar, met a beautiful bouncing boy and, not even knowing his name, went home with him, eyes full of stars, for the standard night of mad, passionate love. In the morning, Wyeth, all aglow, anxiously inquired, "When will I see you again? What's your name?" Shoving Wyeth out the door, Bouncing Boy extruded a coy but curdled smile, and responded, "What name would you like it to be?"

But Enough About Me . . . How Do *You* Think I Look?

It's hard to escape the impression that by and large, gay men looking for partners are concerned with *nothing* but looks, and indeed, one elaborate study, by Paul Sergios and James Cody,[4] found that, at least at the initial social level, this is exactly the case. One hundred Los Angeles-area gay men in their twenties and thirties were rated by a panel of investigators for physical attractiveness and "social assertiveness." They were then sent in pairs to a two-hour tea dance, during which they were to consort primarily with their randomly assigned partners. Following the dance, each man was asked to rate his partner for overall desirability and asked whether he wished to see the partner again. Some time later, the men were followed up to see whether they had made efforts to see their partner again. The data were statistically analyzed using a technique called the analysis of variance.

The results can be summarized simply: the rated attractiveness of a man's assigned partner accounted completely for whether he liked the partner, and whether he tried to see him again. "Social assertiveness" was irrelevant to the decision. This held for both attractive and ugly men: both were interested only in whether the date was good-looking.

This brittle superficiality held true despite the fact that the tea dance forced assigned partners into far more prolonged personal contact than the standard noisy bar ever does. Gays often blame the 'bar environment'—in which one can hardly hear the partner speak, let alone 'really get to know him'—for their cruisy superficiality. This study, in which that factor was removed, gives the lie to the old excuse.

But even a good-looking man is just faking it if he's not *young*. The extreme store gay men set by youth, and the contempt they shower on those wayward enough to grow older, has us all running scared of aging, to an extent that looks pathological—and here, if nowhere else, we speak of the majority of gays. Bizarre distortions of perception and behavior result. In the personals, (futile) subtraction of up to twenty years from one's age is almost expected; even one of the authors—normally incorruptible where truth is concerned—has been known to shave a little off the top of his birth date. One very young New York City boy, homosexually active since puberty, spent his entire sixteenth birthday riding trains through the city and weeping for his lost youth.

In compensation, gay men wage war against each calendar month as though they were reenacting the Battle of the Marne. Although there are no studies to prove it, they probably comprise the majority of male consumers of vitamin nostrums, exercise machines, bronzers (a.k.a. men's pancake make-up), toupees and hair transplants, and face-lifts. To an extent, the effort pays off: gay men really do look younger and neater than their straight counterparts.

But it is, sooner or later, a losing battle, and when it's lost, the result is more gay misery. If the aging straight woman has played her cards right, she'll have children, if not a husband, to fall back on; too many gay men, however, scorning their age peers in the insatiable quest for youth, fall between the two stools of youth and age and end up old, alone, and unhappy. Is this a lifestyle to encourage?

7. MISBEHAVIOR IN RELATIONSHIPS

"There are hundreds of young men who want just what you do," he said, "but they are afraid! Cynical! Pessimistic! Self-loathing! Love bids them follow, and they say, 'No! I'd rather spend my evenings in the men's room at Grand Central!' "

—ANDREW HOLLERAN, *DANCER FROM THE DANCE*

Gay love is like the weather: everyone complains about it, but no one does anything about it. Perhaps that's because they don't know the relevant facts.

Just the Facts, Ma'am: Physiopsychological Considerations

Relationships between gay men don't usually last very long. Yet most gay men are genuinely preoccupied with their need to find a lover. In other words, everybody's looking, but nobody's finding. How to account for this paradox?

Part of this is due to the characteristics of male physiology and psychology, which make the sexual and romantic pairing of man with man inherently less stable than the pairing of man with woman. (Sorry if the truth hurts.) C. A. Tripp, in *The Homosexual Matrix*, has written extensively on this subject; here, in simplified form, is some of what he has to say:

First, although it's not fashionable to say so, men and women really are physiologically and psychologically different, in ways bearing cogently on their differing approaches to affairs of the heart and body. On average, a woman's sex drive is less intense than a man's, and less automatically aroused by visual cues. A woman is more sexually susceptible to her emotions than to what she sees. Men, on the other hand, are not only more 'horny'—and more nearly continuously—than are women, but are also aroused quickly and powerfully by the very sight of an 'ideal' mate, and, in this regard, have more highly visual imaginations than do women, making them more prone to temptation in the realm of sexual fantasy. As Germaine Greer remarked in *The Female Eunuch*, "Higgamus, hoggamus, woman's monogamous; hoggamus, higgamus, man is polygamous."

Since women are, in consequence, less likely to fall prey to the random, day-to-day temptation of instant lust than are men, their physiopsychology is a stabilizing factor in the typical heterosexual relationship. Accordingly, relative to heterosexual liaisons, one would expect male homosexual relationships to be unusually frangible, and female homosexual relationships to be unusually stable, and this is just the case. The evidence indicates that the long-lasting, Toklas-Stein type of lesbian relationship is characteristic, in starkest contradistinction to the radioactively brief half-life of the typical gay male alliance.

Second, sexual arousability depends heavily on 'mystery'—the degree to which there still exist between the partners resistances, areas of reticence, new things to find out. Obviously, men are more like other men, physically and emotionally, than they are like women, so there is less 'mystery' and resistance. This tends, on the whole, to cause gay men to tire of their partners (sexually, at any rate) more rapidly than straight men typically tire of their wives. Interestingly, this is even more true of lesbians, between whom passion very quickly dwindles; they seem, though, perhaps because their purely sexual needs are relatively modest, to be easily satisfied with their emotional rapport.

Given all the disadvantages of physiology and psychology under which relationships between gay men labor, it's clear that two men would have to try harder than a man and a woman to 'make things work.' Alas, they don't. Instead, gay men tend to bring to their relationships a raft of misconceptions, neuroses, and unrealistic expectations, and burden their love affairs past the point that they can handle. Consequently, gay men aren't very good at having and holding lovers. We turn now to the seven stages at which a gay man's love life can misfire—beginning with friendship.

First Misfire: 'I Have Thousands of "Friends" . . . To Whom I'm Bitchy And Disloyal'

It's true that gay friendships can be very, very good—one of the comforting things about the otherwise rather sterile gay social scene. We wouldn't wish to deny how blessed we have been with friends, and how often this is the case. Still, that phrase, 'otherwise rather sterile,' says it all. We wouldn't find our gay friendships so comforting, so precious, if they weren't treasured exceptions to the disappointing rule. And the rule is, that the gay man's hunt for genuine friendship within the community can be mighty hard.

It's probably true that before one can get and keep a lover, one must have, at the very least, the capacity to get and keep a friend. And we do mean *friend*, not merely one of the pack with whom you run. Real friendship is, indeed, closer to love than to mere acquaintance—which is why the personal skills required to get and keep (and to *be*) the one are necessary prerequisites for landing (and being) the other; and why no one, in this tightly defined sense of the term, has more than two or three real friends.

Yet many gay men don't seem to see friendship in this way at all. One often runs into 'popular' gay men—usually either model-handsome or Shrill Dolls, or both—leading the sort of hypomanic social life that keeps the little black book bulging and the cordless telephone ringing off the hook, who claim that they have 'thousands' of friends, yet clearly have no idea of what the term really means. To utter a dictum: if a man claims to have thousands of friends, all he really has is an audience. He wouldn't recognize genuine friendship if it gave him a blow job.

This sort of *soi-disant* attitude toward friendship has many causes. First and foremost is the peculiarly shallow way in which gay men tend to select their associates. Almost all gay male relationships, whether with acquaintances, friends, or lovers, within the urban community are based on a sort of sexual test; that is, one meets other men in settings—bars, parties, beaches, et al.—that are all implicitly more or less sexual in nature. One goes to these cruising grounds with both eyes open for another, *attractive* male. If one finds him, and the attraction is mutual, one goes to bed with him. Some of these bed-partners one never wishes to see again; some become one's friends; one hopes that one of them will finally become one's lover. One passes, in effect, all candidates for personal attention through the sieve of sexual attraction.

This has a degrading effect upon gay social—which are also sexual—relations. First, that two men are visually attracted to each other says virtually nothing at all about whether they share anything deeper—and more lasting—in common; social 'relationships' thus sieved through the upper and lower sheets of one's bed tend to be casual and impermanent. Second, the practice of repeatedly going to bed with men about whom one knows, and cares, nothing tends eventually to harden into a habitual shallowness, and a disinclination to judge by more important criteria. The upshot of this is the sort of gay man—we've all known him—who says, 'Well, Karl *is* a bit of a jerk, but he has a *huge* cock: I guess I'll go home with him.'

But third—and by far the worst—the nearly universal use of the sexual test as a means of screening one's associates means that unattractive gay men (of whom there are, of course, millions) have great difficulty even getting to first base. Not only do they find it nearly impossible to land a lover, but difficult even to meet another gay man to make an acquaintance, let alone a friend. Many's the time we've heard our gay associates say something like, 'Ugh! He's such a troll! I don't even want to *meet* him!' Occasionally, we've even been on the receiving end of such a rejection, so we know that it hurts. This sort of thing makes the gay community, for the *real* dogs, a cold, lonely place.

Naturally, it doesn't make it a very nice place for anyone. In a community of shallow social relationships, even the relatively attractive tend to find that they cannot count on their friends not to be disloyal backbiters. The stereotype of the gay man leaving a group of friends and immediately being mercilessly dissected behind his back—'My God, what a loudmouth Marley is! And did you see that tacky *schmattah* he was wearing?'—has at least some basis in reality.

Of course, one cannot blame gay shallowness on the sexual test alone; there are other reasons. For many, the shallowness is an outgrowth of their emotional anesthesia; they cannot open up their emotions to others, because they can't open them up to themselves—and don't want to. Dealing with others honestly on an emotional plane necessarily entails dealing with yourself honestly, and where one's buried emotions are riddled with fear and pain, shallowness seems preferable.

Then, too, there is an interesting parallel between the shallow world of gay friendship and the 1950s world of repressed, unliberated women described so well by Germaine Greer. In those bygone days, it was considerably harder for straight women to be friends with one another; defining themselves, as they had been taught to do by society, solely in terms of their relationship to men, and feeling that 'without a man, I'm nothing!' they tended to see one another more as potential competition than as potential friends. This made for exactly the same sort of shallow, surface-friendly but hostile-to-the-bone relationships that one often sees among groups of gay male 'friends,' who, when they are not pursuing one another, are also potential competition: the same phony, saccharine smiles and cutting remarks, the same poisonous cattiness, the same insincere, grating use of the term 'dear' as though one were wielding a buzz saw.

But it isn't only competition that alienates, it's the pursuit itself. Although women's liberation has made it easier, in recent years, for straight women to put aside their competition and be friends with one another, they *still* find it hard to be friends with straight men, who are pursuing them—if at all—more for their bodies than for themselves. As noted above, the question of sexual attraction tends to blind one to the wider question of personal characteristics. Unattractive straight women—however luminous their personalities—tend to get short shrift from straight men; attractive straight women, pursued because of their looks, find the resulting liaisons unsatisfying and prone to quick breakup on the shoals of personal incompatibility.

As you can see, gay men have the worst of both worlds: they see one another as potential competition *and* as mere sex objects. That gay friendships tend to be even shallower than straight friendships, and that many gay men find that their best and most long-lasting friendships are actually with straights, is not surprising. We are not great believers in the efficacy of consciousness-raising against such deep-seated, inherent problems, but it would seem that if any help is to be found for this problem, it would have to involve leading gay men, somehow, to see one another as human beings. Frankly, we aren't too optimistic.

But we've been talking, here, about a level of relationship less intense than that linking two lovers. If, as we've said, one needs must be able to be a good friend to be able to be a good lover, and gay men find it hard to be good friends, then it's no surprise that gay men fall even further short of the mark in the hunt for love.

Second Misfire: Forever Pursued, Forever Desired

At the lowest level of adaptation to the demands of a mature relationship is the gay man so emotionally stunted that he wants neither a lover nor even impersonal sex. In his heart of hearts, he feels sure that he's worthless and can only suppress this horrible feeling by providing himself with constant reassurance that he is desired sexually. He cannot allow this desire to be put to the test of consummation, whether in the context of a relationship or behind a bush, because then he might not be wanted anymore. Holleran, in *Dancer*, has described this mellifluously:

> The most beautiful Oriental was in fact chaste . . . He came
> each night to avoid the eyes of everyone who wanted him
> . . . and . . . went home alone . . . He wanted to be de-
> sired, not possessed, for in remaining desired he remained
> . . . forever pursued. He knew quite well that once pos-
> sessed he would no longer be enchanted . . .

There's a name for that kind of boy, and his initials are C.-T.

Into this category, too, falls the gay Casanova, or conqueror, who hypes his sense of self-worth by titillating others, or even laying hot pursuit until he takes their affections by storm. Once a 'target' has fallen in love, Cass drops him: the point has been proved: he's lovable. Like a heroin addict, he then needs a new fix, so his 'romantic' history is littered with hearts broken *seriatim*. Few among us have not fallen foul of Cass at one time or another.

Rather another direction, on the whole *slightly* more emotion-ally mature, is taken by the massively promiscuous.

Third Misfire: 'Promiscuity Is a Revolutionary Act!'

Someone once said that a promiscuous person is one who has more sex partners than you do. We don't mean that. By 'promiscu-ous' we mean those who have sex only with anonymous partners. That such people eventually pile up the numbers is beside the point; the important thing isn't the quantity but the quality of their relationships. (Apropos of this, *Christopher Street* once ran a Rick Fiala cartoon in which one man, taking off his jacket, says to another, "I hope this relationship doesn't last too long—I left the motor running.")

What motivates a man to have nothing but impersonal sex is a slightly less extreme degree of the doubt felt by the Casanova, coupled with an inability to communicate effectively with others on an emotional level—which puts him one step ahead of Cass: he's at least aware of the issue. Moreover, the man who has im-personal sex is not attempting to short-change or shaft his partners (pun not intended); there's an undeniably honest parity in his liaisons. Each party gets what he asks for.

Nevertheless, the disinclination to have *any* one-on-one relationships is often an inability to have them, and as such cannot be admired. People so afflicted will go to any extreme to rationalize their inadequacy, even to the extreme of writing books justifying their 'lifestyle' as a revolutionary political statement . . . performance artists of sexual street theater.

Now, we don't want to be unfair; the lurkers in rest rooms, woods, and fens are a far more mixed bag than the above analysis would suggest. Not all of them are emotionally incapable of a one-on-one relationship—some desire such a relationship desperately. Unfortunately, they're unable to conduct their hunt via the ordinary, more 'acceptable' channels—which amounts, pretty much, to the bar-and-party circuit—because they're not good-looking. Specific defects vary—too fat, too lean, too tall, too short, too square-faced, too round-faced, too old (though never too young)— but all, for one reason or another, have been ostracized by the beauty queens, who have decreed that the ugly must cease to exist.

Ugly or otherwise, life and its needs go on, and among those needs is the need for human contact and the desire for a lover. Thus, many apparent devotees of impersonal sex are no such thing: rather, they are further victims of a gay lifestyle that just doesn't work.

Relatively few gay men, however, take their sex lives to such an extreme of the impersonal. Almost all gay men at least *claim* to want a lover—in fact, they harp on the subject. At this developmental juncture, however, the overwhelming majority fall from the way of psychiatric grace, and are lured into the wily web of Mr. Right. This dasher of hopes, this Man of a Thousand Faces, this futilely awaited Godot of the gay community, demands close scrutiny.

Fourth Misfire: The Curse of Mr. Right

Who is he, this unattainable Platonic ideal, this golem stalking our love lives? And why do we continue to yearn for him after he disappoints us time and again? Are we mad?

No, we're just unreasonable. Almost uniformly, a gay man will reject a suitor who fails to pass any one of a large number of ironclad litmus tests. Yet, typically, he isn't honest with himself; if asked what he's looking for, he'll cry, 'Very little! I just need a man who is A, B, and C . . . is that so much to ask?' Well, if it were just A, B, and C, the answer would be, 'No, that isn't too much to ask.' But it usually isn't just A, B, and C; the list often goes to Z, and beyond.

For years, we've played a little game called Numbers with gay friends who whine that they can't find Mr. Right. Numbers is a game of arithmetic, intended to demonstrate to gay men how very few men there actually are in the United States who would fit their conception of Mr. Right, and how unrealistic their criteria therefore are. Our friend tells us what attributes, in some twenty categories, would be *minimally* acceptable to him in a lover. We then make what our friend agrees is a more than generous estimate of the proportion of the population that has those attributes.

For example, a friend may state that he's looking for a

(1) man;	*50% of population*
(2) gay, of course;	*15% of population*
(3) Caucasian;	*80% of population*
(4) over 18, but definitely under 30;	*20% of population*
(5) with a full head	*95%, for that age range*
(6) of straight,	*no more than 80%, for . . .*
(7) naturally blond hair.	*25%*
(8) Eye color is irrelevant, let's say.	*(Thank goodness.)*

(9) Physical condition is important: Mr. Right must be within 10 pounds, on either side, of ideal weight *no more than 75%*

(10) for height—between 5'7" and 6'3"— *85%*

(11) and well toned. *generously, 75%*

(12) His face must be attractively shaped. *33%, tops, to a typical gay man*

(13) He must be reasonably bright—a B.A., or working on it— *50%*

(14) and stably employed. *90% of young B.A. males*

(15) He must be mentally and emotionally stable. *no more than 90%*

If you'll now *multiply* the percentages, you'll see that we've reduced our pool of potential Mr. Rights from 120,000,000 to approximately 44,000—roughly one American man in 3,000! But is this where the winnowing ends? Oh, no. If pressed, most gay men will specify other characteristics their lover must—or must not—have: he must be free of major disabilities (didn't think of that, did you?); mustn't smoke or get drunk; mustn't have too much chest or body hair; must be interested in the arts, the beach, guacamole dip; have a compatible sense of humor; be from the 'right' social background, straight-acting and -appearing, a smart dresser, clean-shaven, circumcised . . . you get the picture. Before we're done, our friend is lucky if he's left with a dozen men in the U.S. who'd fit his bill. Invariably, he's shocked and dismayed. What are the chances of meeting those dozen? And, if he did meet them, would *he* be *their* idea of Mr. Right? Not likely!

Why do gay men do this to themselves? First, because they'd rather live in a fantasy than deal with reality; second, because they've cooled off on so many other men already that they're forced to sustain their hopes with the specific fantasy that if they could just find the *right* man, the romance would stay evergreen (which, as we've seen, it wouldn't); third (and perhaps most significant), it provides a convenient excuse for not trying to find a lover—incidentally justifying promiscuous and impersonal sex—and becomes a habit. The gay man with this habit can walk into any bar, say 'No one here for me!' and walk out.

After all, dealing with a real-life lover's imperfections takes a lot of effort. Face it, people are a hassle. Fantasies are so much more tractable. Thus, the preponderance of gay men stall out at this stage, and spend the next twenty years wandering from bar to bar, humming, "Someday My Prince Will Come."

And yet, despite their caution, some gays compromise their standards and, one morning, wake up next to a lover. What happens then? Do they live happily ever after? Not in this fairy tale!

Fifth Misfire: The Noninvolving, Hassle-Free, No-Fault Lover

When, *faute de mieux,* a gay man finally settles for a merely human lover, the battle for love doesn't end; it begins in earnest. There are several reasons for this.

First, it so happens that, as psychologist Robert Sternberg has shown, relationships are most lasting when A desires B just as much as B desires A; then everything's hunky-dory. Alas, this is rarely the case. Most relationships start with a pursuer, and a pursued; almost inevitably, the pursuer 'takes the whole thing more seriously' than the other party. When the pursued—even if he's enjoying the affair—perceives that the other party is in pursuit, he may feel emotionally threatened, get cold feet, and back off. Unfortunately, when he draws away, the pursuer, naturally anxious and wondering what he's doing wrong, tries to save the already overwatered bud of romance by pouring still more water on it—redoubling his phone calls, unannounced visits, presents, and the like. This is the worst possible approach: it's perceived as 'pressure,' and drives the pursued still further away, and so on, until he runs screaming out the door and is never seen or heard from again. To make a long story short, uneven relationships are —like tall, skinny vases—subject to the law of gravity: once they start to tip over, they tend to go all the way.

Now, these remarks apply to all relationships, gay or straight, but, for some reason—perhaps that gays start out less comfortable with their feelings than straights—this 'falling vase' effect is peculiarly pronounced in gay relationships: a sizable majority of gay men are allergic to any 'premature overinvolvement' on the part of a new sexual partner, and apt to back right off when they see it. Backing out of a budding relationship is an attractive option, and easy to rationalize. The pursuer, being merely human, has faults, and is therefore not Mr. Right—justification in itself for withdrawal; the pursued, if he's been at all faithful, is likely—unless his previous sexual batting average was near .000—to hanker for the relative 'freedom' of promiscuity, so shaking loose to play the field again seems desirable. Whatever the reasons, the majority of nascent romances fall apart over precisely this point.

The magic code word, which we've all heard until we could puke, is *hassles*. What Joe Gay is looking for, he'll tell you, is a 'hassle-free' relationship, in which his lover isn't 'over-involved,' doesn't 'make demands,' and 'gives him enough space.' In reality, no amount of space could ever be enough, because what Joe is really looking for isn't a lover at all, but a handsome, live-in fuck-buddy—a sort of low-maintenance household appliance. When the emotional tie that should be the very *raison d'être* of a relationship obtrudes noticeably upon the arrangement, it ceases to be convenient, poses an emotional threat, and becomes a 'hassle.' Millions of gay men seek 'arrangements' analogous to no-fault auto insurance, from which, at the first hint of trouble, they can just opt out without penalty.

A word, therefore, of cynical but hard-won advice. Should you find yourself the pursuer in a toppling relationship, give up and let it topple. You can't save it by intensifying your pursuit; you can only ensure its complete collapse. Of course, there is one ray of hope. If, the very second you see your beloved backing off, *you* back off yourself—but just a little bit farther—you might be able to turn the same inexorable law of balance to your advantage, and draw him back. Don't count on it, though, or it'll break your heart.

But not all gay men want quite so dehydrated a 'relationship'; some want a genuine, two-way romance, and get it. What happens then? Sooner or later, the roving penis rears its ugly head.

Sixth Misfire: 'The Seven-Week Itch'

Yes, that wayward impulse is as inevitable in man-to-man affairs as in man-to-woman, only, for gays, it starts itching faster. It's a disastrous aspect of human nature that, sooner or later, no matter how fortunate we may be, the bird that we glimpse in the pubic bush starts to look more appealing than the bird that we hold in our hand. And no matter how happy a gay man may be with his lover, he's likely, eventually, to go dowsing for dick.

If, as statistics have often shown, at least two thirds of married men are, at one time or another, unfaithful to their wives, then surely the cheating ratio of 'married' gay males, given enough time, approaches 100%. Men are, after all, as said earlier, more easily aroused than women, who tend to act as a relatively stabilizing influence; a restless gay man is more apt to be led astray by a cute face in the subway or the supermarket. Two gay men are double trouble, arithmetically squaring the probability of the fatal affairette. Then too, the gay community has never had any tradition of faithfulness, or any formally binding ceremony corresponding to straight marriage, to serve as the cement that might hold roving lovers together. In our experience, unfaithfulness between gay male lovers as often as not spells the beginning of the end.

Many gay lovers, bowing to the inevitable, agree to an 'open relationship,' for which there are as many sets of ground rules as there are couples. Admittedly, this can work; a restless lover gets It out of his system, and returns to the man he really cares about more than any other. But it doesn't always work. Sometimes the open relationship is more agreeable to one partner than to the other, who must finally admit that he can't tolerate it, and leave; sometimes its advent is merely a tacit admission that the relationship is no longer one of love in any case, but of sexual and cohabitational convenience. In the latter case, the result may be distasteful: the lovers—we should say, 'roommates'—tend to become mere collaborators on the prowl, helping each other look for tricks to take home for a *ménage à trois*. We knew of a fellow who considered his lover a valuable sexual bargaining chip. He'd go to a club, walk up to an agreeable potential trick, gesture at the lover (whom he'd left standing at the bar), and ask, "Would you like to come home with us? My friend has a nine-and-a-half-inch cock!"

It is, indeed, our impression that when gay relationships last at all, it's in diluted form, as the result of some such accommodation —though not usually one so blatant. But they don't usually last; eventually, one party heads for the door.

Seventh Misfire: The Nonstick, One-Wipe, Disposable Lover

As awful as it may seem, one of the aspects of gay life that our spokespersons have actually seen fit to eulogize is the fact that gay men can feel free to treat unsatisfactory relationships like Kleenex: one blow and out you go! Unfortunately, 'unsatisfactory' covers an awful lot of ground. It can signify anything from, on the one hand, the legitimate gripe that Lover X has expressed an urge to get into snuff sex, to, on the other, the mere fact that one is simply *tired* of Lover X, and wishes to put him back in the box and play with Lover Y. Misfire 7 is the final common pathway for all the earlier misfires, and the usual way in which promising beginnings come to ignominious ends. And when the end has come, it's back to the drawing board!

The Oppression That Lasts: Self-Oppression

As one of our friends, fresh from an unhappy affair, once said, his lower lip trembling: "Men are such pigs!"

And why do gay men behave in this swinish, wholly destructive way? Two reasons: (a) they're selfishly horny—which is to say, they're *men;* (b) they're still scared of revealing their emotions and being hurt—which is to say, they're *gay* men! The superaddition of these two sources of oppression, pain, and fear makes for a cold and lonely society in which people must conceal their feelings not only from one another but from themselves. Which takes us to our next section.

8. EMOTIONAL BLOCKAGE AND ANESTHESIA

> *[T]hat is what we all had in common: No one*
> *was allowed to be serious . . .*
> —ANDREW HOLLERAN, *DANCER FROM THE DANCE*

Welcome to the Waxworks

Any longtime observer of the gay scene—especially that hyper-intensified microcosm called the bar scene—will be familiar with a certain form of abnormal demeanor, striking to the attention because it's seen, in our society, almost solely among gay men—Shrill Doll Syndrome, a.k.a. Tussaud's Disease. Although we will now draw an exaggerated picture, the stigmata of Shrill Doll Syndrome are, in more attenuated form, all too common.

The first thing you'll notice about the Doll is how *stiff* he is. Typically, the body is held, tensely and rigidly, in an unnatural posture reminiscent of department store mannequins (which, it's worth noting, are usually *designed* by gay men). The posture may be effeminate, with arms akimbo or pinky aloft, or bizarrely macho, with chin thrust forward, arms held rigidly at the side, and legs planted apart, as though in the last stages of tetanus. Overmasculine or overfeminine, the posture is an exaggerated pose reflecting self-consciousness and deep bodily discomfort. Occasionally the arms are folded tightly across the chest in a gesture of self-protection.

This muscular rigidity extends to the face—either icily masklike or set, as though for a Fellini close-up, in an affected, dramatic expression. If makeup is worn—and it often is—it will be laid on like a silent screen star's poreless plastic carapace, heightening the unreal, masklike effect and the *soupçon* of Theatre. The vocal cords, also, are strained to the snapping point, the voice either whining and bleating or grinding and grating—in either case, hard, flat, unmodulated, and often nasal.

Though social, and fond of discotheques, pleasure palaces, and other ostensibly 'gay' surroundings, when out on the town the Doll appears to have a miserable time. Alone or with his own set, he tends not to look directly into the eyes of others, even when regaling them with his wit. When not so occupied, he stands in one spot nursing a drink or shambles, aimlessly yet ceaselessly, about the facility. Consequently, the atmosphere of a gay gathering place is often reminiscent of a mausoleum. Straights who wander into such a crypt are sometimes dismayed more by the apparent discomfort of the clientele than by their own discomfort at being in a den of fags. As a straight classmate told us, after peeking into Greenwich Village's "Uncle Charlie's," "The place was packed with these GQ models, just standing around, looking stiff and uncomfortable, and nobody looked at anyone else! Why do you guys go to those places?" Why, indeed?

Yet S & M (Stand and Model) is only one of the Doll's two settings. In a small group, the Doll often emits 'wit,' with which he may be quite gifted. (We use the word 'emits' advisedly; his wit is strictly a one-way broadcast.) Raconteur and comedian, he may keep his clique in stitches. Yet the performance is no more than that of an entertainer to his audience, and reveals little of his true feelings. (Don't try to break into his monologue with a quip of your own. His is not a game for two players, and he will flay you mercilessly if you attempt to trump his hand.) His wit, moreover, is phony, cold, and hostile. His anecdotes reflect unfavorably on their subjects, his barbs insult and sting. His comic forms are satire, sarcasm, and sneering irony. Although you may laugh, the overall effect is overwhelmingly hateful, and you come away from the Doll feeling as far as you could possibly get from actual fellowship and conviviality.

Coupled to Shrill Wit is the Oscar Wilde Pose: an attitude at once shallow and contemptuous, trivializing and condescending. When a Doll practices Oscar Wilde Pose, he manages to suggest that he's above whatever is being discussed, has seen through it, and finds it just too ridiculous and a mad, yawning bore. Whatever topic you raise, the practitioner of Oscar Wilde Pose dismisses it out of hand, and, in contrast with his own jaded affectlessness, makes *you* seem a Lumpen Bumpkin sorely lacking in taste and restraint. A Doll practicing O.W.P. comes across as an animated corpse with Attitude.

The experience of trying to relate to a Shrill Doll, even in the frivolous, supposedly lighthearted atmosphere of a gay party or dance bar, is hauntingly like eating an entire whipped-cream birthday cake: though tasty in tiny bites, it's neither nourishing nor satisfying, while in whole mouthfuls it rapidly becomes unbearable. The Doll can tickle your funnybone, but is incapable of warming your heart.

What's going on here? In effect, the Doll is trying to conceal his emotions, in two ways. First, by tightening his vocal cords and the muscles of his face and body into a premature rigor mortis, he literally 'holds it all in.' Second, by broadcasting an irrelevant bitchery, he bewilders the observer, distracting his attention from any residual signs of true feeling and, for that matter, from the telltale rigidity itself. The Doll's strategy is to let nothing through but a blizzard of pseudo-emotion, keeping a safe distance between the Doll and his threatening audience. (And, it might be added, between the Doll's threatening feelings and his own conscious awareness of those feelings.) But, try as he may, it never quite comes off.

The Syndrome pops up in unexpected places, and unexpectedly ties together seemingly unconnected aspects of the gay character and lifestyle. Typical gay male choices of job and hobby, for example, are made more comprehensible by an understanding of the Syndrome. Because the Doll is too scared to be himself, he must play a role in public at all times. He naturally tends to become preoccupied with role-playing and image management in general.

It is not too much to say that the gay man's predilection for acting and entertaining as careers, his fascination with the great—and thoroughly artificial—actresses of the Big Screen, and his fondness for costumes, are all, in part, consequences of the peculiar need for concealment characteristic of the Shrill Doll.

Gays who behave in a cold and bitchy way, Shrill Dolls and Oscar Wildes, are not trying, at least primarily, to deny the emotions of others; rather, their aim is to shut off awareness of their *own* emotions. They must affect indifference so that they can continue to *feel* indifferent. They must, at all costs, blockade awareness of their own gay fear and pain.

The unpleasant, inescapable fact of the matter is that being gay in the United States in the 1980s has not only sucked—which is bearable—but bitten. For every gay, whatever his circumstances, awareness of his 'deviance,' and its ineluctable social consequences, entails at least *some* fear and pain that straights simply don't have to deal with, or even think about. Gays in our society exhaust a great deal of time and energy in the maintenance of their defenses against all the hydra-headed evils of homohatred cited in Chapter 1. Always aware of their danger, they must quell the ever-present uneasiness, the anxiety, by making light of it all, pretending that nothing really makes any difference to them, that others can't hurt them because they just don't give a damn what people think. They must, in fact, adopt a certain degree of precisely that rigidity, coldness, and indifference which, in their extreme forms, we've called Shrill Doll Syndrome and Oscar Wilde Pose.

But even when tension and control are not extreme, they take time and energy, and they involve the strapping on of the kind of apparatus and armor that, after a while, you don't find so easy to take off. Even a little 'character armor' is a bad thing, leading to what John Rechy, in *City of Night,* called "the ice-age of the heart" —the inability of gays to let down their guard far enough really to open their hearts, to live and love with one another as the brothers they so often claim—and want—to be.

'Nurse! Quick! The Anesthetic!'—The Use of Alcohol and Drugs

Alas, the most lightweight, streamlined, hi-tech character armor —so comfy you'll hardly know you're wearing it!—has a tendency to stiffen up in the joints without regular lubrication. The Syndrome and Pose are not the only outgrowths of gay fear and pain. Just as prevalent, and far more serious, are the use and abuse of alcohol and drugs. Few of us who lived through the bar scene of the late 1970s can be unaware of the extent to which it accepted, and even depended upon, a never-ending IV drip of pills and liquor.

Although the use of illicit drugs—particularly cocaine and its derivatives—has become less socially acceptable in recent years, there's little evidence that it has actually declined; and alcohol, of course, remains, as it has always been, the anodyne of choice for the troubled. Indeed, according to *Advocate* author George De Stefano ("Gay Drug Abuse: Owning Up To A Serious Problem"), gay-oriented psychotherapists estimate that nearly 30% of their patients have significant problems with drug and/or alcohol abuse.

A homosexual who uses a stimulant to produce euphoria and confidence, who takes a depressant—including alcohol—to fog out his thoughts and emotions, is administering himself a medication—specifically, an anodyne for the fear and pain of being gay. In effect, he is supplementing his Doll/Wilde act, using an artificial means to secure a degree of emotional anesthesia unattainable by any effort of the ordinary human will, but, in the face of wanton, ongoing straight hatred, absolutely necessary to forestall emotional collapse. Not for nothing do drunks jocularly refer to the bartender as 'The Doctor,' and rejoice that, after the latter's ministrations, they're 'feeling no pain.' Temporarily.

There are two fears involved in heavy drinking and drugging. The lesser fear is of the gay social scene itself—bar-room jitters, anxiety over the necessity of making approaches and the (well-founded) fear of a cruel rejection . . . even, for some, internalized shame and self-hatred over *being* gay. This lesser fear leads to a lesser abuse of alcohol and drugs, although it's still a real problem. The greater fear, however, is not of one's fellow gays, but of the antigay world through which one must move on a daily basis —with all the tension, and the anticipatory dread of catcalls and violence, and the loss of family love, friendship, employment, and housing that homophobia and homohatred may imply. This greater fear is what leads to the greater abuse of alcohol and drugs.

As with so many maladaptive ways of administering quick, symptomatic fixes to deep-seated social maladies, gay dependence on pills and liquor ultimately makes the problem far worse. Quite apart from the direct harm that such substances cause to body and mind, and thus to social and job performance, emotional anesthesia is itself life-denying and dangerous. It involves resolutely blinding oneself to the unpleasant realities of life, without a clear and unblinking confrontation with which, we are continually exposed to foreseeable, but unforeseen, disaster.

Beyond the Valley of the Shrill Dolls

If life must be lived beneath a hard, thick plating of emotional antitank armor, it might as well not be lived at all. Let's resolve to create a plan and a lifestyle that will allow us to lay to rest our fears and shrug off our armor, and, unlike the contentedly sightless inhabitants of Plato's lightless cave, venture forth from the Valley of the Shrill Dolls into the relative light and warmth of human brotherhood—however scary the foray might be, and however many times we might get hurt. If even one reader takes our plea to heart and seeks help, whether within himself or in a psychiatrist's office, for his emotional frigidity or his alcoholism or drug addiction, the depressing task of writing this chapter will have been 100% worthwhile.

9. REALITY-DENIAL, NONSENSICAL THINKING, AND MYTHOMANIA

*[W]e queens loathed rain at the beach, small cocks, and real-
ity . . .*

—ANDREW HOLLERAN, *DANCER FROM THE DANCE*

As we've seen throughout this book, American gays are regularly subjected to hostility, which causes them fear, anger, and
pain; in order not to be constantly miserable, they have to find
ways to shut these bad feelings off, or out. We've already explored
many of the ways in which they do this: a haughty, affected indifference, pills and liquor, shallow relationships, and the like.
Clearly, what these maladaptive behaviors reflect in common is
the need to *deny emotional pain.*

But there's a more efficient way to skin this monster: reality-
denial. Gays who can somehow contrive to *deny the reality* of the
hostility around them need feel no such pain in the first place. In
their fantasy, there is no hostility, hence no fear, or anger, or pain
—which obviates the necessity of putting them out of one's mind.
As we'll explain, fantasyland is where millions of gays live.

Now, everyone, straight or gay, is prone, at times, to visit the
realm of fantasy: to believe what *feels good* rather than what is *true.*
Daniel Katz, writing in *Public Opinion Quarterly* ("The Functional
Approach to the Study of Attitudes"), has analyzed this tendency
to select beliefs on a functional, rather than an evidential or logical, basis; the primary reason people believe a given thing, he
finds, is that it makes them feel good, rather than bad. Yet gays
are, on the whole, more prone to pick and choose their beliefs in
this way than straights are; this is because homohatred causes
gays to feel more fear, anger, and pain than most straights have to
put up with. Consequently, reality-denial is a characteristically
gay misbehavior. In this section, we'll explain how reality-denial
reveals itself in bad sense, and why it may be healthy for the
individual gay, but lethal to the gay community as a whole.

How Reality-Denial Elicits Bad Sense, with Some Startling Examples

Reality is always there, staring you right in the face. This makes it hard to deny. In order to shut it out or explain it away, you have to indulge yourself in some pretty serious mind games, ignoring or twisting what you see, hear, and think, no matter how peculiar this may look to impartial outsiders. Just as denying painful *feelings* distorts gay social behavior in a characteristic way, so denying painful *realities* distorts gay intellectual behavior. Although we've seen this pattern of intellectual distortion many times, for many years, in many gays, it's not easy to come up with a label for it. For all its deficiencies, we can manage nothing more evocative than the old-fashioned term your grandmother may have pounded you with—'bad sense.'

Gays reveal several major forms of bad sense in their actions, conversation, and (political) writing. Some of these are:

• Wishful thinking. *This, the axle around which reality-denial revolves, is self-explanatory: believe whatever you like, rather than what you ought to know is true. For example, to this day we're frequently told that "straights no longer hate gays; the majority of straights have recognized our unique worth, and actually respect and like us as much as they do anyone else." (A verbatim quote.) And, according to R. D. Fenwick's* Advocate Guide to Gay Health, *"Despite the horror stories . . . anal intercourse is a perfectly safe and beautifully expressive way for two men to have sex." A dangerous notion, clearly untrue even in 1983.*

Wishful thinking can be carried to surprising extremes. Very effeminate gay men have assured us they're 'never picked out and harassed for being gay.' Half a dozen times, we've been walking in public with one of these, when he was loudly, clearly, and unmistakably 'fag-baited' by hostile teens. (E.g., 'Suck my cock and die, you fucking faggot!') Each time, our companion either failed to notice—a feat so amazing, we must suppose he screened reality out at a preconscious level—or declared, with every appearance of confidence and conviction, "Those boys are just jealous of me, because I'm so good-looking and fashionably dressed!"

By-the-bye, the 'straights-will-love-us-if-we-love-ourselves' theory, addressed earlier, is another example of wishful thinking. But what won't work for one dweeb against ten bullies won't work for one million dweebs against one million bullies.

• Paranoia. *This—the flip side of wishful thinking—reflects a desire to* simplify *the reality of homohatred by blaming it on a small coterie of fantastically evil oppressors. It reveals itself in a predilection for conspiracy theories. Thus, the CIA is accused of having invented and deliberately spread AIDS as part of a government plot to kill all gays. Or AIDS is said to be no more than a mutant form of syphilis, deliberately deployed against gays by the same folks who charted the progress of the old-fashioned variety, in untreated blacks, at Tuskegee. And so forth. Somehow, blaming one's misery on an evil few—who could, in theory, be identified and expunged—is more comforting than the dreary truth: that homohatred is widespread, deep-seated, and very, very hard to target and root out.*

• Illogic. *So common it needs neither example nor explanation. We've all had arguments in which our gay interlocutor made point after point unrelated either to our logic or his own. Why? Because if you pay attention to the rules of logic, you're sometimes forced to accept conclusions you don't like. Consequently, gays often decry logic as life-denying, imprisoning, and constraining. What it constrains them toward is the unpalatable truth. So it has to go.*

• Emotionalism. *One effective way of making the truth go away is to use wild, over-emotional rhetoric. Gays who 'argue' in this way hope to shout down facts and logic with irrelevant expressions of personal passion. Gay newspapers afford many examples. Bob Nelson, attempting in* Gay Community News *to prove that progay advertising is 'bad' ("Advertising Our Way to 'Acceptance' "), used words like "odious," "putrescent," and "ugh," then skipped the rails of logical relevance completely, demanding, "Have you ever been in a gay disco full of sexy men when a Whitney Houston record comes on? Have you ever gone to a lesbian fashion show where the women wear leather and slinky silky things and scream in joy and sisterhood?" He closed by exclaiming, "If we don't love ourselves, no one else will love us. VIVA NOSOTROS!"*

. . . which had about as much to do with the issue under discussion—whether advertising is good or bad for gays—as it did with the price of pork in Peru.

• Unfounded notions. *To what crackpot idea do gay people* not *gravitate? Being themselves outcasts and opponents of the establishment, their attraction to a notion increases in direct proportion to the extent to which it is discredited and debunked by authority figures. Thus, gays are fond of New Age and occult beliefs, as well as any and all others that have no*

basis in, or have actually been disproven by, science: fruitarianism; astrol-
ogy, numerology, and pyramidology; the Tarot; 'vibes' from crystals; and
various questionable forms of 'healing.' In fact, certain healers, whatever
their sexual orientation, seem to recognize that gays are an eager market
for their services. An example: Greenwich Village was recently flooded
with "Dolphenvision" flyers advertising "Dolphin Facilitated Workshops,"
in which one "swims with the dolphins . . . to experience their playful,
spontaneous, loving, and gentle world." A "heart-centered journey to the
light within, guided by . . . the wisdom of our soul," will supposedly
"heal and transform old hurts and limitations." Yeah, likely. But this sort
of thing appeals to gays: its smarmy sweetness and wide-eyed optimism
give them hope, and make the world, and their lives, seem so much more
pleasant than they really are.

So much for bad sense, which flees reality for never-never land,
and works vigorously to deny facts and logic. Good sense, therefore, is its opposite: that no-nonsense attitude toward reality that
keeps its eyes open for serious problems, and, when it sees them,
learns the *facts*, analyzes them *logically*, and tries to discover and
apply a vigorous, workable solution.

This definition is so important, we'd like to emphasize the itali-
cized terms. *Facts* are hard-core data, from reliable, documentable
sources—public records, scientific journals. They consist, in large
part, of such boring, ungay things as absolute numbers and statistics. *Logic* is the straightforward, inarguable, mandatory set of
rules propounded by Aristotle around 300 B.C. It tells you how to
grind all possible true conclusions from a collection of facts.

You ignore either at your peril.

But even if you know the facts, and attempt to analyze them
logically, your attempt will fail if you don't keep emotionalism in
its place. Many gays find this hard to do. Most have spent so
many years repressing their feelings that the ability to feel and
voice their honest emotions is—understandably—precious to
them. They place an exaggerated emphasis on their emotions, val-
uing them above 'mere' logic, and eventually come to believe that
truth is what they feel it to be. And this is, of course, nonsense.
Feelings tell you nothing whatever about the truth; for every individual who feels in his heart that *x* is decidedly true, there is

another individual whose auricles and ventricles tell him that x is decidedly *false*. As a Michelin guide to reality, feelings are worthless.

It's important that it be crystal-clear what we mean by saying that 'feelings are worthless.' We don't mean you should try to act, day in and day out, like a robot. Rather, we mean that when you're trying to solve a serious problem, you should put your feelings aside until you've reasoned your way to a solution. Your feelings *are* important; in the last analysis, factual, logical thinking exists only in order to *serve* your feelings, not vice versa. But for reasoning to serve effectively, it must be left alone to do its job in peace.

Now, we've made a lot of bald assertions we can't prove; they come from personal experience. Ultimately, the persuasiveness of our description walks on two legs: striking examples, and your own gut-level recognition. We suspect that the mortifying truth is this: most readers with good sense will find that our observations are corroborated by their own experience, and require no further demonstration; most readers with bad sense will be unconvinceable by any power of demonstration whatever. Good sense is like eyesight: those who've never had it will never understand it.

We've dealt, here, primarily, with cocktail-party nonsense, which can do relatively little harm. In fact, for the individual gay, it's healthy. Unfortunately, once again, what's healthy for the individual can be most unhealthy for the community. The *danger* of bad sense is that it's not just chattered over cocktails, but also from the pages of national magazines and popular books, whence it does a tremendous amount of damage. It tells gays what they want to hear, not what they ought to hear; it alternately lulls them to sleep, and persuades them to support or follow disastrous courses of action.

Bad Sense Writ Large: Gay Authors

Gay journalists and authors provide us with a sort of horn-o'-plenty of wishful thinking and cock-eyed assessments of the social and political reality in this country, expressed not only in editorials but in the pages of the 'radical' books they like to publish, such as Mark Thompson's *Gay Spirit: Myth and Meaning.* This anthology of screeds by gay 'thinkers,' past and present, focuses on issues like "Who are we gay people? Where do we come from and where have we been? What are we for?" As vaguely as they're phrased, these are legitimate questions. The answers, however, are quite a different kettle of fish.

Harry Hay, for example (justly revered by gays as the founder of the Mattachine Society), thinks it "glaringly clear that the traditional hetero male-dominated subject-object consciousness is bankrupt," and declares that "we gay folk" are the answer: "a species variant with a particular characteristic adaptation in consciousness whose time has come!" Comments: where it's not simply false, this is meaningless. What can we make of the jawbreaker, "traditional hetero male-dominated subject-object consciousness," other than that Mr. Hay apparently dislikes logic and would prefer to substitute emotion? This is typical gay rhetoric, inflated with lighter-than-air emotional gas, sailing away into the stratosphere of unreal things.

James Broughton exclaims, angrily, that "Most gay activists . . . want acceptance . . . to be absorbed in the social fabric of the heterosexual mainstream." Sounds pretty good to us! But no—"this is ass-backwards. We should be considering what *we* can do for *them,* how we can free them from their misery and wrongheadedness . . . [their] shameless greed and . . . passion for war." Comments: Get with the program, James! First, "they" don't want what "we" have to offer, as should be obvious to anyone with one eye on the reality meter. Second, what *do* "we" have to offer? "They" hardly have a lock on the patents for "greed" and "war." As a group, latter-day American gays are arguably even more selfish, and greedy for material things, than are straights; as for "war," we cite (1) various homosexual warrior castes—such as the gay Greeks of the Trojan War—of the ancient world; (2) the highly homosexual Nazi SS; and (3) the pain and hatred peddled by apologists for gay sadomasochism, for whom the leaders of our community long ago rolled out the welcome wagon. Don't tell us that gays are peace-loving; we've seen *Drummer* magazine!

Edward Carpenter, though, were he writing in the present day, would win the door prize for wishful thinking: "It is possible that the Uranian [gay] spirit may lead to something like a general enthusiasm of humanity, and that the Uranian people may be destined to form the advance guard of that great movement which will one day transform the common life by substituting the bond of personal affection and compassion for the monetary, legal, and other external ties which now control and confine society." Comments: Carpenter seems to be saying that gay people love each other more than straights do (a dubious proposition), and that, because of this, someday, in some unspecified way, we'll all be able to live without money or laws (an illogical conclusion).

Lest we fail to feel sufficiently good about ourselves, Malcolm Boyd calls for the telling of the "untold stories of gay saints"; "Hibiscus" assures us that "people who are gay verge on being angels." Shades of Saints Genet, Gide, and Cocteau! Who are these gay "saints" and "angels"? Where do they hang out? The Boston Ramrod, perhaps? The Boy-Bar? Forty-second Street and Times Square?

But this is shooting fish in a barrel. Cheap shots aside, we have a point to make: these writers, admired as the intellectuals of our community, don't write sensibly. The above quotes seem more the product of wishful than of logical thinking. Terms are undefined, and undefinable; statements refer, not to facts, but emotions, or, indeed, to one another: verbal choochoo trains, chasing one another 'round and 'round on a circular track. As such, the above selections, though exaggerated, are representative of the work of the sort of gay people who get invited to speak and write: strong on verbal fluency, weak on logic, swayed far more heavily by the emotional than the practical.

The Fish Rots from the Head Down: Reality-Denial at the Very Top

When you find a given failing even in a community's best and brightest, you suspect its overwhelming prevalence among the great unwashed. In this context, it's noteworthy that Alan Turing, Oscar Wilde, and perhaps Leonardo da Vinci—each, in his own time and unique vein, among the most brilliant minds the gay community has ever produced—*all* embroiled themselves in serious legal trouble by carrying on indiscreetly with young men. Da Vinci stood trial; Wilde was imprisoned, destroying his personality and career; Turing, chemically castrated by order of the court, killed himself.

Arguably, each of these great men knew the law of his time, had ample scope to conduct his affairs in the same discretion and privacy employed by lesser mortals, and, having a first-rate mind, must have known, on some level, that flaunting his 'deviation' in the public's face was an ideal way of losing his reputation, career, freedom, even life. Yet, for the sake of what, we cannot fathom, each man threw caution—and with it, everything else—to the winds.

It's remarkable that these geniuses—the very cream of the human crop—could fail so devastatingly to see their world as it really was, and to exercise minimal restraint. In our view, their failure argues wishful thinking. Some might call it 'the courage of the individual to stand alone against oppression,' but, judging actions by the practical criterion of their consequences, it looks awfully foolish.

And on the clay feet of their betters, more humble gays continue to bumble along.

Myths: The Lies by Which We Live

> *There is something feeble and a little contempt-*
> *ible about a man who cannot face the perils of*
> *life without the help of comfortable myths.*
>   —BERTRAND RUSSELL,
>   *HUMAN SOCIETY*
>   *IN ETHICS AND POLITICS*

The gay penchant for unrealistic thinking is more than annoying: it's fatal. Urban gays who *must* wake up to the reality of
growing straight oppression if they are to avert the several really
ugly possibilities waiting in the wings of the 1990s prefer instead
to continue sailing in the sunlight, heedless of all storm warnings.
Toward this end, they have—unconsciously, we're sure—evolved
a series of fatuous myths justifying their continued refusal to involve themselves, financially or otherwise, in the struggle for our
social and political rights. Taken together, these myths have para-
lyzed the community's collective will to organize. We outline
them so that when the reader next encounters one, he will recognize it and react as he would to a cockroach: by stomping it.
(Verbally, of course.)

Myth No. 1: There is no problem. Many gays deal with the problem
of antigay hatred by denying it. They'll tell you that straight acceptance of gays is already here and here to stay. (With the exception, of course, of a few backwaters that don't count—like the
South, the Breadbasket, all rural areas . . . in short, everything
between New York and San Francisco.) A variation on this theme
is that all the right people—the enlightened, the influential, the
power elite—already accept us, so the vulgar masses don't matter.

These incorrigible optimists tend to live in urban centers packed
with fellow gays. They lose their perspective. In a few of their
favorite cities, it seems that straights *have* learned to live alongside
them—sort of—and they falsely suppose that this trend is nationwide.

Myth No. 2: There is a problem, but it's getting better naturally. Certain Pollyannas, untroubled by the gathering storm, rest in the calm and sunny conviction that sooner or later gay rights will come to those who wait . . . and wait. They just know this will happen, because, they say, people are basically logical and good, whereas homohatred is illogical and bad. From this perspective, homohatred is seen as a temporary evil, a sort of historical head-cold or grumpy mood, sure to pass away of its own accord. Hence, the liberation of gays is as inevitable as the steady progress of mankind. Ah, the steady progress of mankind! Marx said something similar about the impending worldwide proletarian revolution—about 130 years ago. This optimism about the Hand of History relieves lazy denizens of the gay-ghetto set from the responsibility and trouble of speeding things up. Somewhere en route to this comforting delusion they have forgotten that ignorance and illogic and wicked prejudice tend to cling forever with bloody fingertips unless someone works very, very hard to stamp them loose.

Myth No. 3: There is a problem, but gay Messiahs will solve it for us. Well, goodness, look at all those fanatical activists, courageously exposing themselves to danger and ignominy, our Brave Boys on the Front . . . they're always spouting off on TV and leading rallies in Washington and leaving piles of pamphlets in the bars. And what about the Human Rights Campaign Fund, lobbying for us at the Capitol? They're obviously kicking up a storm. The future seems to be in good hands. We'll just lie low and cheer them on.

Although, as we've noted, the National Gay and Lesbian Task Force and kindred 'national' organizations scarcely exist for lack of funding, the relatively high visibility generated *in the bars* by their appeals for aid has the paradoxical effect of making them seem real and vital organizations, hardly so near death's door as to require immediate fiscal transfusion. So let George do it.

Myth No. 4: There is a problem, and books like After the Ball *cause it.* As we noted earlier, one of the most pernicious of gay myths is the magical idea that if gays could just *learn to like themselves*, then straights would like them, too. In this scheme of things, which is drawn directly from the psychobabble racks at the local book-store, gay self-hatred makes for straight hatred of gays. When gays learn to feel good about themselves, straight oppression will just—evaporate!

Naturally, the last thing the comfortably deluded want to hear is anything that might shatter their delusion. Consequently, articles and books like ours, which tell the gay community that all is *not* well, that we are in danger, and—worst of all—that we are partially at fault, come in for savage attack from the brokers of political correctness. We now turn to these blind leaders of the blind.

10. GAY POLITICAL FASCISM AND THE OPPRESSION OF P.C.

> *For the truth, you get beat up.*
> —YIDDISH SAYING

In C. S. Lewis's *The Screwtape Letters,* a fictional devil remarks, of himself and his hellish colleagues, that:

> We direct the fashionable outcry of each generation against those vices of which it is least in danger and fix its approval on that vice which we are trying to make endemic. Cruel ages are put on their guard against Sentimentality, feckless and idle ones against Respectability, lecherous ones against Puritanism. The game is to have them all running about with fire extinguishers whenever there is a flood, and all crowding to that side of the boat which is already nearly gunwale under.

While we wouldn't go so far as to call them devils, so it has been with the leaders of the gay press and their activist sidekicks—heavily overlapping groups, in fact—for twenty years. Ever since we began to read and listen to such, we have felt strongly that *something* was horribly wrong—myopic, overemotional, and destructive—with their whole worldview and tactics. For the purposes of this book, articulation has become absolutely necessary, yet, even now, the closest we can come to a general, overall statement is to declare that our leaders have a bad case of Bad Attitude. We don't doubt that they believe they're absolutely right, but we can't agree; rather, we feel that, collectively, they've taken the wrong road and, by their (often successful) attempts to shape gay political strategy, and their public utterances, done lasting damage.

How to describe this Bad Attitude? Here is a bill of particulars:

• The clique of authors, journalists, and bush-league troublemakers called, collectively, 'gay leaders and spokespersons' consistently tends to define the overall situation of gays *vis-à-vis* straights solely in oppressor/victim terms (revealing, and preserving, an 'oppression' or 'siege' mentality)—a dichotomous, black/white, friend/foe, with-us-or-against-us attitude, leaving no room for fine shades or legitimate differences of opinion, and leading inevitably to antagonism and hotheadedness, to confrontation and martyrdom. They see straights as always and only our enemies, to be fought tooth and nail—not as people, whose mixed feelings about gays can be disentangled and (potentially) turned to our advantage.

• Their tendency to see the gay-straight relationship solely in terms of blind, opposed extremes makes them chronically angry and gives them a taste for violence in speech and action—ostensibly to 'extract concessions from straights,' but actually to discharge their overflowing anger. They call for sit-ins, obstruction, even physical force, as means of solving our problems. They make threats and wave their fists. They are confrontational rather than cooperative. Their passive-aggressive posture is at once whining and belligerent, paranoid and demanding. Their strident emotion and irrational rhetoric puts straight authorities off, and, anger begetting anger, intensifies the hostility of the straight mainstream.

• They're psychologically frozen in a bygone era, in which self-hatred really was *the* gay problem, and refuse to recognize that this battle has, on the whole, become one of secondary concern; that now we're confronted by a whole *new* set of issues, some of which have to do with our liking ourselves altogether too much; that self-criticism is, by now, healthy and necessary; that it's time to stop thinking in terms of past grievances, and start thinking in problem-oriented terms, time to stop raising consciousness, and start raising money. Darrell Yates Rist's *Gay Life* essay, "On Hating Ourselves," warns us yet again of this omnipresently lurking evil, which he apparently finds in any criticism of gay excess. Half-amused, half-disdainful, and wholly condescending, he describes a friend as "self-hating" because he's "offended" by the "Drag, leather, and near-nudity" of a Chicago gay pride parade—also featuring a drag queen handing out "cock-shaped candies" to small children.

• The radical gay cadre persists in seeing all issues in terms of an outmoded and inapplicable Marxist framework, which is not only annoying to reasonable people but the infallible sign of a rigid and simplistic mind. (Marxism itself, as a doctrine, is by no means simple; but naïve belief in its properties as a panacea *is* simplistic.) Speeches and articles analyzing gay-straight relations in Marxist terms do nothing but drag an ideological red herring—and one, at that, in an advanced state of decay—across the path of pragmatism.

• They reject all criticism of the community itself, not only by straight outsiders but by gay insiders, using exactly the same tactics of oppression employed by our straight oppressors: lying, smearing, shouting down, refusing the right of reply, name-calling, and counterstereotyping (imputing to all 'enemies' the same indiscriminate grab-bag of characteristics). Their counterattacks have the same curiously formulaic, sloganeering quality in which their far-right enemies excel: be the criticism large or small, the critic straight or gay, the diagnosis is always the same cheap shot: *you're a homophobe!*—and you must also hate women, blacks, and all other oppressed minorities. Larry Kramer was tarred and feathered in this way (see below).

• They attack straight authorities so uniformly, immoderately, and unreasonably that they forfeit our right to be taken seriously. They bite even those hands that are trying, within the constraints of the system, to feed us, when those hands don't dish up the exact and complete menu they have in mind. Yet the hard, cynical political facts are that politicians who openly embrace us with all three arms simply *cannot* get elected to the really powerful, high-level, national offices—such as President of the United States. Politicians must, even if they're on our side, occasionally stand apart from us in order to be able to 'smuggle' their sympathies into office. Such an all-or-nothing attitude on the part of gays puts our would-be friends in an impossible position and severely damages our long-range interests.

For example, when Governor Michael Dukakis, responding to political pressure from conservative groups, attempted to enunciate a state foster-parents policy that in fact *allowed* adoption by gay would-be parents on a *sub rosa* basis, gay leaders filled the newspapers and airwaves with their embittered plaints, attacking Dukakis as a back-stabber. Essentially, they demanded that he take an impossible position. One doesn't hear this sort of thing from an experienced gay politician like Barney Frank, who knows how to compromise.

• Acting as pied pipers of radicalism, they take us all to blind extremes in rejecting the values of morality and family structure, leaving us with no values or community structure to replace these, and taking us with them into the complete void of individual isolation and communal amorality. They know how to tear down, but not how to rebuild.

• They dare presume to 'speak for' the whole community, yet reject the right of 'silent majority' gays to equal and accurate representation in their publications, allowing us to be tarred by straight pundits with a broad communal brush. Although they embarrass us, they insist upon dragging us down with them. They proclaim us self-haters, frauds, and hypocrites. They respect our lifestyle even less than straights respect their own. Even in the authors' own experience, gay media organs which attack us harshly often either flatly refuse us, or finesse us out of, our right to reply.

• In editorials and feature articles, they applaud, abet, second, and promote ugly, extraneous behaviors of rank-and-file gays (narcissism, hedonism, promiscuity, bathhouse sex), hail these as our 'lifestyle,' and attempt to sell this bill of unwashed goods not only to gays themselves, but to straights, as though *this were what it meant to be gay.* They define our lifestyle in terms of sex, help create a community in which we cannot find love, and then express surprise and anger when straights condemn us as animals who live only for fucking. Randy Shilts' *Band* affords numerous cases: for example, "a leftist Toronto newspaper published a story on 'rimming as a revolutionary act.'" When gay doctor Dan Williams warned the community, in 1980, that its extreme promiscuity posed a significant epidemiological threat, "he suffered [gay media] criticism as a 'monogamist.'" Similarly, the inevitable

public-health decision to force closure of gay bathhouses continued to provoke an editorial storm of childish name-calling and
threats, as late as 1985. (And, astoundingly, in Boston as late as
1989!)

• They label all attempts to get along with the straight community as 'collaboration' and 'selling out,' apparently preferring op-
positional belligerence for its own sake—as though we could ever
live happily in a society we affect to despise. To them, assimilation
is a dirty word; they would rather live in a ghetto of gay ortho-
doxy than find Jesse Jackson's "common ground."

The above behavior becomes comprehensible when placed in
its proper historical context. The contemporary gay press is an
outgrowth of the Stonewall era, in which certain fringe elements
of the gay community—so irremediably far out of the straight
mainstream that they had no hope of 'passing'—got fed up with
police harassment and fought back. This is well known. What
hasn't been so clearly perceived is that it was, by and large, the
same hopelessly out-of-the-closet individuals who founded, or coopted the pre-existing, gay press. Having (as they saw it) no option
of getting along, they made a career out of fighting back, becoming professional revolutionaries and makers of trouble. Marxist
ideology fit their oppression mentality like a glove. Naturally,
their politics and tactical recommendations have been highly confrontational ever since. Equally naturally, having invested a lot of
emotion in their struggle, and in their role as gay leaders, they
resent any hint that their approach is outmoded. Yet, however
historically inevitable it was that they would be the first gays to be
ejected from the closet and into leadership positions, they nevertheless are not representative of the comportment, lifestyle, values, or needs of the enormous preponderance of gays, who are,
except for what they like to do in bed, just like everyone else.
More mainstream gays themselves resent being represented by
those with whom they have little in common, and whom they do
not like.

No single illustration of the above remarks really makes our
point; our observations were made on the basis of enormous num-

bers of similar illustrations, heard and read over a fifteen-year period. The following illustrations—chosen virtually at random—might be multiplied a thousandfold without either depleting the stock or, really, significantly furthering the persuasiveness of our remarks.

Boyd McDonald: The Politics of the Grotty

All right, so we can't get away with citing Boyd McDonald—editor of *Meat, Flesh, Sex, cum,* et al., and *Straight to Hell: The Manhattan Review of Unnatural Acts*—as a bad example, without confessing that we've read his filth. We have. We also pick at scabs, and for similar reasons. But we oughtn't. McDonald's works constitute an *egregious* example—of bad attitudes, both social and political; of the sort of deliberately provocative, antagonistic parading, before the straight community (his works have actually been retailed by major bookstores), of all that is slimiest and most shameful in gay behavior.

The graphic sexual content of his correspondents' outpourings, though bad enough (his books would never pass the Mother Test —that is, 'Would I want my mother to read this?'), is as nothing compared to his sociopolitical posturing. What is McDonald's plan for improving our relations with straights? No weak-kneed conciliator, he! His "journal of revenge therapy" enunciates a policy of "calling them names," and advises readers, "You can't beat them but at least hassle them." Ridiculing the very notion of heterosexuality, he reiterates the old saw that "there ain't no such thing as straights," just closet queers carrying out their "sexual assignment."

Elsewhere, he airs his visceral contempt for gays who don't think that public sex is advisable; as postscript to a *cum* 'article' entitled *"Etudiant* licks cum off 'filthy' terlet floor," he calls these backsliders "a new type of prude, the gay homophobe . . . softcocked, hard-hearted creatures, cold-assed and hot-tempered, themselves oppressors of homosexuals." In short, when serious people don't agree with his flippant attitudes on serious matters, he calls *them* names, too.

Significantly, hardly a word of affection or love is breathed in this vomitorium of polymorphous perversity; a straight person reading this would be convinced for all time that gays are compulsive deviants who don't know what love means. It is, furthermore, hardly too much to say that it was exactly the sort of gross self-indulgence McDonald professes to admire that led to the explosion of AIDS in the 1980s. Yet he still breathes fire against his critics; in McDonald's simplistic world, any suggestion of decorum or restraint is tantamount to absolute oppression.

Larry Kramer vs. AIDS vs. the Gay Press: Kill the Messenger

When, in 1978, at the very height—and close—of the pre-AIDS disco era, New York-based gay author Larry Kramer published *Faggots*, his merciless (and mercilessly funny) dissection of the more dishonest and scabrous side of urban gay life earned him the undying hatred of the P.C. gay press. In essence, the novel had weighed the gay lifestyle in the balance, and found it wanting—in purpose, direction, vision, honesty, charity, maturity, and decency. His characters whine about finding a lover, yet live only for sex; spewing a mishmash of self-justifying psychological jargon, they lie to themselves and to one another. As protagonist Fred Lemish writes, "I have seen the future, and it shits."

Kramer also wrote, with amazing prescience—but the prescience of a Cassandra is usually punished before the fact, and rarely remembered afterward—that gays were going to have to change their lives "before you fuck your[selves] to death." As Shilts relates in *Band*, this sort of thing didn't sit well with the gay community, especially its media. Excoriated in print and in person—one Fire Island grocery store proprietor snarled at him, "You're trying to ruin the island"—Kramer was essentially ostracized for years, his book actually banned in gay Manhattan bookstores; when, alarmed by the emergence of AIDS and the blithe, reckless intransigence of gay men, he organized the Gay Men's

Health Crisis to warn and inform, his actions were taken by many as more hysterical fabrication cut from the same old bolt of cloth. Wrote Robert Chesley in the *New York Native,*

> "Basically, Kramer is telling us that something we . . . are doing . . . is causing Kaposi's sarcoma . . . Being alarmist is dangerous . . . but there's another issue here . . . the concealed meaning of Kramer's emotionalism is . . . that gay men *deserve* to die for their promiscuity . . . [his] subtext is always: the wages of gay sin is death . . . [What he is expressing is] gay homophobia and anti-eroticism."

For trying to get gay men to believe what they preferred doggedly to ignore—that AIDS is, indeed, spread sexually, and that promiscuity had become a guarantee of early death—he was denounced by large numbers of New Yorkers as 'alarmist' and 'sex-negative'; he was also accused of saying 'I told you so.' The fact that he had every *right* to say it cut no ice. Eventually, he was driven out of the organization he'd helped create.

The whole Kramer/*Faggots*/AIDS episode is an instructive example of the gay community's characteristic bad sense, its strident emotionalism and wishful thinking; it also illustrates the extremes of distortion and name-calling to which the gay leadership will go to punish the politically incorrect. Perhaps most instructive of all, though, is a consideration of the circumstances of Kramer's subsequent 'rehabilitation,' which occurred only upon the production of his play, *The Normal Heart;* its implicit criticism of gays was easy to ignore in the harsh, brilliant light of his explicit damnation of our homohating federal government. When Kramer was attacking gay foibles, he was a self-hating, 'antisex' monster, for whom no denunciation was quite bad enough; when he turned his lash against our straight enemies, whose delay in fighting AIDS had killed so many of us, he was suddenly welcomed back like the Prodigal Son.

To be fair and evenhanded, we'd like to point out that not all gay leaders behave so badly. Across the board, the winds of change seem to have begun to blow. The gay dinosaurs of P.C. are becoming an endangered species, overrun by more recent and flexible life-forms. *Christopher Street,* for example—probably the closest thing the gay community has to a 'highbrow' publication— has, especially in recent years, given over precious pages to gay writers with 'politically incorrect' views, and no longer seeks to enforce an ideological tyranny over its authors. A new hard-headedness has also begun to emerge in the long-range planning of the national gay organizations, which—as suggested in previous chapters—have begun to de-emphasize ideology and to re-emphasize practicality—a realistic, 'whatever works' approach, born out of a newfound sense of urgency. We are pleased and honored to be part of that movement.

o   o   o

We have now reviewed a long, long litany of misbehaviors—ten in all. It seems clear that the misery and bad p.r. resulting from gay misbehavior are ample reason for taking it to task in a lengthy chapter. As we've said above, all the carefully controlled image-management in the world will not produce lasting effects on straight attitudes toward gays if gays don't change in actuality as well as in image. We make no apology for the pain with which these shoes fit.

o

CLEANING UP OUR ACT

[W]hat we really needed all along was a massive change of heart.
—WHITLEY STRIEBER AND JAMES KUNETKA,
WARDAY

Presumably, the first part of this chapter has convinced the reader that the gay community has flaws, and could stand to clean up its act. He is unlikely to applaud any of the Ten Misbehaviors. (If he does, we suggest that his head be examined by an ear, nose, and throat man for the presence of foreign objects or uncooked lumps.) But it's one thing to point out what's wrong, and another to set it right. Our objective is not just to yammer on about gay misbehavior, but to suggest a new, self-policing social code for the gay community, and a new plan for the structuring of that community's 'family' life.

1. A SOCIAL CODE? OR, COMING ACROSS WITH SOME VALUE JUDGEMENTS

The code we have in mind is eminently practical. It focuses not on the hypothetical attitudes, values, and states of mind underlying the Misbehaviors, but on specific acts. In other words, we don't say, 'Be this—don't be that!' (an injunction too vague to follow); rather, we recommend, 'Do this—don't do that!' If a person consistently does the right thing, he will eventually be the right thing.

We're quite serious about the gay community policing itself, and suggest something radical: that our readers not only and follow the social code, but encourage others to do the same, *reprove them verbally when they fail to do so.*

Now, this will elicit screams of outrage from gays who've learned, as their sole lesson of manners and morals, that the one thing one mustn't do is tell other people how to behave. We couldn't disagree more. The major reason that there are so many overt assholes in this country, indulging in overt assholery, is the fact that non-assholes mind their own business too much—in effect, yielding the floor to the creeps . . . who never mind their own business.

Creeps misbehave because it gets them what they want. They will not *cease* to misbehave until misbehavior ceases to be worth their while. Since the laws cannot punish lower-order misbehavior, it is left up to the victim and the bystander to mete out punishment. The only form of punishment available to private citizens, yet not intolerably disruptive, is social censure. And, when applied sufficiently frequently and harshly, public embarrassment can be mightier than many a sword.

Alas, social censure isn't used nearly as frequently as it ought to be, either by gays or straights. Most of us either fall victim to, or witness, outrageous acts of rudeness and injury many times a day, yet, beyond muttering to ourselves beneath our breath, we say nothing. Why? We're chicken. We don't want to cause a scene. We don't want to be thought prigs. And we certainly don't want to get punched in the face.

Yet it's our responsibility to speak up. And personally, we've found that when we denounce outrageous acts in public, the perpetrator is usually staggered, and the audience—which may share our annoyance—as often as not applauds. Moreover, onlookers are emboldened to speak out, in the future, themselves.

So speak up! Every time you see a fellow gay violating the social code, say, as sharply as you see fit, 'I don't like or respect that! Other people don't respect that! I don't want my friends to behave that way! It's hurtful—to you, to me, to gays everywhere. So cut it out!' Instead of privately deploring the cheap antics you see going on around you, put your popularity on the line, and speak up for what you believe. It's as simple as that.

There is, of course, a *right* way to speak up. Always be a model of politeness—admittedly difficult, but, like so many difficult feats, one can learn to pull it off with practice. We suggest you start small, by advising smokers in no-smoking sections of buses, trains, and plains to extinguish their fire.

Perhaps you're laughing incredulously. Perhaps you're exclaiming, 'Puh-lease! *I'm* not going to lose my friends, even if I agree with your code!' But what you don't condemn, you condone, and for what you condone, you're responsible. Yes, you may lose friends, but do you really want to be the kind of worm who fears the loss of friends like that?

Now, we're not demanding that you agree with every provision of the social code. Disagreement is inevitable, and actually desirable. We're not trying to domineer, but to awaken. We want you, and all gays, to think about these things, to think out your own code, to live by it, and, yes, to share it with others. We'd rather see the specific provisions of the social code rejected and replaced by conscientious folk with strong beliefs of their own, than simply rejected—and replaced with nothing at all—by those who have *no* beliefs, and don't want any.

But make no mistake: push *has* come to shove. It's time for gays to pick one side or the other: the jerks and creeps, or the good guys. The social code may not change the world, and certainly won't immediately. Very likely it will never have a major effect on everyday life in, say, Greenwich Village. But it's a start.

o   o   o

Before a social code can be translated from blueprint into reality, we must actually *have* a society—not just a ghetto—in which we can live with one another as brothers and sisters, not as mere sardines coldly and coincidentally co-inhabiting the same tin—because, rhetoric to the contrary, we can't be brothers and sisters until our 'community' really is a family.

A SELF-POLICING SOCIAL CODE

Rules for Relations with Straights

I Won't Have Sex in Public Places.

I Won't Make Passes at Straight Acquaintances, or at Strangers Who Might Not Be Gay.

Wherever Possible and Sensible, I Will Come Out—Gracefully.

I Will Make an Effort, When Among Straights, Not to Live Down to Gay Stereotypes.

I Won't Talk Gay Sex and Gay Raunch in Public.

If I'm a Pederast or a Sadomasochist, I'll Keep It Under Wraps, and Out of Gay Pride Marches.

If I'm a Transvestite, However Glamorous, I'll Graciously Decline Invitations to Model Lingerie for "Oprah" or "Donahue."

Rules for Relations with Other Gays

I Won't Lie.

I Won't Cheat on My Lover—or with Someone Else's.

I'll Encourage Other Gays to Come Out, But Never Expose Them Against Their Will.

Tested or Otherwise, I'll Practice Safe Sex.

I'll Contribute Money in Meaningful Amounts to the Gay Cause.

I Will Not Speak Scornfully or Cruelly of Another's Age, Looks, Clothing, or Social Class, in Bars or Elsewhere, Lest I Reveal My Own Insecurities.

When Forced to Reject a Suitor, I Will Do So Firmly but Kindly.

I'll Drop My Search for Mr. Right and Settle for What's Realistic.

I Won't Re-Enact Straight Oppression by Name-Calling and Shouting Down Gays Whose Opinions Don't Square with Mine.

Rules for Relations with Yourself

I'll Stop Trying to Be Eighteen Forever and Act My Age; I Won't Punish Myself for Being What I Am.

I Won't Have More Than Two Alcoholic Drinks a Day; I Won't Use Street Drugs at All.

I'll Get a Stable, Productive Job and Become a Member of the Wider Community Beyond the Gay Ghetto.

I'll Live for Something Meaningful Beyond Myself.

When Confronted by Real Problems, I'll Listen to Common Sense, Not Emotion.

I Will Not Condone Sexual Practices I Think Harmful to Individuals or to the Community Just Because They're Homosexual.

I'll Start Making Some Value Judgments.

2. BACK TO PLATO: A MODEST PROPOSAL TO RESURRECT THE 'TRADITIONAL GAY FAMILY'

The family unit—spawning ground of lies, betrayals, mediocrity, hypocrisy and violence will be abolished. The family unit, which only dampens imagination and curbs free will, must be eliminated.
                    —MICHAEL SWIFT, "FOR THE HOMOEROTIC
                        ORDER," IN *GAY COMMUNITY NEWS*

The above, cited in the *Boston Herald* (February 25, 1988) by Visigothic columnist Don Feder in an article entitled "AIDS, gay politics and the family," is a bottled-in-bond example of the gay extremist rap on the evils of The Family. Luridly overstated as it is, it's fairly representative of the line taken by gay media radicals —angry people, perhaps damaged by emotionally sick families and blinded to the family's good side, who feel compelled to turn their fear and loathing into a sort of social philosophy of absolute individuality. Unfortunately, they play right into the hands of homohaters—always hungry for ammunition—and allow the entire community to be advertised as emotionally ill. Feder, taking as his text both Swift's rabid froth and a set of ill-considered remarks by Boston City Councillor David Scondras, whips up a whole three-ring circus of denunciations of those disgusting homosexuals, who live only for themselves and *admit* that they're trying to destroy the American family. Intones Feder, "Heterosexuals who prattle about gay rights should wake up and smell the wine fermenting for the orgy!"

Must gay pundits really reinforce such idiotic misconceptions? Their antifamily rhetoric doesn't make even bad sense. The sad truth is that, in real life, absolute individuality produces only absolute isolation and absolute loneliness. Even the gay media gurus realize that they must offer some sort of substitute vision, of a 'gay family life' with acceptable contours. Having rejected the idea of the 'family unit' as a basis for the social support network, the gay gurus, and the masses to whom they preach, seem to envision something like the following as the expected, desirable course of social events in a gay man's life.

Having a Gay Old Time: How Life Is Lived in a Fairy Tale

The Fairy Tale of Gay Life runs something like this: first, our gay boy—call him Skipper—severs all pre-existing ties with his sick, stultifying family and with straight society in general, and moves to an inner-city gay ghetto, in order to 'live among his own.' (Skipper's vistas are, of course, limited . . . essentially, to Boston, New York, San Francisco, or Los Angeles.) Once settled in an appropriate Manhattan townhouse, Skipper sets about drawing to him a circle of gay friends, who will bolster his mental health with understanding and emotional support. Theoretically, his main base of operations in this process is the gay bar. Here, utilizing his presumptive physical attractiveness—and, *n.b.*, if he's *not* good looking, the whole prescription fails—Skipper turns a series of tricks, who become his friends and—a few of them—his lovers. Skipper takes his waning sexual attraction to each of these lovers as a sign of inadequate 'chemistry,' and waits in expectation for *the* lover, Mr. Right, whose correct chemistry can, of course, be distinguished from that of fool's gold by the unwaning passion it evokes. Then Skipper and Mr. R., a happy little community of two, sail off into the sunset for a permanent plenitude of hot, discord-free sex, until death do them part.

Now, if you ask a young gay man just what he expects out of gay life, you'll never hear him outline the Fairy Tale quite so baldly; if he did, he'd realize at once how naïve he was: the Tale cannot withstand close scrutiny. And yet, if, by dint of klieg lights and dental tools, you extract from him an admission of his expectations, you will find that this scenario, however fuzzily conceived and expressed, is, at bottom, what he has in mind.

Of course, for the majority of gays, this is *not* what actually happens. Although many migrate to the gay ghettos, the unattractive have little or no success in the bars, and the *Male Guide to Fashion/In Touch* models, though they do turn a long, long series of tricks, have great difficulty in forging lasting friendships with their own narcissistic, bitchy, rejecting kind. And for very few are the last words of the tale 'and they lived happily ever after.' The result is widespread disillusionment and unhappiness.

As though all this weren't bad enough, AIDS has dealt a near-mortal blow to the whole system, which depends, in theory, upon the 'sexual test' described earlier. Previously, if Skipper saw a likely fellow, he'd bed him, and see whether it 'worked.' Now that they can't trick with both regularity and impunity, millions of Skippers in this nation's cities are either standing around in bars or sitting home—in either case, alone—entirely at a loss as to how to proceed. AIDS simply wasn't in the original script, and few ad libs are coming to mind.

In short, the gay lifestyle—if such a chaos can, after all, legitimately be *called* a lifestyle—just doesn't work: it doesn't serve the two functions for which all social frameworks evolve: to constrain people's natural impulses to behave badly and to meet their natural needs. While it's impossible to provide an exhaustive analytic list of all the root causes and aggravants of this failure, we can asseverate at least some of the major causes. Many have been dissected, above, as elements of the Ten Misbehaviors; it only remains to discuss the failure of the gay community to provide a viable alternative to the heterosexual family.

One of the major reasons the gay lifestyle doesn't work is that, when gays form relationships at all—and they do so far less frequently than the wishful thinking of popular mythology would have it—they form them for the wrong reasons, with the wrong people, of the wrong ages.

The best basis for a relationship (whoa! a value judgment!) is each party's desire to *give* to the other—and not just sexually, but of love, support, and, not least, wisdom—with the intent of helping his lover to develop, grow personally, become the best he can be. What sort of man doesn't give a damn whether his lover is great or small? If you really love, you grieve to see your beloved lesser and lower than the larger, higher self he might be.

But many of the (rare) 'lasting' gay relationships we've known haven't been like that at all. Too many gay men stick together in pairs not for love, but for sexual convenience: having a ready cock to suck, and *not* having to stand in the Man-Hole for five hours every Saturday night. Not surprisingly, when that ready cock loses its youth and mystery, and with them its capacity to arouse, the convenience is foregone, the cock bundled back into its Calvin Kleins and sent packing, and the sterile barhopping resumed.

Some—the very young and attractive, hence sexually success-ful, and/or the congenitally shallow—find that such a lifestyle gives them what they want; they may see it as not only viable but exciting and desirable. But its essentially stunted nature, its fool-ishness and pathos, and, finally, the misery that it brings by the age of thirty-five or forty at the latest, are cruelly patent to the vast majority who have, in Holleran's words in *Dancer,* "been cast out of the communion of saints."

The gay community has no generation-to-generation continuity; rather, at all times it comprises two distinct groups, the one sealed away from the other by disdain: the young and attractive, who pair off only with the young and attractive, and the old and ugly, who pair off with nobody. One moves, too, from the first group to the second with startling suddenness, and no hope of turning back. Having lived for five years by the two-edged sexual sword, one dies by it—a poetic but unnecessary and excessive justice.

Strikingly enough, those who die by the sexual sword seem to learn little or nothing from the ordeal. So many gays seem silly, superficial, little wiser at fifty than at twenty. Age seems to bring *some* people insight, self-control, heightened capacity for love, ele-vation of ethical stature—but there's no queen like a silly old queen! We are reminded of Robert Reinhart's gruesome *Christopher Street* piece ("Solos: A Suite") about the seventy-year-old dying in the hospital, who, at this supremely critical juncture, can offer no more uplifting subject for conversation than a laundry list of all the penises he's fellated in his long, action-packed life. His awe-inspiring vacuity seems, in a way, the natural conclusion of the gay life cycle, and a horrible warning to us all.

Of course, some older men *do* distill wisdom from experience, and find that, though they never previously suspected its existence, let alone its importance, they now have something genuine to give, and, out of a desire for purpose and fulfillment, want to give it to a youth who will be not only lover, but proxy for the child the older man will never have. Tragically, such a man finds that it is now *too late*. Even these—who once, in their callow youth, rejected the very company of older men in favor of a lying will-o'-the-wisp—are now rejected in their turn, finding no one to whom to pass on their hard-earned gifts of knowledge and charity.

This wretched situation is the natural, normal, ineluctable consequence of the complete absence, in the gay lifestyle, of anything corresponding to family. This entrains in turn an almost limitless array of associated evils: the community, as a whole, fails to grow in wisdom, or in the dependent capacity to protect itself, with the years; the prevailing mood of the individuals who make up that community becomes one of self-absorption and self-pity without charity or mercy for others, narcissism and loneliness, unrestrained folly, and a lack of communal solidarity, either emotional, political, or fiscal.

The 'traditional nuclear family' is, admittedly, defective, the source of much suffering and neurosis. But it also serves good and necessary social ends. Depending on how you look at it, the drinking glass of the nuclear family is half empty or half full. Emotionally damaged gays, however, have insisted on seeing it as *totally* empty. Unable to conceive of a family except in nuclear terms, they have thrown out the concept altogether—and, blinded by their hatred to its value, have replaced it with no structure at all.

But 'the family' is no more limited, structurally, to the traditional nucleus than it is, functionally, to regimentation and oppression. Any first-year student of anthropology can tell you that the nuclear family isn't, and never has been, the major familial structure among human beings, either in the world as a whole or in this country right now, in which fewer than 15% of the population are living in circumstances anything like the misnamed 'traditional family.' Around the world, children are raised not only by Mom and Pop, but by Mom alone, Pop alone, extended matriarchies or patriarchies of great size, in the case of the kibbutzim of Israel—who are, be it noted, strikingly free from neurosis—communally, and by each adult in turn. These families differ in their special advantages and disadvantages, but they all attempt to serve the same ends.

Between the claustrophobia of the nuclear family, on the one hand, and the asphyxiating airlessness of the gay ghetto, on the other, there is a whole panoply of possible choices for the integration of one's own life with those of others and of society as a whole. Gays should take a second look at these choices. Some of them have worked remarkably well, in the past, for homosexual males.

Gay Love Among the Pagans: An Overview*

Twentieth-century post-Christian America's crazy abhorrence of homosexuals is by no means representative. Most of the world's cultures, through most of history, have either ignored homosexuality altogether, or approved of it . . . within prescribed formats, in a fashion that advanced—or at least didn't conflict with—the broader interests of society as a whole.

The city-states of sixth-, fifth-, and fourth-century-B.C. Hellas—Athens, Sparta, Thrace, *et al.*—were a case in point. Although classical scholars, bowing to the prejudices of our own time, have made outrageous attempts—including gross and deliberate mistranslation—to hide the truth, voluminous records, in the form of pottery-painting, everyday graffiti, popular plays, court transcripts, and philosophical works from the likes of Plato, prove beyond any reasonable doubt that among our ancient Grecian forebears, average Joes (or Jasons) were expected, from time to time, to feel, and to act upon, homosexual as well as heterosexual desires.

---

* In producing the following thumbnail sketch, we have referred frequently to Ken Dover's densely written but authoritative *Greek Homosexuality* and advise the interested reader to follow suit.

But—and this is the important point—Greek homosexuality was only approved within clear-cut normative bounds. That is, homosexuality was as institutionalized, as regulated by social expectations, as subject to the sanctions of approval and disapproval, and even—under special circumstances—the law, as was heterosexuality. The purpose of this normative regulation, as with that of any universal behavior, was the greater harmony and happiness of the community . . . which twentieth-century gays seem to have forgotten. (Albeit with good reason: if you outlaw homosexuals, homosexuals will act like outlaws!)

The ancient Greek model seems to have worked something like this. As an attractive boy—of, say, sixteen or so—passed through puberty (which, for nutritional reasons, occurred much later in those days than it does now) into youth, his boyish looks would attract the attention of an older, presumably more mature and established, man—of, say, thirty or so. The adult—following the youth about, observing him at his work and play, and so forth—would form an estimation of whether the youth's character were as attractive as his body and face. If it were not so, it would be dishonorable to favor the youth with further attentions. If it were so, the adult would begin to 'court' the youth, with conversation, presents, and the like, of whose meaning the youth would be readily aware. During this courtship, the youth would, in turn, form an estimation of the adult's character, as to honesty, integrity, maturity, courage, and the like—in short, the age-old virtues we all (should) admire. Should the adult not come up to snuff, the youth would refuse his presents and send him packing. (Or not— but failure to do so would be a sign that the youth's motivation was mercenary—a state of affairs tantamount, for the Greeks, to male prostitution, which was legally punishable.)

If, however, the youth found the adult as worthy as the adult found him, he might agree to become the beloved *(eromenos)* of his adult lover *(erastes)*—an alliance partaking equally of the qualities of father-son, teacher-student, and big brother-little brother relationships . . . with the superadded bond of explicitly sexual love. As with all relationships, that of the *erastes* and the *eromenos* entailed an understood exchange: the youth would share his beauty and enthusiasm, the adult his strength, security, and guidance—as well as more tangible assets, including training in arms, a position in the adult's business, and so forth. Both parties would benefit to an extent beyond mere genital relief. From the point of view of the community, as well, this arrangement discharged a natural need—for homosexual gratification—in a manner advantageous to public character and morality.

Note well that homosexual relations were *not* considered desirable or respectable *outside* this framework of unequal ages and statuses. For example, sexual acts between agemates were disapproved, at least in Attica: the exchange of orgasmic gratification, alone, was considered insufficient rationale for such a relationship, and therefore mere self-indulgence—the point being, perhaps, that agemates couldn't *teach* each other, and therefore contributed nothing, via their relationship, to the community as a whole. In Sparta, Thrace, and some of the other, more military city-states, sexual relations apparently did occur, with approval, between fellow soldiers; here, of course, the love bond, stimulating greater loyalty, bravery, and comradeship-in-arms, could be justified as contributing to the defense of the overall society.

Similarly, it was understood that when the *eromenos* became a full-fledged man—and had absorbed all the (socially valuable) teaching that the *erastes* could impart—he would cease to be a lover, and would marry a woman and sire children. Neither his nor his former *erastes'* marriage, however, would end their friendship, nor prevent either one of them from forming a fresh alliance, in turn, with a younger male . . . and so on.

Something like this, suitably updated (that is, without the wife and kids), is what we tentatively recommend as a new ideal for gay men—a family structure of their own.

Objection, Your Honor!

Hostile readers may argue that our Return to Plato is pure pie in the sky, and half-baked pie at that; that men—especially gay men

—want what they want, and that neither they nor we can change what they want; and, specifically, that twenty-year-old men will never desire thirty-five-year-old men, nor thirty-five, fifty.

This argument is, however, nothing more than the ancient outcry of the Cynic against the Idealist, and obviously defective. What once was, can be again, for human nature doesn't change. But, although we'll admit that no such change is very likely to happen soon, there are two plausible reasons why it is possible, and perhaps even feasible.

First, it's very clear that what young gay men want in a mate is determined as much by the vividly expressed sexual ideals of the community, in arts and media, as by any innate sexual imperative. Indeed, in fostering a cult of youth, our community has *already* achieved a biologically unwarranted and exaggerated idealization of the extremely young as sexual partners. This is, itself, an arbitrary and cultivated ideal. There is, in fact, absolutely nothing intrinsically more attractive about eighteen than about twenty-eight; it has simply been declared to be so, as a point of fashion. Yet, to the preponderance of gay men, that decade spans the difference between being at the center of the world, and falling off its edge into the abyss.

If we can, through media manipulation and the expression of age-related prejudice, create a self-sustaining cult of youth, we can create, alternatively, a cult of middle age, or, to press the point, old age. It's a matter of becoming aware of, and understanding, the prevailing norms and expectations that have shaped our desires, and reshaping them, in turn, to suit the development of a more desirable sociosexual pattern, and a viable, stable social infrastructure. It's a matter of glamorizing a look more appropriate to the bodies and careers of middle-aged men, who cannot, after all, spend the rest of their lives playing softball. It's a matter of shaping *ourselves* to reveal our natural attractiveness in good health, lest illness make us prematurely hideous. As a matter of fact, all of this will happen, to an extent, in any case—the gay population is, on average, getting older, *pari passu* with the graying of America as a whole. The economics of a marketplace that keeps one eye on demographics will force such a shift in emphasis, where failure to do so would throw away money.

Second, our Return to Plato is not, at least initially, a matter of getting youth to find middle age *sexually* attractive. Among the Greeks, the *erastes* solicited the love of the *eromenos* through demonstration of what he had to offer *over and above* sexual intercourse: practical and occupational aid, wisdom, kindness, and love. Remember, it was considered shameful for a youth to submit to the advances of a man who, though attractive, was otherwise unworthy. The idea was that once the lover had gained the beloved's love, desire might follow—which is the way it should be, and, apparently, the way it often was.

Translating, somewhat cynically, into the terms of the late twentieth century, this means that if we wish to resurrect the 'traditional gay family,' we must provide suitable incentives. We must find a way of incorporating into gay norms the expectation that an honorable, loving man of middle years, once established in the world, will seek out a younger lover with whom to share his good things, not only by helping him financially—perhaps putting him through school or giving him a leg up in business— but by shaping his character and increasing his wisdom. If a man is really worthy of love, and not grossly disfigured, it is not fatuous or out of line with human nature to believe that such an arrangement will win him the love of at least one youth who is himself worthy.

We would envisage this Return to Plato as necessarily occurring in the context of a very great change in the circumstances under which gays meet each other—which are overdue for an overhaul, in any event. Currently, gays have almost no way to meet one another in sizable numbers except at the traditional venues: which means, pretty much, drinking and dance bars. These venues, by their nature, encourage mate selection on the basis of physical appearance and discourage selection on any other basis. (You can't get to know a fellow you've met at a dance bar by *talking* with him—it's too damned loud; you can't suggest going somewhere else to talk without leading him to believe—and reasonably so, given our cultural mores—that you mean to do a good deal more. This would result in disappointment, and possibly an ugly scene. Parties are better, but those who throw them have a perverse tendency to attempt to reproduce the atmosphere of a bar, as though that were the desirable norm.) What we need is some sort of normal framework of sharable activities—sports, arts, games, intellectual discussion—corresponding, if we may be a tad whimsical, to the ancient Athenian Forum—within which gay men can meet on the basis of shared interests, and reveal their character (and not just their tits and asses)—in a natural way.

To sum it up, gays are blinded to the possibilities of human relationships by their stubborn, selfish refusal to recognize that mere sexual arousal is insufficient reason to have sex with a man; one should be motivated by the desire to share, to give as well as take. (We are reminded of the old Charles Schulz "Peanuts" cartoon, in which Lucy van Pelt shows Linus her "git" list; this, she explains, is what she's gonna "git" for Christmas. "Where," asks Linus, "is your 'give' list?" Lucy stares blankly at him for an entire frame, then, panicked, screams, "What? What? 'Give' list!? What are you talking about??") All viable social structures throughout history, including homosexual social structures, have been founded on such give and take, the desire for which can and should be prior to sexual desire. Although we're cynical indeed about the inclination of American gays to change, regarding the *possibility* of Returning to Plato we retain our ideals.

We propose such a Return not merely to suggest a new social pattern more pleasant and advantageous than the old, but as a challenge to those straight Americans who, arrogating to themselves the right to define the word 'family,' have declared unfit and invalid any social unit other than that comprising one heterosexual father, one heterosexual mother, and 2.3 protoheterosexual children, all living under the capacious roof of a raised ranch house in suburbia. A major weapon in their arsenal of arguments against homosexuality has been that it 'threatens the family,' and can't sustain a viable society. Rather than counter their criticism by challenging them with a reworked, fit, and viable 'family' of our own, like fools we've chosen to abandon the 'family,' implicitly ratifying the heterosexual patent on the concept. The Return to Plato is a first stab at such a reworking. We hope that gays will take second and third stabs, and eventually lay before the mainstream a gay family unit that cannot be sneered away.

If our gay readers either detest this idea or like it very much, then it's almost certainly for the wrong reasons. The very young will grimace in disgust at the idea that they should pollute their smooth-skinned beauty with the embraces of old men (although we do not mean 'old,' merely 'older'). Yet there's nothing intrinsically ugly about the healthy face and body of the man of thirty-five; it's the *un*healthy appearance resulting from years of overindulgence and undernutrition—obesity, coarseness, and the bloated, ropy, mottled look of chronic disease—and not middle age itself, that is repellent. Tired old queens with nothing to give but a toothless mouth will be as delighted as the young are disgusted, and equally without justification. What they want to give isn't what they should be giving; what they should be giving, they don't have. A great deal of growing up has to be done on both sides.

To a dirty mind, nothing is clean. We go on record, here and now, as stating explicitly that **we do not advocate adults having sex with minors under any circumstances whatever.** What we do advocate is adults forming the sexual relationships which they must and should form anyway within a reciprocal framework of age differences that will maximize not sex per se, but all that is good and fine and honorable and decent in human relations, setting a standard higher, and with a much stronger and more logical rationale, than that of the much-praised nuclear family itself.

○
CODA: RIGHTS AND RESPONSIBILITIES

Responsibility, n. A detachable burden easily
shifted to shoulders of God, Fate, Fortune, Luck,
or one's neighbor.
—AMBROSE BIERCE, *THE DEVIL'S DICTIONARY*

Stop up your ears as you may, you can't shut out the sound of American minorities demanding their rights. Strain as you will, you won't hear a single American voice calling out for responsibilities. (This is one of the great defects of human nature, found in exaggerated form in our society, especially.) But rights and responsibilities go hand in hand, or should. Any parent knows, intuitively, that to raise a mentally healthy, well-behaved, and happy child, it should earn every right accorded it by the acceptance of a matching responsibility. Accepting this scheme of things is one of the components of maturity. For twenty immature years, the gay community has shrieked for rights while demonstrating an alarming degree of irresponsibility. If gays expect straights ever to accord them their rights, this is one of the things that must change. **We must cease to be our own worst enemies.**

JUMPING TO
CONCLUSIONS

Life is, in fact, a battle. Evil is insolent and strong; . . . goodness very apt to be weak; folly very apt to be defiant; . . . imbeciles to be in great places, people of sense in small . . . But the world as it stands is no illusion, no phantasm, no evil dream of a night; we wake up to it again for ever and ever; we can neither forget it nor deny it nor dispense with it.

—HENRY JAMES

Don't try conclusions with me, faggot!

—BUBBA, WAYLAYING YOU BEHIND
THE LOCAL 7-ELEVEN

Henry James is, as they say, taking the bull by the tail and facing the situation squarely; and so must we. We can neither forget nor deny that the world is chock-a-block full of Bubbas and worse, in places high and low. We have responded to them with a book that is part battle cry, part battle plan.

If our call to arms has differed from most gay tracts in its curt demand for pragmatic action rather than endless polemics on sexual philosophy, this is simply because we think that gays must, at this moment, prefer reveille to reverie. We've seen countless schemes for the greening of gay America come (to nothing) and go over the years; and, sadly, each has put us in mind of Herbert Spencer's tragedy of the Beautiful Theory murdered by a Gang of Brutal Facts. The plan of this book, on the other hand, has been deliberately constructed to put theory in league with facts. If the thinking is sound, then only the doing remains.

There is little more to be said, by way of conclusion. We don't wish to burden you with the usual, dreary, pro forma summation that you may expect with dread; and we *can't* give you the 'magic key,' the missing psychoactive ingredient, transforming arid schematics to *fait accompli,* that you surely would like. Perhaps, like Tracey Ullman, we should simply shout, "Go home! All of you! Go home!"

Because that is exactly what you must now do: Go home (if you're not already there) and make a decision. Either take it upon yourself to do something constructive or else stand out of the way, in the shadows, as you've done for a lifetime. Whether or not you choose to take action—to work the alchemy that will transmute the base metal of our design into something more precious and real—will depend upon whether or not you've found our arguments compelling. Chances are, if you've read this far, you have. But if you haven't, let this concluding chapter offer a final appeal.

Hmmm. Perhaps a little dreary summation would be in order after all . . .

IT'S NOT NELLY TO BE NERVOUS

As we said in the Introduction, we are at a crossroads.

It's usually a mistake to open or close a book with the pompous declaration that Humanity (or America; or Women; or Eskimos . . . or Gays!) is at a crossroads. In a very real sense, we're *always* at one sort of crossroads or another. Still, some crossroads are a bit more portentous than others, and the next several years would certainly seem to qualify as a potentially serious turning point, for good or ill.

The two main factors that will decide whether gays find this country's sociopolitical climate more or less salubrious in the 1990s are the balance of power between the nation's conservative and liberal forces, and the course taken by the AIDS epidemic. As we write this, the '80s surge in homohatred, as indexed by Gallup, has finally leveled off a bit (albeit at its highest levels since the Stonewall riots). This evidently has come *pari passu* with a leveling off in alarm over the heterosexual spread of AIDS. (We are, in fact, surprised and heartened by the generally restrained reaction of the straight community, so far, to the epidemic; the antigay backlash could be—and may yet become—far worse.)

Although this certainly affords us a sort of breathing space, there's an excellent chance that it will prove temporary, lasting just long enough to let us fill our lungs with air before we go down again—and not, one prays, for the last time. As nearly as we can determine, the facts are that (a) there is little likelihood that an effective drug or vaccine will be developed for AIDS in the next decade; (b) virtually all those infected with the AIDS virus will eventually sicken and die; and (c) several millions will be dead or dying by the turn of the century. If this gruesome scenario ensues, then among those several millions will be several hundred thousand white, middle-class heterosexuals.

Nothing further will be needed for straight hysteria to reemerge. If it does so against the backdrop of hard times and a hard-line conservative administration, then all bets are off as to whether 'it'—'it' being whatever hellish form of antihomosexual oppression you care to name—can or cannot happen here. No matter whose society is involved, crisis inevitably brings hysteria and scapegoating (epidemics being particularly vulnerable to the latter: e.g., the Spanish flu, German measles, and the 'gay plague'). Moreover, the record shows that when our populace and leaders are genuinely scared and mad, the Constitution provides no secure barrier to abuse. One need only recall what was inflicted upon 105,000 Japanese Americans during World War II, with the very explicit consent of the U.S. Supreme Court.

We're not saying that this *will* happen, of course; we're saying that you must be *prepared* for it to happen. Rather than denying the very possibility, position yourselves in such a way as to ensure that the worst *doesn't* happen. Rather than sneering, 'Concentration camps? Don't be paranoid!' take action to make sure that camps remain in the realm of paranoia and do not make their appearance instead on the cover of *Newsweek*. The price of freedom really is eternal vigilance; complacency, its downfall. Think of your vigilance as a sort of condom worn to prevent infection with totalitarianism. Be safe, not sorry. The Waging Peace campaign is part of a positioning strategy to ensure that you *won't* be sorry.

In many respects, the gay community's current outlook on straight oppression is uncomfortably reminiscent of nearly *everyone's* outlook on the threat of nuclear war. Despite—perhaps because of—the undeniable fact that we've been straddling the rim of the atomic volcano since the '50s, we've got used to it (or, in our terms, become 'desensitized'). We put it out of our minds, and go about our daily affairs. Perhaps, as Thomas Disch once observed, "Nothing can be terrifying for years on end." But this, of course, leads to serious oversight. Ignoring an omnipresent danger increases the likelihood of its coming to pass. In the words of a survivor of nuclear holocaust, in James Kunetka and Whitley Strieber's novel *Warday,*

> Remember, back in those days it just seemed like there was nothing you personally could do. The solutions *now* to our problems *then* seem obvious. But in those days we were all very different people. We were dulled by living under the Sword of Damocles for nearly half a century. We had done the worst possible thing—gotten used to an incredible and immediate danger . . . But it didn't feel that way, not in those sunny, treacherous days.

While, in the broader scheme of things, virulent oppression of gays is hardly Armageddon, its storm clouds can, in the same way, gather with startling quickness if we acquiesce. And in any event, for the growing number of gays beaten or knifed to death on the streets, antigay oppression might as well *be* Armageddon. The point for gays is simply this: the AIDS scare rode into town this morning, and it will soon be high noon. Keep a sharp eye.

THE AGENDA FOR CHANGE, REVISITED

It surely is not enough, however, to hunker down and wait for high noon at the crossroads. We must push ahead, and this means knowing exactly which road we want to travel. Getting our bearings and setting a course is what this book has been about, even if the authors' cartography has sometimes seemed, to the reader, hard to follow.

Like Martin Luther King, Jr., we have a dream, and, donkeylike, we've been drawn along by it as though by a carrot on a stick. Unlike King's, our dream doesn't stop with blacks and whites and browns and yellows, but embraces sexual orientations as well. It's the dream we outlined in Chapter 1's Agenda for Change, and we want you to dream it, too.

In brief, we're fighting for a tomorrow in which it simply doesn't occur to anyone that there's anything more unusual about being gay than about preferring praline ice cream to double dutch chocolate; in which it would be as bizarre to point your finger and yell 'Queer!' as to point your finger and yell 'Certified public accountant!' We want, as others want, to be seen and judged, first and foremost, as individuals—as "Bruce, whom I like because he's kind and honest"—and only second, third, or not at all, as nameless members of the group called homosexuals. We want, at the very worst, to be let alone; at best, to be liked, valued, and welcomed into the family of man.

Is that so much to ask for?

Specifically, we want straights to believe that we no more choose gayness than they do straightness; that it's a valid and healthy condition; and that, when treated with respect and friendship, we're as happy and psychologically well adjusted as they are. We want them to realize that we look, feel, and act just as they do; we're like hard-working, conscientious Americans with love lives exactly like their own. We want to be seen as the brothers and sisters, daughters and sons, friends and coworkers, and—yes—fathers and mothers of straight Americans: a valued part of

American society, a part whose culture, heroes, and news are worthy of attention and respect.

We want straights to revoke all laws criminalizing sex acts between consenting adults, as the abhorrently arrogant and invasive barbarisms they are; no legal double standard in the content or application of such laws must be permitted. We want straights to provide for us, by special legislation and affirmative action if need be, the same rights to public speech and assembly, to work, shelter, and public accommodations, to legal marriage and parenthood, that straights enjoy. What is sauce for the straight gander must be sauce for the gay goose.

We want straights to cease giving the avuncular wink to the taunting, harassment, and brutalization of gay youths and adults, whether in the school, on the street, in the boardroom or the Oval Office, or from the stage and screen. We want them to denounce, to ostracize such discrimination with the same distaste and embarrassment as they now accord racism and anti-Semitism. When an Eddie Murphy or Sam Kinison sneers at gays and says they give him the creeps, the audience must jeer him from the stage and onto Skid Row. When an Administration admits to a "giggling factor" over the "gay plague" of AIDS, it must be booted from the White House into the gutter where it belongs.

Again, are we asking anything that others don't expect as their right and due?

And while we're at it, let us reiterate bluntly what it is that we're *not* fighting for.

We're *not* fighting for the right to suck and fuck, in full public view, with as many one-minute stands as we can possibly line up end to end, until our mouths and anuses are sore and we're all dying of syphilis and AIDS. We're fighting for the right to love and marry, not merely to blast away with our 'hot love-guns.' We're *not* fighting to eliminate community ethics, to live like selfish brats, narcissistically and meanly. We're fighting for the right to put our arms around each other, not to put each other down. We're *not* fighting to eradicate Family; we're fighting for the right to *be* Family. We're fighting to be decent human beings who might conceivably pass the Mother Test—that is, persons we'd be proud to bring home to Mother, who would be genuinely pleased to meet us. We're fighting not only for America's love and respect, but to become people unquestionably *deserving* of America's love and respect . . . and one another's, too.

And whether *that's* too much to ask or not, we must demand it of ourselves.

So keep all this as clearly before your eyes as St. Augustine's vision of the City of God. We know exactly what we want; we have an unanswerable right to it. Though denied that right by bigots, we arrogate it, willy-nilly, and will do whatever must be done to secure it.

ONLY YOU CAN IGNITE SOCIAL FIRES

But who, you ask, is going to make all this Neat Stuff come about? In answer, we'd like to share one last, homely childhood anecdote.

One of us can recall being elected fifth-grade class president. It was an appointment he hadn't asked for and certainly didn't want. The teacher announced the electoral results, called a class meeting, sat back, and folded her arms. The eleven-year-old president asked the assembled students, "Well, what would you like to accomplish?" A dead, mortifying silence ensued. He stared at the students, and they stared back with blank, bovine expressions— apparently expecting him to perform card tricks, or pull a rabbit from his hat—for ten solid minutes. The eventual, angry consensus was that Mr. Kirk was "the worst president this class ever had!"

Our point, of course, is that you can't very well read this book and snort, 'What sort of leaders are Madsen and Kirk! They haven't *done* anything!' *We* are not going to pull the rabbit of social change out the silk hat of this book; *you* are. Nobody else can do the job for you. Having read, pass the message on. You want to help change straight minds? Then speak to your own acquaintances, contact national gay organizations and media projects, volunteer money, time, sweat, and courage. You want to help change gay life for the better? Then monitor its quality in your own community, and encourage your gay friends (and yourself) to better behavior.

Now, this being a nation of spectator sports and fat-bottomed spectators, such a call to action may sound foreign, improbable, even preposterous. After all, we are asking you to change a nation under your own steam. And where, for that matter, is the steam supposed to come from? Your patriotism and sense of fair play? Your homophile zeal? Benevolent love of your gay brothers and sisters? *Agape?*

No, few are motivated over the long haul by zeal or saintliness. Yet sufficient motivation is found in Chapter 1, and all around you: the sustaining emotional steam that comes not from Love but from Rage.

It's practically a Western tradition to close one's call to arms with the sugary invocation of love as the best way to move mountains. Well, love is an excellent end in itself, but it isn't half so compelling as a means. Over history, love has severed no colonies from their mother countries, nor overthrown any czars, nor obliterated any Nazis, nor produced any civil rights movements. You may discount what the pious tell you, because it is actually *rage*, not love, that lay behind all those progressive events.

Like all emotions, rage has its purposes, and its time and place. When a situation becomes intolerable, an oppression unbearable, when millions do not even *dare* to cry out beneath the heel of injustice, *rage is the appropriate response.* Fury galvanizes. It spurred the authors to think through our community's predicament. Now it must drive all of us to decisive action. America in the 1990s is the time and place for rage—ice-cold, controlled, directed rage. If we have deliberately agitated you in the pages of this book, it was not to see you sputter and fume impotently, nor run about chanting slogans and breaking windows in an extemporaneous *Kristallnacht.* That belongs to the movement's excessive, heedless past. Rather, it was to help equip you with the motive power—the psychic gasoline—to do what must now be done, soberly, skill-fully, quickly.

For, you see, the ball *is* over. On the twentieth anniversary of Stonewall, they are finally putting up the chairs, packing off the punch bowl, and tossing out the celebratory bunting. The masks have come off, and the ridiculous evening gowns have made their last exit. The beautiful room is empty. Tomorrow, the real gay revolution begins. So go home, get changed, and be at the station by eight.

NOTES

CHAPTER 1

1. P. H. Gebhard and A. B. Johnson, *The Kinsey Data: Marginal Tabulations of the 1938–1963 Interviews Conducted by the Institute for Sex Research* (W. B. Saunders, 1979). For a smaller, but more recent, survey that produced much the same results as Kinsey's, see M. G. Shively and J. P. DeCecco, "Sexual Orientation Survey of Students on the San Francisco State University Campus," *Journal of Homosexuality,* 4/1 (Fall 1978): 29–39.

2. Statistics about America's participation in various recreational activities come from the Roper Organization's *Roper Reports* 1987-1, 17.

3. In their 1978 study, *Homosexualities* (363–68), Bell and Weinberg found that, among their sample, gays were only slightly more liberal and Democratic, and somewhat less religious, than their straight counterparts. They obtained, for instance, the following comparisons between gay white males and straight white males:

	GAY	STRAIGHT
• *Democrat*	*36%*	*36%*
Republican	*17%*	*21%*
• *Liberal*	*75%*	*69%*
Conservative	*20%*	*29%*
• *Not at all/not very*		
religious	*51%*	*44%*
Moderately/very		
religious	*22%*	*26%*

4. Roper Organization, *Roper Reports* 1987–2, 49 (Question 14x, y).

5. We are quoting Robert Massa's review, "Straight and Narrow," *Village Voice* (6/30/87), 57, of Kaier Curtin's *We Can Always Call Them Bulgarians: The Emergence of Lesbians and Gay Men on the American Stage* (Alyson, 1987).

6. The results of the Harvard-Stanford study are reported by Florence Skelly, "To the Beat of a Different Drum," *Harvard Magazine* (March–April 1986), 26.

7. In a survey by Roper (*Roper Reports* 1986–10, 39 [Question 68]), 73% of males and 69% of females in America stated that not only is "living in homosexual relations" unacceptable behavior for themselves, but it's also categorically wrong for others to engage in as well. Also, see the poll reported in "American Views of Gays: Disapproval, Sympathy" *Los Angeles Times* (12/20/85), wherein 73% of respondents stated that homosexuality is wrong. By contrast, in a recent poll roughly 80% of the French public indicated that homosexuality was not offensive to them. See "AIDS Spread: A Matter of Mores?" *Boston Globe* (7/7/86).

8. "Pornography: A Poll," *Time* (7/21/86), 22.

9. The poll was conducted by the Gallup Organization in November 1985, as reported in the *New England Mirror*, 1/52 (December 1985), 2. A college survey turned up similar results: see "Young 'Conservatives' Like Reagan But Not GOP," *San Diego Union* (12/22/87).

10. The National Opinion Research Center at the University of Chicago asked a national sample, in 1985, what they thought of "sexual relations

between two adults of the same sex," and heard the following answers. Such relations are:

Always wrong	*73.0%*
Almost always wrong	*3.9%*
Wrong only sometimes	*6.8%*
Not wrong at all	*13.3%*
Don't know	*3.1%*

See *General Social Surveys, 1972–1985: Cumulative Codebook* (NORC/Roper Center, 1985), 224.

11. One protracted case is described in "D.C. Appeals Court Issues Landmark Ruling: Rights of Gay Students Affirmed at Georgetown U." *The Advocate* (12/22/87), 13; and "Rehnquist OKs Delay for Georgetown on Gay Issue," *San Diego Union* (12/25/87). The latter article, incidentally, was printed next to a story about a maniac who murdered and dismembered a boy prostitute. The adjoining Georgetown piece began with an almost audible sigh of relief: ". . . Rehnquist yesterday *spared* Georgetown University temporarily from having to provide two homosexual rights groups with equal access to campus facilities and services." (Stress added.)

12. Based on statistics given in the NORC's *General Social Surveys, 1972–1985*, 110–11.

13. These statistics are derived from the following sources: Roper Organization, *Roper Reports* 1985–7, 47 (Question 46), and 1987–2, 3 (Question 47); Florence Skelly, "To the Beat of a Different Drum," *Harvard Magazine* (March–April 1986), 26; "American Views of Gays: Disapproval, Sympathy," *Los Angeles Times* (12/20/85); "Future Shock: The AIDS Epidemic," *Newsweek* (11/24/86), 32–33.

14. Several clauses of the Family Protection Act are excerpted in Kevin Gordon et al., eds., *Homosexuality and Social Justice*, rev. and expanded (San Francisco: The Consultation on Homosexuality, Social Justice, and Roman Catholic Theology, 1986), 116–17.

15. From a Gallup survey (March 1987), as reported in William Schneider, "Homosexuals: Is AIDS Changing Attitudes?" *Public Opinion* (July–August 1987), 27.

16. Ibid.

17.   Joseph Harry, "Homosexual Men and Women Who Served Their Country," in John P. DeCecco, ed., *Bashers, Baiters, and Bigots: Homophobia in American Society* (New York: Harrington Park Press, 1985), 117–25.

18.   See "Future Shock: The AIDS Epidemic," *Newsweek* (11/24/86), 33. See also "Confronting AIDS on the Job: High Court Enters Debate over Employer Responsibility and Employee Rights," *Boston Globe* (3/8/87); and "Survey Finds a Clash on AIDS in Workplace," *New York Times* (2/7/88).

19.   The San Francisco attack is described in Elizabeth Ogg, *Changing Views of Homosexuality*, Public Affairs Pamphlet No. 563 (1978), 2. The lesbian attacks, and the list of implements, are documented in Kevin Gordon et al., eds., *Homosexuality and Social Justice*, 87. The New Jersey incident was reported in "N.J. Teens Arrested for Anti-Gay Assault," *The New England Mirror* 2/14 (4/30/86), 2. The butcher-knife murder is recounted in Gene-Gabriel Moore, "North Carolina's War Against Gays," *Christopher Street*, No. 121 (1987), 17. The Boston and New York attacks were described to us by victims or their acquaintances. For a long list of similarly grisly attacks on gays, see the two-year report of the Gay & Lesbian Discrimination Project of the New York City Commission on Human Rights (November 1983-October 1985).

20.   Straights who wish to learn more about life on the margins—for gays as well as other discredited types—should read Erving Goffman's classic study, *Stigma: Notes on the Management of Spoiled Identity* (Simon & Schuster, 1963).

CHAPTER 6

1.   Paul Gebhard and Alan Johnson, *The Kinsey Data: Marginal Tabulations of the 1938–1963 Interviews Conducted by the Institute for Sex Research* (Philadelphia: W. B. Saunders, 1979), *passim.*

2.   Gebhard and Johnson, op. cit., and virtually all broad-based surveys of more recent years, converge on a prevalence of at least 15% for homosexual desires and behavior in the adult male American population.

3.   More exact figures are available, if desired, from the annual *Statistical Abstract of the United States.*

4.   Paul Sergios and James Cody, "Importance of Physical Attractiveness and Social Assertiveness Skills in Male Homosexual Dating Behavior and Partner Selection," *Journal of Homosexuality*, Vol. 12, No. 2 (Winter 1985–86): 71.

BIBLIOGRAPHY

ADLER, MARGOT. *Drawing Down the Moon.* Beacon, 1986.

Advertising Age. "Media Update." 5/26/86.

Advocate. "D.C. Appeals Court Issues Landmark Ruling: Rights of Gay Students Affirmed at Georgetown U." 12/22/87.

———. "Helping Gay Street Youth in New York." 2/16/88.

———. "So They Say." 6/24/86.

———. "Supreme Court Hears Arguments in Gay-CIA Case." 2/16/88.

———. *Alan Turing, The Enigma.*

ALTMAN, DENNIS. *AIDS in the Mind of America.* Doubleday, 1986.

———. *The Homosexualization of America.* St. Martins, 1982.

ALVAREZ, WALTER. *Homosexuality and Other Forms of Sexual Deviance.* Pyramid, 1974.

American Psychiatric Association, Council on Statistics and Nomenclature. *Diagnostic and Statistical Manual of Mental Disorders,* 3rd Edition (DSM-III). American Psychiatric Association, 1980.

BARNES, FRED. "The Politics of AIDS." *New Republic,* 11/4/85.

———. "White House Watch: The Juicy Bits." *New Republic,* 6/6/88.

BAYER, DONALD. *Homosexuality and American Psychiatry: The Politics of Diagnosis.* Basic, 1981.

BELL, ALAN; WEINBERG, MARTIN. *Homosexualities: A Study of Diversity Among Men and Women.* Simon & Schuster, 1978.

BELL, ALAN; WEINBERG, MARTIN; HAMMERSMITH, SUE. *Sexual Preference: Its Development in Men and Women.* Indiana University, 1981.

BEM, DARYL. *Beliefs, Attitudes, and Human Affairs.* Brooks/Cole, 1970.

BENNETT, MARTIN. "I'm Gay . . . O.K.?" Last Days Ministries, 1984.

BERMAN, RONALD. *Advertising and Social Change.* Sage, 1981.

BIERCE, AMBROSE. *The Devil's Dictionary.* Quoted in Shapiro.

"Blueprint For Health." Advertisement series. Great Lakes Products, 1985.

Boston Globe. "Catholic Priests and AIDS." 2/5/87.

———. "Reagan Slow to Take Lead in Fight on AIDS." 4/1/87.

BROOKS-KIDD, CAROLYN; CABLE, YVONNE. "Dolphin Facilitated Workshops." Flyer. Dolphenvision, 1988.

BRONSKI, MICHAEL. *Culture Clash: The Making of Gay Sensibility.* South End, 1984.

BULL, BART. "Antihero: Ev Mecham." *Spin,* 5/88.

BURROUGHS, WILLIAM. *Queer.* Penguin, 1985.

———. *The Ticket That Exploded.* Grove, 1962.

BUTLER, SAMUEL. *Hudibras.* (1663). Quoted in Shapiro.

CHESLER, PHYLLIS. *Mothers on Trial: The Battle for Children and Custody.* Seal, 1987.

CHESLEY, ROBERT. Letter to the editor. *New York Native,* n.d. Quoted in Shilts.

CHRISTIAN FAMILY RENEWAL. Fundraising letter. Stafford, Virginia, n.d.

CLECKLEY, HERVEY. *The Mask of Sanity.* Mosby, 1964.

CRISP, QUENTIN. *The Naked Civil Servant.* New American Library, 1983.

CROWLEY, MART. *The Boys in the Band.* Dell, 1968.

CURTIN, KAIER. *We Can Always Call Them Bulgarians.* Alyson, 1987.

DAVIDSON, SARA. "On Tour with Rock Hudson." *New York Times Magazine,* 5/3/87.

DANNECKER, MARTIN. *Theories of Homosexuality.* Gay Men's, 1981.

DE STEFANO, GEORGE. "Gay Drug Abuse: Owning Up to a Serious Problem." *Advocate,* 6/24/86.

DECECCO, JOHN, ed. *Bashers, Baiters and Bigots.* Harrington Park, 1985.

DECTER, MIDGE. "The Boys on the Beach." *Commentary,* 9/80.

DENNENY, MICHAEL. "Gay Politics: Sixteen Propositions." In Michael Denneny et al., eds., *The Christopher Street Reader.* Wideview/Perigee, 1983.

———. "Oedipus Revised." *Christopher Street,* No. 105.

DERSHOWITZ, ALAN. "Emphasize Scientific Information." *New York Times,* 3/18/86.

DISCH, THOMAS. *Fun with Your New Head.*

DOVER, KENNETH. *Greek Homosexuality.* Vintage, 1980.

DOYLE, SIR ARTHUR CONAN. *Sherlock Holmes: The Complete Novels and Stories.* Bantam, 1986.

DREW, PAUL. "Alternative Market: Low Ratings, High Profits." *Billboard,* 7/7/86.

DULLEIA, GEORGIA. "Gay Couples' Wish to Adopt Grows, Along With Increasing Resistance." *New York Times,* 2/7/88.

DWORKIN, ANDREA. *Intercourse.* Free Press, 1987.

ELLUL, JACQUES. *Propaganda: The Formation of Men's Attitudes.* Vintage, 1965.

Equal Times. "Telephone Troubles." 8/26/88.

FEDER, DON. "AIDS, gay politics and the family." *Boston Herald,* 2/25/88.

FENWICK, R. D. *The Advocate Guide to Gay Health.* Alyson, 1983.

FESTINGER, LEON. *A Theory of Cognitive Dissonance.* Rowe, Peterson, 1957.

FIALA, RICK. Cartoon, in *And God Bless Uncle Henry and His Roommate Jack (who we're not supposed to talk about),* Avon, 1978.

FITZGERALD, FRANCES. *Cities on a Hill.* Simon & Schuster, 1986.

FREIBERG, PETER. "Antigay Violence Jumped in 1987, Studies Report." *Advocate,* 7/19/88.

———. "In Depth: PLGTF [Philadelphia Lesbian and Gay Task Force] Media Project." *Advocate,* 4/15/86.

———. "New Report on Hate Crimes." *Advocate,* 12/22/87.

FRIEDMAN, JEANETTE. *Rock Hudson.* New American Library, 1986.

FRITSCHER, JACK. "Beach Blanket Surf-Boy Blues." *William Higgins' California,* 1/1, 1983/84.

GAINOR, PAUL. "Picket the Pope!" *Advocate,* 6/9/87.

GALLUP, GEORGE, JR. *Gallup Poll.* 4/12/87.

GATES, PHYLLIS. *My Husband, Rock Hudson.* Doubleday, 1987.

GAY AND LESBIAN DISCRIMINATION DOCUMENTATION PROJECT (OF THE NEW YORK CITY COMMISSION ON HUMAN RIGHTS). *Two-Year Report on Complaints of Sexual Orientation Discrimination.* (November 1983–October 1985).

GEBHARD, PAUL; JOHNSON, ALAN. *The Kinsey Data: Marginal Tabulations of the 1938–1963 Interviews Conducted by the Institute for Sex Research.* W. B. Saunders, 1979.

GELDER, LINDSY VAN; BRANDT, PAM. "AIDS On Campus." *Rolling Stone,* 9/25/86.

GITECK, LENNY. "Is This Any Way to Run a Movement?" *Advocate,* 6/10/86.

———. "The Traitors Among Us: Horror Tales in D.C." *Advocate,* 9/29/87.

GLAAD [Gay and Lesbian Alliance Against Defamation]. "Kellogg's Gay Bashing: It Ain't 'Nuttin', Honey.'" *GLAAD Bulletin,* 7–8/88.

GOFFMAN, ERVING. *Stigma: Notes on the Management of Spoiled Identity.* Simon & Schuster, 1963.

GOLDSTEIN, RICHARD. "State of Emergency: Gay Life 1987." *Village Voice,* 6/30/87.

GORDON, KEVIN. "Religion, Moralizing, and AIDS." In Kevin Gordon, ed., *Homosexuality and Social Justice, Reissue of the Report of the Task Force on Gay/Lesbian Issues, San Francisco,* Consultation on Homosexuality, Social Justice, and Roman Catholic Theology, 1986.

GREER, GERMAINE. *The Female Eunuch.* Bantam, 1971.

GREIF, MARTIN. *The Gay Book of Days.* Lyle Stuart, 1982.

HADLEIGH, BOZE. "Scared Straight." *American Film,* 1–2/87.

HARRIS, ROBERT. Letter to the editor. *New York Daily News,* 10/6/85.

HARRY, JOSEPH. "Homosexual Men and Women Who Served Their Country." In DeCecco.

HART, JEFFREY. "Ivory Foxhole." *Hopkins Bulletin,* 3/87.

HELMS, JESSE. "Only Morality Will Effectively Prevent AIDS from Spreading." *New York Times,* 11/23/87.

HENRY, LEWIS, ed. *5000 Quotations for All Occasions.* Blakiston, 1945.

HIRSCHFELD, MAGNUS, ET AL. *The Sexual History of the World War.* Cadillac, 1946.

HITCHENS, CHRISTOPHER. "It Dare Not Speak Its Name: Fear and Self-Loathing on the Gay Right." *Harper's,* 8/87.

HOFFMAN, NICHOLAS VON. *Citizen Cohn.* Doubleday, 1988.

HOLLERAN, ANDREW. "Anniversary." *Christopher Street,* No. 121.

———. *Dancer From the Dance.* Bantam, 1978.

HOWE, FISHER. "What You Need to Know About Fund Raising." *Harvard Business Review,* 3–4/85.

INSKO, C. A. *Theories of Attitude Change.* Appleton-Century-Crofts, 1967.

International Advertising Association. *Controversy Advertising: How Advertisers Present Points of View in Public Affairs.* Hastings, 1977.

JACKSON, REV. E. W., SR. "Detracting from Merits of Black Civil Rights." Letter to the editor. *Boston Globe,* 2/17/87.

JAMES, HENRY. *The Portable Henry James,* ed. M. D. Zabel. Viking, 1951.

KAFKA, FRANZ. "The Animal in the Synagogue." In *Parables and Paradoxes,* Schocken, 1961.

KATZ, DANIEL. "The Functional Approach to the Study of Attitudes." *Public Opinion Quarterly,* 24, 1960.

KATZ, LEE. "Motivating the Major Gift." *Fundraising Management,* 8/88.

KAZIN, ALFRED. "A Farewell to Art: Hemingway, by Kenneth S. Lynn." *New Republic,* 7/13/87.

KENNEDY, HUBERT. "The 'Third Sex' Theory of Karl Heinrich Ulrichs." *Journal of Homosexuality,* 6/1–2, 1980/81.

KILPATRICK, JAMES. "Aren't We Overreacting to AIDS?" Universal Press Syndicate, 6/9/88.

KINSEY, ALFRED; POMEROY, WARDELL; MARTIN, CLYDE; GEBHARD, PAUL. *Sexual Behavior in the Human Female.* W. B. Saunders, 1953.

KINSEY, ALFRED; POMEROY, WARDELL; MARTIN, CLYDE. *Sexual Behavior in the Human Male.* W. B. Saunders, 1948.

KIRK, MARSHALL; PILL, ERASTES [pseud. Hunter Madsen]. "Idols of the

Tribe: Rank and Cold War in the Gay Community." *Christopher Street*, No. 77.

———. "Waging Peace: A Gay Battle Plan to Persuade Straight America." *Christopher Street*, No. 95.

KLEPPER, MICHAEL. *Getting Your Message Out: How to Get, Use, and Survive Radio and Television Air Time*. Prentice-Hall, 1984.

KRAFFT-EBING, R. VON. *Psychopathia Sexualis*. Physicians and Surgeons, 1928.

KRAMER, LARRY. *Faggots*. New American Library, 1978.

———. *The Normal Heart*. New American Library, 1985.

KUROPAT, ROSEMARY. "Challenge Bigotry: A Two-Part Proposal for Gay Community Organizing and Positive Message Advertising." Unpublished ms. for GLAAD, 1986.

LANDERS, ANN. "Don't Assume Son's Pal Is Gay." Syndicated column, 3/6/87.

Lesbian and Gay Media Advocates. *Talk Back! The Gay Person's Guide to Media Action*. Alyson, 1982.

LEVENSON, MICHAEL. "The Nayman of Noland." *New Republic*, 7/6/87.

LEVITT, E.; KLASSEN, K. "Public Attitudes Toward Homosexuality: Part of the 1970 National Survey by the Institute for Sex Research." *Journal of Homosexuality*, 1/1, 1974.

LEWIS, C. S. *The Screwtape Letters*. Macmillan, 1961.

LONG, SCOTT. "Terror in the Stalls." *Harvard Gay and Lesbian Newsletter*, 4/3, 1986.

Los Angeles Times. "American View of Gays: Disapproval, Sympathy." 12/20/85.

LOWEN, ALEXANDER. *Narcissism: Denial of the True Self.* Macmillan, 1985.

LYNN, KENNETH. *Hemingway: A Biography.*

MASSA, ROBERT. "Straight and Narrow." *Village Voice*, 6/30/87.

McDONALD, BOYD. *cum.* Gay Sunshine, 1983.

———. *Flesh.* Gay Sunshine, 1982.

McGUIRE, WILLIAM. "The Nature of Attitudes and Attitude Change." In G. Lindzey, E. Aronson, eds., *Handbook of Social Psychology*, Addison-Wesley, 1969.

MILL, JOHN STUART. "On Liberty." In *The Utilitarians*, Doubleday, 1973.

MILTON, JOHN. "Lycidas." Quoted in John Brunner, *The Sheep Look Up,* Harper & Row, 1972.

MITCHELL, DAVID. "Balls." In McDonald, *cum.*

MOLLOY, JOHN. *Dress For Success.* Warner, 1975.

MOORE, GENE-GABRIEL. "North Carolina's War Against Gays." *Christopher Street,* No. 121.

MORDDEN, ETHAN. "The Homogay." *Christopher Street,* No. 77.

MOULTON, POWERS. *2500 Jokes For All Occasions.* Garden City, 1942.

MURPHY, MARY. "The AIDS Scare: What It's Done to Hollywood and the TV You See." *TV Guide,* 10/22/88.

MUSTO, MICHAEL. "Mandatory Macho: Butching Up Is Not a Liberated Act." *Village Voice,* 6/30/87.

NAIMAN, ARTHUR. *Every Goy's Guide to Common Jewish Expressions.* Houghton-Mifflin, 1981.

National Gay Task Force. *Twenty Questions About Homosexuality.* 1978.

National Gay and Lesbian Task Force. *Gay Rights Protections in the United States and Canada.* 1987.

———. *Privacy Project Fact Sheet.* n.d.

National Opinion Research Center (NORC). *General Social Surveys, 1972–1985: Cumulative Codebook.* NORC/Roper Center, 7/85.

NELSON, BOB. "Advertising Our Way to 'Acceptance'." *Gay Community News,* 6/21/86.

New England Mirror. "Members of 'Iron Fist' Expelled from University of Chicago for Anti-Gay Harassment." 8/5/87.

New York Times. "The Aesthetic Realism of Eli Siegel Is True." Advertisement. 8/6/76.

———. "AIDS Emerging As A Key Issue For Campaign '88." 4/2/87.

———. "Brookline Diocese Joins Homosexual-Bill Fight." 2/7/86.

———. "Employers Endorse AIDS Guidelines." 2/18/88.

———. "200,000 March in Capital For Gay Rights and More AIDS Money." 10/12/87.

Newsweek. "Everything but Shouting 'Fire': Colleges Grapple with the Limits of Free Speech." 10/20/86.

———. "Future Shock: The AIDS Epidemic." 11/24/86.

———. "Gays in the Clergy." 2/23/87.

———. "Have Gays Taken Over Yale? The President Responds in a Letter to Alums." 10/12/87.

———. "Kids and Contraceptives." 2/16/87.

———. "Savior on the Right?" 1/19/87.

———. "The Grossest Guys on the Airwaves." 11/17/86.

Ogg, Elizabeth. "Changing Views of Homosexuality." *Public Affairs Pamphlet* No. 563, 1978.

Olson, Wayne. "Defeating the Enemy: Some Guidelines—Do's and Don'ts in Confronting Homophobia." *Christopher Street,* Spring 1986.

Peck, M. Scott. *People of the Lie.* Simon & Schuster, 1983.

People Magazine. "A Frank Biography Finds That Leonard Bernstein's Passions, Like His Talents, Are Endless." 5/4/87.

Peyser, Joan. *Bernstein: A Biography.* Morrow, 1978.

Pomeroy, Wardell. "The Diagnosis and Treatment of Transvestites and Transsexuals." *Journal of Sex and Marital Therapy,* 1/3, 1975.

Principe, Ginnine. "The Sharon Kowalski Story." *Equal Times,* 8/26/88.

Rechy, John. *City of Night.* Ballantine, 1963.

———. *The Sexual Outlaw.* Grove, 1977.

Redman, Alvin. *The Wit and Humor of Oscar Wilde.* Dover, 1959.

Reid, John. *The Best Little Boy in the World.* Ballantine, 1973.

Reilly, Joseph. Letter to the editor. *Boston Globe,* 3/29/87.

Reinhart, Robert. "Solos: A Suite." *Christopher Street,* No. 77.

Reiss, E., ed. *The Esthetic Realism of Eli Siegel and the Change From Homosexuality.* Definition, 1986.

Rich, Frank. "The Gay Decades." *Esquire,* 11/87.

Rist, Darrell. "On Hating Ourselves." In Eric E. Rofes, ed., *Gay Life,* Doubleday, 1986.

Rofes, Eric. *'I Thought People Like That Killed Themselves': Lesbians, Gay Men, and Suicide.* Grey Fox, 1983.

Roper Organization. *Roper Reports,* 1979–9; 1985–7; 1986–10; 1987–1; 1987–2.

Rueda, Enrique. *The Homosexual Network: Private Lives and Public Policy.* Devin Adair, 1982.

RUSSELL, BERTRAND. *Human Society in Ethics and Politics.* Quoted in Shapiro.

RUSSO, VITO. "Mark Thompson on the Myth and Meaning of Gay Spirit." *Advocate,* 12/22/87.

SANDLA, ROBERT. "Gays in the Theater." *Advocate,* 6/9/87.

SCHELLING, THOMAS. *The Strategy of Conflict.* Oxford University, 1960.

SCHNEIDER, WILLIAM. "Homosexuals: Is AIDS Changing Attitudes?" *Public Opinion,* 7–8/87.

SCHULENBURG, JOY. *Gay Parenting.* Doubleday, 1985.

SCHULTZ, ROBERT. Letter to the editor. *New York Times Magazine,* 5/31/87.

SEGELL, MICHAEL. "Your Mental Love Map." *American Health,* 12/87.

SERGIOS, PAUL; CODY, JAMES. "Importance of Physical Attractiveness and Social Assertiveness Skills in Male Homosexual Dating Behavior and Partner Selection." *Journal of Homosexuality,* 12/2, 1985/86.

SHAPIRO, NAT, ed. *Whatever It is, I'm Against It.* Simon & Schuster, 1984.

SHIELDS, S.; HARRIMAN, R. "Fear of Male Homosexuality: Cardiac Responses of Low and High Homonegative Males." In DeCecco.

SHILTS, RANDY. *And the Band Played On.* St. Martin's, 1987.

SHIVELY, M. G.; DECECCO, J. P. "Sexual Orientation Survey of Students on the San Francisco State University Campus." *Journal of Homosexuality,* 4/1, 1978.

SILVERSTEIN, CHARLES; WHITE, EDMUND. *The Joy of Gay Sex.* Simon & Schuster, 1977.

SKELLY, FLORENCE. "To the Beat of a Different Drum." *Harvard Magazine,* 3–4/86.

Statistical Abstract of the United States, annual.

STILES, B. J. "AIDS: How a Problem Became a Priority." *Foundation News,* 3–4/86.

STRIEBER, WHITLEY; KUNETKA, JAMES. *Warday.* Warner, 1984.

SULLIVAN, ANDREW. "Flogging Underwear." *New Republic,* 1/18/88.

SUN TZU, "The Art of War." Published as R. L. Wing, trans. and ed., *The Art of Strategy,* Doubleday, 1988.

SWIFT, MICHAEL. "For the Homoerotic Order." *Gay Community News,* 2/15/87.

THOMAS, CAL. "Houston Gay Rights Showdown." *Boston Globe,* 1/19/85.

THOMPSON, MARK, ed. *Gay Spirit: Myth and Meaning.* St. Martin's, 1987.

THORSON, SCOTT (as told to Thor Leifson). *Behind the Candelabra.* Dutton, 1988.

THORSON, SCOTT. "How Liberace Fooled the World About His Love Life." *Star,* 10/27/87.

Time. "Methodist Maneuvers." 12/28/87.

———. "Milestones." 7/10/85.

———. "Pornography: A Poll." 7/21/86.

TOCQUEVILLE, ALEXIS DE. *Democracy in America,* ed. J. P. Mayer. Doubleday, 1969.

TRIPP, C. A. *The Homosexual Matrix.* New American Library, 1987.

U.S. News & World Report. "The Hot New Politics of AIDS." 3/30/87.

VANDERVELDEN, MARK. "Civil Disobedience: Are We Entering a New Militant Stage in the Struggle for Gay Rights?" *Advocate,* 9/29/87.

Wall Street Journal. "Advertisers Retreat from Making Direct Pitch to the Gay Market." 1/26/88.

War Conference [of national gay and lesbian organizations]. "Final Statement of the War Conference." Held at Airlie House, Warrenton, Virginia, 2/28/88.

WATNEY, SIMON. *Policing Desire: Pornography, AIDS, and the Media.* University of Minnesota, 1987.

WEEKS, JEFFREY. *Sexuality and Its Discontents: Meanings, Myths, and Modern Sexualities.* Routledge & Kegan Paul, 1985.

WHITE, EDMUND. *States of Desire.* Dutton, 1980.

WILDE, OSCAR. Letter to Leonard Smithers. Quoted in Shapiro.

———. *The Picture of Dorian Gray.* In Richard Aldington and Stanley Weintraub, eds., *The Portable Oscar Wilde,* Viking, 1955.

———. "The Soul of Man Under Socialism." In *De Profundis and Other Writings,* Penguin, 1986.

○　　　○　　　○　　　○　　　○

ABOUT THE
AUTHORS

MARSHALL KIRK graduated from Harvard University in 1980. He gave up a National Science Foundation fellowship in order to write full time. A researcher in neuropsychiatry, logician, and poet, Kirk has worked with Johns Hopkins' Study of Mathematically Precocious Youth, designed aptitude tests for adults with 200+ IQs, and spent years trying to figure out what makes gays tick.

HUNTER MADSEN, PH.D., is a public-communications expert who has taught on the Harvard faculty, designed commercial advertising on Madison Avenue, and guided strategy for the Positive Images Campaign—America's first national gay advertising effort. He has spent years trying to figure out what makes the public tick.